Map
Appreciation

Map
Appreciation

MARK MONMONIER

Syracuse University

GEORGE A. SCHNELL

The College at New Paltz
State University of New York

Prentice Hall, Englewood Cliffs, New Jersey 07632

Library of Congress Cataloging-in-Publication Data

MONMONIER, MARK
   Map appreciation.

   Includes bibliographies and index.
   1. Maps.   I. Schnell, George A., (date).
II. Title.
GA105.3.M65 1987   912   87-12619
ISBN 0-13-556052-7

Editorial/production supervision
   and interior design: *Kathleen M. Lafferty*
Cover layout: *Photo Plus Art*
Manufacturing buyers: *Paula Benevento and Margaret Rizzi*

 © 1988 by Prentice Hall
A Division of Simon & Schuster Inc.
Englewood Cliffs, New Jersey 07632

Printed in the United States of America

10 9 8 7 6 5 4 3 2 1

0-13-556052-7   01

PRENTICE-HALL INTERNATIONAL (UK) LIMITED, *London*
PRENTICE-HALL OF AUSTRALIA PTY. LIMITED, *Sydney*
PRENTICE-HALL CANADA INC., *Toronto*
PRENTICE-HALL HISPANOAMERICANA, S.A., *Mexico*
PRENTICE-HALL OF INDIA PRIVATE LIMITED, *New Delhi*
PRENTICE-HALL OF JAPAN, INC., *Tokyo*
SIMON & SCHUSTER ASIA PTE. LTD., *Singapore*
EDITORA PRENTICE-HALL DO BRASIL, LTDA., *Rio de Janeiro*

To Armin Lobeck, Erwin Raisz, and Arthur Robinson
twentieth-century pioneers in American university cartography

Contents

CHAPTER FOUR

Maps of the Atmosphere   *109*

CHAPTER FIVE

Population Maps   *160*

CHAPTER EIGHT

Old Maps   *291*

CHAPTER NINE

Dramatic Effects with Maps   *331*

CHAPTER TEN

Computer Maps   *370*

APPENDIX A

Temperature Conversions

APPENDIX B

Sources of Maps and Cartographic Information

Glossary

Index

Preface

Our title, *Map Appreciation*, reveals our purpose: to show the reader that the map is both a useful tool and an object of visual gratification. We also intend to combat cartophobia, a dysfunction akin to math phobia. Although map use seems unavoidable in many everyday circumstances, some adults (young and old) are uneasy with maps or use them improperly. Others regard maps as mysterious, viewing with awe both well-conceived maps and cartographic monstrosities. Through the examples and discussion in our 10 chapters, we hope to promote an informed appreciation of maps and to make the reader a more effective consumer of geographic information. We are also concerned that cartography takes its proper place in the liberal arts; the liberally educated person should be able to understand and take pleasure in good maps, as well as in good music, good drama, good literature, and good painting.

This book is not a text explaining how to make maps, nor is it a treatise on how to read maps of the landscape or maps showing statistical data. Our focus is not on technique, but on use. With a wide variety of examples we explore the role of maps in many areas that touch people's lives directly or indirectly. Our survey reveals, for instance, the importance of maps to realtors, planners, military tacticians, public administrators, diplomats, earth scientists, legislators, journalists, librarians, educators, hikers, and historians—to name a few. Even some prestigious universities—which for decades have lacked departments of geography—have large, distinguished, and well-used map collections. The great array of maps produced by government at all levels is further evidence that maps are necessary simply because many facts and concepts are best shown on a map.

Whereas a text on cartographic technique or design might be organized to reflect the various types of map symbols or stages in the mapping process, our book is organized systematically to reflect the various types of phenomena portrayed by maps. After an introductory chapter presenting the basic cartographic concepts of scale, symbols, and perspective, succeeding chapters discuss photographic and remotely sensed maps of land cover; topographic and landform maps; maps of weather and climate; maps of the human population occupying the planet; the role of maps in relationships between nations and the use of maps within nations to provide municipal services, record ownership of land, collect taxes, and protect the environment; the rich history of cartography and the fascinating hobby of map collecting; the use of maps to communicate spatial information and ideas in news reporting, advertising, political propaganda, and literature; and the ways in which electronic technology is changing the use and storage of mapped data.

Our own biases and experiences, our assessment of what might be most relevant to the reader, and the economics of textbook publishing limit the range of examples in this book. Many of our case studies examine maps of regions in which we reside; for example, in Chapters 7 and 8 we discuss New Paltz, New York, and Syracuse, New York, in order to provide a geographic focus for comparing types of municipal maps and examining the evolution of map accuracy. This apparent parochialism should not obscure the fact that similar examples (with no great differences) are available for most other parts of North America. Collecting a corresponding set of local examples for the reader's home area is a reasonable (and, we hope, pleasant) challenge to both student and instructor. This book's use of black-and-white illustrations reflects not only the high cost of color illustrations, but also the poor reproduction quality of, for example, a seven-color map mimicked through standard four-color process printing. Again, we encourage the student and the instructor to overcome this limitation through some meaningful project, such as visiting a university map collection, ordering maps and atlases from several government agencies and private publishers, or merely perusing the fine full-color maps found in many inexpensive atlases and weekly news magazines. Our focus on maps of the United States produced in this country is deliberate, providing examples of phenomena and cartographic products likely to be most meaningful to our principal reader, the American undergraduate. Nevertheless, we strongly encourage study of foreign maps produced outside the United States, many of which (particularly among those printed in color) are far better than American maps in design and execution.

A good text should open doors, not close them. We hope that the reader will take seriously these suggestions to develop a personal map collection and to use map libraries. We also recommend reading several of the many good books about the history of maps and about map making. Particularly useful is

Phillip C. Muehrcke's *Map Use: Reading, Analysis, and Interpretation* (Madison: JP Publications, 1978). Muehrcke's book provides more details about mapping and map reading than we have space to discuss here and is an obvious second step for the reader who finds our examples and insights interesting and helpful. At the end of each chapter we list a number of other references that the map enthusiast might consult.

Map Appreciation has two principal uses in college instruction. In a course concerned specifically with map appreciation, the instructor might supplement our discussion by having students examine atlases and flat maps and undertake exercises in map reading, with an emphasis on local examples or on any particular geographic or cartographic topic in which the instructor is particularly interested or competent. In a general survey course on geography as an academic discipline, the instructor might use this book in connection with a world atlas or with a few paperbacks that treat specific applications. Map appreciation is an ideal focus for an introductory geography course designed as part of a core of liberal arts courses; maps and mapping are a distinctive element of geographic methodology, and map study promotes both graphicacy (that is, graphic literacy) and an enhanced understanding of physical and social processes that make the world an interesting, but sometimes hazardous, place in which to live.

Many colleagues have provided useful advice, guidance, and encouragement. Thomas W. Hodler and Alan M. MacEachren offered helpful suggestions at the beginning of the project; and Robert B. Kent, Michael P. Peterson, and Richard D. Wright gave our finished manuscript a careful reading. Michael Kirchoff supervised production of both new artwork and facsimile reproductions at the Syracuse University Cartographic Laboratory. We are indebted to Mike and his staff: Marcia Harrington, Margaret Vance, Nancy Doolittle, Serge Marek, and Steve Segal. Numerous firms and government agencies, identified in the captions, provided the many example illustrations essential to a book with this focus. At Prentice Hall we appreciate the assistance of Betsy Perry, who helped us launch the project; Jennifer Schmunk, who provided continuity; Kathleen Lafferty, who guided the project through copyediting and production; and Dan Joraanstad, Jeanne Hoeting, Nancy Forsyth, Curtis Yehnert, and Bob Sickles, who contributed their experience in marketing and production.

Mark Monmonier
George A. Schnell

CHAPTER ONE

Introduction

Why do humans draw maps? An answer to this seemingly naïve question becomes obvious when a stranger asks for directions. Giving clear directions is seldom easy for many of us, unless the destination is in plain sight or just down the road. Our verbal directions are often garbled or too lengthy for the questioner to remember. Perhaps out of frustration, we resort to equally vague arm-waving as a way of describing turns, curves, or complex intersections. A two-dimensional drawing would be more helpful than our words and sign language. Both the confused stranger and the well-meaning giver of directions often wish they had the paper and pencil to create a quick map.

Maps organize spatial information for convenient use. Among the best examples of cartographic organization is the road map, which travelers use first to choose and then to follow a route. As a scale model of part of the earth's surface, the road map is a masterpiece of purposeful selection, designed to aid drivers of motor vehicles. Such maps confine themselves to towns, recreational attractions, landmarks, and the highways that connect them. To show much more detail would clutter the visual image and confuse the driver. To promote a desirable clarity, road maps sacrifice some geometric accuracy by separating symbols for places and things that in reality are much closer.

Printing a map on a flat, foldable sheet of paper, instead of on a rigid, spherical (and expensive) plate, further distorts the representation; however, in cartography such distortion is not only unavoidable, but also tolerable because of the advantages a flat map provides the viewer. Although more accurate than flat maps in a narrow, geometric sense, bulky globes representing the whole earth can portray little more than continents and oceans, international boundaries, gross physical features, major cities, and a few transportation routes. They reveal less than half the earth to the viewer at once, and must be turned. In contrast, portable, inexpensively published flat maps of the whole earth or of particular regions—on single sheets of paper, in atlases, and in the storage cases of reference libraries—can show at a glance a far wider variety of detailed geographic phenomena, both natural and social: from global atmospheric circulation and continental drift, to waves of battle during World War I, to patterns of political instability in the Middle East, to changing residential patterns in cities. Although some people have difficulty refolding them, flat maps have for years been marvels of efficiency in the storage and retrieval of information related to many aspects of human experience.

MAP APPRECIATION

By "map appreciation" we mean a basic understanding not only of the ways maps can serve the individual, but also of the role maps play in geography and other sciences, public administration, mass communications, and historical research. With its focus on the orchestration of symbols and its goal of enjoyment based on knowledge of principles, history, and the varieties of human expression, map appreciation is much like music appreciation. The informed map reader, like the informed listener, better appreciates the symbolic "symphony" of geographic detail that a map provides. The music-lover with catholic tastes not only understands the role of electronic music in modern society, but also knows where and when to savor the delights of baroque ornamentation, progressive jazz, and the hammer dulcimer. The music aficionado must listen beyond hard rock and Muzak, and the map enthusiast must look past the road atlas and the Associated Press locator map. As with any form of art or communication, careful study of maps and their principles, purposes, or modes leads to insight, discretion, and personal fulfillment.

As a scholarly focus, map appreciation is different from map making: the former addresses consumption, whereas the latter concerns production. Like music appreciation, map appreciation requires no talent and develops no instrumental skill. The map enthusiast needs neither to survey nor to draw: although the study of maps promotes critical insight, it need not make the student a good designer. Nonetheless, an enhanced appreciation of maps should improve the motivation and job satisfaction of those who make maps for a living.

Map appreciation is also distinct from map use. Many people use maps with little understanding of the basic principles, purposes, and modes of cartographic expression. Military officers, geologists, county clerks, meteorologists, real-estate agents, and taxi drivers often have only a job-specific knowledge of maps. Map appreciation does not follow from map use, although map use—in the field, as in the sport of orienteering—can be a sure way to appreciate some types of map, if not maps in general.

Map appreciation is also different from the history of cartography, although both subjects are concerned with temporal change and the evolution of the map-maker's science and art. Like other historians of technology, the historian of cartography is deeply committed to explaining the development of methods and artifacts and to understanding their relationship to society and events, to cause and effect. Because skills in using source materials develop slowly, the historian tends to concentrate on a particular era, type of map, or part of the world—for example, sixteenth-century navigation maps of Latin America. The map enthusiast, in contrast, is far more a generalist than a specialist and investigates maps as a hobby or interest, not as a profession. In this sense, the map aficionado is a consumer rather than a producer of research on cartographic history. Moreover, map appreciation is concerned very much with the present, whereas the history of cartography traditionally has ignored contemporary maps in favor of times well before the recent past.

Finally and emphatically, map appreciation is not map collecting. Like the historian of cartography, the serious collector tends to specialize. For some very serious collectors the principal motive is profit, not pleasure or scholarship. Rare maps, after all, appreciate in value, and investing in maps is a good way to protect financial resources against inflation. Although most collectors also enjoy the maps in their collections, too often they are only interested in the ornate and the scarce and ignore the mundane and the commonplace. In contrast, the mapophile appreciates both old and new, rare and plentiful. If such a person collects maps, the theme is likely to be contemporary and the maps are likely to have little economic value—at least not yet. (Someday, quite likely, Rand McNally products will be every cent as valuable as, say, Coca-Cola memorabilia are today.)

Map Skills and the Educated Person

For over two decades British educator William Balchin has argued that school curricula should group geography with English and mathematics as foundation subjects for pre–college-level education. Balchin notes that the four types of basic intelligence—verbal, social, numerical, and visual-spatial—have their respective "educated counterparts": literacy, articulacy, numeracy, and *graphicacy.* These four skills involve written and oral modes of communication, manipulation of numbers, and route finding and environmental exploration through map reading and the use of pictures and other graphics.[1] Balchin defines graphicacy as "the communication of spatial information that cannot be conveyed

[1] W. G. V. Balchin, "Graphicacy." *American Cartographer* 3, no. 1 (April 1976), 33–38.

adequately by verbal or numerical means."[2] Since the tools of graphicacy—maps, diagrams, photographs, and various spatial documents—are the very basis of geography, says Balchin, geography should be the academic home of graphicacy.[3]

Recently one advocate of graphicacy in general education at the college level observed that much of the instruction in graphic methods for processing and displaying numerical information occurs in cartography or quantitative techniques courses that are designed explicitly for geography majors. Jo Margaret Mano went on to suggest a course, "Maps and Graphics: Measures and Symbols," directed toward helping a general audience at the freshman-sophomore level integrate numerical topics and geographic examples. By learning about maps and other graphics, Mano asserted, students who are often unable to fully understand diagrams in newspapers and textbooks should become more competent consumers and begin to use graphics in their writing assignments.[4]

In his own cogent remarks about the value of cartography in liberal education, Arthur Robinson, an influential writer on the technology and philosophy of mapping, offers a definition of cartography with general appeal: "the creation of a map for the use and enjoyment of the educated individual."[5] By "liberal education," Robinson means "guiding the individual's personal development toward greater understanding of, and abiding curiosity about, all aspects of the world in which we live, while heightening the individual's ability to think rationally and to feel emotionally—and, hopefully, to know the difference."[6] Many topics, geographical and other, are clearer in graphic terms than in verbal terms; and many verbal presentations are immeasurably clearer when thoughtfully prepared graphics accompany them. Therefore, studying graphic presentation is as important as studying effective speaking.[7] Finally, Robinson reminds us that maps are more than factual tools and that they do possess emotional and intellectual appeal. Indeed, he maintains that maps should receive the kind of analysis that instructors and students have long applied to literature, for example, in order to involve students more personally in cartographic skills and perspectives.[8] Those who have experienced the rigors of setting cartographic

---

[2] Quoted in David Boardman, *Graphicacy and Geography Teaching* (Beckenham, Kent: Croom Helm, Ltd., 1983), preface, from Balchin's presidential address to the Geographical Association in 1972.

[3] Balchin, "Graphicacy," p. 33.

[4] Jo Margaret Mano, "Geography and General Education," presentation at the Middle States Division, Association of American Geographers, West Chester, Pennsylvania, October 1984.

[5] Arthur H. Robinson, "The Potential Contribution of Cartography in Liberal Education," in *Geography in Undergraduate Liberal Education, A Report of the Geography in Liberal Education Project* (Washington, D.C.: Association of American Geographers, 1965), p. 34.

[6] Ibid., p. 34.

[7] William Morris Davis, "The Colorado Front Range: A Study in Physiographic Interpretation," *Annals of the Association of American Geographers* 1 (1911), 21–83; ref. on p. 33, quoted in Robinson, "Potential Contribution of Cartography," p. 35.

[8] Robinson, "Potential Contribution of Cartography," p. 46.

objectives, compiling information, preparing a rough draft, evaluating the draft and its design, and submitting a finished map are better able to appreciate maps and better prepared to use maps intelligently.

Geography and the study of maps are more popular abroad than in the United States. In the United Kingdom, A. Stewart Fotheringham's research shows, geography ranked fifth in popularity in high schools at the ordinary level (O-level) and eighth among all subjects at the advanced level (A-level) in 1979.[9] Subjects in which more British students take O-level and A-level examinations than in geography include several subjects that British schools require—in particular, English and mathematics. Geography was the sixth most common major that incoming British university students selected in 1979. According to Fotheringham, the single most important reason for geography's popularity in British higher education is the high status of the discipline in the schools: British teachers are trained and certified in geography and accord the subject recognition equal to the recognition they give history and chemistry. Almost all British students study geography in elementary school and are able to take geography courses in high school.

Recognizing that American colleges will not attract many geography majors among freshmen until elementary and secondary schools institute a stronger geography curriculum, the Association of American Geographers and the National Council for Geographic Education published *Guidelines for Geographic Education*. Directed toward both elementary and secondary levels of education, these helpful guidelines include one assertion particularly pertinent to map appreciation:

> Geographers use many research tools. They are, in some cases, similar to other social and physical science methods, but geographers have a special expertise in using maps to portray and study a variety of locations and distributions. Reading, interpreting, and making maps are skills integral to geographic education and to acquiring geographic knowledge.[10]

Certainly those who consider themselves liberally educated should explore and appreciate the value of such skills and knowledge.

Maps: Misunderstood and Unappreciated

Just as racial, ethnic, and religious prejudices are often the products of ignorance, so mistrust and abhorrence of certain academic subjects often result from lack of familiarity and understanding. "Math anxiety," for example, which ed-

[9] A. Stewart Fotheringham, "Geography in the United Kingdom," *Professional Geographer* 36, no. 4 (November 1984), 482–85.

[10] Joint Committee on Geographic Education of the National Council for Geographic Education and the Association of American Geographers, *Guidelines for Geographic Education* (Washington, D.C.: n.d.), p. 2.

ucators have diagnosed and are attempting to treat, results from fear and dislike of mathematics. A map anxiety appears to be afoot as well, although it is less obvious—perhaps because elementary and high school teachers either have little occasion to confront it or, in some cases, choose to ignore it. Both maps and mathematics are languages of sorts, and, like English, Spanish, or German, can be used effectively only when the individual is grounded in its vocabulary and grammar. Map skills, like numerical skills, are related not only to basic ability, but also to experience with maps and to attitudes about maps and map use that both elders and peers communicate to the individual.

An individual's differing abilities and interests in certain subjects also seem related to the dominance of either the left or the right hemisphere of the brain, a topic still debated among psychologists. Cartographic educator Phillip C. Muehrcke has advanced the notion that environmental awareness depends upon both "rational-analytical-logical thought" and "intuitive-holistic-ecological thinking."[11] He notes that psychologists have demonstrated that distinctive cognitive styles of processing information are associated with parts of the brain—analysis of information with the left side and synthesis of information with the right side. The logical left hemisphere relates to high levels of skill in language and mathematics, whereas the holistic right hemisphere relates to intuition and visual-spatial aptitudes. Cartographic education, however, demands the combination of logical and holistic thought, as mapping is both science and art.

The right hemisphere–left hemisphere dichotomy seems particularly strong in journalism. Some journalists are "word people," who react negatively to nonverbal symbols such as photographs and informational graphics. Others, fortunately, use both sides of their brains and comprehend and appreciate the role of maps in communicating spatial facts and ideas. Both print and electronic journalism, however, are now reflecting a resurgence of interest in graphics of all types in the 1980s—largely because of color television, video recording, and computer graphics. The print media are making increased use of maps. Of particular note are the maps in the *New York Times* and *USA Today*, national newspapers with marked differences in editorial style and depth of coverage. Despite its often staid, gray appearance, the *New York Times* was not only a leader in the use of graphics, but also an early and loyal advocate of maps that communicate the spatial complexities of local, national, and foreign news stories. Designed for impatient, on-the-go readers called "scanners," the more colorful *USA Today* employs maps and other graphic devices to a much greater extent than do its competitors. Its weather page (see Figure 4-16 in Chapter 4) has inspired many local papers to adopt detailed regional weather maps, often in color, and to use more graphics of all types. Network television news programs, local TV weather forecasts, and national weekly news magazines employ informative maps as an essential part of their services. This wide adoption of maps

---

[11] Phillip C. Muehrcke, "An Integrated Approach to Map Design and Production," *American Cartographer* 9, no. 2 (October 1982), 109–22.

in mass communications seems likely to foster a wider public acceptance and appreciation of maps. Perhaps graphicacy has a chance after all!

CARTOGRAPHIC VARIETY AND THE STRUCTURE OF THIS BOOK

As this book demonstrates, in a helpful sequence of topics, the variety of maps is extremely wide, the places where maps may be found are many, and the uses to which people can put maps are legion. Before initiating our survey of cartographic functions, we conclude this introductory chapter with a systematic examination of basic map elements—including scale, projection, and graphic symbols—and a short survey of the roles maps play.

The next two chapters treat maps of the land surface—including the most basic and some of the most advanced types of cartographic representation. Chapter 2, "Photomaps and Remotely Sensed Images," describes relatively recent developments in an increasingly valued area of cartography—from conventional black-and-white air photographs to the myriad remotely sensed images today's rapidly changing technology produces from satellite platforms and scanner systems. Chapter 3, "Maps of the Landscape," complements the discussion of photomaps by exploring the many cartographic methods used to describe the earth's surface with conventional line maps—from photomaps and early pictorial representations to topographic maps, physiographic diagrams, and maps of land use and land cover. Added to these customary treatments are a section on landscape architecture and the presentation of several topographic vignettes depicting the results of natural agents and human activity in landscape modification.

Chapter 4, "Maps of the Atmosphere," reminds the reader that the earth's atmosphere, unlike the earth's surface, is visibly changing by the hour. The dynamism of the atmosphere requires symbols more varied than those needed to represent tangible surface features of the earth. Topics in Chapter 4 include elements and controls of weather and climate, weather maps, climate maps, and a review of atmospheric maps used in everyday life.

Population study is essentially the study of number, distribution, and composition, as well as the changes in these elements resulting from the interworkings of mortality, fertility, and migration. Chapter 5, "Population Maps," which deals with the cartographic representation of these phenomena, includes a survey of the uses of population maps in planning and marketing.

The next two chapters address maps and government. "Political Maps," Chapter 6, discusses maps as tools for describing and analyzing international and intranational events and phenomena. Its topics include maps and geopolitics, propaganda, boundaries, the law of the sea and landlocked states, nation-building, elections, and the constitutional imperative in the United States to establish and maintain congressional districts apportioned on the basis of population distribution. Chapter 7, "Maps of the Municipality," which focuses on local governments, explores the use of maps to help govern, control, permit, and approve all manner of land use, development, and improvements. Maps are often legal documents serving to define boundaries, ownership, and district jurisdiction and to answer many questions that arise frequently in even the smallest, least complicated minor civil divisions. In the thousands of municipalities that dot North America, maps occupy the time and command the attention of millions of officials and interested citizens.

Maps also have value for humanistic scholars, antiquarians, and collectors. Chapter 8, "Old Maps," provides a concise introduction to the history of cartography, with emphasis on the many approaches adopted by scholars, a review of major works, and a chronology of selected events in cartographic technology. The second half of the chapter is devoted to map collecting for the professional and amateur, the map historian, or the hobbyist.

Chapter 9 describes "Dramatic Effects with Maps," whether achieved by the art department of a daily newspaper to heighten interest in a story, by the advertising agency attempting to convince potential customers of its client's locational advantage, or by the political or environmental group promoting a cause or idea. Chapter 9 has a dual function: to whet the reader's appetite for (and heighten the reader's appreciation of) maps as illustrations and to warn the reader that geographic reality can be distorted for a variety of reasons, good and bad.

"Computer Maps," Chapter 10, completes the book and helps prepare the reader for a future in which automated cartography could well make maps more numerous, more functional, and more visually effective. The chapter begins with an explanation of computer cartography—from map production to the storage and display of digital geographic data, including the role of telecommunications—and concludes with a discussion of computer cartography's advantages and disadvantages and the challenges it poses for educators and policymakers.

When read in sequence, these ten chapters provide an orderly flow of facts and concepts, an appropriate chronology, and a logical grouping of subjects. Photomaps, for example, are easy to understand but are often not as revealing as conventional "line maps." Presented first, photomaps thus herald the need for maps that tell more about the land surface by employing symbols at a higher level of abstraction—for example, maps of the landscape and the atmosphere. Population, political, and municipal maps portray, in part, the human use of the physical earth. Old maps, presented later in the sequence, allow the reader to gain some knowledge of the subject before delving into the manner in which cartographers in times past dealt with problems of compilation and presentation and into the ins and outs of map collection. Like old maps, dramatic maps focus upon symbols rather than upon the rudiments of cartography. Computer mapping is appropriately placed at the end of the book, since the subject not only is on the frontier of cartography but also requires grounding in traditional cartography to be appreciated.

ELEMENTS OF THE MAP

As a scale model, the map projects a spherical surface onto a plane and represents real features with graphic symbols. Cartographers employ the three basic elements of scale, projection, and symbolism to portray spatial distributions and geographic relationships. Since most maps represent phenomena on the earth, we begin with a short introduction to the shape of our planet and its spherical coordinates, latitude and longitude.

The Earth: Grid and Shape

Rotation about its axis gives the spherical earth two basic reference points, the North Pole and the South Pole. The locus of points equidistant from the poles defines the equator, which divides the earth into two equal hemispheres. The equator is a *great circle,* the largest circle possible on a sphere. Every sphere such as the earth contains many great circles—an indefinitely large number, in fact— each formed by the intersection of the sphere with a plane through its center. The equator, however, is the only great circle in a plane perpendicular to the earth's axis.

    Latitude, one of the earth's two spherical coordinates, is based on the equator. Through each point on the sphere passes a unique plane parallel to the equator and perpendicular to the axis. These parallel planes are many, and each intersects the spherical surface to define a circle called a *parallel.* Except at the equator, a parallel is a *small circle*—smaller than a great circle. Only one parallel passes through a point, and that parallel is referenced by its angular position north or south of the equator, as Figure 1-1 illustrates. This angle, or latitude, is measured in degrees north or south of the equator. Washington, D.C., with

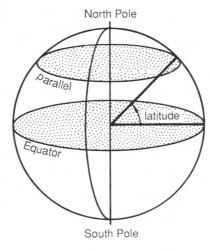

Figure 1-1 View of the earth showing the relationship of latitude and the parallels to the equator, the axis of rotation, and the poles.

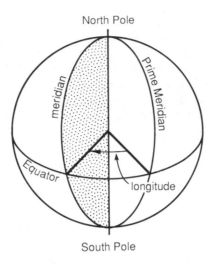

North Pole

South Pole

Figure 1-2   View of the earth showing the relationship of longitude and the meridians to the prime meridian, the axis of rotation, the poles, and the parallels.

a latitude of almost 39°N, lies about 12° closer to the equator than to the North Pole.

Along each parallel are many points, all with the same latitude. Through each of these points passes a unique perpendicular grid line called a *meridian*. On the surface of the sphere, meridians intersect parallels at right angles. Each meridian runs from the North Pole to the South Pole and is half a great circle. The earth has an indefinitely large number of meridians, all of which meet at the poles. Except at the poles, a single, unique meridian passes through each point on the sphere. The point's unique combination of intersecting meridian and parallel provides a precise description of its location. A grid of uniformly spaced meridians and parallels is called a *graticule*.

One meridian, designated the *prime meridian*, is the basis for measuring *longitude*, the angle that uniquely identifies each meridian, as Figure 1-2 shows. Longitude is measured east or west of the prime meridian, and ranges from 0° to 180°, the approximate location of the International Date Line. The world contains no natural prime meridian, but the former ascendancy of Great Britain as a world power and leader in navigational astronomy led to an international agreement accepting a common reference meridian through the Royal Observatory at Greenwich, England.[12] With a longitude of 77°W, Washington, D.C., is very much closer to Greenwich than to the International Date Line.

Although we usually think of the earth as a perfect sphere, the distance between the poles (12,713.5 km) is actually shorter than the earth's diameter at the equator (12,756.3 km). Thus the earth is shaped rather like a ball of gouda cheese that is somewhat flattened at the top and bottom. This shape is not surprising to geophysicists, who consider our planet not a rigid solid, but a gob

---

[12] See Derek Howse, *Greenwich Time and the Discovery of the Longitude* (Oxford, Eng.: Oxford University Press, 1980).

of very viscous fluid spinning about its axis like a slow merry-go-round subject to the outward pull of centrifugal force. Geodesists, who make precise measurements of both the locations of places and the shape of the earth, have shown that a cross section through the earth's rotational axis more closely resembles an ellipse than a circle. An ellipse has two extreme radii: a *semi-major axis*, which represents the distance from the earth's center out to the equator, and a *semi-minor axis*, which represents the shorter distance from the earth's center to one of the poles. As Figure 1-3 shows, rotating this ellipse about the shorter axis yields a three-dimensional figure called an *ellipsoid* or *spheroid*, which approximates the flattening of the earth at the poles and provides a mathematical model of the planet's shape on which to base map projections.[13]

The earth, of course, is not a smooth ellipsoid: the land is generally higher than the sea. With mean sea level as the *datum,* or reference point, elevations on earth range from -400 m ($-1,312$ ft) in the Dead Sea to 8,854 m (29,028 ft) at Mount Everest. Both Mount Everest in the Himalayas of Asia and many other mountain ranges around the world are hundreds of miles away from the ocean. To determine the elevations of such mountains relative to a distant sea level, geodesists have developed a hypothetical three-dimensional surface called the *geoid*, which represents the shape of a smoothed, sea-level world. At each point the geoid approximates the water surface on a hypothetical canal that is part of a hypothetical network of canals connected to the oceans without locks or rapids.[14] Geodetic measurements of the geoid indicate that the general shape of the earth resembles a pear, with a mid-latitude bulge in the southern hemisphere, a slight depression at the South Pole, and a slight protrusion at the North Pole. As Figure 1-4 shows schematically, these departures from the ellipsoid are minor when compared to the marked vertical differences between ellipsoid and sphere.

Precise measurements of latitude and longitude require expensive, lengthy astronomical observations and are carried out in only a few places. An ellipsoid and a series of precise ground measurements called a *control survey* carry the precision of these "anchor" measurements to other locations.[15] Flat maps of the world, a country, or one of the large states in the United States are conveniently

---

[13] Most formulas for small-scale maps are based on the sphere, but ellipsoidal formulas are appropriate for large-scale maps, on which horizontal accuracy might be affected by the flattening of the earth at the poles. For the formulas of some common projections, as well as a concise description of each projection's properties, see John P. Snyder, *Map Projections Used by the U.S. Geological Survey*, Geological Survey Bulletin no. 1532 (Washington, D.C.: U.S. Government Printing Office, 1982).

[14] For a fuller discussion of the geoid and geodetic measurement, see Desmond King-Hele, "The Shape of the Earth," *Science* 192, no. 4246 (25 June 1976), 1293–1300; and Petr Vanicek and Edward J. Krawiwsky, *Geodesy: The Concepts* (Amsterdam: North-Holland Publishing Company, 1982), pp. 97–122.

[15] See, for example, C. B. Breed and G. I. Hosmer, *Principles and Practice of Surveying, Volume II: Higher Surveying*, 8th ed. (New York: John Wiley & Sons, 1962).

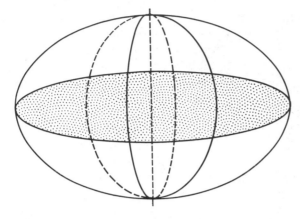

Figure 1-3 The ellipse, which in cross section better accommodates the flattening of the earth at the poles, describes a three-dimensional ellipsoid when rotated about its minor axis.

based on the less complicated spherical model of the earth, but detailed maps of smaller regions require an ellipsoidal model for the accurate assignment of latitude and longitude. Geodesists have proposed several slightly different ellipsoids, each of which seems to work better for some regions than for others.

Different ellipsoids can create noticeable differences in detailed maps of one small area, as illustrated in Figure 1-5, which shows two intersections for the meridian and parallel that define the mapped area's upper right-hand corner. The corner at which the map boundaries meet is based on what geodesists call the North American Datum of 1927, which is based in turn on an ellipsoid British

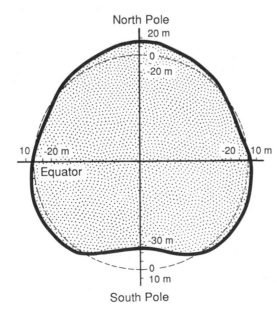

Figure 1-4 Cross sections showing the deviations between the geoid and an ellipsoid. (Adapted from Desmond King-Hele, "The Shape of the Earth," *Science* 192, no. 4246 [25 June 1976], 1293–1300.)

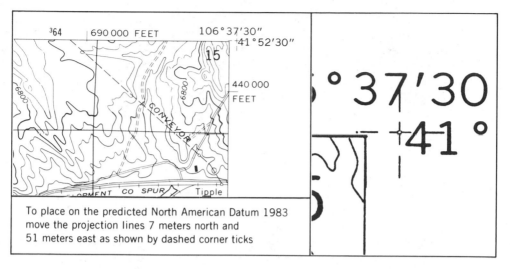

Figure 1-5 Example of differences in latitude and longitude for different reference ellipsoids. Because the North American Datum of 1983 would assign points spherical coordinates slightly different from the North American Datum of 1927, quadrangles bounded by meridians and parallels might have slightly different limits in future years. For now, however, the practice is to use the old quadrangle boundaries, but to show estimated locations for the new corners. In this example the mapped area is bounded by positions based on the North American Datum of 1927, but the new corner is shown by dashed cross-ticks adjacent to the old corner (as in the upper left and enlarged at the right). The map's explanation includes a printed description of the shift in corners (lower left). (From Dana, Wyo., U.S. Geological Survey 7.5-minute topographic map, 1:24,000, 1971, photorevised 1982.)

geodesist Alexander Clarke developed in 1866.[16] To the right of this obvious corner is a small dashed-line cross representing the same latitude and longitude. This new corner, which represents a position 7 m (23 ft) north and 51 m (167 ft) east of the old corner, is based on the North American Datum of 1983 (NAD-83, for short), which employs a new reference ellipsoid, the Geodetic Referencing System 1980 (GRS 80). Different ellipsoids yield different spherical coordinates, and shifting the ellipsoid shifts the corners of the quadrangle mapped. In the 1960s and 1970s, highly precise observations using orbiting satellites and electronic distance-measuring instruments indicated that the 1866 Clarke ellipsoid led to systematic errors in latitude and longitude, and that a new ellipsoid, with slightly different lengths for its semi-major and semi-minor axes,

[16] A *datum*, in a general sense, is a number or geometrical object that serves as a reference or base for measurement. For a discussion of the origin of the North American Datum of 1927, see William Bowie, "The Triangulation of North America," *Geographical Journal* 72, no. 4 (October 1928), 348–56.

substantially reduced the errors.[17] Map users concerned with accuracy must learn to read carefully the text printed outside the map frame on topographic and other government maps. This "collar information" mentions the datum on which the map is based and thus might explain why some features on a new map fail to match their counterparts along a common border with an older map. Map enthusiasts should appreciate the efforts of geodesists and cartographers to improve the accuracy of their products.

Scale

If you ever have to guess the identity of a hidden map and are allowed to ask 10 questions with yes-or-no answers, you should first determine the map's scale. Scale, perhaps the single most important property of a map, limits both the type of information portrayed and the size of area shown. Scale indicates actual length on the earth of a distance represented on the map. Thus scale suggests how many kinds of geographic feature can be depicted by nonoverlapping graphic symbols and what kind of information may have to be suppressed to avoid clutter. Because sheets of paper are limited in size, a map's scale also suggests how large a portion of the earth a sheet of paper can accommodate: on identically sized sheets of paper, for example, the larger the scale, the smaller the area shown.

Scale is a ratio of distance on the map to linear distance on the earth. When expressed as a ratio, units of distance must be the same and can be omitted: whether 1 centimeter represents 10,000 centimeters or 1 inch represents 10,000 inches is immaterial, for in both cases the scale is 1 to 10,000, more commonly written as 1:10,000 or 1/10,000.

Scale involving nonequivalent units of measurement can be stated verbally. With British units, verbal statements such as "1 inch represents 2,000 feet" and "1 inch represents one mile" are convenient ways of expressing the common map scales of 1:24,000 and 1:62,500 (or, more precisely but less common, 1:63,360). Map users should avoid sloppy jargon such as "1 to 200" in referring to a scale in which 1 inch represents 200 feet. With metric units, of course, map distances relate more easily to ground distances. For example, a scale of 1:500,000 readily converts to 1 centimeter representing 5 kilometers.

The common bar scale represents scale graphically, with the length of the horizontal scale representing a certain distance on the ground. A simple bar scale representing five kilometers on the earth, for example, might consist of an appropriately scaled horizontal line with vertical tick marks at both ends, the label "0" over the left-hand tick, the label "5" over the right-hand tick, and the label "km" centered below the line. Often bar scales also show intermediate

---

[17] Committee on the North American Datum, National Research Council, *North American Datum* (Washington, D.C.: National Academy of Sciences, 1971), pp. 6–24.

distances, with tick marks graduated on one side in kilometers and on the other side in miles. A graphic scale is both easy to use and a safe and convenient standard by which to enlarge or reduce a map. If, for example, an artist draws and labels a map with the ratio scale 1:5,000, an editor who is a self-styled "word person" who seldom talks to map makers could change the map's dimensions in a way that makes the label incorrect. If the map's width were reduced from 8 cm to 6 cm, the scale would then become 1:6,667, in spite of what the label indicates. With a bar scale, which can be reduced proportionately and remain accurate, the artist protects the map against editorial ignorance, herself or himself against possible embarrassment, and the reader from confusion or a serious mistake.

Whether a scale is considered "large" or "small" depends upon the size of its fractional representation, not upon the size of the denominator. The fraction $\frac{1}{2}$ is larger than the fraction $\frac{1}{4}$, and the scale 1:10,000, or 1/10,000, is larger than 1:50,000, or 1/50,000. Thus large-scale maps tend to be more detailed, covering smaller areas, than small-scale maps.

Geography thrives on cartographic generalization. The map is to the geographer what the microscope is to the microbiologist, for the ability to shrink the earth and generalize about it is as important to the study of people and their environment as the ability to magnify objects and note cellular structure is to the study of disease and genetics. The microbiologist must choose a suitable objective lens, and the geographer must select a map scale appropriate to both the phenomenon in question and the "regional laboratory" in which the geographer is studying it. Figure 1-6 shows the range of choices as a spectrum of common cartographic scales. Among the very largest, least generalized scales are those for floor plans illustrating furniture in a living room or seats in a concert hall. Where a square 20 cm (8 in.) on a side represents a square room 5 m (16 ft) along each wall, the scale is 1:25. Few maps are this detailed, however. At the other extreme we might have maps on postage stamps or the tiny figure of a projected globe in a newspaper logo, with a mere 4-cm (1.6-in.) line representing the 40,000-km (25,000-mi) equator at a truly small scale of 1:4,000,000,000. Maps this generalized can accommodate little more than a crude graticule and vague continental outlines. Most map scales, however, fall within a narrower range—between 1:1,000 and 1:200,000,000.

Projection

Transforming the spherical surface of the earth into a flat plane can play havoc with map scale. In general, map projection distorts shapes, areas, angles, directions, distances, and, quite naturally, scale. Because of the stretching, compressing, and tearing needed to flatten the sphere, scale varies from point to point. Moreover, scale in one direction away from a point commonly differs from scale in another direction. Although scale variation in a large-scale map

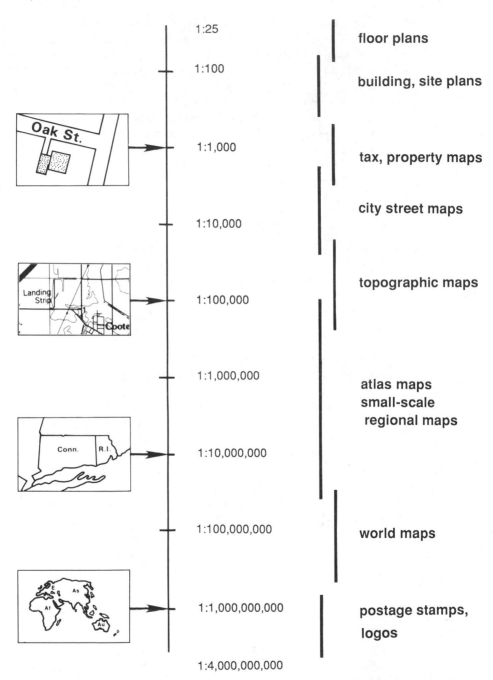

Figure 1-6 Spectrum of cartographic scales, with selected examples and ranges for common applications.

of a small area may be negligible, on a small-scale map of the world or a continent spatial distortions are blatant, but not necessarily detrimental. For some applications the distorted flat map is far more useful than a globe.

We may view map projection as a two-stage process. The first stage reduces the earth in scale to a comparatively small globe. The second stage transfers meridians, parallels, coastlines, boundaries, and other features from the globe onto a surface that can be flattened—a so-called *developable surface*—which is placed around or through the sphere. Three kinds of developable surface plane, cylinder, and cone—yield the three distinctive map grids Figure 1-7 illustrates. When centered to touch the globe at one of the poles, the plane produces a distinctive pattern of converging, straight-line meridians and concentric parallels called the *polar azimuthal* projection. When centered at the equator, the cylinder yields an *equatorial cylindrical* projection, with a set of parallel, straight-line parallels perpendicular to a set of parallel, straight-line meridians. When oriented with its apex over a pole, the cone provides a graticule of concentric, part-circle parallels and diverging, straight-line meridians. In a sense, the conic perspective is the most general and straightforward, for the plane and the cylinder can be viewed as an extremely flat cone and an extremely tall cone, respectively.

Other orientations of the developable surface produce radically different graticules, as Figure 1-8 shows. Azimuthal projections may be *equatorial*, to focus on a hemisphere, or *oblique*, to highlight distances or directions from a specific center. Oblique cylindrical projections are rare, but *transverse cylindrical* projections are common in large-scale topographic maps. In the transverse case the cylinder touches the globe along two opposite meridians.

In general the map's scale equals the globe's scale only at the point or line of contact. The orientation of the developable surface to the globe is important because distortion increases with distance from the point or line of contact. Thus

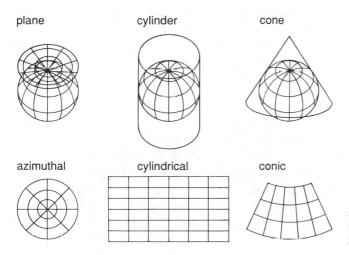

Figure 1-7 The three developable surfaces and their characteristic graticules.

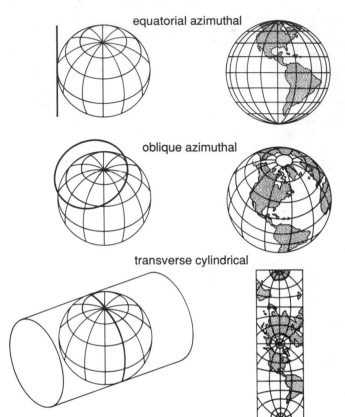

Figure 1-8 Other common orientations of the plane and cylinder to the globe, with examples of the resulting graticules.

an azimuthal projection, which touches, or is *tangent* to, the globe at its center, has low distortion near the center and relatively high distortion toward the periphery. For this reason, and because the graticule looks appropriate, geodesists prefer polar azimuthal projections for polar areas. A conic projection is tangent to the globe along a *standard parallel*, away from which in either direction distortion becomes larger, as evident on the left side of Figure 1-9. Conic projections can accommodate most mid-latitude countries, such as the United States. An equatorial cylindrical projection, tangent at the equator, has low distortion in the tropics and high distortion near the poles, which are stretched from points into lines as long as the equator. Good for mapping continents that straddle the equator, such as Africa and South America, equatorial cylindrical projections are also used for world maps, on which the distortion of sparsely inhabited polar regions is usually tolerable. In contrast, a transverse cylindrical projection is tangent along a meridian, which lies at the center of a long, thin, north-south belt of low distortion. A transverse cylindrical projection is ideal for Chile, Delaware, and other regions with a pronounced north-south elongation.

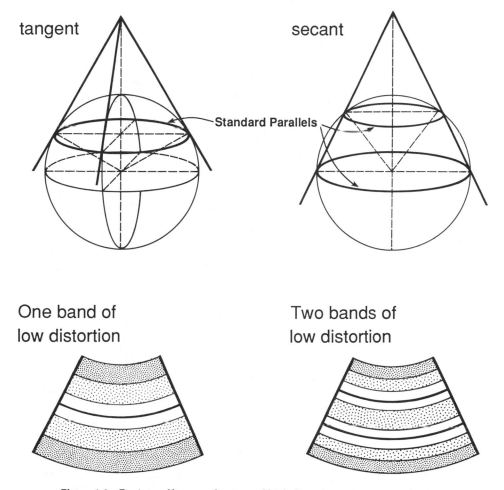

Figure 1-9 Regions of low, moderate, and high distortion on tangent and secant conic projections.

Making the developable surface pierce, rather than merely touch, the globe can lower overall distortion. A cylinder or cone *secant* to the globe has an additional line of contact, and a secant azimuthal projection touches the globe along a line rather than at a single point. On the average, places on a secant projection lie closer to a line of contact than do places on a tangent projection and are less distorted. A mid-latitude country such as the United States is particularly well served by a secant conic projection with both standard parallels within its borders to produce a broader zone of low and medium distortion, as evident on the right side of Figure 1-9.

Flat maps distort shapes, distances, directions, areas, and angles, as Figure 1-10 illustrates. All map projections distort gross shapes such as national bound-

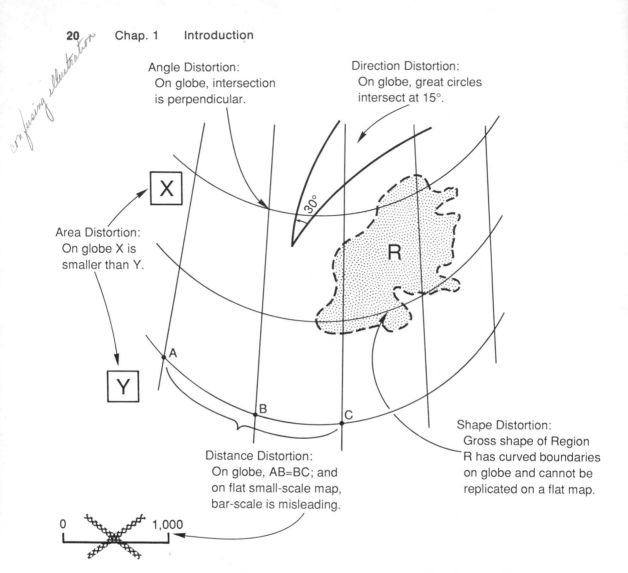

Angle Distortion:
On globe, intersection
is perpendicular.

Direction Distortion:
On globe, great circles
intersect at 15°.

Area Distortion:
On globe X is
smaller than Y.

30°

X

R

Y

A

B

C

Shape Distortion:
Gross shape of Region
R has curved boundaries
on globe and cannot be
replicated on a flat map.

Distance Distortion:
On globe, AB=BC; and
on flat small-scale map,
bar-scale is misleading.

0   1,000

Figure 1-10 Examples of the five types of cartographic distortion caused by projection from a spherical to a flat surface.

aries and continental outlines. Moreover, all projections distort most if not all distances, and the map user must understand that a stated scale of, say 1:50,000,000, holds only for the standard lines, where the developable surface is in contact with the globe. The stated scale is for the hypothetical "stage-one" globe and should not be used to estimate distances between places. Unless both places lie along a noncurving standard line, never attempt to measure the direct distance between places as a straight-line distance between map symbols. If a map is to show true distances, it may do so only for one point, the center of an *azimuthal equidistant* projection, on which all radiating straight lines are great circles with true scale. Equidistant and all other azimuthal projections also pre-serve directions in the sense that the angles between great circles intersecting at the center are the same on both map and globe. At other points on azimuthal projections, and on other projections in general, one cannot measure angles between great-circle routes on the map. Although no projection can preserve distances or directions everywhere, *equivalent,* or *equal-area,* projections preserve all relative areas, and *conformal* projections conserve all angles. Yet no projection can be both equivalent and conformal, and some are neither.

Equal-area projections are required whenever the map user might compare the sizes of countries or other territories, such as coniferous forest or agricultural land. Relative area also affects the packing of map symbols and visual estimates of density. Equivalence is particularly necessary for dot-distribution maps, on which one dot represents a fixed number of people, hogs, acres of land, or other countable phenomena. Dot maps rely upon an accurate relative packing of dots to depict an accurate picture of relative density. For example, if each of two regions with 500,000 hogs on 500 km² of land was represented on the map by 50 dots, the two groups of dots should be similarly spaced to suggest similar densities. But if the map were to distort areas, one region might have its dots spread over a noticeably larger part of the map to suggest a markedly lower density.

Systematic shrinking of oversize areas can make a projection equivalent. On an equatorial cylindrical projection, for instance, evenly spaced parallels result in exaggerated polar zones (see Figure 1-11a). Making successive parallels closer in poleward latitudes is one strategy for preserving relative area (Figure 1-11b). Bending the meridians inward to produce a *pseudocylindrical* projection (Figure 1-11c) also reduces the size of polar areas and can make a projection equivalent. But this bending severely distorts shapes for mid- and upper-latitude places far to the east or west of the *central meridian,* near which distortion is comparatively minor. Although poor for world maps, pseudocylindrical pro-jections with converging meridians provide low-distortion portrayals of places along the equator and the central meridian. Careful positioning of the central meridian yields effective regional projections for Africa, South America, and Asia. Giving each major region its own locally centered pseudocylindrical pro-jection yields regional lobes that can be joined together along the equator in an *interrupted* projection, with the map of the oceans torn apart to provide low overall distortion for continental land masses (Figure 1-11d). Perhaps the most widely used interrupted projection is J. Paul Goode's interrupted homolosine projection, which also breaks each lobe into two separately projected regions at 40° to permit optimal low-distortion representations of 12 separate zones.[18]

---

[18] See, for example, J. Paul Goode, "The Homolosine Projection: A New Device for Portraying the Earth's Surface Entire," *Annals of the Association of American Geographers* 15, no. 3 (September 1925), 119–25; and Mark Monmonier, *Maps, Distortion, and Meaning,* Resource Paper no. 75-4 (Wash-ington, D.C.: Association of American Geographers, 1977), pp. 16–18.

A: Equatorial cylindrical with
exaggerated polar areas

B: Equatorial cylindrical
adjusted for equal areas

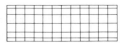

C: Pseudocylindrical equal-area

D: Interrupted cylindrical

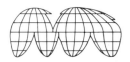

Figure 1-11 The intense distortion of area in poleward regions on an equatorial cylindrical projection (A) can be removed by decreasing the relative spacing of poleward parallels (B) or bending the meridians toward a central meridian to form a pseudocylindrical equal-area projection (C). Further reduction of shape distortion results from dividing the world into a number of lobes, representing each on its own locally centered pseudocylindrical projection, and joining the projections along the equator in an interrupted projection (D).

Conformal projections preserve angular relationships within extremely small areas around points by making the scale equal in all directions away from each point. Although map scale must vary from point to point across the map, these variations are negligible for the comparatively small area shown on a standard, large-scale topographic quadrangle map. Estimates of ground distance based on measured map distances thus can be as accurate as measurement techniques, symbol placement, and paper shrinkage or swelling allow. On large-scale conformal maps, circular objects remain essentially circular, straight lines represent direct routes, and intersecting straight lines portray measurable bearings. In addition to their use for large-scale maps, conformal projections are preferable for world and regional maps of the atmosphere and oceans in order to minimize distortion of the shapes of pressure cells, wind and current directions, and weather fronts. Although no flat map can portray shapes and curves exactly as they appear on the globe, conformal projections always provide perpendicular junctions of meridians and parallels and tend to distort routes and gross shapes less than other projections.[19]

Two conformal projections are particularly useful for navigation. The *Mercator* projection in the equatorial case, as Figure 1-12 shows, has the useful property of straight lines that are *rhumb lines*, or lines of constant geographic

[19] Although parallels and meridians meet at right angles on conformal projections, a graticule with perpendicular junctions is not sufficient evidence that a projection is conformal.

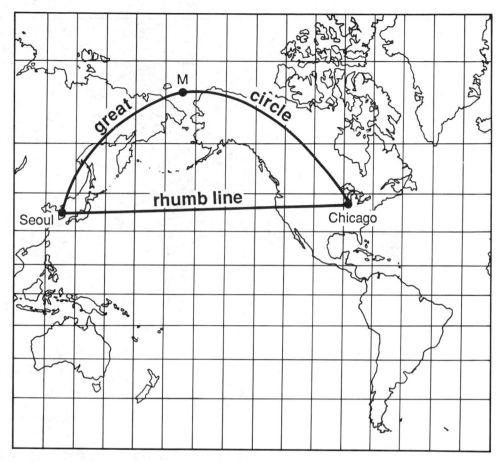

Figure 1-12 On the equatorial Mercator grid a straight line is a rhumb line, showing a line of constant geographic direction between two points. Great-circle routes generally appear as curved lines. A great-circle route can be approximated by two or more segments, which the navigator can follow with relative ease.

direction.[20] Moreover, these rhumb lines intersect the meridians at an angle equal to their true bearing. Thus to obtain his or her bearing a navigator need only draw a line between two points and measure the angle east or west of a meridian to this rhumb line. Following that bearing with an accurate compass, corrected to show true north, should take the navigator from one point to the other. Although the Mercator projection provides the most easily navigated route between points, it does not show the most direct route because a rhumb

[20] Rhumb lines are also called *loxodromes*. They would be "lines of constant compass direction" were all compasses corrected for *magnetic declination,* the departure of magnetic north from true north. The north magnetic pole does not coincide with the North Pole, at which the axis of rotation intersects the earth.

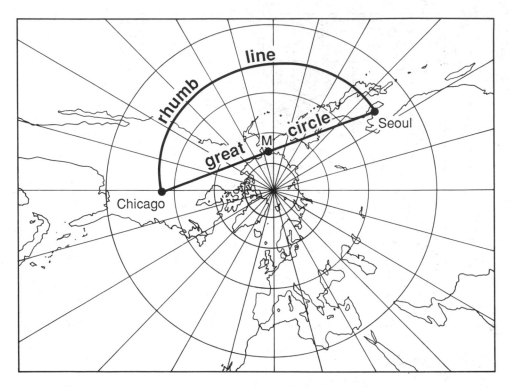

Figure 1-13   On a gnomonic projection straight lines represent great circles. A direct, great-circle route may be broken into two segments at some midpoint *M*, so that each segment can be portrayed on the Mercator grid as a straight line.

line is not a great circle but part of a spiral.[21] To complement the Mercator map, the navigator uses a *gnomonic* projection, on which straight lines portray great-circle routes. As Figure 1-13 shows, the navigator can identify intermediate points along a direct route on a gnomonic map and transfer them to the Mercator grid. Each segment now has its own rhumb line, and the navigator must change course at these intermediate points. A journey broken into two or more easily followed segments is more direct than a simpler route represented by a single rhumb line; yet the route is much easier to navigate than a great-circle route, along which direction is constantly changing. Gnomonic projections are particularly useful for planning or illustrating intercontinental circumpolar airline routes, which appear with inexplicable dogleg bends on most world maps.

Despite these advantages, both the Mercator and the gnomonic projections

---

[21] If the direction is true north or true south, the rhumb line coincides with a meridian, and thus follows a great circle. If the direction is true east or true west, the rhumb line coincides with a parallel, and thus follows a small circle. Otherwise the rhumb line is a spiral; if followed indefinitely, the rhumb line would continually circle the globe, converging toward but never quite reaching one of the poles.

grossly distort areas on their periphery and should not be used as general-purpose base and wall maps. Poleward areas are so distorted on the equatorial Mercator projection that Greenland appears as large as South America and the poles cannot be shown because they lie at infinity. This pattern of distortion has been useful to political fringe groups concerned about the threat of communism, who dramatically portray bloated, ominous, red-colored representations of the Soviet Union and the People's Republic of China on Mercator maps. Even more serious is the area distortion on the gnomonic projection, which cannot show an entire hemisphere on a finite sheet of paper. Neither projection provides a suitable general view of continental land masses, unless the inherent magnification of area can be made to serve an ideological viewpoint. Map viewers must appreciate the limited value of map distortions and be wary of their misuse.

Plane Coordinates.   Rectangular x, y-coordinates are convenient for plotting locations on graph paper or with a computer-controlled plotter and for computing distances between points.[22] When all places of interest are on a single map sheet, a local coordinate system is conveniently anchored at the lower left-hand corner of the mapped area, with the x-axis along the bottom edge. When a series of large-scale maps portray a large area, such as an entire state, a more formal plane-coordinate scheme is needed. Yet the many large-area coordinate systems in use have much in common with the simple, one-sheet x, y-grid system. As Figure 1-14 shows, a plane-coordinate system is designed for a specific zone and is based upon a particular map projection centered somewhere within the zone to minimize distortion and promote accurate distance calculations. This center is the *true origin* at which the grid lines coincide with the intersecting meridian and parallel. In order to provide x- and y-coordinates that are always positive, the cartographer references the system's *eastings* (x) and *northings* (y) to a *false origin* outside the zone. Because the quadrangles portrayed on individual map sheets of the series are bounded by meridians and parallels, which generally do not coincide with grid lines, tick marks are printed in the collar along the edges of the mapped area. By drawing straight lines across the map between corresponding tick marks, the map user can construct the grid on any map in the series.

The most widely used plane-coordinate system is the Universal Transverse Mercator (UTM) grid, defined worldwide for all places between 80°S and 84°N.[23]

---

[22] One can compute distance from plane coordinates according to the Euclidean distance formula from analytic geometry. Take the difference between the x-coordinates of the two points and the difference between the two y-coordinates. Square each difference, add these squared differences, and take the square root of the sum.

[23] The Universal Polar Stereographic (UPS) grid system, used for polar areas, is based on an azimuthal projection. For a fuller discussion of the UTM and UPS plane coordinate systems, see Porter W. McDonnell, Jr., *Introduction to Map Projections* (New York: Marcel Dekker, 1979), pp. 122–29.

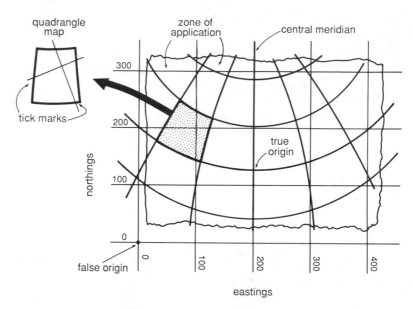

Figure 1-14   Properties of a plane-coordinate system include a zone of application, a projection with a local central meridian anchored to the grid at the true
origin, and a false origin from which one measures eastings and northings.
Because meridians and parallels generally do not coincide with grid lines, the
plane-coordinate grid appears tilted on quadrangle-format map sheets, bounded
by meridians and parallels.

This interpolar area is divided into 60 long, thin, north-south trending zones,
each 6 degrees of longitude in width and numbered eastward starting at zone
1 between 180° and 174°W. Washington, D.C., at 77°W, is in zone 18, which
extends from 78°W to 72°W, with its central meridian at 75°W. Separate transverse Mercator projections centered on each of the 60 central meridians provide
low distortion within the zones.[24] For places in the Northern Hemisphere the
false origin is on the equator at a point 500 km west of the zone's central meridian. Thus Washington, D.C., with an easting (x-coordinate) of approximately
323 km E, lies to the west of the center of zone 18—323 km E is *less east than*,
or west of, 500 km E. Its northing (y-coordinate) of 4,307 km N is its grid distance
north of the equator. For places in the Southern Hemisphere, the equator has
a northing (y-coordinate) of 10,000 km N, and all places farther south have lesser
northings. Thus a place in Australia, say, with a northing of 7,000 km N would
lie 3,000 km south of the equator.

U.S. Geological Survey quadrangle maps, both orthophotoquads (see
pages 45–47) and topographic maps (see pages 81–83), provide either UTM grid
lines across the map or tick marks along the edges, in blue. Figure 1-15 illustrates

[24] Distortion is reduced further by making the projection secant, with the transverse cylinder
piercing the globe along two small circles equidistant from the central meridian.

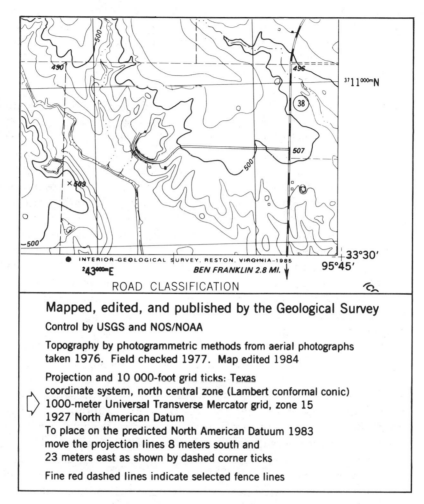

Figure 1-15   Examples of labeled UTM grid lines and differences in orientation between grid lines and the meridians and parallels that bound most quadrangle maps. The UTM grid lines labeled have coordinates of 243,000 m E and 3,711,000 m N. Explanation printed in the collar, below the mapped area of the quadrangle map, notes that grid spacing is 1,000 m and that the area is within zone 15. On older maps the user must construct grid lines from blue tick marks at the edge of the mapped area. Not all grid lines or tick marks are labeled, but the interval is constant, and the user can count up or down, as appropriate, from the labeled grid references. (From the Petty, Tex., U.S. Geological Survey 7.5-minute topographic map, 1:24,000, 1984.)

that, for 1:24,000- or 1:25,000-scale maps, grid or tick marks are spaced at intervals representing 1 km. The military developed the UTM grid to facilitate locational referencing and gunnery calculations. The UTM grid is used widely by both federal and state agencies for tying special-purpose mapping projects, such as land-use inventories, into the existing series of topographic basemaps.[25]

Map Symbols

Symbols on maps differentiate features and make geographic information visible. Symbols must be large enough for the map reader to see clearly, and thus they inherently distort the features they depict. Consider, for example, a country road 9 m (30 ft) wide that a 1:24,000-scale map represents as a line 0.5 mm (0.02 in.) in width. If the width of the line were a true reflection of the roadway, the actual pavement would be 12 m (40 ft) wide. This slight exaggeration does not hinder the faithful reproduction of the road's curves at 1:24,000, but at the smaller scales of 1:100,000 and 1:250,000 the same line symbol would mimic highways with the improbable widths of 50 m (167 ft) and 125 m (420 ft), respectively. Small-scale maps cannot show tight curves and complex interchanges in detail, as Figure 1-16 demonstrates with 1:24,000- and 1:100,000-scale representations of the intersections between two interstate highways. Symbol-induced generalization can be even more severe when a map encumbers a linear feature without width, such as a shoreline, with a line whose width would be more suitable for a 10-lane highway.

Symbols on flat maps have zero, one, or two dimensions. *Point symbols*, with zero dimensions, are located at points, which in geometry have neither width nor area. Some point symbols represent true geometric points, such as sample points in a field survey, whereas others represent areas such as cities, which small-scale maps identify only by point locations. Point symbols may be used within recognizable areal units, as when pie charts are positioned within each state or county boundary, and an individual point symbol might represent the averaged location of several objects, as when dots on a dot-distribution map each portray 5,000 hogs. *Line symbols*, with the dimension of length, are useful for portraying not only boundaries, limits, and routes, but also the form of a three-dimensional surface on a plan view or block diagram. *Isolines*, which allow maps to represent surfaces that sometimes are difficult to visualize, include contour lines to show elevation, isobars to show atmospheric pressure, isohyets to show precipitation, and isochrons to show time. A contour line, for example, would show elevations at 300 m, and contours at a variety of elevations would

---

[25] UTM coordinates reference points along the perimeter of irregularly shaped areas, as well as defining the lower left-hand corners of square grid cells. New York State's LUNR (Land Use and Natural Resource) Inventory, one of the earliest geographic information systems for environmental data, stored land-use information by square-kilometer grid cells identified by UTM coordinates. Other environmental data bases use UTM coordinates also. See Roger F. Tomlinson and others, *Computer Handling of Geographical Data* (Paris: UNESCO Press, 1976), pp. 110–24.

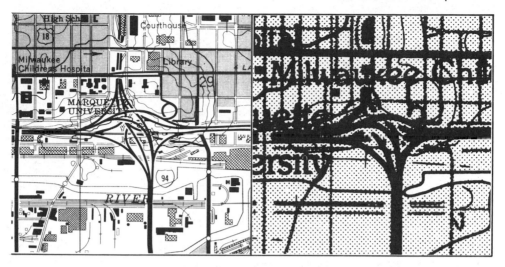

Figure 1-16   Freeway interchange shown with generally complete roadway detail at 1:24,000 (left) must be represented by a highly generalized symbol at 1:100,000 (right). (From Milwaukee, Wisc., U.S. Geological Survey 7.5-minute topographic map, 1:24,000, 1958, photorevised 1971 (left); and Milwaukee, Wisc.-Mich., U.S. Geological Survey metric topographic map, 1:100,000, 1980 (right).)

portray the land surface. *Area symbols* are two-dimensional, and may represent zones on an isoline surface, such as the area between the 20- and 40-cm isohyets on a map of rainfall, and political or administrative territories or natural features, such as lakes or deserts.[26]

Another important symbolic distinction is between qualitative and quantitative phenomena—in other words, between distributions that differ in kind and by degree. *Qualitative* distributions include soil type, dominant religion, language, and land use—traits for which places are neither more nor less than one another, merely different. In contrast, *quantitative* distributions involve geographic differences in amount or intensity—for example, population density, number of farms, and annual average temperature. Quantitative distributions may be either absolute counts or magnitudes, such as the number of farms, or intensity measures, such as median farm size or the average value of farmland and buildings. Intensity measures include medians, ratios, percentages, densities, and rates of change. Cartographic symbols suited to qualitative data tend to represent quantitative data poorly. Where the distribution is quantitative, some symbols are appropriate for showing magnitudes, whereas others are more suited to depicting intensity.

[26] Three-dimensional symbols include molded plastic relief maps portraying exaggerated terrain variations, but high production costs and difficulties with storage and portability limit the number of three-dimensional maps.

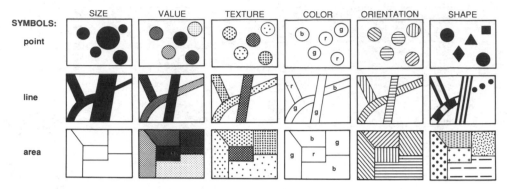

Figure 1-17 Jacques Bertin's six visual variables. In the "color" column, r, g, and b refer to the hues red, green, and blue.

To provide a theoretical framework for relating symbols to geographic phenomena, the French cartographer Jacques Bertin identified the six visual variables shown in Figure 1-17.[27] Symbols differing in size are particularly suited to portraying magnitudes at points, whereas those varying in value, or graytone, are ideal for representing intensities for areas. Quantitative line symbols can rely upon size and value to express variations in magnitude or intensity. Shape is particularly useful for qualitative point symbols, especially if pictorial shapes can be used to show churches, oil barrels, or dairy cattle. Pictorial symbols are easy for the map user to memorize and make frequent references to the map key unnecessary. Texture is effective for qualitative area symbols: differences in the shape of the small repeated pattern element effectively signal differences in type of area. Shape or texture variations are appropriate for qualitative line symbols. Point symbols are useful in portraying orientation—wind, currents, and other directional phenomena. Color is a complex symbol that can be particularly effective when red, green, blue, and other hues portray qualitative differences.[28] Because map viewers do not readily organize hues in a single spectral sequence, contrasting colors tend to frustrate the map viewer even if they make the map look pretty. Never assume that a visually attractive map will be easy to use.

In the decades ahead computer graphics will make the static, single-view map less necessary than it has been in the past. With a powerful microprocessor called a *graphics engine* the map viewer will be able to examine on a flat screen a three-dimensional model of a surface, rotating and tilting it at will. Cartographic animation will portray the evolution of settlement patterns and other spatial-temporal distributions. Automobile navigation systems will keep track of the driver's location on a dashboard screen so that awkward folded maps

[27] Jacques Bertin, *Semiology of Graphics: Diagrams, Networks, Maps,* trans. William J. Berg (Madison: University of Wisconsin Press, 1983), pp. 60–97.

[28] For a concise discussion of the role of color as a cartographic variable, see Borden D. Dent, *Principles of Thematic Map Design* (Reading, Mass.: Addison-Wesley, 1985), pp. 343–67.

need never be opened in traffic.[29] Digital atlases stored on videodisks will make thousands of maps available for display on large, flat wall panels, used for both information and entertainment. New, timely displays and datasets can be "downloaded" through direct broadcast satellite (DBS) systems or two-way fiber-optics telecommunications networks.[30] With more maps stored in digital form, map users will become their own cartographers and control the scale, projection, and symbolism of the maps they view.

Whatever a map's form may be, the map viewer must remember that a cartographic symbol is a graphic mark subject at some stage in its development to human error. Figure 1-18, which presents the State College, Pennsylvania, area as portrayed on different editions of the Harrisburg 1:250,000-scale topographic map, demonstrates that graphic marks on maps have no more a claim to ultimate truth than do typographic statements in newspapers or books. The 1957 map in this sequence portrays a fictitious rail line. Instead of deleting this spurious feature from the 1965 edition, the map's authors indicate that the rail line has been abandoned. Subsequent field inspection and examination of historical records revealed that a railroad never ran directly from State College to Dale Summit. Although a railroad once ran south to Pine Grove Mills in the 1920s, that branch was gone by 1950 and was never rebuilt. Whether this error was perpetrated by sloppy interpretation of air photos or by the wishful thinking of a railroad buff turned cartographer we may never know. Other figments of the cartographic imagination include the "paper streets" on some urban maps, which reflect roadways planned but never built. Most maps are trustworthy, but as small, inexpensive, easily manipulated surrogates, map symbols are much more prone to mistakes, inadvertent shifts, and fabrication than are the real objects they represent.

PRINCIPAL ROLES OF THE MAP

As already discussed, the map is fundamentally an efficient *instrument of communication*, a device humans use when words or gestures alone are inadequate. As a spatial object designed to be seen, the map excels in conveying relative positions or locations. The map is efficient for spatial search, too, for the eyes can move around freely to note neighbors and detect alignments, sequences, gaps, or boundaries. Although we can organize information in a variety of helpful ways—alphabetically, for example, as in a telephone book or city directory— the spatial organization provided by a map or an aerial photograph "map" clearly is more efficient for certain purposes. As used by the media to describe news events and by novelists as a backdrop for fictional happenings, the map

[29] See, for example, Robert C. Haavind, "Etak: Navigating Cars with Video Maps," *High Technology* 5, no. 4 (April 1985), 10–11.

[30] See Mark Monmonier, *Technological Transition in Cartography* (Madison: University of Wisconsin Press, 1985), pp. 171–78.

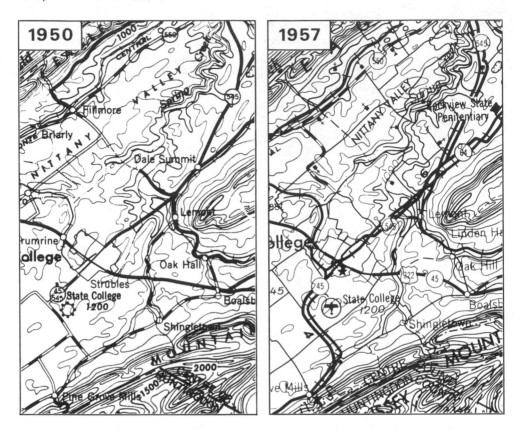

Figure 1-18 Sequence of excerpts from four maps showing the unexplained emergence on the 1957 edition of a symbol for a nonexistent railroad and an apparent attempt to "correct" the error on the 1965 edition with the symbol for an abandoned railroad. (From Harrisburg, Penn., U.S. Geological Survey 1:250,000 series map, editions for 1950, 1957, 1965, and 1969.)

can be a highly dramatic communicative tool. Because many marketing campaigns and battles for minds involve spatial phenomena, advertisements and propaganda often use the map as an instrument of persuasion.

Maps play a variety of roles, with the most basic of maps being part of the *infrastructure* of society—in a sense like pages in an owner's manual for the citizen. For instance, street maps help us find our way around our city and county, and highway maps point out various routes, direct or scenic, between places. Our tax dollars build these roads, but we need maps to use both local streets and interstate highways efficiently. Within our home community, maps help us find parks and other recreational facilities, and once we are there, other maps direct us along nature trails or point out the locations of the pool, zoo, or picnic grove. Communities lacking accurate, up-to-date maps of water and sewer

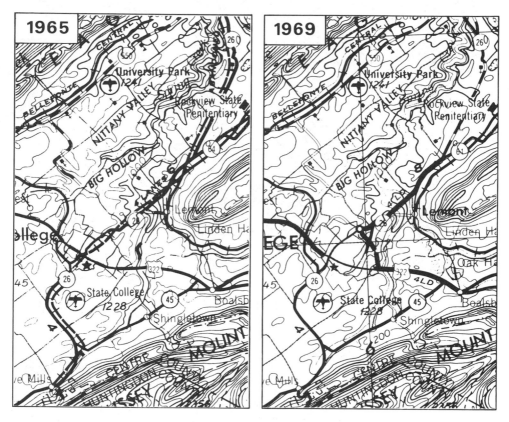

Figure 1-18 (*continued*)

lines, storm drains, and gas and electric lines provide inadequate public utilities services to the taxpayers. Even private companies map their utility lines, so that a crew repairing a water main break does not rupture a gas line or disrupt telephone service; and ideally the plot plans of all homeowners' lots should map such features, for general knowledge and in case of malfunction or emergency.

Maps also are indispensable as *research tools*. In fields as diverse as epidemiology and transporation, researchers find maps useful in defining and describing distributions and spatial patterns and in analyzing geographic associations. As an example, Figure 1-19 illustrates the areal correlation between the distribution of unirrigated cotton in the southern United States in 1929—a peak year before cotton acreage began to decline—and the temperature and moisture factors that combine to set the perimeter for cotton farming. As shown on the map, the 200-day frost-free isoline sets the northern limit: areas poleward of this line simply have too short a growing season. The isoline describing an annual average of 20 in. (51 cm) of rainfall sets the western limit; this is the minimum

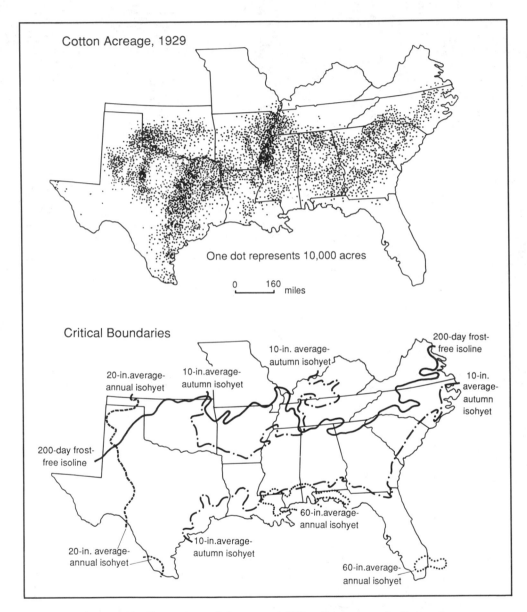

Figure 1-19 Comparison of the map of 1929 cotton acreage in the southern United States (above) with a number of climatic maps led to the detection of the environmental perimeters for economic nonirrigated cotton farming (below). (Cotton map from the 1929 *Census of Agriculture;* perimeter map compiled by authors.)

moisture requirement unless the crop is irrigated. The 10-in. (25-cm) average autumn rainfall line sets the eastern and southern limits, for more rainfall than this in the autumn tends to damage the crop. Without maps to describe the limits of cotton production, the verbal or written description would necessarily be long and more difficult to follow. Moreover, as in this example, maps can be used to discover tolerances and to suggest hypotheses.

Maps also serve as *graphic icons,* symbolizing an attachment to or a concern for place—as in the artwork that introduces "news briefs" in newspapers, in corporate logos, in business letterheads and packaging materials of all sorts, in state highway signs, and on the sides of police cars and other municipal vehicles. Often only the most schematic outline of a state or country, or the graticule of meridians and parallels, is sufficient to suggest a specific place or the world at large. A number of colleges and universities use maps on their catalogs and letterheads to associate their campuses with the states that provide both students and legislative appropriations. Cartographic icons come in all sizes. As wall decorations, maps are not only useful geographic reference works, but also useful illustrations of political organization, marketing activity, or sympathetic concern. Like exposed brickwork, hanging plants, and oak woodwork, maps can add to the ambiance of a restaurant, and, like photos of mountains and children in native costumes, maps can enhance a travel brochure. As products of science and art, maps are useful tools and sources of endless enjoyment.

FOR FURTHER READING

BALCHIN, W. G. V., "Graphicacy," *American Cartographer* 3, no. 1 (April 1976), 33–38.

BOARDMAN, DAVID, *Graphicacy and Geography Teaching.* London: Croom Helm, 1983.

GREENHOOD, DAVID, *Mapping.* Chicago: University of Chicago Press, 1964.

MONMONIER, MARK, *Maps, Distortion, and Meaning.* Resource Paper no. 75-4. Washington: Association of American Geographers, 1977.

MONMONIER, MARK, *Technological Transition in Cartography.* Madison: University of Wisconsin Press, 1985.

MUEHRCKE, PHILLIP C., *Map Use: Reading, Analysis, and Interpretation.* Madison: JP Publications, 1978.

SNYDER, JOHN P., *Map Projections Used by the U.S. Geological Survey,* Geological Survey Bulletin no. 1532. Washington, D.C.: U.S. Government Printing Office, 1982.

THROWER, NORMAN J. W., *Maps and Man.* Englewood Cliffs, N.J.: Prentice-Hall, 1972.

CHAPTER TWO

Photomaps and Remotely Sensed Images

Many map makers think of air photos as source materials, not as maps. After all, they point out, a map has crisp, uniform symbols and either accurate or purposefully controlled distance relationships, while aerial photographs, in contrast, show all terrain features but lack "interpretation." Although useful for military intelligence and a wide range of measurement tasks in civil engineering, agronomy, forestry, and urban planning, air photos were once considered aesthetically and geometrically inferior to their more sophisticated cartographic offspring, the topographic map and the land-use map. Yet advances in electronics, aeronautics, and rocketry have expanded the photomap's content and uses—and improved its reputation in the cartographic community. Far from being merely "raw" pictures of terrain, modern aerial imagery can be timely, informative, visually attractive, geometrically accurate, and more geographically complete than most other maps. The enhanced reputation of such maps extends as well to the conventional, black-and-white aerial photograph, which has changed little from the air photos photogrammetric pioneers created in the early twentieth century.

This chapter examines both conventional air photos and their newer, more varied photographic and electronic cousins, collectively termed *remotely sensed imagery*. We emphasize the geometric distortions of both air photos and satellite images and the variety of films and sensing systems: an understanding of these principles is fundamental to the use of aerial and satellite imagery, applications of which we discuss in the chapters on weather maps, municipal maps, and old maps. Our treatment of conventional imagery includes discussion of how the reader might obtain and use local photographic coverage. Remote sensing is evolving so rapidly that currently available imagery is probably a poor representative of what the user may easily obtain in the not-too-distant future; thus this chapter also introduces such basic concepts as spectral signatures, resolution, and active and passive sensing systems.

CONVENTIONAL IMAGERY

Air photos are almost as old as manned flight and not much older than improved cameras and photographic emulsions. William Henry Fox Talbot, Joseph Nicéphore Niepce, and Louis Jacques Daguerre invented photography in the 1830s. In 1858 the French photographer Gaspard Felix Tournachon took the first recorded aerial photograph, not from an airplane, but from a balloon. A mere 6 years after Orville and Wilbur Wright's short but historic flight at Kitty Hawk, North Carolina, in 1903, Wilbur Wright and a newsreel photographer took the first photographs from an airplane. During World War I both sides used aerial photographs extensively, and in the early 1920s technicians and scientists who had received training in the military explored a variety of civilian applications. Inventors in Europe and North America devised numerous aerial cameras and plotting instruments during the 1920s, and government mapping organizations such as the U.S. Geological Survey experimented with the photogrammetric production of highly accurate topographic maps. By 1934, when the American Society of Photogrammetry was formed, aerial photographs were used widely for agriculture, forestry, geology, highway design and construction, military intelligence, topographic mapping, and urban planning. Today several hundred firms in the United States are in business to supply original aerial photography to federal, state, and local governments; public utilities; forest resource corporations; and other clients.

Format, Scale, and Resolution

The standard air photo is a black-and-white photographic print, on paper, approximately 23 cm (9 in.) square. Centered along each side of the picture is a *fiducial mark*, the image of one of four markers embedded in the camera (see Figure 2-1). The two perpendicular lines connecting opposite fiducial marks intersect at the *principal point*, where the optic axis of the camera pierces the film plane. In a *vertical* aerial photograph, the principal point on the film plane records the image of the *ground nadir*, the point directly below the camera on the earth (see Figure 2-2). In practice, however, the optic axis is rarely in a true perpendicular to the horizontal plane of the earth, and some degree of *tilt* results. Measured as the angle between the optic axis and a plumb line through the

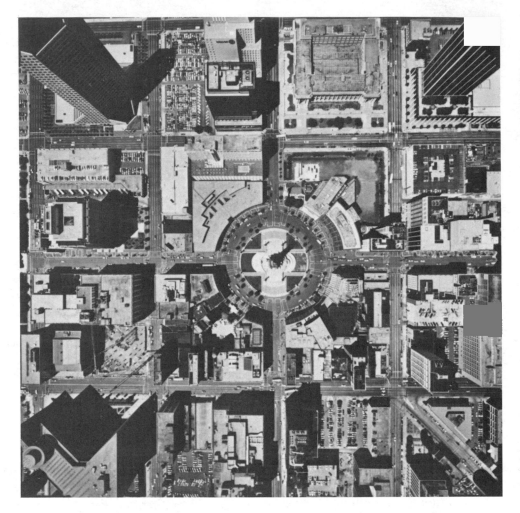

Figure 2-1 Large-scale vertical aerial photo illustrating distortion inherent in the perspective of aerial photography. Tops of buildings are displaced outward from their bases in this view centered on Monument Circle in Indianapolis, Indiana, taken from the comparatively low altitude of 360 m (1,200 ft). (Courtesy of Woolpert Consultants, Dayton, Ohio.)

center of the camera's lens, tilt generally should not exceed 3 degrees for an air photo to be considered vertical.

The scale of an aerial photograph depends upon the focal length of the lens and upon the flight height. The ratio of focal length to flight height equals the ratio of the length of a photographed image to the length of the object this image represents (see the shaded triangles in Figure 2-2). Thus for a photograph taken with a 150-mm (approximately 6-in.) lens from an altitude of 3,000 m (10,000 ft), the scale is 1:20,000. The most common scales are between 1:4,800

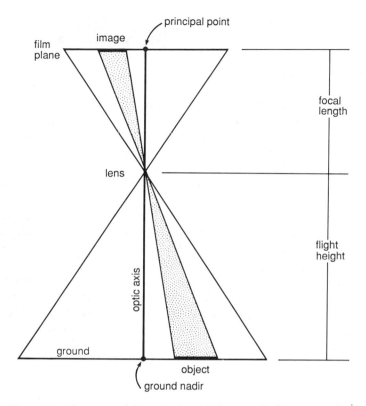

Figure 2-2 Geometry of the vertical aerial photograph, showing an object within the photographed area and its image on the photograph.

and 1:25,000, although enlargements to as much as 1:600 monitor insect damage to urban vegetation. Scales between 1:4,800 and 1:10,000 are most useful for urban planning. At 1:5,000, a house 15 m (50 ft) long is represented by a 3-mm (0.12-in.) mark, and a road 10 m wide is shown by a 2-mm line. At this scale a 23- by 23-cm (9- by 9-in.) format represents a ground area of approximately 1.3 km² (0.5 mi²).

Films for conventional black-and-white photography are sensitive to reflected light in the visible part of the spectrum, but haze-reducing filters screen out most of the blue light and require a greater sensitivity in the red part of the spectrum so that a fast shutter can provide a sharp, unblurred image of the ground. Films for aerial photography are designed for medium resolution, good tonal contrast, and sensitivity to a wide range of illumination. Flying on clear days with little turbulence, skilled pilots usually take air photos between 10 A.M. and 2 P.M. so that shadows will not hide much of the ground. Some shadow is useful, however, to provide a rough impression of the heights of trees and buildings. Air photos commonly are sold as paper prints—sometimes with the choice of either a glossy or a semi-matte finish—and as positive film transparencies. Glossy prints, on single-weight paper, provide a clearer view of the landscape, but semi-matte prints, on double-weight paper, are more durable.

Geometry and Distortion

Like a photograph taken with an ordinary camera, an aerial photo is a perspective view: as the left side of Figure 2-3 shows, the rays of light reflected from features on the ground converge on the camera's lens and then diverge as they approach the film plane. As a result, scale varies, and air photos do not portray distances between points with a constant scale, as do conventional topographic maps. Large-scale maps represent the positions of various points on the land surface as if they were all lying on the same horizontal plane, called a *datum plane*—although, of course, many points actually differ in elevation (see Figure 2-3, right). Such maps, produced by the U.S. Geological Survey and other government survey agencies, are called *planimetric maps*. A planimetric map portrays the distance between two points as the distance between the perpendicular, or *orthographic*, projections of these points onto the datum plane. Neither the map nor the photo shows the overland, or surface, distance from one point to another. On the photograph the distance between the images of the points is a function of several factors, including their distances from the ground nadir, the difference between the elevation of each point and the elevation of the horizontal datum plane, and the scale of the photo. Computed as f/H, the scale S is valid only for the datum plane at distance H below the point at which the picture was taken. Because of the convergence of the light rays through the

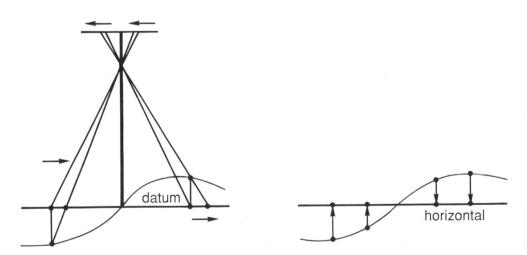

Figure 2-3 A vertical aerial photograph (left) displaces the apparent positions of objects radially inward, if below the datum, or radially outward, if above the datum, because the lines of projection converge through the lens of the photo. A planimetric map (right) places all points on a horizontal plane by lines of projection perpendicular to that plane.

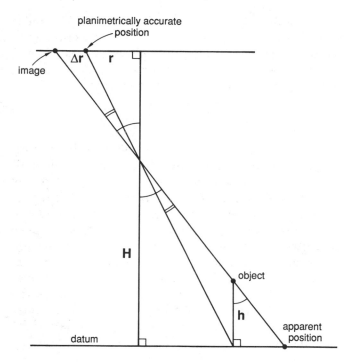

Figure 2-4 Schematic diagram showing equivalent angles used to derive the equation relating radial displacement Δr to flight height H, height h of the object above the datum, and distance r from the principal point to the planimetrically correct position of the image.

camera's lens, points above the datum plane are displaced outward from their true, planimetric positions, as Figure 2-3 shows, and points below the datum are displaced inward. For a vertical photograph this shift in apparent position is termed *radial relief displacement* because images are shifted along a straight line radiating from the principal point.

From the geometric relationships that Figure 2-4 illustrates we can derive the formula

$$\Delta r = (h/H)(r + \Delta r) \approx (h/H)r$$

which relates the displacement Δr on the photo directly to the elevation h of the object above the datum, and the distance r on the photo from the principal point to the image, and inversely to the flight height H. In general, then, distortion will be greater near the edge of the photo—particularly so in mountainous regions, where sides of steep hills facing away from the ground nadir might be hidden from view. When the flight height is great, as with the U.S. Geological Survey's National High-Altitude Aerial Photography (NHAP), taken at about 12,000 m (40,000 ft) above the terrain and available as 23- by 23-cm (9- by 9-in.) prints at a scale of 1:58,000, displacement is slight, and for most purposes can be ignored. Yet with conventional aerial imagery taken at, say, 3,000 m (10,000 ft) and a scale of 1:20,000 and enlarged to 1:5,000, the image of the top of a building 70 m (230 ft) tall near the perimeter of the photo will be displaced about 1 cm outward from its foundation. (A similar effect is evident in the images of tall buildings along the left and bottom edges of Figure 2-1.) Relief displacement is perhaps the principal reason why cartographers, traditionally concerned with planimetric accuracy, have had difficulty regarding the air photo as a map. When we use aerial photography, then, we should expect some variation in scale, particularly when the scale of the photo is large and the terrain is hilly.

Stereoviewing

Relief displacement limits the usefulness of single aerial photographs, but increases the value of a pair of photos that overlap somewhat in the area covered. Two photos taken at the same altitude at different but not-too-distant points permit the viewer to see a three-dimensional model of the terrain in the region of overlap. As in binocular vision, each eye views a scene containing the same objects. The distance between corresponding images formed on the retinas is slightly greater for the closer object, and the eye-brain system converts these distances into perceptions of relative elevation. For persons with normal vision, Figure 2-5 demonstrates this *stereoscopic effect*. Stare at the two parts of the upper half of the figure and focus your eyes as if looking into the distance. When the corresponding images fuse, you should see a pyramid, with its apex clearly above its base. Look in the same way at the two parts of the lower half of the figure; here you should see a pit, with the point at the bottom well below the

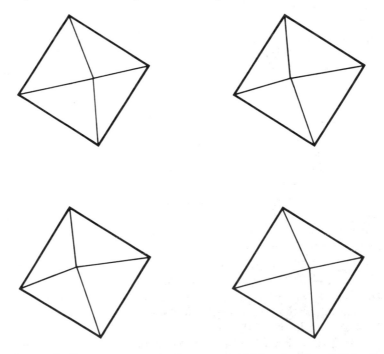

Figure 2-5   Stereograms representing a pyramid (above) and a pit (below).

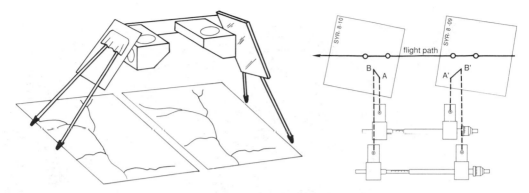

Figure 2-6   A mirror stereoscope (left) can be used to view two successive, overlapping aerial photographs. A stereometer (right) can be used with the stereoscope to measure parallax displacement, the difference between *A-A'* and *B-B'* of a vertical object.

pit's rim. Note that the pattern of displacement for these two stereograms is consistent with the perspective of a single vertical photo: the images of the top of the pyramid are displaced outward, away from each other, whereas the images of the bottom of the pit are displaced inward, toward each other. This effect, called *parallax displacement*, permits stereoviewing with the naked eye, but a stereoscope that magnifies the images promotes visual fusion and provides a sharper, more detailed view of the landscape.

Researchers in photogrammetry have developed many useful techniques and machines for measuring parallax displacement and converting this measurement into a precise estimate of the difference in elevation between points. One of the simplest photogrammetric instruments is the *stereometer* (see Figure 2-6), which the photogrammetrist can use with a mirror stereoscope and a pair of overlapping photos to estimate elevation differences. These estimations can then serve as the basis for estimating slope, tree height, and other landscape traits of interest to geologists and foresters.[1]

The *stereo plotter* is a more complex instrument, at which an operator can view a three-dimensional stereomodel and trace the path of a line of constant elevation around a hill or valley (see Figure 2-7). As the photogrammetrist follows the line, the stereoplotter draws the corresponding contour line. Stereoplotters are highly useful for compiling topographic maps: in addition to plotting relief contours, these machines facilitate the accurate planimetric plotting of buildings, roads, railways, streams, shorelines, forest boundaries, and other prominent features readily identified in the stereomodel.[2]

[1] For a discussion of the use of a stereometer, also called a parallax bar, to measure elevation difference and slope, see John Wright, *Ground and Air Survey for Field Scientists* (Oxford, Eng.: Clarendon Press, 1982), pp. 204–10.

[2] For a comprehensive discussion of stereoplotting instruments, see Chester C. Slama, Charles Theurer, and Soren W. Henriksen, eds., *Manual of Photogrammetry*, 4th ed. (Falls Church, Va.: American Society of Photogrammetry, 1980), pp. 545–722.

Figure 2-7 Zeiss C100 Planicomp Analytical Plotting System, with photogrammetric viewer (right), printer and CRT terminal (left), and minicomputer and disk unit (rear). (Courtesy of Carl Zeiss, Inc.)

Orthophoto Maps

An instrument called an *orthophotoscope* can remove relief displacement and thus produce air photos, called *orthophotos*, that are planimetric maps. The concept of the orthophotoscope is straightforward: measure parallax difference and then expose an enlarged negative of the overlapping part of one of the two photos so that each small picture element, about 5 mm^2, is relocated to its true planimetric position. If, for instance, relief displacement moved a relatively high feature radially outward 4 mm from the principal point, on the resulting *orthophoto* the image of this feature would be shifted radially inward 4 mm. In essence, then, the orthophotoscope copies the aerial photograph piece by piece to yield a planimetric map providing a continuous-tone, photographic image of the landscape. Because steep hill slopes near the edge of the photo and facing away from the principal point may be hidden, orthophotos for areas of high relief may include blind spots—features invisible on both parent photos—for which the orthophotoscope could not measure the parallax difference. For this reason orthophoto products generally are not available for areas of mountainous or very rough terrain or for urban areas with many high-rise buildings.

Computers and modern electronic sensors have relieved the photogrammetrist of many tedious, by-rote chores, including the production of orthophotos. Electro-optical machines can scan the stereomodel systematically, cell by cell, to detect corresponding images on both photos and thus to measure parallax differences automatically. With the first practical mechanical-optical orthophotoscopes, developed in the 1950s at the U.S. Geological Survey, a trained operator required several days to generate an orthophoto for the overlap portion of a stereomodel, and USGS considered orthophotomaps useful but not economical. The electronic orthophotoscopes introduced in the 1970s could produce an orthophoto of the same area in a matter of hours, including time for set-up and film processing. Moreover, modern orthophotoscopes produce not only planimetrically correct photographic images, but also automatically plotted contour charts and *digital elevation models,* arrays on magnetic tape or disk containing terrain elevations at the intersections of evenly spaced grid lines. Digital elevation models have a wide variety of applications in terrain analysis, remote sensing, hydrologic modelling, and regional planning.[3]

Orthophoto technology produces a variety of different photo-image maps. Photogrammetrists can reproduce orthophotos as photographic prints or halftones to be printed lithographically along with overprinted map grids, place names, route numbers, contour lines, and symbols to emphasize roads and indicate boundaries. Natural or artificial color can enhance the image. Masking to suppress the photo image and enhance contrast is an effective way of making labels and other symbols recognizable where the photographic image is relatively dark. Of course cartographers must be careful to avoid adding too many closely spaced symbols, particularly in urban areas, where even a traditional line map is likely to have a high density of features.

The U.S. Geological Survey produces two principal types of photo-image map in a standard quadrangle format. The *orthophotomap* includes contours and locally appropriate color enhancements such as blue for water, greenish blue for wetlands, green for forest, and brown for relatively dry, nonforested areas. Such maps' coverage is highly selective, with emphasis on low-relief coastal or desert areas having little or no urban development. In 1985, orthophotomaps were available for fewer than 800 of the 53,549 7.5-minute quadrangles in the contiguous states. In contrast, the less visually enhanced, less expensive, black-and-white *orthophotoquad* covered about 67 percent of these quadrangles.[4] Based upon an aerial photograph taken at about 12,000 m (39,000 ft) above the center of the quadrangle, a 1:24,000- or 1:25,000-scale orthophotoquad has a map grid

---

[3] For a discussion of digital elevation models and their uses, see James R. Carter, *Computer Mapping: Progress in the '80s* (Washington, D.C.: Association of American Geographers, 1984), pp. 21–23; and Atef A. Elassal and Vincent M. Caruso, *Digital Elevation Models,* Circular no. 895-B (Reston, Va.: U.S. Geological Survey, 1983).

[4] Copies of most orthophotoquads are available only as diazo prints, reproduced in a manner similar to building plans. In 1987, one could purchase lithographically printed maps for approximately 6 percent of the 36,000 orthophotoquads available.

Figure 2-8 Photographically reduced southwest portion of Ashland, Pennsylvania, 7.5-minute orthophotoquad. (U.S. Geological Survey, 1976.)

and collar similar to 7.5-minute series topographic maps. Orthophotoquads contain only a few labels and symbols, mostly lines to indicate state and county boundaries and numbers to identify principal highways. These photomaps usually name the most important topographic features and settlements (see Figure 2-8). A typical orthophotoquad can be produced more rapidly and less expensively than a new topographic map. For many areas orthophotoquads provide the only reasonably current, detailed coverage, and the U.S. Geological Survey has used orthophotoquads to provide temporary coverage until modern topographic maps can be produced. For many applications, such as tax assessment, site selection, and environmental conservation, photomaps are often preferable to conventional line maps, which provide far less information about land use and land cover.[5]

"Flying" Aerial Imagery

Understanding how aerial photography is "flown" is vital to its acquisition and use. Except for highly specialized applications—in which, for example, a helicopter might be used to obtain a photograph centered at a specific point—most conventional aerial imagery is available in parallel strips of overlapping photos taken from fixed-wing aircraft flying along carefully planned flight lines (see Figure 2-9). A 60 percent *forward overlap* of photos along the same flight line is

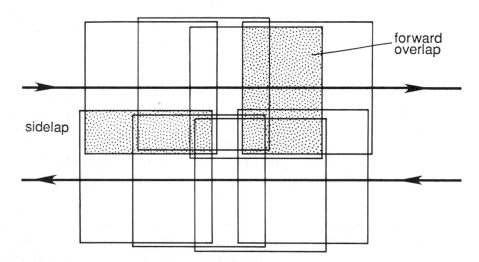

Figure 2-9   Typical specifications for aerial photography require 60 percent forward overlap between successive photos on the same flight line and 30 percent sidelap between photos on adjacent flight lines.

[5] For discussion of the design and uses of orthophotomaps, see Norman J. W. Thrower and John R. Jensen, "The Orthophoto and Orthophotomap: Characteristics, Development and Application," *American Cartographer* 3, no. 1 (April 1976), 39–56.

required for stereoviewing. Flight-line orientation is usually east-west. When a project area is long and narrow, another flight-line orientation requires fewer turns by the aircraft, covers the area with significantly fewer exposures, and provides fewer strips of overlapping photos. Each additional flight line adds to the number of frames. An approximately 30 percent *sidelap* of neighboring flight lines is normally needed so that all photos can be tied to a common datum plane with comparatively few carefully surveyed *ground control* points.

The wary purchaser of aerial photographs must look for photo coverage that contains minimal variation in scale, particularly where terrain elevation fluctuates greatly. A comparatively high flight height and a long focal length normally reduce scale variation in hilly areas if the atmosphere is calm and the aircraft is not buffeted by vertical air currents. If the air is turbulent, the photographs will probably have appreciable tilt, the shift of the optic axis from a true vertical (see Figure 2-10) discussed earlier. Although a small amount of tilt is unavoidable, tilt poses difficulties for stereoplotting, and aerial photography contracts commonly specify that the departure of the optic axis from a plumb line shall not exceed 5 degrees for any single photo or average more than 1 degree for a single flight line.[6] *Crabbing*, a rotation of the frame of the photo relative to the flight line, reduces the usefulness of the overlap and should not exceed 10 degrees between consecutive photos (see Figure 2-11, left). Crabbing may occur when horizontal turbulence requires the pilot to turn the plane into the wind a bit to avoid *drift*, the divergence of the flight line from its intended course (see Figure 2-11, right). A typical specification in an aerial photography contract might require that all photo centers fall within 1 cm of their planned positions.

Because tonal variations in air photos should reflect differences in land cover, pilots should not take photographs on days when cloud shadows, haze, air pollution, or snow obscure substantial portions of the area. Such phenomena should obscure no more than 5 percent of the area of any one photograph. Moreover, to minimize tonal variations caused by the shadows of trees or buildings, aerial photography should not be taken too early or too late in the day; the angle between the sun's rays and the horizontal surface should be at least 25 degrees. Inquire about time of day and cloud cover when purchasing from a nonstandard source.

Seasonality is important as well: the intended use of the photographs dictates the time of year at which aerial photography is flown. Foliage is the controlling factor: photography for crop measurement must be taken during the growing season, whereas photography for topographic mapping is best obtained after deciduous trees have lost their leaves, which obscure the ground. Thus

---

[6] In addition, the combined angular deviation between the optic axes of two successive photos in a flight line should not exceed 6 degrees. For an example of the standards used in evaluating aerial photography and in contracts, see Francis H. Moffitt and Edward M. Mikhail, *Photogrammetry*, 3d ed. (New York: Harper & Row, 1980), pp. 497–98.

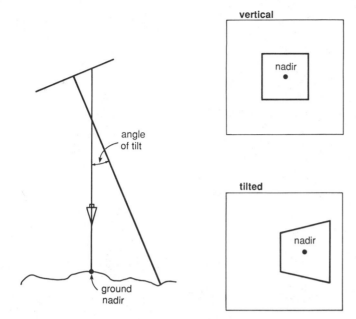

Figure 2-10 Tilt, a departure of the optic axis from a plumb line through the lens, displaces the nadir point from the center of the photo and distorts scale and shape.

the U.S. Department of Agriculture takes aerial photographs—used largely in measuring cropland acreages—during the summer in the North and during the winter in the South; whereas the U.S. Geological Survey and the Tennessee Valley Authority take aerial photographs—used with stereoplotters to obtain elevation contours—in spring or fall. The intended use also affects scale: aerial photography for mapping ordinarily has a scale (1:20,000 or less) that is smaller than that of photography for area measurement (1:20,000 or more), which uses lenses with relatively long focal lengths in order to minimize relief displacement. Most of the conventional aerial coverage of the 48 contiguous states in this country is of the latter type. In counties with even a modest amount of farming,

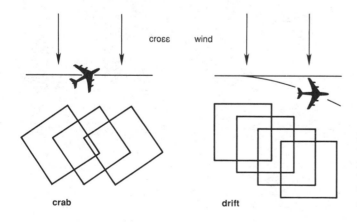

Figure 2-11 Crab (left) occurs when the pilot remains on course by facing into a cross wind, but fails to rotate the camera. Drift (right) occurs when the pilot does not compensate for cross wind and drifts off course.

the local office of the U.S. Agricultural Stabilization and Conservation Service (listed in the federal government section of the blue pages of the telephone directory under "AGRICULTURE, DEPT OF") probably has complete coverage of the county that usually is no more than seven years old. The government allows anyone to examine these aerial photographs at the local ASCS office, which can furnish information on how to order particular prints.

The U.S. Department of Agriculture's Soil Conservation Service uses large-scale aerial imagery to make county-wide *uncontrolled photo mosaics*: carefully assembled collages of aerial photos produced at a common scale and with tilt removed, but with relief displacement still present (see Figure 2-12). (If photogrammetrists used orthophotos to remove relief displacement, the collage would be a *controlled mosaic*.) To create an uncontrolled photo mosaic, the photogrammetrist carefully joins the low-displacement central portions of overlapping individual photographs—to minimize obvious displacements of linear fea-

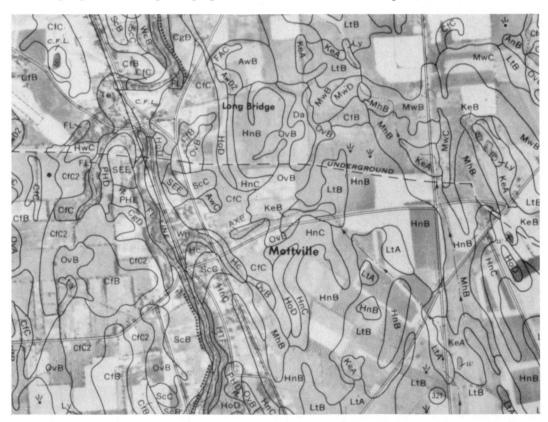

Figure 2-12 Portion of uncontrolled photo mosaic showing boundaries between soil mapping units and classification codes on map in soil survey report. (From a portion of sheet 33 in Frank Z. Hutton, Jr., and C. Erwin Rice, *Soil Survey of Onondaga County, New York* [Washington, D.C.: Soil Conservation Service, 1977].)

tures at the joins—then tapes the collage and photographs it for publication at a scale of 1:20,000 or 1:15,840. Rectangular portions of the mosaic, overprinted with the classification codes and boundaries of soil units, are bound into the soil survey report.

The *index mosaic* is merely a picture of overlapping untrimmed frames assembled with the exposure numbers exposed at the top of each frame (see Figure 2-13). This form of collage is less elegant than the uncontrolled photo mosaic, but is particularly helpful in selecting photos that cover an area of interest. The photogrammetrist photographs the index collage at a scale much smaller than that of the original photos so that a single index sheet covers the entire county. For comparatively large-scale imagery, with proportionately more photographs, the photogrammetrist may have to make several index mosaics.

Another form of index is the *photo index sheet*, a map showing flight lines, center points of individual frames, and exposure numbers, as well as reference features such as minor civil division boundaries and principal roads (see Figure 2-14). A photo index sheet also includes the scale, date, and focal length of the photography, the project and roll numbers, the name of the contractor who flew the mission, and the address from which one can order prints.

Obtaining Aerial Imagery

Obtaining aerial imagery for your local area is usually straightforward, although not as simple as acquiring topographic maps. A single national program systematically produces topographic maps and orthophotoquads, which local dealers and government centers sell from their inventories of maps covering their areas. A wide variety of government agencies and private firms produce and supply aerial photographs, however. Private firms are often willing to sell prints of photographs they originally "flew" for other clients. Rather than purchasing existing imagery, which may be obsolete, organizations undertaking projects such as tax mapping and environmental impact studies may need to hire photogrammetrists to provide them with new aerial photographs. Sometimes photogrammetric firms "fly" photography "on speculation": if one client orders aerial coverage of two-thirds of a county, for instance, imagery of the entire county might be attractive in the near future to a second client. Government agencies—such as the county planning commission, the county tax assessor, and the local office of the U.S. Agricultural Stabilization and Conservation Service—have photo index mosaics and photo index sheets that purchasers may inspect during business hours. Sometimes individual prints can be examined as well. Each agency most likely will have indexes only for the imagery it controls, however.

The U.S. Geological Survey's National Cartographic Information Center (NCIC) and some state governments maintain records of existing aerial photographs, which can be indispensable in finding out what coverage is available and where one may purchase it. These inventories, which are maintained as a

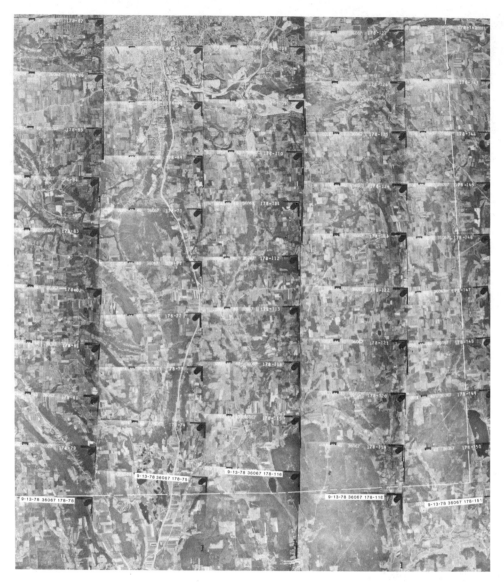

Figure 2-13 Index mosaic. (Photographic reduction of index sheet 4 [of 4], Onondaga County, N.Y., code 36067, U.S. Agricultural Stabilization and Conservation Service.)

service to government agencies and private users alike, list aerial imagery from all sources, including contractors who fly photographic missions on speculation and companies and government bodies that obtain site-specific coverage for environmental impact statements, facilities planning studies, and other projects

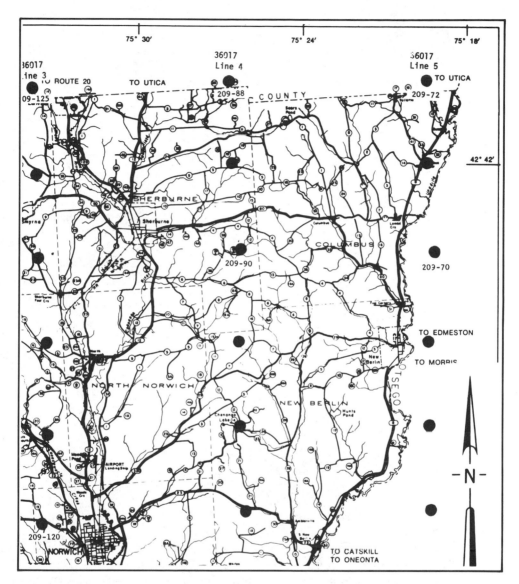

Figure 2-14   Portion of a photo index sheet. Dots are shown for photo centers along two north-south flight lines. The number 209-72, in the upper right corner, is a frame number. (Photographic reduction from index to National High Altitude Photography for Chenango County, N.Y.)

(see Figure 2-15). Not all air photos, after all, are acquired for county-wide or other systematic mapping projects.

The purchaser of aerial photographs may have the choice of paper prints

| 11/78 | | 6" | AREA OF COVERAGE: Skaneateles Lake and shore (See Regional Project 64) |
| | 1:9600 (1"=800') | Pan | VIEW PHOTOS: COE-Buffalo   BUY PHOTOS: COE-Buffalo |

3,4/81		6"	AREA OF COVERAGE: Entire county
	1:9600* (1"=800')	Pan	VIEW PHOTOS: PLAN-Syracuse BUY PHOTOS: PLAN-Syracuse
			* = 1"=200' scale enlargements also available

5/81		6"	AREA OF COVERAGE: E 1/6 of county: quadrangle centered photos covering
	1:80,000 (1"=6667')	Pan	the 7.5' quadrangles of Cleveland, De Ruyter, Manlius, Oran (See Regional Project 79)
			VIEW PHOTOS: No known NY State BUY PHOTOS: NCIC-Reston VA address
			Part of US Geological Survey Project GS-VEWR

5/81 & 4/82	1:80,000 (1"=6667')	6"	AREA OF COVERAGE: NW 4/5 of county: quadrangle centered photos for all
		Pan	7.5' quadrangles except Cleveland, De Ruyter, Manlius, Otisco Valley, Owasco, Skaneateles, Spafford, Tully (See Regional Project 78)
			VIEW PHOTOS: No know NY State BUY PHOTOS: NCIC-Reston VA address
			Part of US Geological Survey Project GS-VEOX

Figure 2-15 Photographic reduction of part of a page in *Inventory of Aerial Photography and Other Remotely Sensed Imagery of New York State* (Albany, N.Y.: Map Information Unit, New York State Department of Transportation, 1983). Entries contain date of photography (month/year), scale, lens focal length (6 in.), film (panchromatic), area covered, and places where one may view or purchase the imagery. COE is the U.S. Army Corps of Engineers; PLAN is the Syracuse and Onondaga County Planning Agency; and NCIC is the U.S. Geological Survey's National Cartographic Information Center. (Used with permission.)

or transparent, reproducible images on film, which are more expensive. Enlargements are sometimes available. Some county planning offices provide enlarged diazo copies within a few days, at a cost of approximately $10 for a 91-by-91-cm (36-by-36-in.), 1:2,400-scale copy of an enlargement from a 1:9,600-scale exposure. Photographically reproduced enlargements and contact prints, which one must usually order from the federal government or the original contractor, may be delivered within 4 to 6 weeks after payment is received. A 61-by-61-cm (24-by-24-in.) contact print ordered from the U.S. Department of Agriculture costs about $10 (Aerial Photography Field Office, Agricultural Stabilization and Conservation Service, P.O. Box 30010, Salt Lake City, UT 84125).

For aerial imagery of the United States held by the U.S. Geological Survey, a computer search of the data base maintained by the National Cartographic Information Center is an expedient substitute for a costly visit to the locality of interest (NCIC, 507 National Center, U.S. Geological Survey, Reston, VA 22092). The service is free. The NCIC asks users to identify their area of interest by state, county, and city or town, as well as by geographic coordinates (latitude and longitude). Submitting a marked map and a statement of the terrain features sought is helpful. The user should specify the level of ground detail desired: either low altitude, large scale for maximum detail; or high altitude, small scale for minimum detail. Users may request overlapping p⁻⁻tos for stereoviewing

```
                    Eros Data Center                          Report No. OL001-1
                 Sioux Falls, South Dakota  57198            Date:  4/19, 1984
              Contact Number 0464636016     Terminal T83A22   Time:  08:50
                 Alk--Monmonier                               Page:  1


        11 Accessions                          Polygon Retrieval


      Latitude   Longitude   Latitude   Longitude   Quality   Cloud-Cover   Recording-Tech    Scale
      N43D03M    W76D10M                               5         30%           Vertical      LE 160D00


                        Data Type    Photo-Index


  Imagery-Type               Scene   ID Film/Index-Type  Quality Cloud  Expo-Date   Scene-Scale   Microform

  Aerial-Mapping-Standard B590350950168    B&W MI/B      **8**   00%   10/18/59     1:60,000     0000950168
  Corner Point Coordinates=#1:N43D00M00S W078D00M00S #2:N43D00M00S W076D00M00S #3:N44D00M00S W076D00M00S #4:N44D00M00S W078D00M00S

  Aerial-Mapping-Standard 1VEQX00670086    B&W PI/A      **8**   00%   05/07/81     1:80,000     0000670086
  Corner Point Coordinates=#1:N43D00M00S W076D15M00S #2:N43D00M00S W076D00M00S #3:N43D15M00S W076D00M00S #4:N43D15M00S W076D15M00S

  Aerial-Mapping-Standard 1SWGI00440106    B&W PI/A      **8**   00%   05/21/72     1:20,697     0000440106
  Corner Point Coordinates=#1:N43D00M00S W076D15M00S #2:N43D00M00S W076D07M30S #3:N43D07M30S W076D07M30S #4:N43D07M30S W076D15M00S

  Aerial-Mapping-Standard 1VKX000360648    B&W PI/A      **8**   00%   05/07/56     1:23,828     0000360648
  Corner Point Coordinates=#1:N43D00M00S W076D15M00S #2:N43D00M00S W076D07M30S #3:N43D07M30S W076D07M30S #4:N43D07M30S W076D15M00S



                    Eros Data Center                          Report No. OL001-1
                 Sioux Falls, South Dakota  57198            Date:  4/19, 1984
              Contact Number 0464636016     Terminal T83A22   Time:  08:50
                 Alk--Monmonier                               Page:  2


                        Data Type    Photo-Single


  Imagery-Type            Scene ID    Frame(s)  Film-Source   Qual Cloud  Expo-Date   Scene-Center-Point  Scene-Scale   Microform

  Aerial-Mapping-Standard B005390010018  18   B&W-09.0"    **8**   00%  06/02/60   N43D02M50S  W076D10M02S 1:10,707  0000000000
  Corner Point Coordinates=#1:N43D02M12S W076D10M51S #2:N43D02M14S W076D09M11S #3:N43D03M28S W076D09M15S #4:N43D03M24S W076D10M55S

  Nasa-Aircraft-Standard   5750020854031  4032  CIR-09.0"   **8**   00%  05/07/75   N42D57M12S  W076D07M04S 1:127,000  0001580685
  Corner Point Coordinates=#1:N42D50M0DS W075D57M16S #2:N43D04M36S W075D57M10S #3:N43D02M54S W076D18M52S #4:N42D48M18S W076D14M58S

  Nasa-Aircraft-Standard   5730010199807  9812  CIR-09.0"   **9**   00%  03/23/73   N42D57M42S  W076D05M24S 1:132,000  0001760520
  Corner Point Coordinates=#1:N42D50M24S W075D54M54S #2:N43D05M30S W075D55M18S #3:N43D04M30S W076D16M12S #4:N42D49M48S W076D14M30S

  Nasa-Aircraft-Standard   5730010199813  9813  CIR-09.0"   **8**   00%  03/23/73   N42D57M24S  W076D11M24S 1:128,000  0001760521
  Corner Point Coordinates=#1:N42D50M48S W076D00M30S #2:N43D05M30S W076D02M24S #3:N43D03M36S W076D22M18S #4:N42D49M18S W076D19M48S

  Nasa-Aircraft-Standard   5730010199793  9799  CIR-09.0"   **8**   00%  03/23/73   N43D08M00S  W076D13M48S 1:130,000  0001760507
  Corner Point Coordinates=#1:N43D14M48S W076D24M42S #2:N43D00M00S W076D22M54S #3:N43D01M30S W076D02M42S #4:N43D16M12S W076D05M00S

  Nasa-Aircraft Standard    5720006323342  3343  CIR-09.0"   **9**   10%  08/20/72   N43D03M23S  W076D06M46S 1:132,000  0001721949
  Corner Point Coordinates=#1:N43D07M05S W076D20M16S #2:N42D53M35S W076D12M28S #3:N42D59M29S W075D53M40S #4:N43D12M47S W076D01M04S

  Nasa-Aircraft Standard    5CITY06323343  3343  CIR-09.0"   **8**   10%  08/20/72   N43D04M02S  W076D07M04S 1:130,354  0001721950
  Corner Point Coordinates=#1:N43D08M40S W076D20M32S #2:N42D54M10S W076D13M24S #3:N42D59M22S W075D53M38S #4:N43D13M53S W076D00M42S
```

Figure 2-16   Result of an NCIC search for air photos covering point at 43°3′N, 76°10′W in Syracuse, New York. This search found five black-and-white photos and six color-infrared (CIR) photos. Search results include latitude and longitude of each photo's center and corner points.

and may specify black-and-white, color, or color-infrared imagery (described in the next section); a particular season; and the oldest or the most recent photography. Standard (9-by-9-in.) contact prints are available, as are 2× (18-by-18-in.), 3× (27-by-27-in.), and 4× (36-by-36-in.) enlargements. The successful request yields a list of one or more prints (see Figure 2-16) and their prices; the user then must place a prepaid order. The entire process requires about 4 to 8 weeks, and the cost of a pair of contact black-and-white prints is approximately $12. NCIC also provides microfiche copies of its Aerial Photography Summary Record System (ASPRS), as well as computer-produced maps showing the agency or contractor holding the most recent coverage for various parts of a region. ASPRS includes non-Geological Survey imagery not included in the standard USGS data base.

Obtaining air photos for distant areas is more complicated. Aerial imagery of many foreign countries is usually classified information, and one must have permission from the government in question to obtain it.

SATELLITE PLATFORMS AND SCANNER SYSTEMS

Although conventional black-and-white aerial photography is, and will continue to be, widely used, aerial imagery of the earth's surface has changed greatly because of high-altitude aircraft, artificial satellites, special films, and electronic scanners. Military needs stimulated most of these advances—an unsurprising development, given the military use of aerial imagery that extends back to at least 1859, when Napolean III used balloon photography to plan for the battle of Solferino in northern Italy. Both sides used aerial photography during World War I. By World War II military strategists were attempting to deceive their opponents—and often succeeding—with camouflage and dummy or decoy targets. This deception encouraged the development of camouflage-detection film, which extended the photo interpreter's vision into the near-infrared part of the spectrum, where green paint reflects noticeably less light than does healthy foliage. The advent of artificial satellites and nonphotographic scanner systems in the late 1950s led to a new term, *remote sensing*, first used in 1960 by Evelyn Pruitt, director of the U.S. Office of Naval Research. Pruitt's term distinguished new technology based on electronics and radiation physics from photogrammetry, which relies principally on chemistry and optics. Remote sensing has many civilian uses in agriculture, geology, environmental protection, weather forecasting, and small-scale mapping. Continuing improvement in the ground detail of remotely sensed images and in all-weather/day-and-night systems may eventually extend these benefits to large-scale mapping and local public administration. This section provides an overview of the fundamentals of remote sensing and the variety of map products and applications.

Films, Sensors, and the Electromagnetic Spectrum

Even children ask perhaps the most penetrating question in remote sensing: "Why are trees green?" To avoid confusing the young mind, we might explain first that the eye can see different kinds of light: blue, green, and red. We call these the *additive primary* colors because we can add, say, green light to red light and obtain yellow light. When the proportions of the three primary colors are approximately equal, we see white light. Sun light is white light, generally, and when we reflect it from a mirror we still see white because the mirror does not absorb significant amounts of blue, green, or red. Yet when the sun shines on a tree's leaves, the chlorophyll absorbs more blue and red light than green light. Green is the dominant type of light reflected, and the tree "looks" green.

But what is green? And how does it differ from red and blue? Here we have to delve into a bit of radiation physics and introduce the *electromagnetic spectrum*, shown in Figure 2-17. Visible light is but one of many types of energy referred to as *electromagnetic radiation* and identified by *wavelength*. In a most general sense this energy may be viewed as a pulsating set of perpendicular electrical and magnetic waves—something not easily appreciated without a good course in modern physics. This wave energy has a frequency as well as a wavelength. Green light, for instance, pulsates at about 540,000,000,000,000 cycles

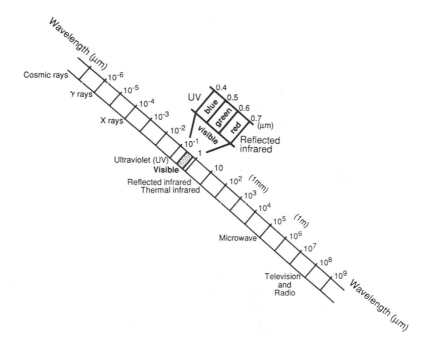

Figure 2-17 The electromagnetic spectrum.

per second. Yet its wavelength of approximately 0.00000053 m, or 0.53 microm-
eters, written 0.53 μm, is used to identify its position in the electromagnetic
spectrum. Our eye-brain system generally will consider light with a wavelength
in the range 0.5 to 0.6 μm as green or greenish yellow; in general discussions
of the spectrum this range is called the *green band*. The eye is not sensitive to
wavelengths shorter than 0.39 μm or longer than 0.77 μm, and the comparatively
narrow part of the electromagnetic spectrum lying between these approximate
limits is called the *visible band*, or *visible spectrum*.

An object can both absorb and reflect the radiation it receives, and usually
it will reflect some wavelengths more fully than others. An object can also re-
radiate some of the energy it receives, commonly at a different wavelength—as
does a stone that absorbs sun light during the day and radiates heat at night.
Some objects can convert one form of energy into another, as in the chemical
reactions whereby green plants manufacture sugar. Because healthy leaves absorb certain wavelengths more readily than others, green vegetation has a characteristic pattern of reflected radiation, the strength of which varies with wavelength, as shown in Figure 2-18. This pattern is called the *spectral signature* of
green vegetation because it differentiates healthy vegetation from other kinds

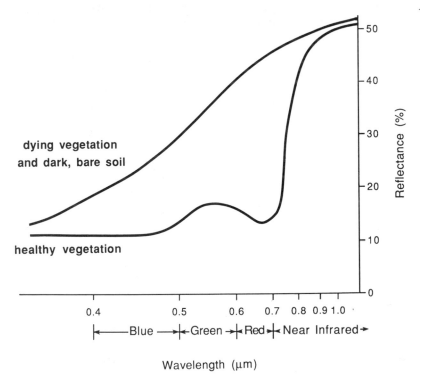

Figure 2-18   Spectral signatures of healthy vegetation and of dying vegetation
and dark, bare soil.

of land cover, such as water, dying vegetation, and the dark, bare soil of a freshly plowed field. Differences associated with the surface geometry and internal structure of broad leaves and needles yield distinctively different spectral signatures for deciduous and coniferous trees. Particularly noteworthy for living plants, however, is a reflectance in the *near-infrared band*, with wavelengths slightly longer than visible light, much stronger than in the green part of the spectrum.

A prime objective of remote sensing research is development of systems for detecting meaningful differences in reflected or emitted electromagnetic energy, especially for wavelengths beyond the range of human vision. One approach is to alter the photographic emulsion so that photosensitive chemical reactions occur, say, in the presence of infrared light, independent of the amount of visible light. *Color-infrared*, or "false color," film was a significant step in both discovering and reporting these differences. Figure 2-19 shows the spectral sensitivities of conventional color imagery and of color-infrared imagery; the three zones in each graph represent separate emulsion layers that produce on the

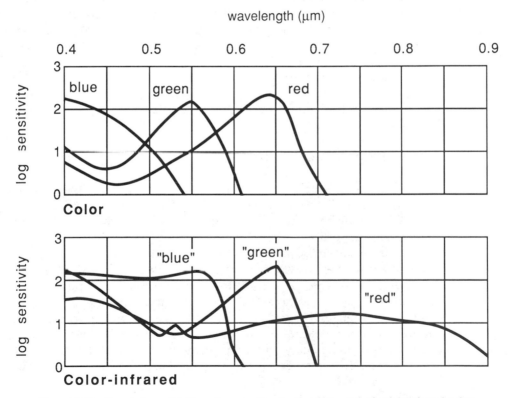

Figure 2-19 Spectral sensitivities of conventional color film, and of color-infrared color film employing a spectral shift to show on photographic prints infrared color the eye cannot see.

print individual layers of blue, green, and red dyes. With standard color film, objects reflecting mostly blue, green, or red light have blue, green, or red images. With color-infrared photography, however, a *spectral shift* occurs: blue objects such as water appear to be black; mostly green objects appear to be blue; red objects appear green; and objects largely reflecting near-infrared energy appear red. In addition to differentiating green paint (shown as a light blue) from leafy vegetation (a vivid red), color-infrared film also eliminates the haze associated with blue light, which the atmosphere readily scatters.[7]

Satellite sensors collect imagery and relay it to earth as a digital or video signal, rather than as a cartridge of unprocessed film (an expensive method used by some intelligence satellites). A satellite scanner commonly has three or more *channels,* each sensitive to a different spectral band. At any single instant energy reflected from a single spot on the ground strikes separate photosensitive devices sensitive to green, red, and infrared light. The scanner converts the energy to an electronic signal and relays the signal to earth, where it is stored on magnetic tape. The tape drives a device that makes photographic prints by reading the reflectance values stored on tape for the green, red, and infrared bands and exposing to proportionate amounts of light the blue, green, and red layers of a color-print emulsion to yield a color-infrared "composite" image similar to those obtained with an aerial camera and color-infrared film. An image analysis system can also read the computer tape and display the recorded scene on a color video screen. Black-and-white prints of individual bands can also be useful in providing a clear differentiation of land and water, vegetated and nonvegetated land covers, as the band-3 Landsat-4 Thematic Mapper image in Figure 2-20 illustrates.

Orbits and Image Geometry

Like conventional aerial photographs and other maps, satellite images are projective views that distort somewhat the spatial relationships of the earth's curved surface. Satellites have two distinct types of orbit, and each orbit has its own characteristic distortion.

An *environmental satellite* gathers atmospheric and oceanographic data while hovering over the same point on the equator in a *geostationary orbit* (see Figure 2-21, left), which permits it to monitor the same scene continually, day after day. A typical weather satellite, for example, transmits every half hour a snapshot-like image of the pattern of cloud cover for the entire North American continent and surrounding oceanic areas. At an altitude of approximately 35,800 km (22,000 mi) the effect of relief displacement is minimal, but the effect of earth curvature is significant. For many weather maps, however, this view is ac-

---

[7] Conventional black-and-white photography employs a haze filter that excludes blue light and other short-wave light rays. As a result, black-and-white aerial photographs usually are much clearer than those taken with standard color film, which is often degraded by haze.

Figure 2-20 Band-3 Landsat-4 Thematic Mapper image of a portion of Washington, D.C., 1:100,000. Very light areas are the Potomac and Anacostia rivers. Paved roads and roofs are very dark, and vegetation is light gray. (Courtesy of U.S. Geological Survey.)

ceptable as an appropriate projection, and the coastlines and state boundaries needed for a frame of reference are superimposed.

An *earth resources satellite*, in contrast, provides less frequent, more detailed coverage for a larger area. This type of satellite has a *sun-synchronous, near-polar orbit* (see Figure 2-21, right), in which it circles the earth many times a day, keeping pace with the rotation of the earth about its axis. Its orbital plane rotates westward as the earth rotates eastward, so that the sun angle of the scene below

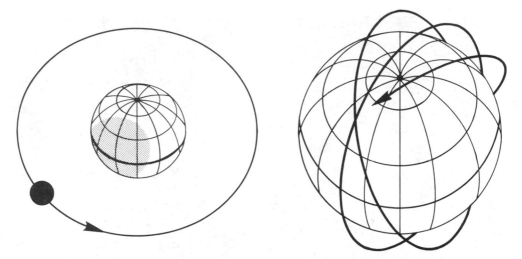

Figure 2-21 A satellite in a geostationary orbit (left) revolves with the rotating earth and hovers above the same spot on the equator to provide continuous coverage of the same scene. A satellite in a sun-synchronous, near-polar orbit (right) revolves at a much lower altitude in an orbital plane that rotates against the angular motion of the earth, so that the satellite crosses the equator at points successively farther west at approximately the same time of day.

is nearly constant. Landsat-4, a typical earth resources satellite, recorded scenes at the equator for a local sun time of approximately 9:40 A.M. After one pass from north to south over the illuminated part of the earth, the satellite orbited around the darkened side of the planet to emerge again in the north along a path crossing the equator about 25 degrees west of, and 103 minutes after, the previous equatorial crossing. Landsat-4 collected imagery at an altitude of about 705 km (440 mi) for a belt 185 km (115 mi) wide. So that relatively detailed coverage could be obtained for all parts of the earth, except polar areas, the same pattern of crossings was not repeated again until 18 days later.

Although relief displacement is minimal for imagery collected from earth resources satellites, other distortions, most significantly that of the earth rotating beneath the satellite, affect the images acquired. Most satellite imaging systems divide the ground swath below the satellite into scan paths, and then divide each scan path into cells. In the scanned image, a single *picture element*, or *pixel*, represents each cell. An oscillating mirror often directs the radiation from successive ground cells along the scan path to photosensitive detectors that measure and record reflectance for three or more spectral bands, or channels. Some multispectral scanners with rotating mirrors can sense several adjacent scan lines simultaneously (see Figure 2-22, left). More advanced systems use a "pushbroom scanner," in which a thousand or more detectors printed on a silicon chip can sample an entire scan path simultaneously, with no need of a mirror (see Figure 2-22, right). Separate linear detector arrays are used for each channel. Whatever

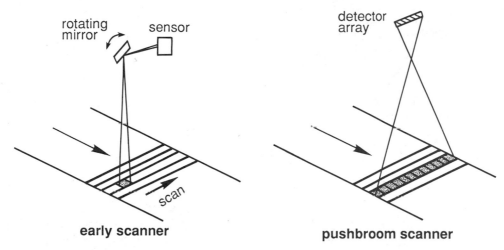

Figure 2-22   Some multispectral scanners use a rotating mirror (left) to direct reflected energy to the sensor from scan spots along parallel scan paths. More advanced pushbroom scanners (right) use linear detectors to record all spots along the scan line simultaneously.

scanning system is employed, successive scan lines are displaced to the left by the rotation of the ground below the satellite; when a group of scan lines is collected into a single *scene* for processing, the cells are not aligned in the customary square grid and the border is a parallelogram, not a rectangle (see Figure 2-23, left).[8] The recorded scene must be "resampled" to produce a rectangular array of pixels suitable for display and analysis on a computer graphics system (see Figure 2-23, right). Resampling, usually to a finer grid (smaller pixel), is common during processing—for example, when the image is changed from one projection to another.

Spatial Resolution

Although stored and displayed by square or rectangular pixels, electromagnetic reflectance values are sensed and recorded for overlapping circular scan spots. The diameter of scan spots, called the *instantaneous field of view* (IFOV), is the basic unit for comparing the resolving power of satellite sensing systems (see Figure 2-23). The IFOV was a comparatively coarse 79 m (260 ft) for the multispectral scanners of Landsat-1, Landsat-2, and Landsat-3. In the Thematic Mapper system aboard Landsat-4 and Landsat-5, the IFOV was an appreciably

[8] Another type of scanner used with earth resources satellites is the return beam videcon (RBV) system, in which separate television cameras view the same scene simultaneously but for different bands. This system records an instantaneous scene for later telemetering to the network of ground stations. Although the resolution is often coarser than resolutions obtained with multispectral scanner systems, the RBV image has greater geometric accuracy. Because of tape recorder failures, RBV systems employed with early Landsats were never used as fully as had been hoped.

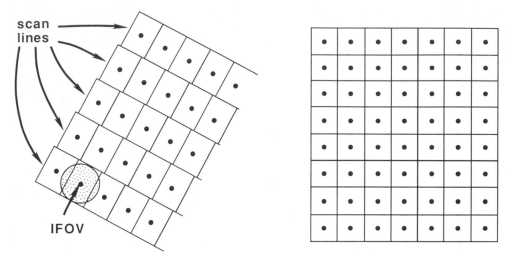

scan lines

IFOV

Figure 2-23 Scan lines displaced leftward by the earth's rotation below a multispectral satellite scanner (left) can be resampled and reformatted to a geometrically correct square grid of pixels (right) for computer processing and graphic display. Because the resampled grid shown here has a smaller pixel, measurements for a single original cell may be assigned to more than one pixel in the new, denser grid.

smaller 30 m (98 ft). Reflectances recorded for the green (0.52–0.60 μm), red (0.63–0.69 μm), and one of the three near-infrared (1.55–1.75 μm) bands have been printed in yellow, magenta, and cyan, respectively, on a 1:100,000-scale map that demonstrates the potential of Thematic Mapper data for intermediate-scale mapping.[9] On that map deep clear water appears blue-black, shallow or turbid water generally is blue, deciduous forests are dark reddish brown, and crops and grasslands are light reddish brown. Fallow or cleared areas, highways, runways, and sandbars are pink, gray, or white, and urban areas exhibit densely mixed patterns. The user can readily identify principal roads, built-up areas, field boundaries, forested areas, streams and canals, and many other land-cover features.

In principle one cannot expect an imaging system to detect an object with a diameter less than twice the IFOV. Of course the sensor might detect a smaller feature if the feature's center falls close enough to the center of the ground spot or pixel that its unique spectral components can be sensed without dilution by neighboring land covers with different absorption characteristics. Yet with sensors collecting imagery from several diagnostic bands and with image processing

---

[9] U.S. Geological Survey, *1:100,000-scale Satellite Image Map of Dyersburg, Tenn.-Mo.-Ky.-Ark.* (Reston, Va.: U.S. Geological Survey, 1983). The Dyersburg satellite image map is based on imagery recorded on August 22, 1982, and the map was published in early 1983 with a conventional 1:100,000-scale topographic map on the other side of the paper. The U.S. Geological Survey produces several experimental maps each year, including photomaps.

systems designed to filter noise, enhance edges, and recognize pattern, both probability theory and controlled experiments with ground data for known features can be marshaled to detect, for example, roadways and structures narrower than the IFOV. In a sense, then, spectral resolution can partly compensate for some deficiencies in spatial resolution.[10]

Continued collection of earth resources data by satellite sensors will permit change-detection studies and mapping based upon data that are multitemporal as well as multispectral. For these applications a comparatively fine spatial resolution will be particularly important because data obtained for two different dates can be resampled reliably to a common pixel grid only if the new resolution is about twice as coarse as that of the individual sets of unitemporal data. Although image analysis systems based on the principles of artificial intelligence might compensate for some of the failings of existing Landsat coverage, the careful monitoring of urban growth and agricultural production will depend upon more detailed remotely sensed data, such as that obtained from traditional fixed-wing aircraft or possibly the multispectral sensors of the Système Probatoire d'Observation de la Terre (SPOT), launched in February 1986 by the Centre National d'Etudes Spatiales in France. The SPOT scanner can be operated in a three-band mode with an IFOV of 20 m (66 ft) and in a single-band, panchromatic "black-and-white" mode with an IFOV of 10 m (33 ft).[11]

Thermal Imagery

Heat is a form of electromagnetic energy, but with a wavelength much greater than that of visible light. Unlike sunlight, heat energy is emitted by all objects with a temperature above absolute zero, and can be sensed electronically and mapped at any hour of the day. The military developed the earliest thermal infrared sensors for detecting enemy soldiers at night. Civilian applications include measuring heat loss from homes and other buildings and delineating the area affected by subsurface fires in abandoned coal mines (see Figure 2-24). A still wider range of applications is possible with highly sensitive thermal sensors because land covers differ in the rates at which they absorb and lose heat. Bare soil, for instance, becomes hotter during the day than water does, but cools

[10] The channels of a sensing system can be optimized for specific applications. The multispectral scanners used aboard the Landsats, for example, were designed to be more nearly ideal for a wide range of geologic investigations than for applications in agriculture, forestry, and land cover mapping. See John R. Jensen, "Urban Change Detection Mapping Using Landsat Digital Data," *American Cartographer* 8, no. 2 (October 1981), 127–47.

[11] For a discussion of the SPOT program and its imagery, see Tomislav F. Milinusic, "France's SPOT Satellite," *Computer Graphics World* 7, no. 7 (July 1984), 43–50; R. Welch, "Cartographic Potential of SPOT Image Data," *Photogrammetric Engineering and Remote Sensing* 51, no. 8 (August 1985), 1085–91; and Michael Courtois and Gilbert Weill, "The SPOT Satellite System," in *Monitoring Earth's Ocean, Land, and Atmosphere from Space—Sensors, Systems, and Applications*, ed. Abraham Schnapf (New York: American Institute of Aeronautics and Astronautics, 1985), pp. 493–523.

Figure 2-24 Thermal scanner images from satellite and fixed-wing aircraft. Satellite image (above) shows upstate New York and southern Ontario. Darker tones are hot and show Toronto, Buffalo, and Rochester. (From the Heat Capacity Mapping Mission satellite, July 4, 1978; courtesy of John R. Schott.) Low-altitude photo (below) is a nighttime image taken for a heat-loss study from 300 m (1,000 ft) with an infrared line scanner. White is hot and indicates spots with significant heat loss. (Courtesy of John R. Schott.)

more rapidly than water after sunset. Incorporation of a thermal infrared band (10.4–12.5 µm) on the Thematic Mapper recognized the potential of thermal sensing systems. With an IFOV of 120 m, about four times the IFOV for the three visible and three near-infrared channels, this thermal channel is particularly useful for mapping differences in soil moisture, type of vegetation, and vegetation stress.

Microwave Imagery

Microwave radiation, with wavelengths between 0.1 and 200 cm, can support "active" sensors, such as radar, that can detect surface form and land cover through clouds, haze, smoke, and darkness. Unlike *passive* systems, which depend upon reflected solar radiation or internally generated or reflected heat radiation, *active* systems generate the energy reflected by the land and recorded by their sensors. A camera with a flash attachment is an active sensing system, but for the large, distant tracts sensed from aircraft or satellites such explosive bursts of visible light are impractical.

More suitable for mapping are microwave systems that transmit and capture electromagnetic radiation with antennas. Because the antennas are aligned with the path of the plane or satellite and emit radiation in a direction perpendicular to the antenna, this technique is called SLAR, for *side-looking airborne radar*. The sensor's scan lines are perpendicular to the ground track of the aircraft or satellite, so that elevated features are displaced outward at a right angle from the nadir line (see Figure 2-25). Transmitted energy is generated in short bursts, so that the same antenna may be used to both transmit and receive. Energy reflected from the land surface is recorded as a digital signal for processing and display. In general, steep slopes facing the sensor will return more "backscattered" energy and appear brighter than slopes facing away. Rough surfaces tend to scatter the radiation in many directions; because little energy is returned, they tend to appear dark. Smooth surfaces that reflect all the energy away from the sensor are darker still. Occasionally a particularly strong, bright return results from a double reflection, say, when the beam is reflected from a parking lot to the side of a building and then back to the sensor. Moisture in vegetation or soil also tends to increase radar reflectivity.

Resolution is a function of antenna length: the longer the antenna, the greater the detail. Because airplanes cannot carry long antennas, a technique called *synthetic aperture radar*, or SAR, is used to simulate the effect of a longer antenna. Signals emitted at regular intervals from a short, 2-m (6.6-ft) antenna are reflected, recorded, and unscrambled by computer to produce images with

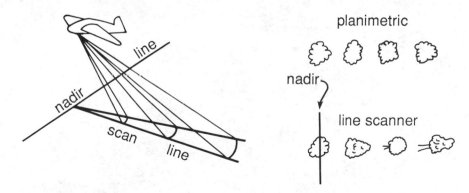

Figure 2-25 Side-looking radar scans outward along parallel scan lines perpendicular to the nadir line (left). Resolution cell increases in size with increased distance from the nadir. Line-scan image displaces vertical features at a right angle outward from the nadir line (right).

the resolution of a non-SAR image possibly only with an antenna 600 m (2,000 ft) long! Comparatively fine resolution is thus possible with antennas not able otherwise to detect features less than a kilometer wide. Figure 2-26 is a SAR image that demonstrates the usefulness of radar imagery for military intelligence, oceanography, and geology. The lighter tones off the tip of the peninsula at San Diego harbor represent kelp beds, which reflect radar waves in a different way than do their surroundings. Note the linear pattern of distortion, with the scale progressively smaller from the bottom to the top of the image—a typical pattern for SLAR images of scenes on one side of the aircraft. *Plan position indicator radar* (PPI) is another type of active microwave imaging system, with a point-source transmitter and a circular pattern of distortion.

Obtaining Remotely Sensed Imagery

Remotely sensed images generally are available in two forms: black-and-white or color-composite prints, and digital data, stored on magnetic tape for computer processing. Government agencies and private firms have obtained many images for experiments or highly specific applications; these images either are not for public distribution or are not advertised. As with conventional aerial photography, remotely sensed imagery of foreign areas commonly is not available without the permission of the government of the territory covered. For the United States, however, Landsat images, photographs from manned NASA spacecraft,

Figure 2-26 Synthetic aperture radar (SAR) image of San Diego harbor. (Courtesy of Westinghouse Electric Corporation.)

and high-altitude color and color-infrared photographs for more than 100 cities are available through the National Cartographic Information Center (507 National Center, U.S. Geological Survey, Reston, VA 22092). NCIC is also a source for 23-by-23-cm (9-by-9-in.) photos from the National High Altitude Photography Program (NHAP). Funded by 14 federal agencies, NHAP provides consistent coverage of the 48 contiguous states in this country by 1:80,000-scale black-and-white and 1:58,000-scale color-infrared imagery valuable for resource evaluation and environmental monitoring.

When ordering Landsat imagery one should generally know the latitude and longitude of the areas for which one is seeking coverage. To facilitate distribution and use of remotely sensed images of the 48 contiguous states, a coverage index map (see Figure 2-27) indicates the path and row numbers for specific *scenes*. The dots on this map show the approximate centers of parallelogram-shaped areas for which one may readily obtain data or photographic images from the National Cartographic Information Center (NCIC) or the Earth Observation Satellite Company (EOSAT, c/o Landsat Customer Services, EROS Data Center, Sioux Falls, SD 57198). One may order these scenes, selected for clarity and minimal cloud cover, as magnetic-tape files; as black-and-white paper prints or film transparencies for the individual bands; or as color-infrared composite paper prints, film transparencies, or 35 mm slides.

In 1985 land remote sensing took a major step with the transfer of the Landsat program to the Earth Observation Satellite Company (EOSAT), a private firm. Whether this was a step forward or a step backward is uncertain, for an

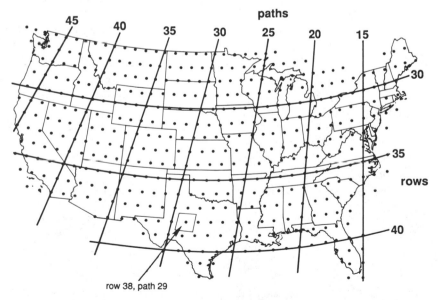

Figure 2-27   Landsat-4 coverage index map references 185-by-185-km scenes by the row and orbital path numbers of a grid of approximate scene centers.

operational remote sensing program seems unlikely to survive without substantial government support in the form of direct grants or purchases of large amounts of expensive imagery.[12] Launching of the first SPOT satellite the following year marked the beginning of international competition in the commercial market for satellite data. With a finer resolution and an office in the United States (SPOT Image Corporation, 1897 Preston White Drive, Reston, VA 22091-4326), EOSAT's European competitor is eager to capture a large share of a market once monopolized by Landsat. Moreover, at both the national and the international level, several important policy issues remain unresolved. These include distribution, pricing, copyright, and restrictions on the sale of politically or militarily sensitive images. Yet whatever policies prevail, photomaps clearly will become still more prominent and more widely used in the future.

FOR FURTHER READING

Barrett, Eric C., and Michael G. Hamilton, "The Use of Geostationary Satellite Data in Environmental Science," *Progress in Physical Geography* 6, no. 2 (June 1982), 159–214.

Campbell, James B., *Mapping the Land.* Washington, D.C.: Association of American Geographers, 1983.

Colwell, Robert M., ed. *Manual of Remote Sensing* (2d ed.). Falls Church, Va.: American Society of Photogrammetry, 1983.

Jensen, John R., *Introductory Digital Image Processing.* Englewood Cliffs, N.J.: Prentice-Hall, 1986.

Lillesand, Thomas M., and Ralph W. Kiefer, *Remote Sensing and Image Interpretation.* New York: John Wiley & Sons, 1979.

Lulla, Kamlesh, "The Landsat Satellites and Selected Aspects of Physical Geography," *Progress in Physical Geography* 7, no. 1 (March 1983), 1–45.

Moffitt, Francis H., and Edward M. Mikhail, *Photogrammetry* (3d ed.). New York: Harper & Row, 1980.

Slama, Chester C., Charles Theurer, and Soren W. Henriksen, eds., *Manual of Photogrammetry* (4th ed.). Falls Church, Va.: American Society of Photogrammetry, 1980.

Townshend, John R. G., "The Spatial Resolving Power of Earth Resources Satellites," *Progress in Physical Geography* 5, no. 1 (1981), 32–55.

Townshend, John R. G., ed., *Terrain Analysis and Remote Sensing.* London: George Allen & Unwin, 1981.

---

[12] See Space Applications Board, Commission on Engineering and Technical Systems, National Research Council, *Remote Sensing from Space: A Program in Crisis* (Washington, D.C.: National Academy Press, 1985).

CHAPTER THREE

Maps
of the Landscape

Map makers use a variety of methods to describe and record the earth's surface cartographically. This chapter discusses the most common cartographic portrayals of landscape, including photomaps, pictorial representations from earlier times, topographic maps, physiographic maps and diagrams, and land-use and land-cover maps. In addition, we discuss the maps and schematic renderings of landscape architects. A series of topographic vignettes focuses on cartographic portrayals of a few famous places and of representative landforms for which processes both natural and human contribute to the landscape's appearance.

CARTOGRAPHIC REPRESENTATIONS OF THE EARTH'S SURFACE

Maps of the earth's surface vary greatly in degree of detail, surface attributes portrayed, and extent to which the cartographer interprets the physical landscape for the viewer.

Photomaps

We discussed aerial photography and remotely sensed imagery in Chapter 2, but mention photomaps here briefly, for the sake of completeness. After all, the simple terrain photograph is the most rudimentary landscape map. Photomaps vary considerably, depending upon whether a photograph is taken from directly above the object (vertical) or a bit to the side (oblique), and whether the film is black-and-white or color. Further, black-and-white film may be sensitive to all wavelengths in the visible band (panchromatic film), to only the green and red portions of the visible spectrum (when a minus-blue filter is used to avoid the clouding effects of haze), or to a substantial part of the nonvisible near-infrared spectrum, in order to detect camouflage or diseased vegetation. Color infrared film, which is partly sensitive to infrared energy and also filters haze, provides the useful but sometimes disconcerting "false-color" image, in which a spectral shift paints areas with healthy vegetation a brilliant red. Other, nonphotographic views of terrain, based on reflected radar energy or the thermal energy that all objects emit, yield photomaps when sensed energy levels recorded on magnetic tape are played back through a film recorder.

Photomaps are continuous-tone images, with tones ranging from white to black or, if in color, from light to dark, as well as across the spectrum of visible hues. The photomap can capture small variations in surface reflectance, and its tonal variations usually are much more subtle than those of the high-contrast line maps reviewed elsewhere in this section. Line maps require a conscious effort by the cartographer to select features, but photomaps merely show what the camera's eye sees; the principal cartographic decisions are the choice of sensor, the flying height, and the time and date of coverage. Yet photomaps are sometimes printed with "cartographic enhancements" such as feature labels and delineated boundaries and shorelines.

More than other kind of landscape map, the photomap embodies the concept of *data*, the plural of the Latin *datum*, meaning "that which is given." In contrast, the other kinds of landscape map discussed in this section reflect an intelligent generalization or interpretation of the earth's surface and are thus akin to the concept of *information*, implying a measure of understanding about process and origin.

Early Pictorial Representations

A line map of the terrain need be neither artistically sophisticated nor based on careful measurement. Before surveying techniques were refined in the eighteenth century, topographers shared many of the professional and cultural biases of portrait artists, who drew what they saw as their attitudes conditioned them to see it. Earlier, more primitive portrayals of terrain had been largely symbolic—for example, the natives of the Marshall Islands used a carefully bound network of sticks and pebbles to represent lines of swell, currents, and islands.[1] Historian P. D. A. Harvey has traced the evolution of the modern

---

[1] For a discussion of primitive topographic maps, see Michael Blakemore, "From Way-finding to Map-making: The Spatial Information Fields of Aboriginal Peoples," *Progress in Human Geography* 5, no. 1 (1981), 1–24.

topographic map through three stages: symbols, such as the stick charts of the Marshall Islanders; pictures, of which Christopher Saxton's portrayal of Kent, Surrey, and Sussex is an illustration (see Figure 8-7); and surveys, which are systematic attempts to inventory major landscape features and organize their map symbols on a carefully scaled grid.[2] Surveys relied on triangulation to compute horizontal distances so that positions could be plotted accurately on large- and medium-scale flat maps. Overland distance always overestimates horizontal distance, an effect more pronounced and more unpredictable for rough terrain. The first great national topographic survey, which in the mid–nineteenth century produced the Geometric Map of France, was possible only through the invention of telescopic surveying instruments and the persistence and foresight of Jacques Cassini and his son, who managed an extensive triangulation survey that led to 173 map sheets at 1:86,400.[3]

Even when based on careful measurement, the topographic maps of the late eighteenth and early nineteenth centuries looked quite different from their modern counterparts. Relief was portrayed by *hachures*, short lines running directly down slope, as Figure 3-1 illustrates. Hachure thickness was proportional to angle of slope, so that steep slopes were portrayed by dark bands of thick, closely spaced hachures and gentle slopes were portrayed by light bands of thin, less crowded hachures. Cartographers based their maps on field notes and surveyed spot elevations, and used standard keys in choosing the hachure width appropriate to a particular angle of slope. Despite this use of guidelines, considerable artistic skill was required to master the technical details, and hachuring was far more subjective than stereocompilation, the basis for present-day topographic maps. Although hachures promote the visualization of terrain by the untrained map reader, the biases of both map maker and map user readily distort the resulting mental picture of a landscape portrayed by hachures.

A change in warfare from the chess-piece strategy of the early nineteenth century to the more independent tactics of Napolean's platoons encouraged the use of hachures, a marked improvement over earlier, less standardized topographic symbols.[4] But military needs were also among the factors responsible for the demise of hachuring. Few cartographers and geographers had the skill required for the proper execution and decoding of hachures; and the symbol's visual heaviness makes the map dark and limits the cartographic portrayal of other features in rugged areas. In contrast, the modern contour map is more precise in its details about surface form, as well as more "open" and graphically receptive to place names and other map symbols. Improved surveying tech-

---

[2] P. D. A. Harvey, *The History of Topographical Maps: Symbols, Pictures and Surveys* (London: Thames & Hudson, 1980).

[3] See Josef V. Konvitz, "Redating and Rethinking the Cassini Geodetic Surveys of France," *Cartographica* 19, no. 1 (Spring 1982), 1–15.

[4] See Francis Burton Harrison, "Early Topographical Maps," *Geographical Review* 14, no. 3 (July 1924), 426–32.

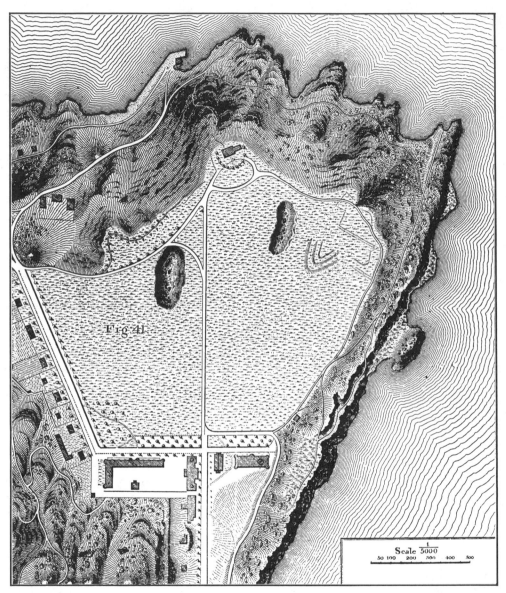

Figure 3-1   Hachures, pictorial symbols, and shoreline contours in an early topographical sketch. (From R. S. Smith, *Manual of Topographical Drawing* [New York: John Wiley & Sons, 1903], plate 5.)

niques provided more land-surface information than hachures could reliably or aesthetically encode, and both engineers and military tacticians demanded more information than hachures could convey. Moreover, artillery became more powerful and accurate in the early twentieth century, and effective gunnery demanded calculations based on more abundant, contoured elevation data. Even so, several small European nations, such as Switzerland and Sweden, still employed hachures on their exquisitely detailed maps well into the twentieth century.[5]

Topographic Maps

With a name derived from *topographos,* the Greek word meaning "to describe a place," the topographic map is not only a useful product for geologists, planners, engineers, geographers, and military tacticians, but also the "mother map" from which many smaller-scale thematic maps are derived.[6] The principal and distinguishing symbol on most topographic maps is the *contour,* a line representing a narrow band of places sharing roughly the same elevation above a *datum,* or fixed reference elevation, usually mean sea level.

Figure 3-2 is a useful aid in understanding contours, which are particularly meaningful when viewed collectively. Some teachers describe the contour by first pointing out the intersection of the three-dimensional land surface with a plane parallel to the horizontal datum plane: the contour is the perpendicular, or "orthographic," projection of this intersection onto the datum plane. Other instructors introduce the contour by asking students to imagine a three-dimensional model of terrain sitting in an aquarium—or by having students actually conduct such an experiment. Water poured into the aquarium establishes a sea-level reference elevation, as the shoreline is traced around the model with a marking pen. Next the water level is raised a fixed amount—the *contour interval*—and a second line is marked. A third, fourth, and other marked lines follow, with each new shoreline a constant vertical distance above the previous level. The perpendicular projection of all of these mutually parallel "shorelines" onto a similarly parallel map plane yields a map of contours, or collectively, a contour map.

Although mathematical purists might argue that the contour represents a geometrically thin line—the locus of points on the land surface at a constant perpendicular distance above the datum plane—the forthright cartographer recognizes not only that the line on the map covers what would be a finite width on the ground, but also that the measurements upon which this line is delineated have, like all measurements, a margin of error. Thus, at a scale of 1:24,000, the 0.13-mm-thick (0.005-in.-thick) contour line on a typical U.S. Geological Survey topographic map "represents" a width of about 3 m (10 ft) on the ground.

[5] See, for example, Everett C. Olson and Agnes Whitmarsh, *Foreign Maps* (New York: Harper & Row, 1944), p. 157 and plates II and V. Although dated, this World War II volume presents an intriguing survey of the content and design of the topographic maps of Europe.

[6] "Mother map," used to denote the original sources of information from which thematic and smaller-scale topographic maps are compiled, was a favorite term of Henry Gannett, the first chief geographer at the U.S. Geological Survey. See, for example, Henry Gannett, "The Mother Maps of the United States," *National Geographic Magazine* 4, no. 4 (31 March 1892), 101–16.

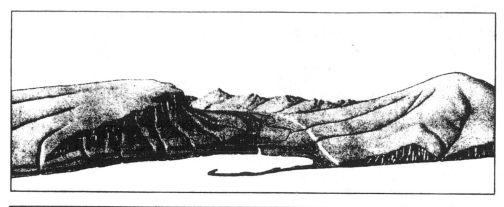

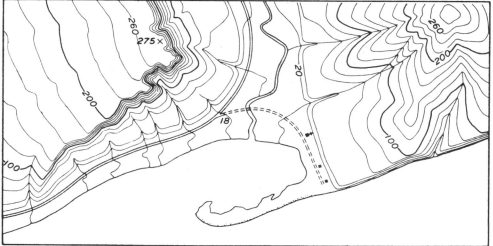

Figure 3-2   In the early twentieth century the U.S. Geological Survey used this pair of oblique (above) and plan (below) views on the back of its topographic maps to explain to users the representation of terrain by contour lines (in the plan view). Plan view is also a planimetric map.

Moreover, the *vertical accuracy standard* for contours requires that the elevation anywhere along the contour line only be within half a contour interval of the true elevation.[7] Fortunately, although a group of adjoining contours might collectively represent slightly erroneous elevations, in concert they tend to provide a usefully accurate portrayal of all but the most minute terrain features.

[7] The United States National Map Accuracy Standards specify that vertical accuracy "as applied to contour maps at all publication scales, shall be such that not more than 10 percent of the elevations tested shall be in error by more than one-half the contour interval," and that horizontal accuracy on maps published at 1:20,000 and smaller scales shall be such that "not more than 10 percent of the points tested shall be in error by more than 1/50 inch (0.5 mm)." The initial standards were issued in 1941 by the Bureau of the Budget. See Morris M. Thompson, *Maps for America* (Washington, D.C.: U.S. Department of the Interior, Geological Survey, 1979), pp. 102–7.

To avoid clutter, very few contour lines bear elevation labels. Usually every fifth contoured elevation is represented by *index contours,* notably heavier lines broken where appropriate by type indicating elevation. Index contours thus have their own contour interval, five times that of the map as a whole. Exceptionally gentle areas in an otherwise rugged region might also have *supplementary contours,* dashed lines spaced at a distance half that of the contour interval.

With their spacing and shape, contours tell us much about the land surface. Consider the contour maps and profiles in Figure 3-3, which represent two perfectly conical hills of equal height. All contours for both hills are perfect circles because all conic cross sections perpendicular to the axis of a cone are circular. Moreover, for each hill the contours have the same center, which also is the perpendicular projection of the cone's apex onto the datum plane. Yet the hill with the steeper sides is represented by more closely spaced contour lines; because their elevations are equal, both cones have the same number of contours, but these must be packed into a smaller outer circle for the steeper hill, which has a shorter horizontal, or *planimetric,* distance from apex to base. Figure 3-3 illustrates a corollary of the spacing rule: the closer the contours, the steeper the slope.

Figure 3-4 demonstrates another law of topographic maps: uniformly spaced contours represent uniform slopes, and irregularly spaced contours represent irregular slopes. Note that the hemisphere in the middle has progressively more widely separated contours from edge toward center than does the cone at its left. The cone has straight sides and a uniform slope, whereas the hemisphere has a steep slope (and close contours) near its base and a more gentle

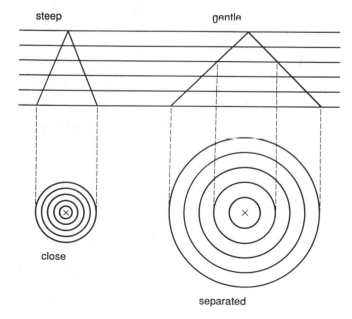

Figure 3-3　Profiles (above) and contoured plan views (below) of two conical hills of equal height.

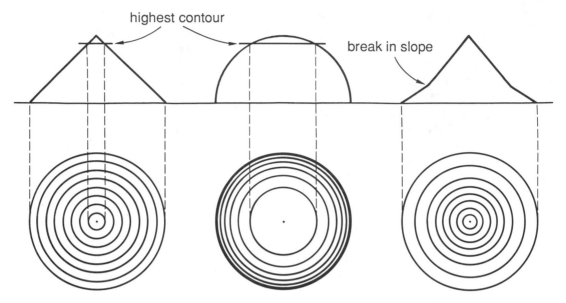

Figure 3-4 Profiles and contoured plan views for a conical hill (left), hemispherical hill (center), and a symmetrical hill with a break in slope (right).

slope (and separated contours) at the top. The hill at the right demonstrates how a shift in contour spacing reflects a break in slope. Note also that for all three hills perfectly circular contours portray perfect radial symmetry: the profile for one of these hills is the same no matter what the orientation of the cross section.

Although not all landforms are models of geometric regularity, the spacing rule is useful nonetheless—for example, in choosing a route up the irregular hill shown in Figure 3-5. Consider, for instance, the two routes from point A, at an elevation of 767, to point B, at an elevation of 856. Route X is longer and generally more gentle because the contours are more widely separated along its path than are the contours on route Y. But note the particularly steep grade along route Y just below point B, where the contours in the direction of ascent are very closely spaced. This section would be most demanding to hikers.

Although a person walking up a hill might prefer a gentle, and generally longer, path, a rolling object descending a slope would seek out the quickest, steepest path, which might twist and turn to follow always the route of locally steepest descent. In theory, such a route on an unvegetated, frictionless slope would intersect contour lines at right angles, as seems generally the case in Figure 3-5 for route Z, which represents the path of steepest descent and least resistance from point B. Note that route Z descends to 767, the elevation of point A, in a shorter distance than does either route X or route Y.

Running water is the most common and influential type of movement

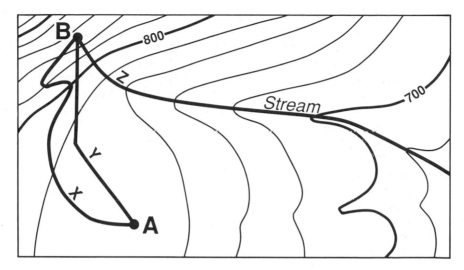

Figure 3-5 Map of irregular terrain illustrating relatively gentle (X) and steep (Y) routes between points A and B, and the path of steepest, most rapid descent (Z) from point B into a stream channel. Contours surrounding the stream form a set of nested vees pointing upstream.

across a landscape not only because surface runoff wears down high elevations and builds up low ones, but also because water collects into stream channels for the efficient drainage of precipitation to larger bodies of water for evaporation and perpetuation of the hydrologic cycle.[8] Streams and rivers commonly have gently sloping channels, in contrast to steeper sided slopes and tributaries. Contours often run almost parallel to the channel; they suddenly cross the channel and quickly reverse direction, so that one must infer the theoretical right-angle intersection rather than see it on the map. As in the lower part of route Z in Figure 3-5, where the path of steepest descent from point B joins the channel, the contours along a stream tend to follow one another in a pattern of nested vees, the points of which are aligned like arrowheads pointing upstream. This veeing of contours upstream is an unfailing clue to the direction of stream flow and an indicator of channels too small or infrequently flowing to be identified on the map with the traditional blue line.

Ordinarily one might assume that a series of roughly concentric closed contours represent a hill, with the innermost contour marking the approximate location of a local high, or *peak*, situated within. But nested closed contours can also represent a topographic depression, not occupied by a lake or pond because

---

[8] Not all rainfall and snowmelt moves into drainage channels as surface runoff. Precipitation that does not evaporate or that plants do not ingest may seep into bedrock for indefinite storage in the ground water reservoir. Ground water may be withdrawn at a well, flow to the surface at a spring, or feed a stream or lake below the surface.

of low precipitation or permeable surface material. Because of the confusion that might otherwise result, cartographers portray depressions with *depression contours* having small perpendicular teeth on one side pointing downslope. Thus one can ascertain elevations by counting downward in the direction of the tick marks. Contour A in Figure 3-6, for instance, is three contours downward from an indexed depression contour with an elevation of 800; if the contour interval is 10, A's elevation is 770. Hill and depression contours on a slope between contours of unlike elevations follow a simple rule: higher for hill, lower for depression. Thus, between bounding contours representing 200 and 210 in Figure 3-7, the elevations of hill contour C and depression contour D are 210 and 200, respectively.

Topographic maps show many kinds of features, not merely surface elevations, and cartographers organize map symbols by color for ready retrieval. The U.S. Geological Survey uses five colors, and five separate printing plates,

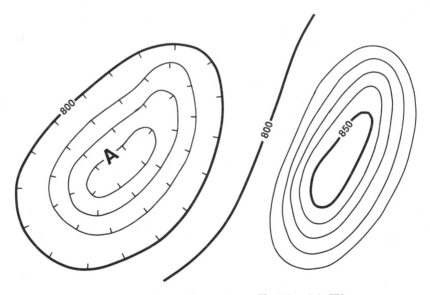

Figure 3-6 Depression contours. Elevation A is 770.

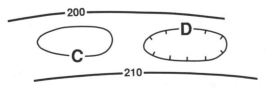

Figure 3-7 Depression and hill contours between contours of unlike elevations demonstrate the rule: higher for hill, lower for depression. Elevation C is 210, and elevation D is 200.

to segregate topographic data.[9] The brown "contour" plate contains contour lines, elevations for index contours, and special symbols for dune areas, mine tailings, and other rough or transient surfaces not readily or predictably portrayed by contour lines. The blue "drainage" plate represents streams, marshes, lakes, rivers, bays, and other "hydrographic features." The green "vegetation" plate shows the extent of woodland, orchard, vineyard, and other tree or brush cover. The red "road classification" plate uses a soft red, pinkish tint to indicated built-up areas for which the map shows only landmark buildings, and includes red lines representing major roads and some land-survey boundaries. The black "culture" plate contains roads, buildings, place names, political boundaries, railways, and other features reflecting human settlement and public administration. On "photorevised" map sheets changes identified on aerial photographs are added in purple on an "update" plate, to reflect new highway, residential and commercial development, and other landscape changes occurring since the previous map edition based on a field survey.[10]

Orienteering, a sport in which competitors race over a wooded or otherwise rugged course with a map and compass, requires special maps showing not only terrain, but also starting and finishing points of the course and several intermediate "control points" as well.[11] As in Figure 3-8, symbols for the course commonly are printed over part of an existing topographic map, but participants sometimes are required as a part of the race to copy the course onto their own maps from a master copy showing the various objectives of the race. A plastic carrying case hung about the neck protects the map from moisture and provides ready access. Orienteering is an excellent way to develop map-reading skills and to acquire a fuller appreciation of both the value and the limitations of maps.

Topographic map sheets commonly cover *quadrangles*, roughly rectangular areas bounded by parallels and meridians. The area covered reflects the series: the U.S. Geological Survey's 7.5-minute series, for instance, has quadrangles spanning 7.5 minutes of latitude (approximately 13.9 km [8.6 mi]) and 7.5 minutes of longitude (approximately 10.7 km [6.6 mi]) to contain roughly 148 km^2 (57

---

[9] For a thorough discussion of standard topographic symbols on U.S. Geological Survey maps, see Thompson, *Maps for America*, pp. 27–122. For a comparable examination of British topographic maps, see J. B. Harley, *Ordnance Survey Maps: A Descriptive Manual* (Southampton, Eng.: Ordnance Survey, 1975). British topographic maps are more detailed than their North American counterparts and include a national series with contours at 1:10,560. For discussion of Canadian topographic maps, see N. L. Nicholson and L. M. Siebert, *The Maps of Canada* (Folkestone, Eng.: William Dawson and Sons; Hamden, Conn.: Archon Books, 1981). The most detailed nationwide Canadian topographic map series is at 1:50,000.

[10] See Thompson, *Maps for America*, pp. 96–102.

[11] For an introduction to orienteering, see, for example, Hans Bengtsson, *Orienteering for Sport and Pleasure* (Brattleboro, Vt.: Stephen Greene Press, 1977), or John Disley, *Orienteering*, 2d ed. (Harrisburg, Pa.: Stackpole Books, 1978).

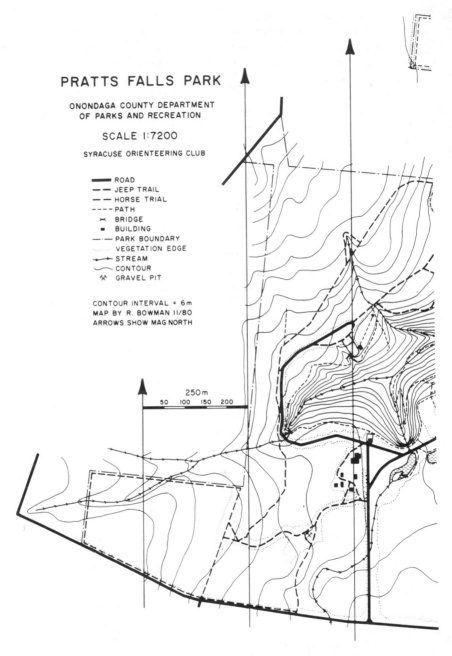

Figure 3-8 Example of an orienteering map. (Portion of the Pratts Falls Park Orienteering Map. Courtesy of Rosemarie Bowman and the Syracuse Orienteering Club.)

mi^2) at a scale of 1:24,000, or occasionally 1:25,000.[12] An older series providing less detail at 1:62,500 with only a quarter as many 15-minute quadrangles has largely been abandoned; but the need for an intermediate-scale topographic map is met by a newer series at 1:100,000, with quadrangles covering one degree of longitude (approximately 85 km [53 mi]) and 30 minutes of latitude (approximately 56 km [34 mi]).[13] A somewhat older, less detailed series at 1:250,000, with quadrangles encompassing one degree of latitude and two degrees of longitude, is still maintained. Each quadrangle bears the name of a prominent city or landscape feature therein. Index maps show quadrangle boundaries, names, and a limited amount of reference information, such as state and county boundaries, principal highways, and locally prominent settlements.[14]

Landform Maps and Physiographic Maps

For large areas mapped at small scales, accurate contours are neither necessary nor desirable. On a small-scale map, earth features can be represented more realistically, if very generally, by adding small, obliquely viewed landform drawings to a conventional, planimetric view of the region. Based upon topographic and other maps, oblique aerial photographs, and copious notes taken while observing the area to be mapped from a plane, the *landform map* is prepared to represent the surface as it might appear in an oblique aerial photograph.[15] The cartographer may fill in the outline of an individual landform with hachures, each short line extending along the slope of the land. Where relief is minimal, as in plains, vegetation and cultivation can be shown. The oblique view of the landform symbols displaces mountain peaks from their location on a planimetric map, and not all landforms can be shown. However, the visual effect is well worth the problems of geometry and the lack of complete coverage.[16]

Figure 3-9, a portion of Erwin Raisz's map, "Landforms of the United

[12] Meridians converge toward the poles, and all United States quadrangles are a bit narrower at the top (North) than at the bottom (South). Moreover, quadrangles are generally narrower as latitude increases. Yet a degree of latitude is much less variable than a degree of longitude. Because the earth is not a perfect sphere and is flattened somewhat at the poles, however, a quadrangle in, for example, Florida, will actually cover a slightly shorter north-south distance than a quadrangle in Maine. Average values given in the text are for quadrangles at about 40°N.

[13] For a discussion of the planning and design of the 1:100,000-scale topographic series, see Clarence R. Gilman, "1:100,000 Map Series, U.S. Geological Survey," *American Cartographer* 9, no. 2 (October 1982), 173–77.

[14] One can obtain index maps and leaflets describing various uses of topographic maps free of charge from the National Cartographic Information Center, U.S. Geological Survey, 507 National Center, Reston, VA 22092. For ready inspection of the index map of your home state, consult a local Geological Survey map dealer, a college reference library, or the reference department of your main city or county library.

[15] Erwin Raisz, *Principles of Cartography* (New York: McGraw-Hill, 1962), p. 79.

[16] Ibid., pp. 79 and 82.

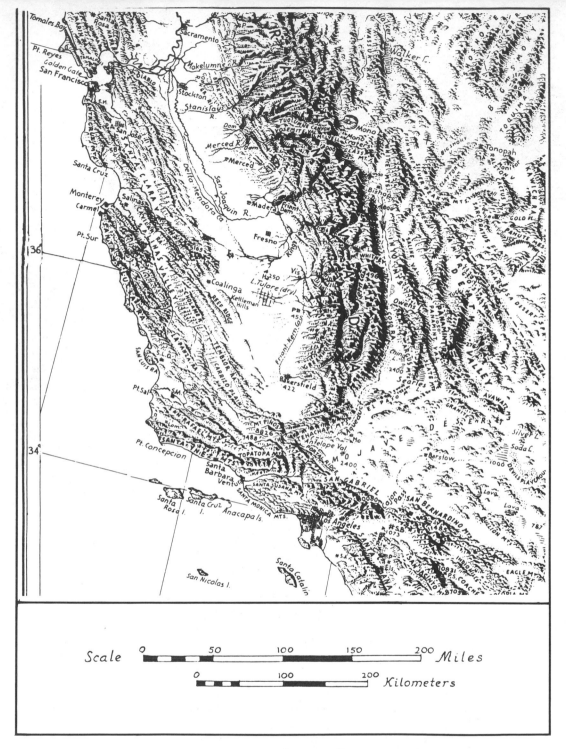

Figure 3-9 The southwestern part of "Landforms of the United States," a physiographic diagram by Erwin Raisz, 6th revised edition, 1957. (Used with permission.)

States," is an excellent example of a landform map. The area of southern California and Nevada shown includes the Coast Ranges, the southern part of the Great Valley, the Sierra Nevada Mountains, the southwestern corner of the Basin and Range Province, and the Transverse Ranges.

Space prohibits a lengthy discussion of this example, but the map contains one particularly well-known element worthy of more than passing mention, the San Andreas Fault. This famous fracture in the earth's crust, brought dramatically into world view by the San Francisco earthquake and resultant fire of 1906, extends 965 km (600 mi) or so southeastward from Point Arena (to the north and outside the area shown in Figure 3-9). Tomales Bay (found in the northwestern corner of the map), separating Tomales Point from the mainland, is located directly along the fault. Indeed, the linear arrangement of troughs, lakes, bays, valleys, escarpments, and narrow ridges is no doubt related to the rift, or fault, zone which extends almost vertically into the earth to a depth of at least 32 km (20 mi).[17] In the southern part of Figure 3-9 the fault is found 80 or more km (50 or 60 mi) inland from Los Angeles.

Armin Lobeck presented a different angle on the area shown in Figure 3-9. In his book, *Things Maps Don't Tell Us*, Lobeck points out that in the San Joaquin River Valley—as well as in valleys of other piedmont (foothills) rivers of the world, such as the Po and the Danube—the course of the stream is much closer to the lower Coastal Ranges than to the higher Sierra Nevada (see Figure 3-10, left). A second fact can be gleaned from this map: the tributaries flowing into the San Joaquin River from the higher mountains to the east are much more numerous than those from the Coastal Ranges. The explanation for this seemingly anomalous situation is found in the right part of Figure 3-10. Lobeck described it:

> High glaciated mountains like the Sierra Nevada, the Alps, the Transylvanian Alps, the Himalayas, and the Pyrenees usually have large streams which carry a great deal of detritus. During the relatively recent Glacial Period, when the glaciers were larger and more numerous than they are at present, the rivers emerging from the melting glaciers were heavily laden with sand and gravel. This load of material was carried down to the foot of the mountains and was there deposited in the piedmont basins in the form of outwash plains or alluvial fans. As the fans spread outward into the basin they forced the main river draining the basin farther and farther away from the foot of the high mountain range.
>
> The smaller mountains, like the Coast Ranges and the Apennines, at whose foot the main river was eventually forced to flow, were never glaciated. Their smaller rivers, therefore, never carried any great quantities of silt into the piedmont lowland. Because of this, no alluvial fans were built at the base of the lower ranges.[18]

---

[17] Robert Wallace, *The San Andreas Fault* (Washington, D.C.: U.S. Government Printing Office, 1977).

[18] Armin K. Lobeck, *Things Maps Don't Tell Us: An Adventure into Map Interpretation* (New York: Macmillan, 1958), pp. 82–83; used with permission.

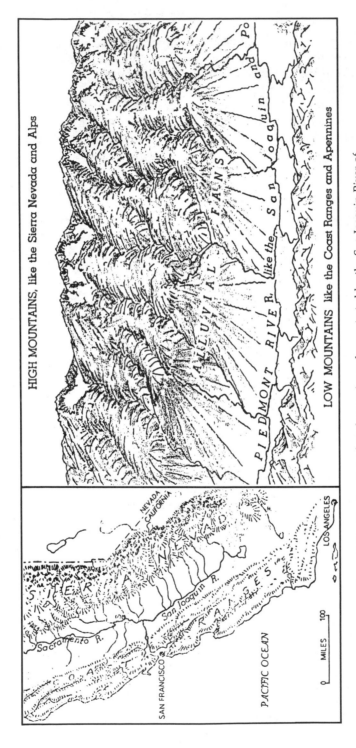

HIGH MOUNTAINS, like the Sierra Nevada and Alps

ALLUVIAL FANS

PIEDMONT RIVER R., like the San Joaquin and Po

LOW MOUNTAINS like the Coast Ranges and Apennines

NEVADA
CALIFORNIA

SIERRA NEVADA

San Joaquin R.

Sacramento R.

SAN FRANCISCO

COAST RANGES

PACIFIC OCEAN

LOS ANGELES

MILES

0   100

Figure 3-10 The location of piedmont rivers demonstrated by the San Joaquin River of California. Diagram at right explains the drainage pattern shown on map at left. (Reprinted with permission of Macmillan Publishing Company from *Things Maps Don't Tell Us* by Armin K. Lobeck, copyright © 1956 by Armin K. Lobeck.)

Lobeck's drawing is a *physiographic diagram* and differs from landform maps, such as that by Erwin Raisz in Figure 3-9, in that the physiographic diagram is drawn with the idea of suggesting the area's origin, whereas the landform map is concerned more with describing the earth's surface than with inferring geologic or geomorphic causes.[19]

Land-Use Maps and Slope Maps

In 1974, the U.S. Geological Survey began a nationwide program of land-use and land-cover mapping. Although experts disagree about the definition of "land use," the USGS cites human "activities on land which are directly related to the land" as having merit. "Land cover" is easier to define because the term literally refers to the natural vegetation and the constructed phenomena that cover the earth's surface.[20]

The need for a general overview of land use and land cover, along with the lack of coordination among federal agencies using and collecting land-use data, led in 1971 to the creation of the Interagency Steering Committee on Land Use Information and Classification.[21] Representatives from the U.S. Geological Survey, the National Aeronautics and Space Administration, the Soil Conservation Service, the Association of American Geographers, and the International Geographical Union worked to develop a classification scheme incorporating conventional data and imagery from satellites. This system is operational at regional, state, and local levels, as well as at a highly generalized national level. Table 3-1 lists the typical data sources by level of classification, which range from highly aggregated, small-scale data based on very high altitude aerial imagery (Level I) to low-altitude data taken at less than 3,000 m (10,000 ft) and at scales exceeding 1:20,000 (Level IV). The Committee envisioned the larger scales, Levels III and IV, as being developed by users interested in local information, right down to the municipality. The large-scale information is compatible with that generated in a nationwide program at Level II by the U.S. Geological Survey, especially its point and line land-use data on map sheets for quadrangles similar to those in its intermediate-scale topographic series.[22]

The Geological Survey's National Mapping Division operates the Land Use and Land Cover Mapping Program. The program was started in the early 1970s and coverage of the 48 contiguous states should be completed by the end of the 1980s. The program produces maps at scales of 1:250,000 and, for some places,

[19] Arthur H. Robinson et al., *Elements of Cartography*, 5th ed. (New York: John Wiley & Sons, 1984), p. 375.

[20] James R. Anderson et al., "A Land Use and Land Cover Classification System for Use With Remote Sensor Data," *Geological Survey Professional Paper 964* (Washington, D.C.: U.S. Government Printing Office, 1976), p. 4.

[21] Ibid., pp. 2–3.

[22] Ibid., p. 6.

TABLE 3-1 LAND-USE AND LAND-COVER CLASSIFICATION SYSTEM, ITS LEVELS OF CLASSIFICATION, AND DATA SOURCES

Classification level	Typical data characteristics
I	Satellite from several hundred km
II	High-altitude data at 12,400 m (40,000 ft) or above (less than 1:80,000 scale)
III	Medium-altitude data taken between 3,100 and 12,400 m (10,000 and 40,000 ft) (1:20,000 to 1:80,000 scale)
IV	Low-altitude data taken below 3,100 m (10,000 ft) (more than 1:20,000 scale)

Source: James R. Anderson et al., "A Land Use and Land Cover Classification System for Use with Remote Sensor Data," *U.S. Geological Survey Professional Paper 964* (Washington, D.C.: U.S. Government Printing Office, 1976), p. 6.

more detailed metric base maps at 1:100,000. Based upon high-altitude aerial photography at a scale of about 1:80,000, the program describes the landscape according to the hierarchical classification scheme shown in Table 3-2. This scheme was designed to be compatible with more detailed land-use mapping from larger-scale conventional photography, as well as with imagery from orbiting satellites at smaller scales. Coverage is provided at Level II of a scheme with four levels (Table 3-1), and the 37 categories at Level II collapse into nine at Level I (Table 3-2). Since at a scale of 1:250,000 one cannot show accurately the extent of all land use and land cover, the minimum mapping unit is 4 hectares (about 10 acres) for urban, water, some agricultural land, and for strip mines, quarries, and gravel pits. Smaller isolated patches and features narrower than 200 m (about 600 ft) are not shown. For all other categories, the minimum area is 16 hectares (about 40 acres) and the minimum width is 400 m (about 1,310 ft).[23] The minimum mapping unit is an objective standard for the cartographers who compile the maps from aerial imagery; it avoids an excessively congested map and promotes uniformity in the content of the more than 400 sheets in the series.

Figure 3-11 illustrates Level-I land use and land cover in an enlarged section of the northeast quarter of the Indianapolis 1:250,000-scale quadrangle. This map is typical of maps produced by conventional interpretation techniques from high-altitude, color-infrared photographs. Figure 3-12 shows the area outlined in the center of Figure 3-11, part of the Maywood, Indiana, 1:24,000-scale quadrangle. Note that the rectangle in the center of the Level-I map includes all or part of less than 20 landscape units, whereas the more detailed Level-II map in Figure 3-12 recognizes over a hundred individual land-cover units for the same

[23] W. B. Mitchell et al., "GIRAS: A Geographic Information Retrieval and Analysis System for Handling Land Use and Land Cover Data," *Geological Survey Professional Paper 1059* (Washington, D.C.: U.S. Government Printing Office, 1977), pp. 2–3.

TABLE 3-2 LAND-USE AND LAND-COVER CLASSIFICATION SYSTEM FOR USE WITH REMOTE SENSOR DATA

Level I	Level II
1. Urban or built-up	11 Residential
	12 Commercial and services
	13 Industrial
	14 Transportation, communications, and utilities
	15 Industrial and commercial complexes
	16 Mixed urban or built-up land
	17 Other urban or built-up land
2. Agricultural land	21 Cropland and pasture
	22 Orchards, groves, vineyards, nurseries, and ornamental horticultural areas
	23 Confined feeding operations
	24 Other agricultural land
3. Rangeland	31 Herbaceous rangeland
	32 Shrub and brush rangeland
	33 Mixed rangeland
4. Forest land	41 Deciduous forest land
	42 Evergreen forest land
	43 Mixed forest land
5. Water	51 Streams and canals
	52 Lakes
	53 Reservoirs
	54 Bays and estuaries
6. Wetland	61 Forested wetland
	62 Nonforested wetland
7. Barren land	71 Dry salt flats
	72 Beaches
	73 Sandy areas other than beaches
	74 Bare exposed rock
	75 Strip mines, quarries, and gravel pits
	76 Transitional areas
	77 Mixed barren land
8. Tundra	81 Shrub and brush tundra
	82 Herbaceous tundra
	83 Bare ground tundra
	84 Wet tundra
	85 Mixed tundra
9. Perennial snow or ice	91 Perennial snowfields
	92 Glaciers

Source: James R. Anderson et al., "A Land Use and Land Cover Classification System for Use with Remote Sensor Data," *U.S. Geological Survey Professional Paper 964* (Washington, D.C.: U.S. Government Printing Office, 1976), p. 8.

Note: USGS uses a one-digit numerical code for Level I and a two-digit code for Level II.

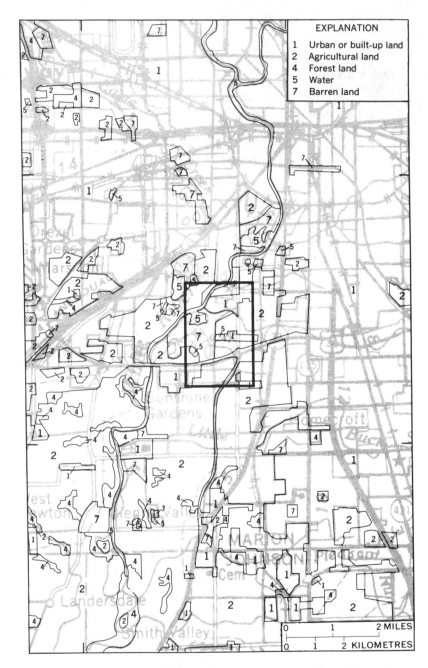

Figure 3-11 Level-I land use and land cover in an enlarged part of the northeast quarter of the Indianapolis, Indiana-Illinois, 1:250,000 quadrangle. The area outlined in the center is the Maywood area, enlarged in Figure 3-12. (James R. Anderson et al., "A Land Use and Land Cover Classification System for Use with Remote Sensor Data," *Geological Survey Professional Paper 964* [Washington, D.C.: U.S. Government Printing Office, 1976], p. 23.)

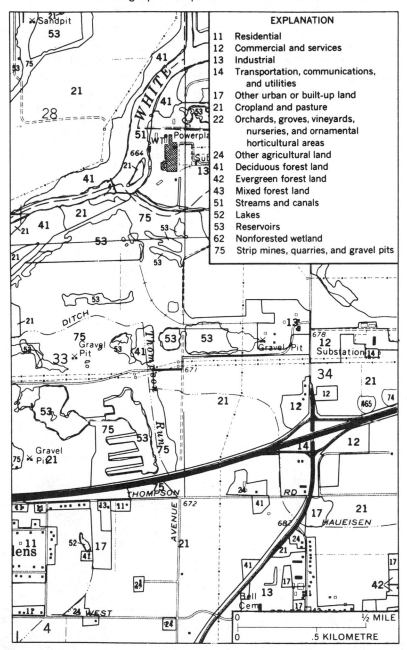

Figure 3-12   Level-II land use and land cover in a part of the Maywood, Indiana, 1:24,000 quadrangle. (James R. Anderson et al., "A Land Use and Land Cover Classification System for Use with Remote Sensor Data," *Geological Survey Professional Paper 964* [Washington, D.C.: U.S. Government Printing Office, 1976], p. 25.)

area. The relationship between Level I and Level II is obvious, and careful study of the two maps heightens understanding of the system.

A map showing just one land-use category can also be quite instructive. For example, Figure 3-13 depicts Level-II Category 75 (strip mines, quarries, and gravel pits) in Lackawanna County, Pennsylvania. The map suggests, among other things, the influence of geologic structure upon miners' access to anthracite and, in turn, the impact of mining on the pattern of stripped land. This part of the Northern Anthracite Field is confined essentially to a northeast-southwest trending valley in which coal was relatively accessible and most intensively mined in earlier times. Despite its relatively late settlement, Scranton became the largest city in the region, largely because of mining operations. The tracts of stripped land Figure 3-13 shows are nearly contiguous and recall the halcyon

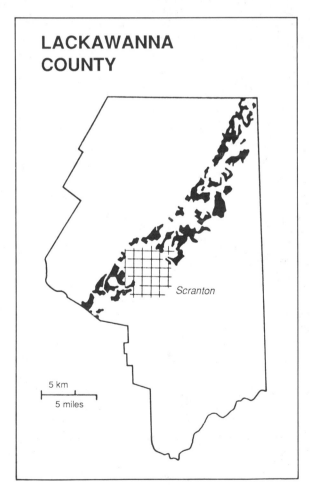

Figure 3-13 Strip-mined land (Category 75 in the Land Use and Land Cover Mapping Program) in Lackawanna County, Pennsylvania. (George A. Schnell and Mark Monmonier, "Coal Mining and Land Use-Land Cover: A Cartographic Study of Mining and Barren Land," in *Pennsylvania Coal: Resources, Technology and Utilization*, S. K. Majumdar and E. W. Miller, eds. [Easton: Pennsylvania Academy of Science, 1983], p. 346; used with permission.)

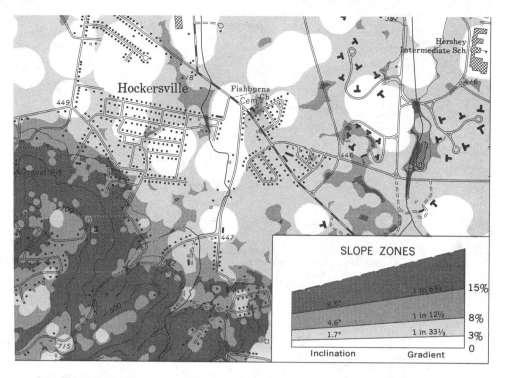

Figure 3-14 Slope map of Hershey, Pennsylvania, at a scale of 1:24,000. (Melvin Y. Ellis, ed., *Coastal Mapping Hnadbook* [Washington, D.C.: U.S. Government Printing Office, 1978], p. 165.)

days of the anthracite industry in the late nineteenth and early twentieth centuries.[24]

Slope maps are, essentially, generalized contour maps that classify slope by aggregating areas of consistent slope to form zones. Slopes can be estimated mechanically by the distance between contours on a topographic quadrangle, or by computer-generated digital terrain data. Planners find slope maps useful for suggesting slopes that promote or inhibit various uses of the land. Large-scale slope maps are especially useful in evaluating land for agriculture and in delineating potential problem areas. For example, farming on a steep slope may lead to excessive erosion or even gullying, and level land with slow drainage and standing water requires special efforts to drain the water when the land is intended for a residential subdivision. Figure 3-14, a slope map of Hershey,

[24] George A. Schnell and Mark Monmonier, "Coal Mining and Land Use-Land Cover: A Cartographic Study of Mining and Barren Land," in S. K. Majumdar and E. Willard Miller, eds., *Pennsylvania Coal: Resources, Technology and Utilization* (Easton, Pa.: Pennsylvania Academy of Science, 1983), pp. 345–46.

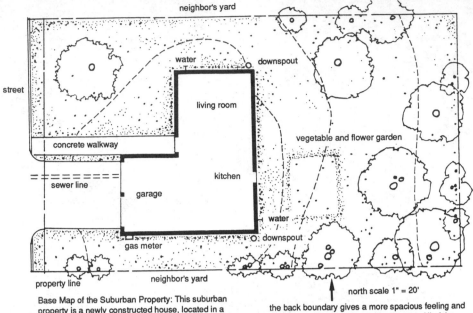

Base Map of the Suburban Property: This suburban property is a newly constructed house, located in a development, with the usual plantings of turf, shrubs and a few small specimen trees. A natural woodland along the back boundary gives a more spacious feeling and provides a nice backdrop to the property. All of the existing landscape features are depicted on the map.

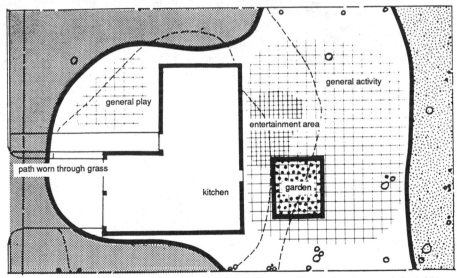

Functional Analysis of the Suburban Property: Because this is a newly occupied landscape, there is not yet an orderly arrangement of existing functions. Activities take place wherever they can.

The driveway, which also serves as a parking area, cannot accommodate more than two cars. The front entry functions poorly. The walk to the street is never used; instead there is a path worn into the grass from the parking area. There is also a large area in front of the house that is essentially wasted. Although the children sometimes play here, it is not encouraged because of its proximity to the street.

The back of the house is used for outdoor eating and entertainment. The back edge of the property is too wet to be used for any activities.

Figure 3-15 Landscape architect's base map (upper left), analysis (lower left), and synthesis (right) of a suburban property. (Reprinted from Carol A. Smyser and the Editors of Rodale Press Books, *Nature's Design,* © 1982 Rodale Press, Inc. Permission granted by Rodale Press, Inc., Emmaus, PA 18049.)

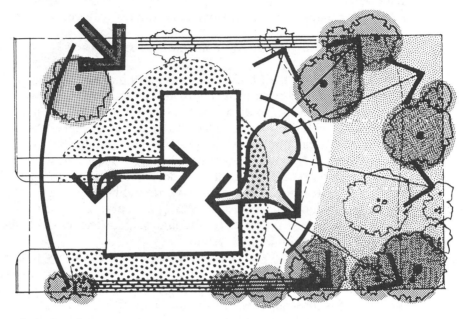

Synthesis:

With all of this information compiled, this synthesis drawing is ready to be used as the information base for the design. Together with the list of needs and wants, it will be used to work out a landscape plan.

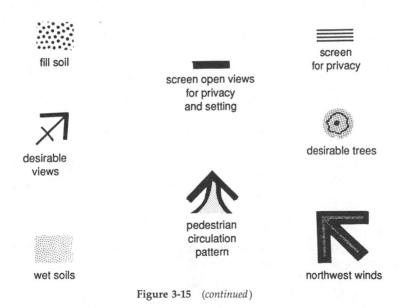

fill soil

screen open views
for privacy
and setting

screen
for privacy

desirable
views

desirable trees

wet soils

pedestrian
circulation
pattern

northwest winds

Figure 3-15   (*continued*)

Pennsylvania, shows ranges of slope percentage by various shades of gray. Some available slope maps distinguish slope zone ranges with color.[25]

Plans and Renderings of the Landscape Architect

The unabashed attempts of humans to modify the earth's surface for more efficient use is perhaps best recorded by the renderings of the landscape architect. To a landscape architect, "landscaping . . . is the arrangement of land for human use, and it involves not only the selection and planting of vegetation, but changes to the contour of the landscape, the placement of buildings, walks and roads and much more."[26] Landscape architecture is thus concerned with the elements of the physical environment—vegetation, soil, water, and rocks—as well as with the humanly constructed aspects of the environment—buildings, walks, walls— as they are combined into pleasant-looking and practical places of residence, work, and recreation. Theoretically, the landscape architect treats each site as a unique entity, an evolving ecosystem.[27]

Figure 3-15 (top left) shows at a large scale, which is easy to perceive and simple to comprehend, a base map of a lot, house, lawn, trees, and shrubs. Note that the map also shows walks, sewer lines, gas meter, water lines for hose connections, downspouts, and contour lines. With this base map, the landscape architect's consideration of the lot can proceed to the manner in which the inhabitants will use the property—the functional analysis, shown in the bottom left of Figure 3-15. Essentially, the area within the heavy line is used space, and the periphery outside the heavy line is unused space. After extensive study of all elements and the wants and needs of the inhabitants, the architect prepares the synthesis map (Figure 3-15, right), which indicates physical problems such as wet soils, along with functional aspects such as northwesterly winds and pedestrian circulation. The synthesis map reflects the owners' visual concerns too: where screening should be considered and where desirable views should be preserved. These maps, combining natural and constructed environments with human needs and desires to make a residence functional as well as pleasant, are quite straightforward and truthful.[28]

The plans in Figure 3-15 differ from stylistic renderings in which the plan, often an oblique diagram complete with landscaping and fences at just the right height and placed well, is in reality an instrument of persuasion. A map or sketch used in this way is intended to transform an idea into an ideal, a sales pitch in which the representation often looks better than the reality it illustrates!

[25] Melvin Y. Ellis, ed., *Coastal Mapping Handbook* (Washington, D.C.: U.S. Government Printing Office, 1978), p. 55.

[26] Carol A. Smyser and the Editors of Rodale Press Books, *Nature's Design: A Practical Guide to Natural Landscaping* (Emmaus, Pa.: Rodale Press, 1982), p. ix.

[27] Ibid.

[28] Ibid.

Figure 3-16   Perspective drawing of peasant row housing near Tianjin, China. (Liu Song-tao and Zhu Bizhen, *Proposed Drawings of Rural Dwellings* [Tianjin, China: Tianjin Science and Technology Publishing House, 1983], p. 5.)

Such materials abound in real-estate offices, developers' mailings, and public hearings before planning boards across North America, Europe, and elsewhere. Figure 3-16 shows a plan for duplex housing for peasants in one of the rural suburbs surrounding Tianjin Municipality, China. The density of such housing is great, so, in reality, the trees in the background of this drawing would most likely be removed to make room for other comparable units. The front yard of these dwellings is of particular interest: the nearest enclosure would most likely be a pig pen, the small structure to its right would be the toilet for the nearest row house, a chicken coop would occupy one of the corners, and the remainder of the yard shown as a lawn with shrubs and trees would probably be a subsidiary vegetable garden for home use.[29] An alert public must be aware of the persuasiveness of selective cartographic images, which developers often present at planning-board or zoning-board meetings with the express purpose of making

[29] Professor Ronald G. Knapp, Department of Geography, College at New Paltz, State University of New York, supplied the above description of the house and grounds. See Ronald G. Knapp, *China's Traditional Rural Architecture: A Cultural Geography of the Common House* (Honolulu: University of Hawaii Press, 1986).

the proposal look better on paper than it has any chance of appearing on the ground.

TOPOGRAPHIC VIGNETTES

The remainder of this chapter presents examples of landscape features portrayed on topographic maps of the U.S. Geological Survey. After a brief essay on their value to tourists as souvenirs, we explore what topographic maps can reveal about a landscape's geological controls, and how old and recent maps can reveal the impact of both catastrophic geologic processes and human settlement. The reader is encouraged to study the original maps, which are in color and thus are able to differentiate features more readily than the black-and-white illustrations presented here.

Famous Places

By recording hills, valleys, streams, roads, place names, and other landscape characteristics, the topographic map is the perfect souvenir of many excursions. A map offers a compact and concise overview of the beach resort, the national park campsite, or the cherished relative's neighborhood. With it the tourist can take home the geographic flavor of the Colorado Rockies, the Nebraska prairie, or the Pennsylvania Dutch countryside. The traveler can easily learn to read the map's standardized topographic symbols, to relate the map to landscape and landscape to map, and to use the map's orderly assemblage of geographic cues to recall pleasant moments and spectacular vistas. Vacationers who return home only with a set of photographs and other conventional tourist bric-a-brac are missing much of the reminiscence about places that detailed, informative maps can trigger. Of course, the "Compleat Tourist" will use the map not only to prompt memory after the trip, but also to plan and explore before traveling.

History buffs in particular should readily recognize the value of modern topographic maps. A map is a convenient base on which to plot waves of settlement and lines of famous battles, and can provide an appreciation of distances and the ruggedness of terrain that early settlers confronted. Although tree cover and even shorelines may have changed, most topographic features are highly stable over the past 200 years or so. In Figure 3-17, for instance, the reconstructed Fort Carillon, better known as Fort Ticonderoga, occupies the point from which the French in the French and Indian War (1754–1763) and the British in the American Revolution hoped to control the principal route along Lake Champlain between Canada and the Hudson River Valley. Guns from the fort, strategically situated on high ground, could block the outlet of Lake George into Lake Champlain.

Topographic maps can be particularly valuable as supplements to photographic portrayals of large national monuments. Andersonville National Cem-

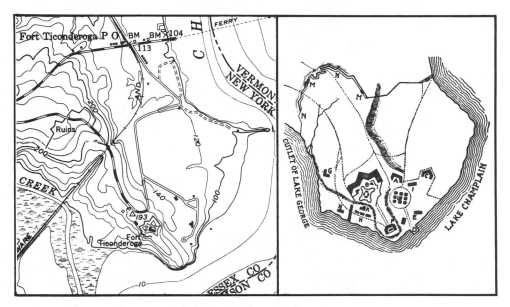

Figure 3-17   Reconstruction of Fort Ticonderoga as represented on a modern topographic map (left), and a representation of the original fort in 1759 (right). (From Ticonderoga, N.Y.-Vt., U.S. Geological Survey 7.5-minute quadrangle map, 1:24,000, 1950; and Justin H. Smith, *Our Struggle for the Fourteenth Colony: Canada and the American Revolution* [New York: G. P. Putnam's Sons, 1907], p. 120.)

etery and Prison Park, in west central Georgia, illustrates this point. Most pictures of the park draw attention to the graves of the nearly 13,000 Union soldiers who perished in this poorly run Confederate military prison during 1864 and early 1865. But the plan view of the park and its surrounding area in Figure 3-18 allows the visitor to appreciate more fully MacKinlay Kantor's vivid historical novel about life in and around the prison.[30] The map also shows the small, pleasantly restored village of Andersonville, which the visitor will also want to experience and recall with the aid of the map.

Hill Cumorah, in upstate New York, is a historic monument of a different sort. Mormons—members of the Church of Jesus Christ of Latter-day Saints—annually hold there a 4-day pageant attended by 100,000 persons. As Figure 3-19 shows, this landform is an elongated hill, called a *drumlin*, which geomorphologists believed was shaped during the Ice Ages by glaciers hundreds of feet thick.[31] Mormons believe that on Hill Cumorah their founder, Joseph Smith, received from the angel Moroni a set of gold plates revealing an ancient North

[30] MacKinlay Kantor, *Andersonville* (Cleveland: World Publishing, 1955).

[31] For a discussion of the drumlin field containing Hill Cumorah, see Jesse W. Miller, Jr., "Variations in New York Drumlins," *Annals of the Association of American Geographers* 62, no. 3 (September 1972), 418–23.

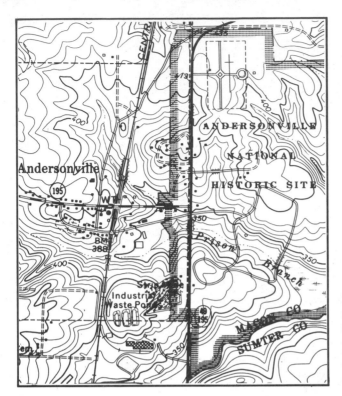

Figure 3-18 Topographic representation of site of the infamous Confederate prison camp at Andersonville, Georgia, during the Civil War. (From Andersonville, Ga., U.S. Geological Survey 7.5-minute quadrangle map, 1:24,000, 1972.)

American civilization that existed 15 centuries ago.[32] These revelations are the basis of the *Book of Mormon*, and a monument at the north end of the drumlin memorializes them and the angel.

Landforms

Although topographic maps are fun for the cartographically initiated tourist, the student of physiography takes them far more seriously. The many and varied U.S. Geological Survey maps at a variety of scales provide numerous clear-cut examples of features, events, and situations that are central to the study of landforms.

Figure 3-20 illustrates that the manner in which streams are patterned may depend upon slope and grain of the land, the kind of rocks that underly their course, and features caused by faulting and folding. These partial topographic sheets selected from the Welch, West Virginia, and Bellefonte, Pennsylvania, 1:62,500 quadrangles are models of dendritic and trellis drainage patterns, re-

[32] William J. Whalen, *The Latter-day Saints in the Modern World* (Notre Dame, Ind.: University of Notre Dame Press, 1964), pp. 27, 43, and 52.

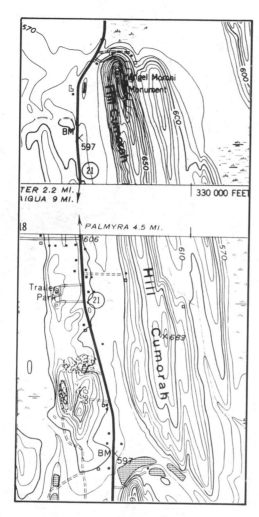

Figure 3-19 Topographic representation, from two adjoining quadrangles, of Hill Cumorah in New York. This illustration demonstrates a cartographic corollary to Murphy's Law whereby features of interest tend to lie astride quadrangle boundaries. (From [above] Palmyra, N.Y., U.S. Geological Survey, 7.5-minute quadrangle map, 1:24,000, 1952; and [below] Clifton Springs, N.Y., U.S. Geological Survey 7.5-minute quadrangle map, 1:24,000, 1951, photorevised 1978.)

spectively. Welch, located on horizontal strata on the Appalachian Plateau of southwestern West Virginia, is drained by streams that take on a dendritic pattern, as in the branching from a tree's trunk. The horizontal structure presents a surface that is relatively uniform in resisting erosion; thus the Welch area is drained by streams that are uncontrolled by the rock structure and that flow in all directions. Bellefonte, located in central Pennsylvania's Ridge and Valley province, is drained by streams whose pattern is the product of strong structural control—that is, an area with subsequent streams such as Bald Eagle Creek, which flows northeastward through the center of the map and into which tributaries flow perpendicularly. This trellis pattern (like the parallel and perpendicular strips of wood that support climbing roses) developed along least resistent strata and was regimented by the folding of originally flat-lying sediments.

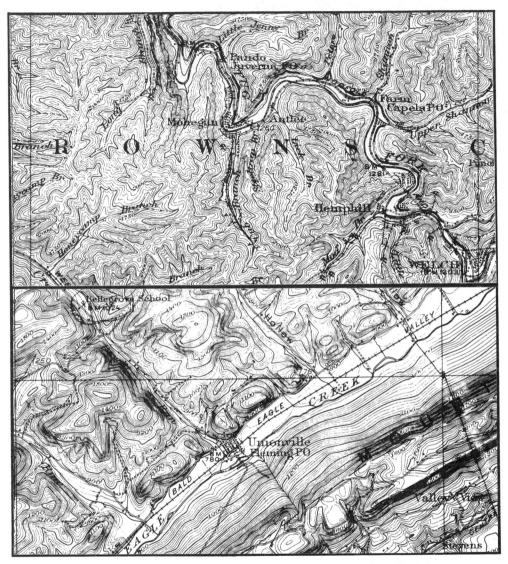

Figure 3-20 An example of dendritic drainage (above) and trellis drainage (below). (From Bellefonte, Pa., U.S. Geological Survey 15-minute quadrangle map, 1:62,500, 1908; and Welch, W. Va., U.S. Geological Survey 15-minute quadrangle map, 1:62,500, 1926.)

Thus these two not very distant places exhibit drainage patterns different in origin and form.

Figure 3-21 illustrates a very distinctive feature, the Cedar Creek Alluvial Fan, located in the Ennis quadrangle of the Rocky Mountains of Montana, less than 160 km (100 mi) southeast of Butte. Note that the relief in the mountainous

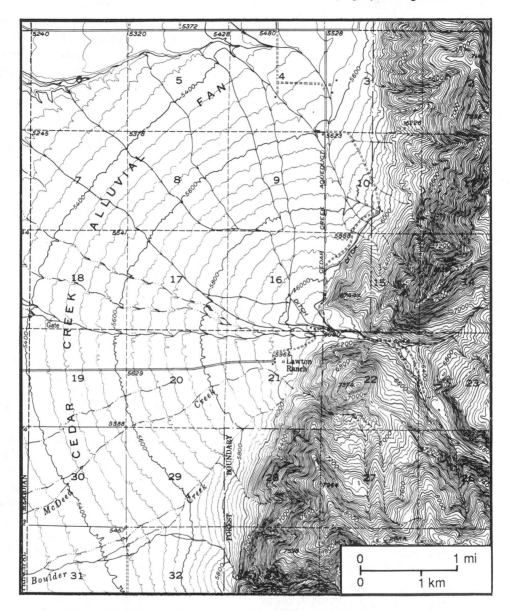

Figure 3-21 Topographic representation of an alluvial fan and radial drainage. (From Ennis, Mont., U.S. Geological Survey 15-minute quadrangle map, 1:62,500, 1947.)

sections shown is great enough for the Geological Survey to have used a 40-ft (about 12 m) contour interval rather than the customary 20-ft (about 6 m) contour interval, yet the surface appears to be covered with contour lines. The elevation at the fan's center is about 5,000 ft (about 1,500 m) but the elevations exceed 9,000 ft (2,700 m) in the map's southeastern section, not more than 5 km (3 mi) from the 5,500-ft (less than 1,700 m) elevation. Indeed, the slope of the fan down from the 6,080-ft (about 1,853 m) benchmark near the fan's apex at the canyon's mouth approaches 47 m per km (250 ft per mi) for the first 3.2 km (2 mi) and flattens a bit to 28 m per km (150 ft per mi) at the fan's western periphery. Slopes such as these are quite typical for alluvial fans.

How did this symmetrical feature come to be? Such fans are not unlike delta formations found where streams issue into a large body of water—the Mississippi River emptying into the Gulf of Mexico, for example—except that these alluvial fan deposits are on land. As a stream flowing down a steep gradient encounters more nearly horizontal terrain, the reduction in slope causes a rather sudden reduction in the stream's velocity, which, in turn, causes deposition at the mountain's base in the shape of a fan. Features such as these are found in many sites in the West and the Southwest of the United States, when conditions are as described above.

Both natural events and human activity can lead to destruction of landforms and landscapes. An earthquake on March 20, 1980, heralded the awakening of Mount St. Helens, one of the volcanic peaks of the Cascade Mountain Range that extends through southwestern Washington. A week later, the volcano began to erupt repeatedly for the first time in 123 years, so that by March 28 two craters had formed. These enlarged over the next few days and eventually coalesced to form an even bigger crater, which continued to grow. On April 3, continuous vibrations of the earth (harmonic tremor) reflecting the movement of molten rock (magma) under the volcano caused part of the mountain's north side to swell up to 150 cm (5 ft) a day. Such activity continued to alternate with periods of quiet until May 18, when a great explosion threw an estimated 4.2 km^3 (1 mi^3) of rock and ash more than 20 km (13 mi) into the air above. As a consequence, an area 13 by 24 km (8 by 15 mi) to the north was flattened (see Figure 3-22). Lava, steam, ash, and gas seeped and flowed from the crater, causing great destruction. Glacial melt caused mud flows that fouled the drainageways and re-formed the lower elevations. By mid-summer, 28 deaths had been reported and 36 persons were missing. Yakima, some 130 km (80 mi) east, was covered with the erupted ash, and ash reached the eastern states within 4 days, as ash clouds began to circle the earth at more than 18,000 m (60,000 ft). Mount St. Helens' peak, almost 3,000 m (9,677 ft) in height before the eruption, was reduced to about 2,500 m (8,400 ft).[33] Careful study of the pre- and post-eruption maps of Mount St. Helens (see Figure 3-22) will allow the reader to recreate the events described above as they caused vast changes over a very short period of time. The most obvious change in the landform itself occurred

[33] U.S. Department of Agriculture, Forest Service, *Mount St. Helens* (Vancouver, Wash.: Gifford Pinchot National Forest, January 1981).

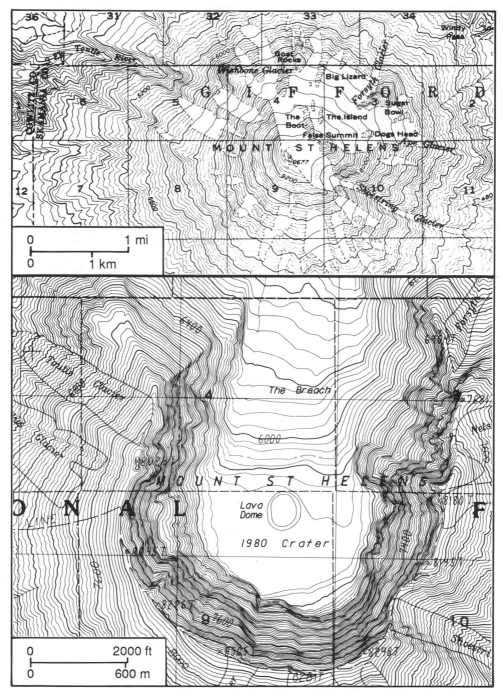

Figure 3-22 Mount St. Helens before (above) and after (below) earthquake and volcanic eruptions, 1980. (From Mount St. Helens, Wash., U.S. Geological Survey 15-minute and 7.5-minute quadrangle maps, 1:62,500, 1958, and 1:24,000, 1983, respectively.)

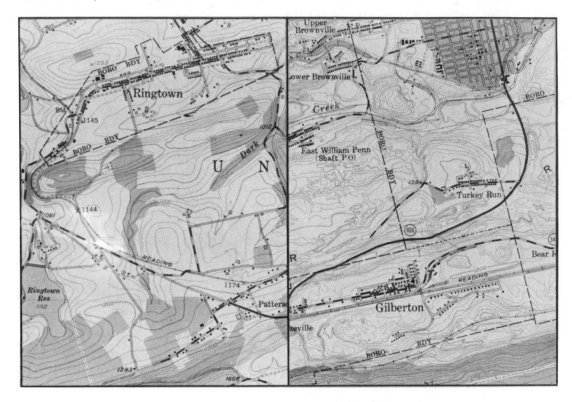

Figure 3-23 Topographic evidence of the role of humans in altering the landscape: an agricultural area (left) and a mined-over site (right). (From Shenandoah, Pa., U.S. Geological Survey 7.5-minute quadrangle map, 1:24,000, 1955.)

to the area immediately north of the original peak, the area described above as having been "flattened."[34]

Figure 3-23, taken from the northeastern corner of the Shenandoah, Pennsylvania, quadrangle, illustrates the effects of human activity on the topography of the small borough of Ringtown and areas to the south of it in the 1950s. Smooth, rounded contours depict an equally smooth, rounded topography sculpted over the millenia by streams. People practiced agriculture there, but judging by the rather large part of the valley devoted to woodlot and the small level area, not in a very productive way. The small reservoir is worth noting, but compared to the topographic complexity of the map to the right, the map to the left shows a tranquil landscape.

As the right part of Figure 3-23 clearly portrays, humans have been busy

[34] A recent article in a new journal contains vivid photographs of both the destructive force of the eruption and the return of vegetation of a surprising diversity. See Jerry F. Franklin et al., "Ecosystem Responses to the Eruption of Mount St. Helens," *National Geographic Research* 1, no. 2 (Spring 1985), pp. 198–216.

digging and piling up earth debris in the area, judging by the predominant irregular, broken contours, with depression contours near low hills. The activity is mining and the product is anthracite coal. After all, the Shenandoah area is part of the Ridge and Valley province of Pennsylvania's Appalachians, where flat lying sediments were folded, causing the surface to wrinkle, and the softer bituminous coal strata to become the harder anthracite as pressure and heat removed volatile materials. The absence of forest cover in the area (shown well on the five-color quadrangle map) is also consistent with mining, since strip-mined land is not immediately hospitable to reforestation: iron pyrite, found in association with coal, produces dilute sulphuric acid and thus deters tree growth in mined-over areas. The complete map depicts numerous small reservoirs, suggesting problems with water, since the small dammed area suggests little depth and low water levels each season in which precipitation is lower than normal.

In addition, both roads and railroads on the map reflect the dominance of coal mining: notice the great number of railroad lines between Upper Browns-ville and Lower Brownsville, most of which converge to the east, indicating their function as sidings where gondolas were loaded and stored until the train was complete. The road immediately north of Turkey Run seems to end nowhere. Actually, this road and others like it on the map were built to accommodate trucks laden with coal, as they end near strip or open-pit mines. (The depressions and hills of mining are very evident in the area near the part of the road just described that extends toward the southwest.) Finally, note the absence of settlement and associated activity along Route 924, the highway extending from Shenandoah southward to Turkey Run and then westward. In the 1950s the anthracite coal industry had suffered from oil's rise in the competition for the home heating market, and the status and outlook of the local economy were not good. Therefore local housing and economic activity were in a slump and growth had given way to decline as other areas became the foci of America's continuing evolution from the Industrial Revolution to the Age of High Technology.[35]

We see the earth's surface daily, and a good way to more fully appreciate the value of landscape maps is to examine carefully the topographic maps for our home areas and for places we visit frequently or recall most vividly. Find on such a map a route you frequently walk or drive. Note how the spacing of the contour lines indicates slope: where the lines are closer, the climb is harder. Note also how the contours bend to show hills and stream valleys. Note as well how other symbols show vegetation, urban development, and whatever features, natural or constructed, make the area distinctive. On a smaller-scale map, covering a larger part of the territory, observe how the map shows the pattern of drainage, steep slopes, transportation routes, and other manifestations of the

[35] The discussion of this quadrangle is based upon an unpublished essay, "The Geography of the Shenandoah Quadrangle," by Peirce F. Lewis, Department of Geography, The Pennsylvania State University, 1967.

human presence. Relate symbols on the map to experiences. Then note what the map can tell you that you did not know. How can the map help you choose a place to live or picnic? How does it suggest and even help explain change in the region? How might you use other maps for armchair exploration of more distant places, including those you have never seen but would like to visit? You read books, newspapers, and magazines daily, but have you ever earnestly attempted to read a map? It can be fascinating. Try it!

FOR FURTHER READING

BIES, JOHN D., and ROBERT A. LONG, *Mapping and Topographic Drafting.* Cincinnati: South-Western Publishing Co., 1983.

ELLIS, MELVIN Y., ed., *Coastal Mapping Handbook.* Washington, D.C.: U.S. Government Printing Office, 1978.

HARLEY, J. B., *Ordnance Survey Maps: A Descriptive Manual.* Southampton, Eng.: Ordnance Survey, 1975.

HARVEY, P. D. A., *The History of Topographical Maps: Symbols, Pictures and Surveys.* London: Thames & Hudson, 1980.

IMHOF, EDUARD, *Cartographic Relief Presentation,* trans. Harry Steward. Berlin: Walter DeGruyter, 1982.

LARSGAARD, MARY LYNETTE, *Topographic Mapping of the Americas, Australia, and New Zealand.* Littleton, Colo.: Libraries Unlimited, 1984.

LOBECK, ARMIN K., *Things Maps Don't Tell Us.* New York: Macmillan, 1956.

MUEHRCKE, PHILLIP, *Map Use: Reading, Analysis, and Interpretation.* Madison: JP Publications, 1978.

NICHOLSON, N. L., and L. M. SIEBERT, *The Maps of Canada.* Folkestone, Eng.: William Dawson and Sons; Hamden, Conn.: Archon Books, 1981.

RAITZ, KARL, and JOHN FRASER HART, *Cultural Geography on Topographic Maps.* New York: John Wiley & Sons, 1975.

THOMPSON, MORRIS M., *Maps for America: Cartographic Products of the U.S. Geological Survey.* Washington, D.C.: U.S. Department of the Interior, Geological Survey, 1979.

CHAPTER FOUR

Maps
of the Atmosphere

The earth's atmosphere, a mixture of gases and suspended particles, is a complex, constantly changing system that no map or chart can fully represent in the way that, say, Erwin Raisz and Armin K. Lobeck portrayed topography or that aerial photographs show the surface of the earth.[1] The symbols needed to map the atmosphere are of a variety well beyond that of symbols employed in topographic mapping. Generally, these atmospheric symbols represent the elements of temperature, moisture, pressure, and wind as they appeared yesterday, appear today and, with much less certainty, will appear tomorrow. On weather maps the mapped symbols represent to the reader conversant with their meaning a spatial summary of the manner in which the elements interact to produce atmospheric conditions at the moment, just recently, or in the near future. While weather maps are concerned with evanescent atmospheric conditions, climatic maps are concerned with atmospheric conditions over a long period of time, or "averaged weather."

Prior to the seventeenth century, meteorology and weather forecasting were based on a melange of Aristotelian philosophy, astrology, mythology, re-

---

[1] These cartographers have contributed much to the way we illustrate the earth's surface. See, for example, Armin K. Lobeck, *Things Maps Don't Tell Us* (New York: Macmillan, 1958); and Erwin J. Raisz, "The Physiographic Method of Representing Scenery on Maps," *Geographical Review* 21, no. 2 (April 1931), 297–304.

ligion, and folklore.[2] Weather science became more nearly exact only with the invention of the thermometer and the barometer. Indeed, prior to our gaining the ability to "sound" the atmosphere and, even more recently, to "fly" it, weather science was limited to the analysis of the lowest altitudes of the earth's atmosphere.

Since both popular interest in and commercial concern about the atmosphere focus on the near future and what forecasts will present, maps take on a position of importance; they describe as well as summarize the place-specific and general pattern of the elements of weather and climate, and contribute in no small way to the study and analysis of the atmosphere. This chapter, which focuses on the cartographic representation of the atmosphere and examines the elements of weather and climate, explores the unique nature of weather maps and climatic maps and presents a review of atmospheric mapping in everyday life.

THE ELEMENTS AND CONTROLS OF WEATHER AND CLIMATE

The measurable attributes of the atmosphere include temperature, precipitation/ humidity, pressure, and winds. These elements are the essentials of the weather report, the weather map, and the weather forecast. In a given place they vary throughout the year. The degree of their variation depends upon myriad factors, not the least of which is latitude. From place to place at any given time atmospheric elements also vary because of other influences that reflect, essentially, the earth's relationship to the sun throughout the seasons, which regulates the receipt and distribution of solar energy on earth. These controlling influences are

> latitude,
> land and water distribution,
> winds and associated phenomena,
> elevation,
> topographic barriers,
> ocean currents.

The latitude of a given place largely determines the intensity of the atmosphere's *insolation*—incoming solar radiation, which generally controls "temperature"—and temperature, in turn, plays a leading role in the humidity and

---

[2] An excellent, brief summary of the influence of the intellectual revolution on the rise of empiricism in studying the atmosphere is found in S. K. Heninger, Jr., *A Handbook of Renaissance Meteorology* (New York: Greenwood Press, 1968).

pressure of that air. Winds, or moving atmosphere, respond to pressure differences, which reflect temperature and moisture levels. Solar intensity—the angular elevation of the sun above the horizon—accounts in large measure for both spatial variation in insolation and change over time in an area's receipt of insolation, although the length of the day, or *duration* (time between sunrise and sunset), solar output, and a number of less important factors contribute as well. The relative importance of latitude and duration in accounting for insolation variations is underscored by the fact that, while all places on earth receive 6 months of day and 6 months of night each year, the equator receives 12 hours of sunlight every day of the year, whereas the poles receive 6 consecutive months of day and 6 consecutive months of night annually. Differences in insolation and temperature at different latitudes on the globe, therefore, must be due to the marked differences in solar intensity—the high angular elevation of the sun at or near the equator and the low angular elevation of the sun at the poles and in the upper latitudes generally.

Figure 4-1, with diagrams of an equinox and a solstice, illustrates well the geographic and temporal differences that affect weather. Variations in intensity of insolation are most important, although variation in duration plays a role in compensating somewhat for the lower sun angle in higher latitudes during their respective "summers." In Figure 4-1, the left diagram illustrates intensity and duration on an equinox, on or about March 21 or September 21. During an equinox—literally "equal night"—the earth receives the sun's radiation directly

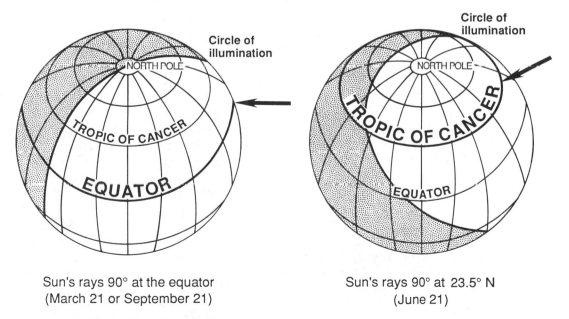

Sun's rays 90° at the equator
(March 21 or September 21)

Sun's rays 90° at 23.5° N
(June 21)

Figure 4-1 Solar radiation received directly at the equator during an equinox (left) and at the Tropic of Cancer on the summer solstice in the Northern Hemisphere (right).

at the equator (at a 90° angle), so that all lines of latitude are bisected and all places on earth receive 12 hours of day and 12 hours of night. At these times, the poles experience a kind of dawn/twilight all 24 hours. Equality of day and night is illustrated on the diagram by the intersection of the circle of illumination and the parallels of latitude: notice that each parallel is bisected and thus half in sunlight and half in darkness. By contrast, the right diagram, symbolic of June 21 or so—the summer solstice in the Northern Hemisphere (and the start of winter in the Southern Hemisphere)—shows the circle of illumination bisecting only the equator, whereas at all other latitudes day and night are of unequal length. The extremes at this time are illustrated by the poles, which are in the midst of either 6 months of continuous "day" (North Pole) or 6 months of continuous "night" (South Pole). Between the fall and spring equinoxes, all Northern Hemisphere sites have longer nights than days, whereas in the Southern Hemisphere, days are longer than nights. Moreover, in the Northern Hemisphere the farther north a place is, the longer its night is. South of the equator, day lengthens as one proceeds poleward.

Several factors combine to produce a latitudinal bias in temperature: the shape of the earth, its revolution about the sun, and the inclination of the earth's axis $23\frac{1}{2}°$ from a line perpendicular to the plane of the orbit. Because of these conditions, in very general terms, temperature decreases with latitude. Cartographers portray this effect with *isotherms*, which are lines connecting points of equal temperature. Like contour lines on topographic maps, isotherms are spaced according to the rate of change across the surface: they are closely spaced when temperature change is rapid or abrupt and widely spaced when temperature change is slow or tenuous. The pattern of isotherms in Figure 4-2 generally shows the world's average temperatures in January and July as changing north-south. Indeed, if the earth were homogeneous in surface and not axially inclined, the lines would look even more like parallels and the earth would have no seasons. Isothermal maps show that the distribution of land and water also has a great effect on temperature patterns, because west coastal areas in the middle and upper latitudes are much less subject to wide-ranging temperatures and because oceanic influences carried ashore by winds result in warmer winters and cooler summers (since large water bodies heat and cool more slowly than land). A comparison of the isotherms as they cross the United States reveals these continental-maritime differences, as coastal areas, notably the western ones, have a comparatively small temperature range, whereas places at mid-continent exhibit significant differences between January and July temperatures. The coast of southern California, for example, has average temperatures in the 50s (10s in °C) in January and in the 60s (teens in °C) in July, in strong contrast to the 60°F (teens in °C) difference between Iowa's respective January and July averages in the 10s (−teens in °C) and 70s (20s in °C). Moreover, topographic features and resultant elevational differences also weigh heavily in producing squiggles in the lines, since topographic barriers block maritime influences (as

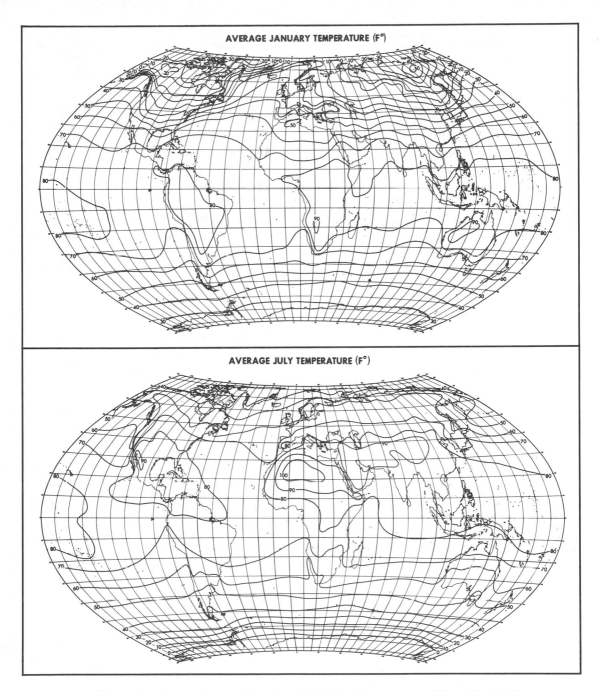

Figure 4-2 Average January (above) and July (below) temperatures (°F) worldwide. The lines are isotherms, which connect points of equal temperature. (From U.S. Department of Commerce, Environmental Sciences Services Administration, Environmental Data Service, *Climates of the World* [Washington, D.C.: U.S. Government Printing Office, 1972, pp. 2–3.]

in the mountainous west of the United States) and produce higher, cooler environments.

Cartographers use *isohyets,* lines connecting points of equal rainfall, to portray the world pattern of precipitation. As Figure 4-3 shows, precipitation is like temperature insofar as the world pattern is very much the product of location with respect to latitude as well as the other controls. Generally, the wettest sites are tropical or subtropical, whereas the driest locales are found at about 20° to 30° north and south, where large-scale atmospheric subsidence and divergence produces an aridity of major proportions and far-reaching consequences: the tropical deserts are all located between these latitudes. Other less-than-humid areas are in the far north and in Antarctica, as well as in extratropical places located great distances from water sources or where mountains effectively block maritime winds. Siberia exemplifies the ways in which distance from water sources and the impact of cold temperatures create low humidity and low pre-

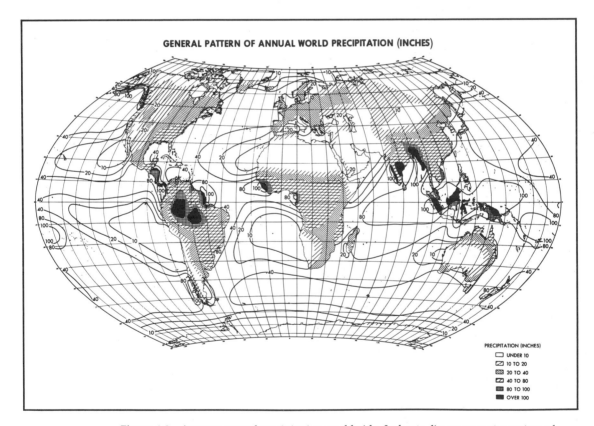

GENERAL PATTERN OF ANNUAL WORLD PRECIPITATION (INCHES)

PRECIPITATION (INCHES)
☐ UNDER 10
▨ 10 TO 20
▧ 20 TO 40
▧ 40 TO 80
▦ 80 TO 100
■ OVER 100

Figure 4-3 Average annual precipitation worldwide. Isohyets, lines connecting points of equal precipitation, enclose the regions. (From U.S. Department of Commerce, Environmental Sciences Services Administration, Environmental Data Service, *Climates of the World* [Washington, D.C.: U.S. Government Printing Office, 1972], p. 4.)

cipitation, whereas the interior of the western United States is an example of topographic barriers blocking the Pacific's influence on an arid and semiarid area.

Figures 4-4 and 4-5 show, respectively, atmospheric pressure in January

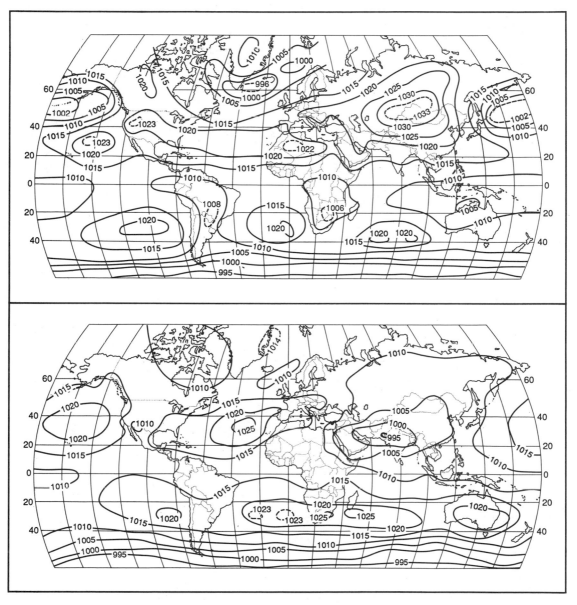

Figure 4-4   Mean sea-level pressure in January (above) and July (below) worldwide. Isobars, lines connecting points of equal air pressure, define the regions.

Figure 4-5 Surface wind patterns in January (above) and July (below) worldwide. The lines represent mean flows.

and July and winds in January and July. Figure 4-4 reduces the pressures to sea level to remove the influence of the fall in the mercurial barometer at the rate of approximately $\frac{1}{30}$ of its height for approximately each 900 ft (about 275 m) in altitude. In this way, the maps in Figure 4-4 represent a statistical surface whose variation in *isobars* (lines connecting points of equal pressure) more nearly reflects atmospheric differences, especially of temperature and humidity.

Despite the relatively low order of predictability of atmospheric conditions in the middle latitudes as compared to the tropics, the location of atmospheric phenomena viewed over time is not random. Indeed, beginning with the control of latitude and adding the other controls as needed, one can construct a reliable model of weather and climate at a world or continental scale. As we move from weather maps to climatic classification and mapping, the reader should gain an understanding of the conditions of the atmosphere and the ways these have been mapped and charted.

WEATHER MAPS: SELECTED EVENTS IN HISTORY

Maps used in atmospheric description and study date back to 1686, when Edmund Halley published his map of trade winds in *Philosophical Transactions*. Halley, an English astronomer and geographer, was editor of the *Transactions* and is best known for his investigations of comets. Following the development of thermometry in the early seventeeth century and of the Fahrenheit and Celsius scales in the mid–eighteenth century, temperature mapping commenced in the late eighteenth century with the systematic recording of temperature. In 1817, Alexander von Humboldt produced a small and primitive temperature map of the Northern Hemisphere. Although Evangelista Torricelli invented the mercury barometer in 1643, atmospheric pressure was not mapped until 1820, when H. W. Brandes plotted deviations from normal pressure. The American Elias Loomis plotted isobars as irregular lines independent of parallels of latitude in 1846. In 1839 O. N. Nelson, a Dane, drew the earliest precipitation map, a map of Europe and Africa employing shadings rather than isohyets, which came into use shortly thereafter.[3]

Before the daily weather map could become a reliable, useful tool, simultaneous observations had to be made at a number of locations, and data collection had to be immediate or nearly so. A long history of experimentation in rapid communications preceded Samuel F. Morse's invention of the telegraph in 1837, and equally crude attempts at making daily weather charts from newspaper accounts began as early as 1820, but not until 1856 did the Smithsonian Institution actually produce weather charts. The first international weather bulletin was published in France in 1857, based on an 11-station telegraphic hookup and 11 other stations that *mailed* the information. The weather maps that began to accompany this bulletin in 1863 represented the first publication of the current weather map. This initial map included isobars and winds; 15 years

---

[3] Arthur H. Robinson, *Early Thematic Mapping in the History of Cartography* (Chicago and London: University of Chicago Press, 1982), pp. 69–76.

later, in 1878, an additional map showing isotherms, clouds, and rain was finally included in the *Bulletin International*.[4]

In 1893 Robert H. Scott, a British official, summarized better the status of the daily weather map in a speech before the Chicago Meteorological Congress. He pointed out the rare use of weather maps and the fact that maps produced in different countries differed in scale and character because of different areas being mapped and different levels of funding for such activity. The French *Bulletin Meteorologique du Nord*, for example, one of the oldest meteorology publications in Europe, was bereft of any maps of any description. Scott described the history of weather reports in the British Isles, beginning at about the time of the American Civil War and their issuance to the public since 1875. These daily reports included maps of pressure, wind, sea disturbance, temperature, precipitation, and changes in temperature and pressure. In 1875, shortly after the organization of meteorological telegraphy, the *Times* of London began publishing copies of weather charts prepared expressly for that newspaper. Indeed, for many years, the *Times* carried the entire cost of the preparation of one of the charts—"a fact which affords strong evidence of the public interest in weather intelligence," said Scott.[5]

With the cooperation of Western Union, Cleveland Abbe collected telegraphic weather reports in Cincinnati in 1870.[6] The local telegraphic company prepared weather maps and distributed a limited number of them for several months in 1870, until the U.S. Signal Office took over the production of weather maps in October of that year. These early maps of the Signal Office were based upon about 30 weather stations, extending from the Atlantic Coast westward to Houston, Omaha, and Cheyenne, northward to Halifax in Nova Scotia, and southward to Havana. They included no isolines and omitted atmospheric pressure, but noted temperature, clouds, precipitation, and wind direction. A month after this beginning at the Signal Office, the official U.S. Weather Bureau began operation with the publication of daily weather maps thrice a day. The bureau added barometric readings to its weather maps from the outset in 1870, isobars a year later, and isotherms in 1872.[7]

Table 4-1 summarizes the information about early weather map coverage

---

[4] Mark W. Harrington, "History of the Weather Map," *Bulletin of the U.S. Weather Bureau*, no. 11, paper read before the Chicago Meteorological Congress, August 21–24, 1893, pp. 327–30.

[5] Robert H. Scott, "The Publication of Daily Weather Maps and Bulletins," *Bulletin of the U.S. Weather Bureau*, no. 11, paper read before the Chicago Meteorological Congress, August 21–24, 1893, pp. 6–9.

[6] The *Dictionary of Scientific Biography* touts Abbe as "the first regular official weather forecaster of the U.S. Government and a promoter of research in atmospheric physics." Abbe served as the model for future meteorologists, and his career reflects the saga of early weather maps in the United States and of early American meteorology in general. See *Dictionary of Scientific Biography*, vol. 1 (New York: Charles Scribner's Sons, 1970. Published under the auspices of the American Council of Learned Societies), p. 6.

[7] Harrington, "History of the Weather Map," pp. 330–31.

TABLE 4-1 WEATHER MAP COVERAGE, 1863–1893

Location	Dates	Location	Dates
Europe	Since 1863	Australia and New Zealand	Since 1877
North Atlantic	1864, 1865, 1873, 1874, 1876, and 1877 to 1887	Australasia	Since 1887
		India	Since 1887
		Indian Ocean	1861 and since 1887
United States and Southern Canada	Since 1871	Algeria	Since 1877
Japan	Since 1883	Northern Hemisphere	From 1877 to 1887
Western Siberia	Since 1889		

Source: Mark W. Harrington, "History of the Weather Map," *Bulletin of the U.S. Weather Bureau* no. 11, papers read before the Chicago Meterological Congress, August 21–24, 1893, pp. 334 and 335.

that Mark W. Harrington presented to the Chicago Meteorological Congress in 1893. The data show a clear Northern Hemisphere bias in coverage, as one would expect at that time.

In 1905 an article in the *National Geographic Magazine,* "Forecasting the Weather and Storms," described the complexity of weather reporting and, more to the point, weather mapping on a daily basis:

> This morning at 8 o'clock . . . the observers at about 200 stations scattered throughout the United States and the West Indies were taking their observations . . . noting the pressure of the air, the temperature, the humidity, the rainfall or snowfall, and the cloudiness at the bottom of the aerial ocean in which we live, and which, by its variations of heat and cold, sunshine, clouds and tempest, affect not only the health and happiness of man, but his commercial and industrial welfare. By 8:15 the observations have been reduced to cipher for purposes of brevity, and each has been filed at the local telegraph office. During the next 30 to 40 minutes these observations, with the right of way over all lines, are speeding to their destinations, each station contributing its own observations and receiving in return, by an ingenious system of telegraph circuits, such observations from other stations as it may require. The observations from all stations are received at such centers as Washington, Chicago, New York, and other large cities, and nearly all cities having a Weather Bureau station receive a sufficient number of reports from other cities to justify the issuing of a daily weather map. . . .
>
> . . . As fast as the reports come from the wires they are passed to the Forecast Division, where a reader stands in the middle of the room and translates the cipher into figures and words of intelligible sequence. A force of clerks is engaged in making graphic representations of the geographical distribution of the different meteorological elements. On blank charts of the United States each clerk copies from the translator that part of each station's report needed in the construction of his particular chart. One clerk constructs a chart showing the change in temperature during the preceding 24 hours. Broad red lines separate the colder from the warmer

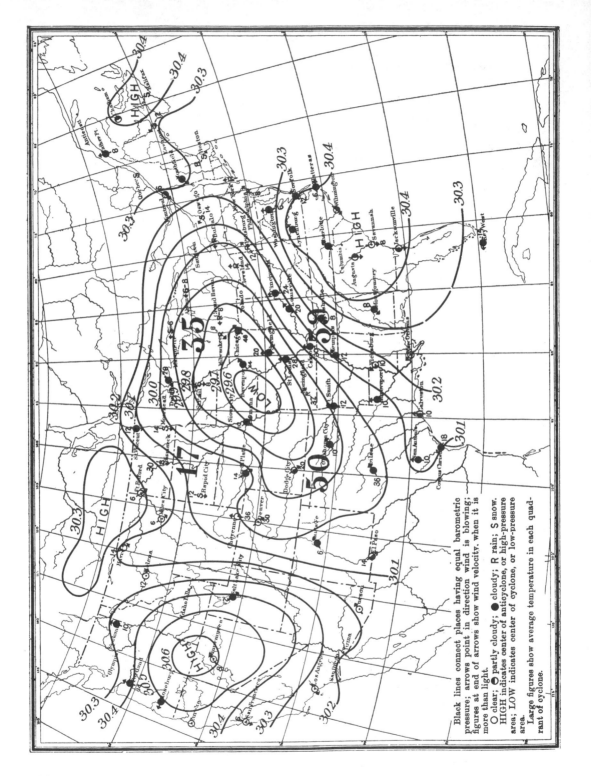

Black lines connect places having equal barometric pressure; arrows point in direction wind is blowing; figures at end of arrows show wind velocity, when it is more than light.

○ clear; ◑ partly cloudy; ● cloudy; R rain; S snow. HIGH indicates center of anticyclone, or high-pressure area; LOW indicates center of cyclone, or low-pressure area.

Large figures show average temperature in each quadrant of cyclone.

regions, and narrow red lines inclose [sic] areas showing changes in temperature of more than 10 degrees. The narrow lines generally run in oval or circular form, indicating . . . that atmospheric disturbances move and operate in the form of great progressive eddies; that there are central points of intensity from which the force of the disturbance diminishes in all directions.

A second clerk constructs a chart showing the change that has occurred in the barometer during the past 24 hours. As in the construction of the temperature chart, broad, heavy lines of red separate the regions of rising barometer from those of falling barometer. Narrow lines inclose [sic] the areas over which the change in barometer has been greater than one-tenth, and so on. . . . This chart is extremely useful to the forecaster, since, in connection with the general weather chart, it indicates whether or not the storm centers are increasing or decreasing in intensity, and, what is of more importance, it gives in a great measure the first warning of the formation of storms.

A third clerk constructs two charts, one showing the humidity of the air and the other the cloud areas. . . .

A fourth clerk constructs a chart called the general weather chart, showing for each station the air temperature and pressure, the velocity and direction of the wind, the rain or snow fall since the last report, and the amount of cloudiness. The readings of the barometer on this chart are reduced to sea-level, so that the variations in pressure due to local altitudes may not mask and obscure those due to storm formation. . . . By drawing isobars for each difference in pressure of one-tenth of an inch the high and the low pressure areas are soon inclosed [sic] in their proper circles. The word "high" is written at the center of the region of greatest air pressure and the word "low" at the center of the area of least pressure. Under the influence of gravity the air presses downward and outward in all directions, thus causing it to flow from a region of great pressure toward one of less. The velocity with which the wind moves from the high toward the low will depend largely on the difference in air pressure.[8]

Figure 4-6 illustrates a turn-of-the-century weather map representing December 15, 1893, at 8:00 A.M. Given the great amount of manual labor involved in the preparation of such charts, and instrumentation that was primitive compared to the automated state of affairs today, their appearance, if not their accuracy, was remarkable.

Passing from military to civilian control in 1891, the Weather Bureau became an agency under the U.S. Department of Agriculture. That the business and industrial community believed the bureau's services were beneficial was revealed by the vast support in the form of petitions requesting adequate funding for the bureau in 1892. Weather forecasting was generally modernized before

[8] Willis L. Moore, "Forecasting the Weather and Storms," *National Geographic Magazine* 16, no. 6 (June 1905), pp. 258 and 260.

Figure 4-6 Weather map showing a winter storm in the United States on December 15, 1893. (From Willis L. Moore, "Forecasting the Weather and Storms," *National Geographic Magazine* 16, no. 6 [June 1905], 268.)

World War II, as hurricane warning matured, river and flood services improved, and agricultural applications expanded. In 1940, the Weather Bureau was transferred to the U.S. Department of Commerce. Over the years, improvements in both its technology and its services have been tied closely to aviation. Better communications and the launching of satellites brought a new age of weather observation, forecasting, and mapping. In April 1960 TIROS I (Television Infra-Red Observation Satellite) was launched into a circular orbit from 700 to 750 km (435 to 468 mi) above the earth's surface. It orbited the globe once every 99 minutes, sending televised images of the earth's cloud cover to tracking stations. This first satellite recorded over 20,000 images before a camera ceased functioning in June 1960.[9] Today earth-orbiting satellites scan part of the earth's surface and transmit the line-pattern image to earth stations every few seconds. On a daily basis, the Satellite Data Service Division of the U.S. Weather Bureau receives hundreds of negatives, films, and digital data on tape for evaluation, storage, and retrospective use, and thereby provides a unique information service.[10] These files contain early TIROS imagery, as well as images from experimental and operational satellites such as Applications Technology Satellites (ATS), Synchronous Meteorological Satellites (SMS), and Geostationary Operational Environmental Satellites (GOES).[11]

MODERN WEATHER MAPS

A note on weather map projections is needed before our discussion of the modern weather map. Cartographers commonly use conformal projections for weather maps because the grid is one in which angles are not distorted locally (that is, within small neighborhoods of points) and are best suited for portraying the movement of dynamic phenomena. Cartographers often use conformal projections for climate maps, not involving movement, as well. While this may be useful for relating weather to climate, these projections are inappropriate when one wishes to relate climate to area and other phenomena commonly shown on an equivalent (or equal-area) projection. Portrayal of climatic information on a conformal projection may underrepresent the tropics and overrepresent the arctic and polar climes.

The atmosphere's circulation is a product of pressure differences much the same way that water on the land flows down slope. Because of the rotation of the earth, wind trajectories *appear* to veer from their straight-ahead path, to the

---

[9] This brief discussion is based on Donald R. Whitnah, *A History of the United States Weather Bureau* (Urbana: University of Illinois Press, 1965), pp. 61–62, 148, 167, 194–95, 238–39.

[10] U.S. Department of Commerce, National Oceanic and Atmospheric Administration, Environmental Data and Information Service, *Environmental Satellite Data from NOAA*, (Washington, D.C., 1981).

[11] Ibid.

right in the Northern Hemisphere and to the left in the Southern Hemisphere (the Coriolis Effect). The effect is absent only along the equator. Therefore, winds flow from high to low pressure zones in a spiral pattern, moving counterclockwise into lows in the Northern Hemisphere and clockwise into lows south of the equator. This atmospheric movement, termed *cyclonic* (into lows) and *anticyclonic* (out of highs), is discussed when we examine weather maps later in the chapter. Figures 4-4 and 4-5 illustrate not only the movement of the air from high toward low pressure and the Coriolis Effect, but also the seasonal shifts in the placement of highs and lows and wind flows: see Asia in winter and in summer and note the flow off the continent in January and onshore in July, a phenomenon creating a noteworthy difference in precipitation called the *monsoon* (a seasonal reversal of winds over land and nearby seas).

When two or more masses of air different in temperature, humidity, and pressure come into contact, the boundary between them is called a *front*. Figure 4-7 provides a graphic summary of the kinds of weather fronts and their brief life cycle. It will repay careful study, since one can understand much of the dynamism in the atmosphere only by understanding the nature of fronts and the manner in which they interact to produce *disturbances* or, as they are commonly called, *storms*. As discussed earlier, pressure differences in the earth's atmosphere cause air to move out of high-pressure centers in a clockwise fashion and into low-pressure centers in a manner defined as counterclockwise in the Northern Hemisphere. (Flow direction is reversed south of the equator because the direction of change in the speed of rotation by latitude is likewise reversed— that is, in the Northern Hemisphere the speed diminishes northward compared with a southward diminution in the Southern Hemisphere.) When atmosphere moves south and east from Canada into the warmer United States, it carries the cooler, drier, heavier characteristics of polar or arctic air to lower latitudes and, as depicted in the upper-left section of Figure 4-7, creates a cold front. Notice that, in mapped cross section, the cold front is a wedge of cold air invading areas occupied by warmer, lighter, often more humid air, which it forces aloft. As it rises, the warm air cools, condenses and, often, precipitates. The upper right quarter of Figure 4-7 shows a warm front, created in the eastern United States by the invasion of warm moist atmosphere from over the South Atlantic or Gulf of Mexico. As the cross section indicates, the warm air overrides cooler, heavier, drier air and forces it to retreat slowly. As before, the warm front is characterized by a disturbance, as the warm air flowing northward ascends, cools, condenses, and often precipitates. On the map, the line with triangles pointing in the direction of advance represents a cold front. A line with less threatening semicircles represents the warm front, which is generally slower and less turbulent than the cold front. The lower left quarter of Figure 4-7 depicts a *stationary front*, in which the dissimilar masses are not really converging but are moving in opposite directions side-by-side. This creates a kind of meteorological stalemate that ends only when one of these fronts gains hegemony and moves toward the other. The lower right section of Figure 4-7 shows an

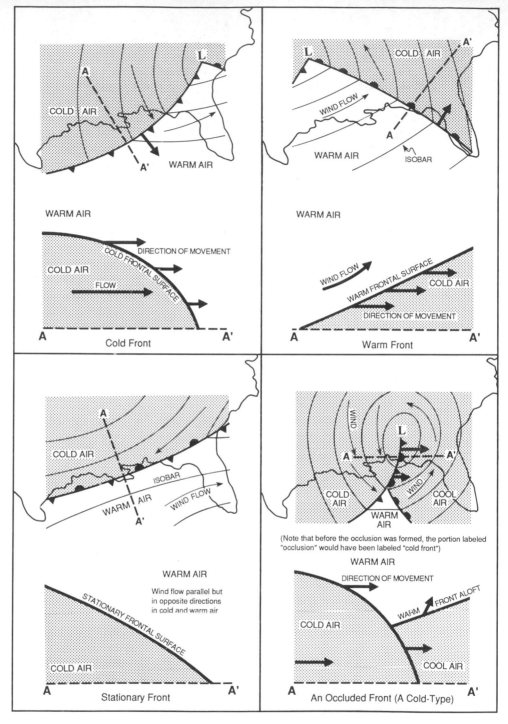

Figure 4-7 Types of fronts, top views and cross sections. (Redrawn and adapted from U.S. Department of the Air Force, *Weather for Aircrews*, AF Manual 105-5 [Washington, D.C.: 1962], pp. 8-4–8-5.)

occluded front in which the cold front has overtaken the warm front and is forcing it off the surface of the earth, signaling the coming dissipation of the system.[12]

This brief, graphic summary points up many things, perhaps the most important of which is that change is the rule in our earth's atmosphere: as a frontal system moves across the landscape at some 24 to 34 km (15 to 20 mi) an hour, colder, drier, heavier air replaces warm, humid, light air in the case of cold-front invasion and vice-versa for warm fronts. Such change characterizes the middle latitudes, where arctic-polar air masses battle with tropical-subtropical atmospheres daily. Although fronts seldom "produce weather" above the lower troposphere—say 4,500 to 6,000 m (15,000 to 20,000 ft) above sea level—the jet streams, high speed "rivers" of atmosphere circling the earth at some 9,000 to 12,000 m (30,000 to 40,000 ft) determine the placement of a front, or the zone of transition. Warm air often lies to the south and the east of jet streams, colder atmosphere to the north and the west.

The modern surface weather map is illustrated by the daily weather map for February 22, 1984, in Figure 4-8. Figure 4-8 also contains (lower left) a map of 500-millibar height contours (a constant-pressure chart at about 5,500 m (18,000 ft) above sea level that is used to determine past conditions, wind speed and direction, temperatures, frontal movements, clouds, precipitation, and areas of icing, turbulence, and thunderstorms), along with wind direction and speed at those heights; a map (middle right) of the highest and lowest temperatures for the stations; and a map (lower right) of precipitation areas and amounts.

For each reporting location, the main map provides a station model, of which Figure 4-9 provides an enlarged example for clarity. Basically, the circle in the model illustrates percentage of cloud cover by the degree of the circle's opacity, and an associated symbol reveals cloud type. The direction of the line extending from the circle indicates wind source, and the feathers and pennants on the line indicate wind speed. Numbers placed around these symbols refer to temperature, pressure, precipitation, and a series of associated facts. (All temperatures in Figures 4-8 and 4-9 are in degrees Fahrenheit, except the temperatures on the 500-millibar map, which are in degrees Celsius; see Appendix A for a temperature conversion chart.)

As an example, look at the data for Shreveport, Louisiana. The horizontal line with the "barb" identifies cirrostratus clouds, not increasing and not covering the sky. The upper right number indicates barometric pressure (1,010.2 millibars, since the first 10 is dropped), and the upper left number shows an air temperature of 50°F (10°C). The circle is one-quarter opaqued, indicating two- or three-tenths cloud cover. The line extending from the circle signifies wind direction (southwest) and speed (10 knots, given the single "feather"). Try identifying the other symbols for Shreveport using the specimen station model in Figure 4-9.

---

[12] Much of this discussion is adapted from U.S. Department of the Air Force, *Weather for Aircrews*, AF Manual 105-5, (Washington, D.C.: 1962), pp. 8-1–8-7.

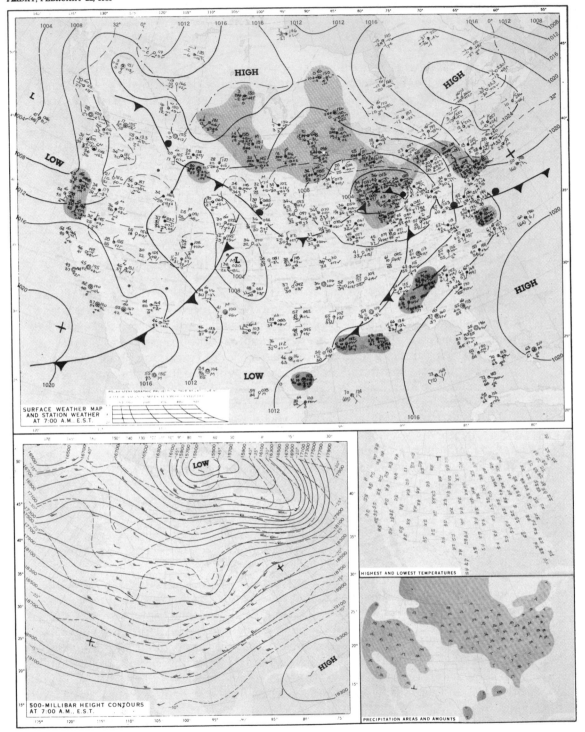

Figure 4-8 Daily weather map of United States, February 22, 1980. (From U.S. Department of Commerce, National Oceanic and Atmospheric Administration, Environmental Information and Data Service, *Daily Weather Maps, Weekly Series* [Washington, D.C.: U.S. Government Printing Office, 1980].)

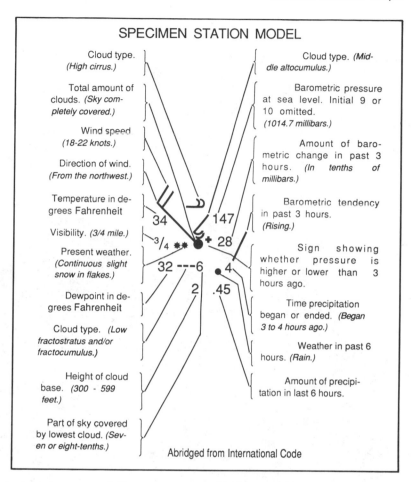

Figure 4-9 Specimen station model.

The map of February 22 is typical of that time of year in terms of well-defined highs off the coast of Florida and in two locations in Canada; lows appearing amidst the highs; and several frontal systems in evidence. Figure 4-10, a satellite image taken at 6:00 P.M. (1800 hours) on February 21, illustrates the cloud cover and, when compared with the maps, the placement of pressure cells and fronts. The satellite image in Figure 4-10 and the daily weather map in Figure 4-8 are quite similar in showing the succession of cold fronts—one extending north and east from New Mexico and the other north and east from the southern part of Texas—with practically cloudless skies between. (See Chapter 2, "Photomaps and Remotely Sensed Images," for a detailed discussion of the subject.)

Clearly, improved observations, more reliable forecasting, and better capability in storm and flood warning continue to require accurate, rapidly pro-

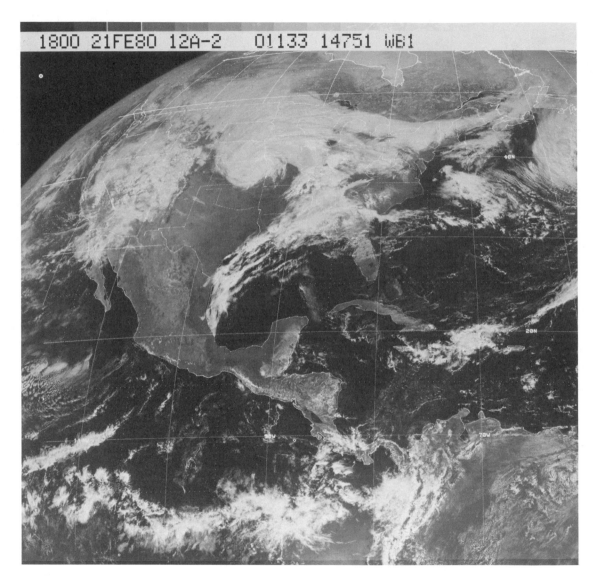

Figure 4-10 Geostationary Operational Environmental Satellite (GOES) image taken at 6:00 P.M. E.S.T. on February 21, 1980. GOES operates at 36,000 km (22,300 mi) above the earth and is synchronized with the earth's rotation to appear stationary over a point. Normally, GOES transmits every 30 minutes, but in severe weather it relays images as often as every 3 minutes for limited areas.

duced maps and charts. The weather report and the weather map are of interest to just about everyone, and the interest grows as we travel and communicate more often and with greater and greater speed.[13]

MAPPING CLIMATE

Heat and moisture, the manner in which these atmospheric elements change over time in a given place, and the differences in them from place to place over time provide the general focus for climatology. As stated earlier, weather can be defined as the atmosphere's momentary conditions and short-term trends, whereas climate reflects longer-term atmospheric conditions and dynamics—"averaged weather," so to speak. Perhaps one of the best ways to demonstrate the difference between weather and climate is to examine graphically the basic data, temperature and rainfall of specific years for a given place—say, New York City in 1982 and 1983. The two charts in Figure 4-11 are quite similar in terms of temperatures, but as a quick inspection of the precipitation bars reveals, very different in terms of rainfall. Indeed, the ratio between normal annual precipitation in New York City and the great amount of precipitation in 1983, a record year, is almost 2:1. The climate of New York City, while based upon weather data such as those shown in Figure 4-11, is revealed through long-term observations and average temperatures and amounts of precipitation.

Extremes of weather affect assessments of climate, but the great variability in atmospheric conditions around the world may be lost in the averages that are the basis of climatology. Mean temperature and rainfall data can obscure the detrimental effects of extreme values. Figure 4-12 illustrates global extremes of weather and climate through a rich litany of atmospheric highests, lowests, mosts, and leasts—from places where constant conditions make weather observing and forecasting repetitious exercises, to places where unbelievably rapid changes have occurred and where, on a daily basis, change is the rule. The "hottest" and "coldest" places on the earth according to these records are found in El Azizia, Libya—with a recorded high of 136°F (57.8°C) *in the shade*—and Vostok, Antarctica, with a recorded low of −127°F (−88.3°C). During the International Geophysical Year of 1957–1958, a group of participants from the United States and 11 other countries observed the temperature reading at Vostok. Chances are good that lower temperatures have occurred there or elsewhere

[13] Copies of "Explanation of the Daily Weather Map" are available from National Oceanic and Atmospheric Administration, Central Logistics Supply Center, 619 Hardesty Street, Kansas City, MO 64124. Daily Weather Maps, Weekly Series, are available by annual subscription from the U.S. Government Printing Office, Washington, D.C. 20402. Single copies are also available. According to a recent letter to the editor of *Weatherwise* from a federal employee, the Daily Weather Maps are now based on a reduced data base, since budget cutting has resulted in closed weather stations, part–time operations for some stations, and staff cuts. See "Letters" in *Weatherwise* 38, no. 6 (December 1985), 293.

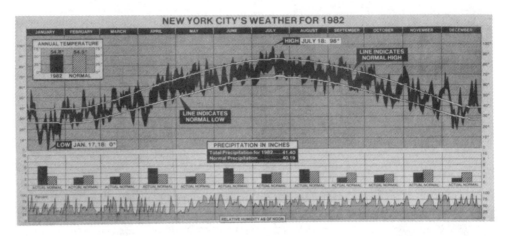

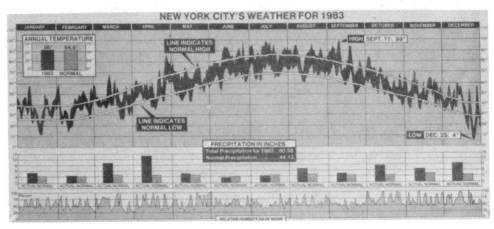

Figure 4-11   New York City's weather for 1982 (above) and 1983 (below), showing actual and normal monthly and annual data. (From the *New York Times*, Sunday, January 9, 1983, p. 36, and Sunday, January 8, 1984; Copyright © 1983/1984 by the New York Times Company. Reprinted by permission.)

in Antarctica, but have gone unnoticed and unrecorded; the same could be said for the earth's highest temperature. As for precipitation, several boxes in Figure 4-12 are noteworthy. The "wettest" place on earth, using average annual data, is Mt. Waialiale on the Island of Kauai, Hawaii, with 460 in. (1,150 cm) annually. This annual average pales, however, when compared to the record rainfall of Cherrapunji, India: 1,042 in. (2,605 cm) in a 12-month period and 366 in. (915 cm) in one month! At the other extreme, Arica, Chile, experiences an average annual rainfall of just 0.03 in. (0.075 cm). Iquique, Chile, also in the extremely arid Atacama Desert of western South America, "boasts" no rain over a 14-year period.

Such data reflect a broad base of absolute meteorological quantities against which the averages used in the study of climate gain significance. As stated in *Climate and Man: The 1941 Yearbook of Agriculture*, a classic in climatology, climate is inextricably related to vegetation and soils, the variety and distribution of which have important geographic associations and significant influence on settlement and activity:

> Three great patterns dominate the earth and are of tremendous importance to man—the pattern of climate, the pattern of vegetation, and the pattern of soils. When the three patterns are laid one upon another, their boundaries coincide to a remarkable degree because climate is the fundamental dynamic force shaping the other two. . . . A fourth pattern laid upon the three is that of human culture, or civilization. Though modern man has some freedom to vary this pattern because of his control of other forces, he too cannot go beyond certain limits set fundamentally by climate.[14]

Although the yearbook was written more than four decades ago, the fact that it places climate at the center of human-environment relationships gives it a timelessness, a modernity. After all, heat and moisture are crucial for all organisms, both flora and fauna, and these same climatic elements contribute to the degradation and modification of the earth's mantle to produce soils; soils' variety is also controlled by the "parent material" from which the soil is produced.

Wladimir Köppen's system of climatic classification is most likely the best known and most used vehicle for cartographically summarizing these ideas at a world scale. The Köppen System has special relevance in a book about maps because it lends itself to graphic representation. Peirce Lewis, a recent president of the Association of American Geographers, touts the merits of the Köppen climatic classification system as a teaching device: "By reducing numerous rainfall data to simply stated and easily compared formulae, it emphasizes the orderliness of the world's climatic pattern, and helps relate climates to gross patterns of world vegetation. . . . Köppen's symbols constitute a kind of universal vocabulary which must be understood if one is to read the climatological literature intelligently."[15]

Table 4-2 defines the five major types of climate that the Köppen System embraces: polar, dry, humid tropical, humid mesothermal, and humid microthermal. The order in which one reviews these climatic types in classifying the weather station data is critical if the beginner is to proceed through the scheme easily, with little chance of error. The tree diagram in Figure 4-13 is an abridged and simplified key to the order in which one might review station data

[14] David I. Blumenstock and Warren C. Thornwaite, "Climate and the World Pattern," in *Climate and Man: The 1941 Yearbook of Agriculture*, U.S. Department of Agriculture (Washington, D.C.: U.S. Government Printing Office, 1941), p. 98.

[15] Peirce F. Lewis, "Dichotomous Key to the Köppen System," *Professional Geographer* 13, no. 5 (September 1961), 25.

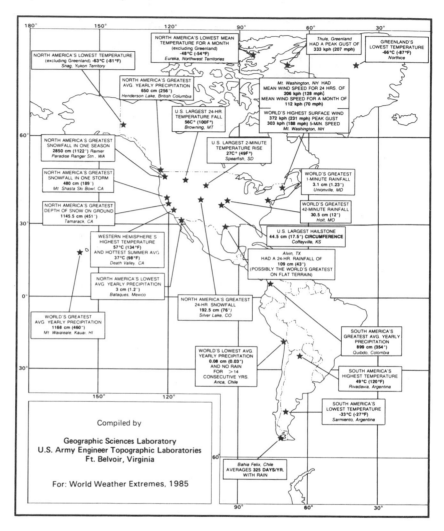

Figure 4-12 World weather extremes. (Courtesy of the Geographic Sciences Laboratory, U.S. Army Engineer Topographic Laboratories, Fort Belvoir, Va.)

in determining climatic type.[16] The reason for the order concerns function. Polar climates (E) come first because they are determined wholly on the basis of temperature, ignoring other criteria, and are thus easily classified. Classifying dry climates, arid or semiarid (B), involves determining a statistical boundary between steppe (semiarid) and humid climates (A, C, and D) by means of an estimating equation designed to gauge the effect of temperature on rainfall and, ultimately, on soil moisture as it permits or inhibits vegetational growth of var-

---

[16] Ibid., pp. 29–30.

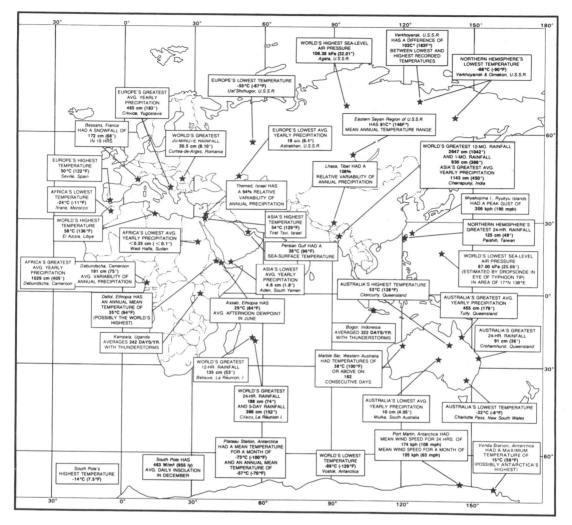

Figure 4-12   *(continued)*

ious kinds. A sixth category, undifferentiated highland (H), is employed because of the rapid change in climate that occurs in areas of rugged local relief. At the world scale, a map without such a category would be cluttered in mountainous regions where a profusion of many climates (associated with rapid change in temperature) over a small map area would render the map confusing to say the least. Thus H is used where slope invokes rapid change and allows for classification of individual stations in the usual manner, although they are not mapped.

The system becomes easier to understand when the reader considers how the classifier proceeds in using it. With Table 4-2 and Figure 4-13 for reference,

TABLE 4-2 THE KÖPPEN SYSTEM OF CLIMATIC CLASSIFICATION

E: *Polar climates.* Average temperature of warmest month less than 50°.
  ET: Tundra. Average temperature of warmest month exceeds 32°.
  EF: Ice cap. Average temperature of warmest month less than 32°.
B: *Dry climates.* This type is determined by whether annual rainfall exceeds, is equal to, or is less than statistical boundaries between steppe-humid and steppe-desert. These boundaries are based on an estimation of evaporation rate and the impact of temperature on soil moisture.
  BW: Desert. ⎫
  BS: Steppe. ⎬ See equations below for definitions.
              ⎭
        Tertiary symbols used with B are as follows:
        h: Tropical desert or steppe. Average annual temperature exceeds 64.4°.
        k: Middle-latitude desert or steppe. Average annual temperature less than 64.4°.
Formulas for estimating steppe-humid and steppe-desert boundaries:
  (*t* = average annual temperature)

Rainfall distribution	Boundary	
	Steppe-humid	Steppe-desert
even	$r = 0.44t - 8.5$	$r = \dfrac{0.44(t) - 8.5}{2}$
at least 70% in warmer 6 months	$r = 0.44t - 3$	$r = \dfrac{0.44(t) - 3}{2}$
at least 70% in cooler 6 months	$r = 0.44t - 14$	$r = \dfrac{0.44(t) - 14}{2}$

These equations are employed as follows:

$$\begin{array}{r}r \\ r/2\end{array} \left. \overline{\underline{\begin{array}{l}\text{if annual rainfall} > r\text{, station is humid (A,C, or D)} \\ \text{if annual rainfall} \leq r \text{ but } > r/2\text{, station is steppe (BS)} \\ \text{if annual rainfall} \leq r/2\text{, station is desert (BW)}\end{array}}}\right.$$

A: *Humid tropical.* Coolest month's temperature exceeds 64.4°.

Af: Tropical rainforest. Driest month's rainfall at least 2.4 in.
Am: Tropical monsoon. At least one month's rainfall less than 2.4 in. Dry season compensated for to some extent by wet season.
Aw: Tropical savanna. At least one month's rainfall less than 2.4 in.

  If station is not Af, Am/Aw determination is based on following formula:

$$a = 3.94 - arf/25$$

where *arf* is annual rainfall.
This equation is employed as follows:

$$a \left. \overline{\underline{\begin{array}{l}\text{if rainfall of driest month} > a\text{, station is Am} \\ \text{if rainfall of driest month} < a\text{, station is Aw}\end{array}}}\right.$$

C: *Humid mesothermal.* Average temperature of coldest month exceeds 26.6°, but is less than 64.4°. (Warmest month exceeds 50°.)
  Cf: Humid subtropical. No dry season, and driest month of summer has more than 1.2 in. of rainfall.
  Cw: Subtropical monsoon. Dry and mild winter. 70% or more of rainfall in warmer 6 months.

TABLE 4-2 (*continued*)

Cs: Mediterranean subtropical. Dry summer. 70% or more of rainfall in cooler 6 months.
Tertiary symbols used with C are as follows:
a: Hot summer. Warmest month's average temperature 71.6° or higher.
b: Warm summer. Warmest month's average temperature less than 71.6°, and four months or more above 50°.
c: Cool summer. Less than four months with temperatures over 50° (that is, 1 to 3 months over 50°).

D: *Humid microthermal.* Average temperature of coldest month less than 26.6°. (Warmest month exceeds 50°.)

Df: Humid continental. Cold winter, humid in all seasons, and driest month of summer gets more than 1.2 in. of rainfall.

Dw: Humid continental, dry winter. 70% or more of rainfall in warmer 6 months.
Tertiary symbols used with D are as follows:
a, b, and c: These are the same as those used with C above.
d: Subarctic. Winter extremely cold, average temperature of coldest month less than −36.4°.

H: *Undifferentiated highland.* These stations may be classified, but because of rapid change brought on by relief, are not shown on the map except as "H."

Sources: In preparing this modified Köppen guide, the following texts were consulted: Glenn T. Trewartha, *An Introduction to Climate* (New York: McGraw-Hill, 1954), pp. 225–26, 381, 382–83; and Howard J. Critchfield, *General Climatology,* 2d ed. (Englewood Cliffs, N.J.: Prentice-Hall, 1966), p. 155. Also consulted was Peirce F. Lewis, "Dichotomous Key to the Köppen System," *The Professional Geographer* 13, no. 5 (September, 1961), 25–31, from which the order of classification was taken.

Note: Not all of the symbols are described here and some of the statistical boundaries have been modified. Temperatures in degrees Fahrenheit, precipitation in inches. For an example of a Metric Köppen Key, see Howard J. Critchfield, *General Climatology,* 4th ed. (Englewood Cliffs, N.J.: Prentice-Hall, 1983), p. 156.

Metric equivalents are:

64.4°F = 18°C	71.6°F = 22°C
32°F = 0°C	50°F = 10°C
9°F = 5°C	26.6°F = −3°C
2.4 in. = 6 cm	−36.4°F = −38°C
	1.2 in. = 3 cm

let us classify the following hypothetical weather station in which monthly and annual temperature figures (T) are in degrees F, and all precipitation figures (RF) are in inches. Annual figures (YR) are average annual temperature and rainfall.

	J	F	M	A	M	J	J	A	S	O	N	D	YR
T	54.5	55.5	57.2	60.6	64.1	67.3	72.2	73.3	71.8	66.9	60.6	55.5	63.3
RF	2.9	3.3	2.7	1.0	0.4	0.1	0	0	0.2	0.6	1.1	2.9	15.2

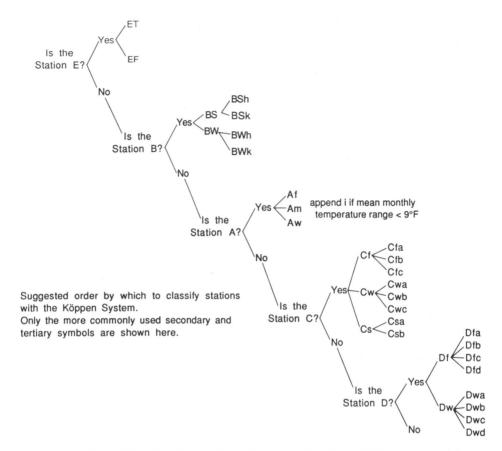

Figure 4-13 Tree diagram illustrating the order of classification suggested for the Köppen System.

Step 1. Is the station E? No, since the warmest month (August at 73.3°) has a mean temperature of more than 50°F.

Step 2. Is the station B (arid or semiarid)? This step requires use of the formula for differentiating between semiarid (or steppe) and humid climates. In order to do this, we must first determine whether the rainfall for the year is concentrated in a particular six-month period. A high-sun maximum means that 70 percent or more of the annual precipitation falls from April through September in the northern hemisphere (and January through March and October through December in the southern hemisphere). If neither high- nor low-sun period receives 70 percent or more, the distribution of rainfall is considered to be even. This formula reflects the effectiveness of rainfall under different temperature regimes, or the effect of evaporation on soil moisture as it, in turn, controls vegetation. Notice that the northern hemisphere low-sun period (January through March and October through December) received 13.5 in. of rainfall, which exceeds the required 70 percent (70 percent of 15.2 = 10.64 in. of rainfall, and 13.5 > 10.6). Therefore, the formula $r = 0.44t - 14$ (in which r is a statistical boundary between steppe and humid types and t is average annual temperature) is utilized to decide whether the station is BS (steppe) or A, C, or D (humid). Thus,

$$r = 0.44t - 14$$
$$= 0.44(63.3) - 14$$
$$= 27.85 - 14$$
$$r = 13.85 \text{ (the humid-steppe boundary)}$$

and

$$\frac{r}{2} = \frac{13.85}{2} = 6.925 \text{ (the steppe-desert boundary)}$$

In practice, then, we apply the values as follows:

	if annual rainfall $> r$, (>13.85, in this case) the station is A, C, or D (humid)
r is the humid-steppe boundary, or 13.85	if annual rainfall $\leq r$ (13.85) and $> r/2$, (6.925 in this case) the station is BS (steppe)
$\dfrac{r}{2}$ is the steppe-desert boundary, or 6.925	if annual rainfall $\leq r/2$ ($\leq$6.925 in this case) the station is BW (desert)

Since 15.2 (total annual rainfall) is greater than 13.85 (the value of r), the station is not B, so it must be A, C, or D.

Step 3.   Is the station A, C, or D? Since the coldest month (January, 54.5°F) is less than 64.4°F, the station is not A (tropical humid). Notice that although several months are below 64.4°F in temperature, no month has an average temperature as low as 26.6°F. Thus the first letter of the station in question is C (humid mesothermal), with a temperature less than 64.4°F, but more than 26.6°F in the coolest month (which happens to be January in this example).

Step 4. Is the station Cf (no dry season), Cw (dry winter), or Cs (dry summer)? Recall that we identified a low-sun maximum in Step 2. Thus the station is Cs, or dry summer subtropical, since January, February, March and October, November, December receive more than 70 percent of the annual amount.

Step 5. Is the station Csa, Csb, or Csc? It happens to fall into the second category, Csb, or subtropical with cool summers. The last letter, b, means that the temperature of the warmest month is less than 71.6°F, but at least four months are above 50°F. We can now specify that the station is dry-summer subtropical with cool summers—Csb (also called Mediterranean subtropical). This station happens to be Los Angeles, California (35°N, 118°W). Find the approximate location in Figure 4-14, the map of the Köppen System, and check the climate type.

Figure 4-14, the map of the Köppen System, may at first appear to be a mishmash of climates spread over the earth without rhyme or reason. Nothing could be farther from the truth: the map portrays the pattern of climate as a product of the interworkings of the controls discussed earlier—especially latitude, the relationship between earth and sun. For example, the tropical rainforests (Af) straddle the equator—unsurprisingly, given their 64.4°F mean

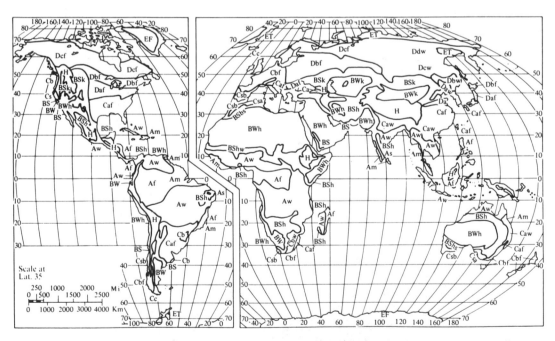

Figure 4-14 Climates of the continents based on the Köppen System. (From Albert Miller et al., *Elements of Meteorology*, 4th ed. [Columbus, Ohio: Charles E. Merrill, 1983], p. 260. Copyright 1970, 1975, 1979, and 1983 by Bell & Howell Company; used with permission.)

monthly temperature requirement. Note also the location of polar climates (ET and EF) at the northern and southern extremes, where low insolation produces low temperature much of the year. Tropical deserts (BWh) occupy equally rational locations: under the subtropical high pressure cells where atmosphere subsides and diverges at the surface. In subsiding, the air is compressed, and becomes warmer and thus capable of holding more water vapor; its relative humidity decreases and it becomes an evaporating atmosphere. All this is quite consistent with the environments found in the Sahara, Sonora, Atacama, Victoria, and other tropical deserts of the world. The Köppen System, although called a climatic classification scheme, is really much more, because vegetation is directly related to climatic type and soils are not unimportant in the ecology of natural vegetation.

MAPS OF THE ATMOSPHERE IN EVERYDAY LIFE

Interest in the atmosphere transcends the daily weather map, although that service provided by public as well as private agencies remains immensely popular. As this section reveals, our interest in atmospheric maps and phenomena ranges from insolation to insulation—from a growing interest in solar heating to a new interest in reducing heat losses in our buildings. As we spend more time in outdoor recreation, we become more concerned with the physiological effects of extreme temperatures; as we learn more about the causes and consequences of pollution, topics such as acid rain invade our consciousness and call for action to reverse the environmental impacts of our industries and utilities. Although Figure 4-15 shows a small number of examples of the many major weather disasters that have occurred in the United States, two noteworthy aspects of the map underscore the degree to which we are influenced by the vagaries of the atmosphere and the myriad effects such events have on us. Specifically, no state is exempt from these occurrences, as the lists shown cover the map; and the disasters range from floods, to freezes, to windstorms and droughts, and from hurricanes and tornadoes to mudslides and ice storms. This section begins with a discussion of weather maps in newspapers and proceeds through a series of brief accounts of maps that we encounter in our daily lives.

Weather Maps in Newspapers

Newspapers provide a source of information about the state of the atmosphere in the recent past, the present, and—in the forecasts—the near future. Their audience seems never to tire of the weather report. Ranging widely, reasons for wanting to know the forecast include, among others, the traditional decisions about umbrellas and attire (boots, coats, hats), whether to cook out or not, and whether to spend the weekend at the beach or in the mountains. House painters, roofers, builders, traveling salespeople, and others have a financial stake in the

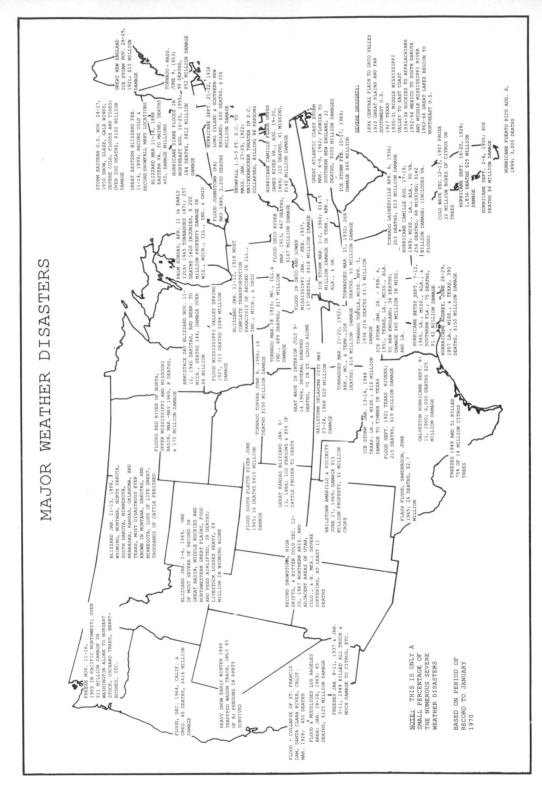

Figure 4-15 Major weather disasters in the United States. (From John L. Baldwin, *Climates of the United States* [Washington, D.C.: U.S. Government Printing Office, 1974].)

daily weather, which ranges from conditions that prohibit work altogether to conditions that create hazards and lost time. Thus all daily papers carry a weather section because of the demand for such information by the public.[17]

USA Today, a national daily launched by Gannett Newspapers and published in a growing series of markets since September 1982, has upgraded the usual newspaper treatment of weather information. Its weather page includes a full-color presentation of "Weather Across the USA," complete with map; "Four-Day Highlights" by state; an additional map with an accompanying text illustrating and describing a meteorological condition of interest; an "Area Weather Close-Up" for 24 cities across the land; "Yesterday's World Weather" for 50 foreign cities; and an "Extended Forecast" for each of seven national regions (see Figure 4-16). Rather than continuing with our description of the project, let us turn to an excellent account of "A Typical Day" at *USA Today's* weather page offices, published recently in *Weatherwise*:

"A typical day on the page begins around 10:30 A.M. and ends around midnight at the earliest. . . . A morning meeting brings together all the editors of the paper to begin blocking out the . . . front page . . . and it is decided whether the weather is a front page candidate. . . . USA TODAY receives all the state wires in addition to the national services. . . . To make the front page, a draft of the weather story must be in the hands of the national editor in time to make the 5:30 P.M. editors meeting. . . . A page 1 story is always separate from what will appear on the actual weather page. . . ."

"To compose the weather page," wire service reports are called up at about 2:30 P.M. The editor/writer then calls Accu-Weather, a private weather service, for a briefing on the forecast. At about 3:30 P.M., Accu-Weather supplies, by telephone line, a sketch map of isotherms and projected highs for the next day. A second map of frontal situations and weather features is also sent. Although used in writing the story, the highs, lows, and fronts are not shown on the main map because the readers want a forecast and not an analysis.

At about 8:00 P.M., the 16 closeup forecasts for major cities are sent by Accu-Weather, along with world weather and the 50 states' forecasts. At that time the subject of the feature focus is chosen—the map below the main map.

After the isobaric map is received, the artist begins work on the maps and illustrations. When seeking a format during the time when the page was being developed, 50 to 60 layouts were reviewed. The color scheme is produced from the Accu-Weather isobars, as the artist selects the map from six views of the United States and cuts plastic sheets to match various isobars to create the map's color scheme. In addition, a three-dimensional map is drawn for the weather focus story.

Before the map is transmitted by satellite to the production plants, color matches between key and map areas are checked and labels are proofed. Finally

---

[17] For an interesting account of the use and value of weather reports in the mass media, see W. J. Maunder, *The Value of the Weather* (London: Methuen, 1970), pp. 274–85.

Figure 4-16 The weather page, *USA Today*, April 24, 1984, p. 10A. (Reprinted with permission of *USA Today*.)

composed, the graphics and weather stories are combined to produce the page before midnight. Since the page is sent by satellite to several printing plants around the country, mistakes cannot be corrected; thus, proofreading and checking are accomplished with great care. Attempting to publish a weather page written by people who know the subject has resulted in a weather map which is "exciting news and good reading."[18]

Maps of the Effects of Air Pollution: Acid Rain

Home and industrial heating systems, power plants, smelting of some ores, volcanic eruptions, and motor vehicles produce sulfur oxides and nitrogen oxides which, after being transported in the atmosphere, return to the earth as pollutants in acid rain (or acid snow). In addition to damaging crops, forests, and buildings in North America, Europe, and Asia, this acidic additive wreaks havoc with aquatic life.[19] At one time, acid rain was believed to be concentrated in eastern North America and Scandinavia, but recent studies in the Soviet Union indicate that lakes in the Soviet Northwest have experienced an increase in water acidity. Although estimated at just 4 percent of the USSR, the area affected is equivalent to Sweden and Finland in area.[20] Figure 4-17, a map of acid-sensitive areas in North America, clearly demonstrates that the places affected are not only producers themselves but also are "down wind" of other producers. Note that Ohio and western Pennsylvania are in the "moderate" category, but are clearly among the most heavily industrial parts of the continent. In contrast, Maine, New Hampshire, and Vermont, hardly heavy-industry centers, are in the region of "high sensitivity."[21]

As one reads about acid rain, the state of New York and in particular its Adirondack Mountains are mentioned as foci of the problem. In a recent publication describing each state's situation, the National Wildlife Federation summarized New York's plight very well. The report states, in part, that the major source of acid rain in New York is apparently the Ohio Valley, and that less than 15 percent of the sulfur afflicting the state originates in New York and New Jersey. Be that as it may, sources in New York itself emitted over a million tons

[18] Edward F. Taylor, "All the Weather That's Fit to Print: Telling the Weather Story," *Weatherwise* 36, no. 2 (April 1983), 52–59. Used with permission. (Note: Weather Services Corporation now supplies USA TODAY with data for its weather page.) See also, "Doing Something About the Weather," *Design*, no. 12 (Summer 1983), 3–13, for an excellent description of how several daily newspapers tackle their weather page.

[19] G. Tyler Miller, Jr., *Living in the Environment* (Belmont, Calif.: Wadsworth, 1982), pp. 414–15.

[20] Theodore Shabad, "Acid Rain Reported Over Soviet Union," *New York Times*, April 24, 1984, p. C2.

[21] For a recent summary of the problem with acid rain in a variety of countries and regions, see Sandra Postel, *Air Pollution, Acid Rain, and the Future of Forests*, Worldwatch Paper 58 (Washington, D.C.: Worldwatch Institute, March 1984).

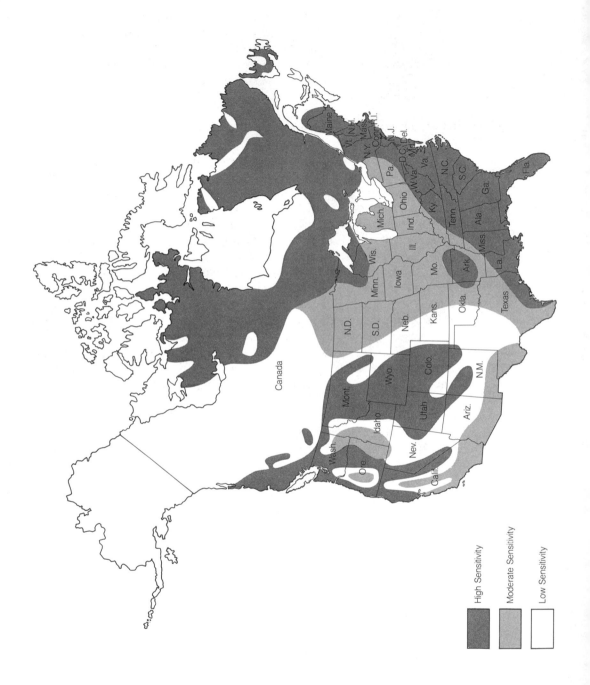

High Sensitivity

Moderate Sensitivity

Low Sensitivity

of sulfur dioxide in 1980. Needless to say, New York's precipitation acidity and associated environmental conditions render the state extremely vulnerable to the effects of acid rain; indeed, average rainfall in New York is 25 times more acidic than unpolluted rain, and the Adirondack region is listed among the largest sensitive lake areas in the eastern United States.[22]

The effects on New York's aquatic system are legendary: 212 lakes and ponds in the Adirondacks have suffered loss of sport fish, and another 256 are in danger of a similar fate. The pH levels, tested in 40 lakes in the 1930s, were less than 5.0 in just three lakes, and four lakes had no fish. By the 1970s, almost half of these lakes had pH levels under 5.0 and 52 percent had no fish. At higher elevations the problem gets worse: almost all lakes are without fish! The effects on forests may be as serious: nutrient losses from soils exceed the additions brought by precipitation; soil acidity increases; and lessened annual growth, abnormal growth, and die-back have affected a variety of Adirondack species. As for health effects, acid rain has the potential to leach metals such as mercury and lead into watersheds and metals such as copper and lead from pipes into water supplies. Figure 4-18, a map of the alkalinity of surface waters in New York (a good indicator of the sensitivity of surface waters), based on 1982 EPA data, clearly illustrates the intensity of the problem in the Adirondacks and lends definition to the broad areas of "high sensitivity."[23] Maps will no doubt play an important role in describing and documenting the extent of acid-rain damage to natural and built environments, and are likely to offer valuable assistance in the analysis of sources of pollution, atmospheric dynamics, and the areas likely to be fouled in the future.

Maps of the Atmosphere Used in and about the Home

After briefly examining cartographic summaries of snow load in New York, this section focuses on a series of topics about which the public has shown growing interest—heating fuel consumption, insulation in the home, and solar heating. Maps of degree-days, R-values, and sunshine have become more popular simply because fuel oil now costs six or seven times more than it cost some 20 years ago and the consumer, by necessity, seeks greater efficiency and reduced costs for home heating. These subjects will doubtless become even more important

[22] National Wildlife Federation, *Acid Rain: Its State By State Impact* (Washington, D.C., 1984), p. 9. Used with permission.

[23] Ibid., pp. 11–13. Used with permission.

Figure 4-17   Areas of the United States and Canada that are sensitive to acid deposition. (Redrawn from G. Tyler Miller, Jr., ed., *Living in the Environment*, 3d ed. [Belmont, Calif.: Wadsworth, 1982], p. 416. © 1982 by Wadsworth, Inc. Reprinted by permission of Wadsworth Publishing Company, Belmont, California 94002.)

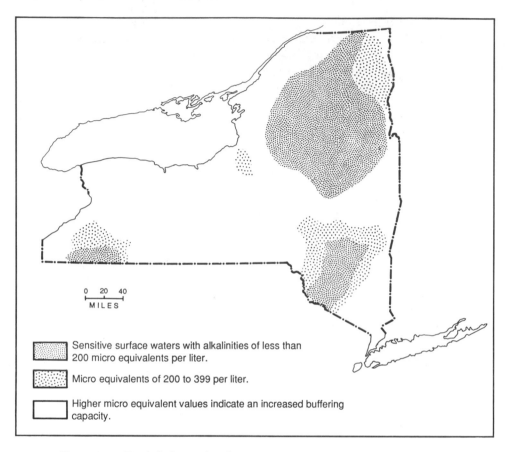

Sensitive surface waters with alkalinities of less than 200 micro equivalents per liter.

Micro equivalents of 200 to 399 per liter.

Higher micro equivalent values indicate an increased buffering capacity.

Figure 4-18   Total alkalinity of surface waters in New York State, 1982. (Redrawn from National Wildlife Federation, *Acid Rain: Its State by State Impact* [Washington, D.C.: National Wildlife Federation, 1984], p. 11. Used with permission.)

to the population as the costs of necessities such as fuel, electricity, and natural gas continue to spiral upward and to consume a greater proportion of our expendable income.

Snow Load.   The *New York State Uniform Fire Prevention and Building Code* requires all construction to conform to minimum construction standards in order to withstand the load of accumulated snow during the winter. Figure 4-19 presents the code's interesting map of snow-load zones in the state. For example, if the snow load for a region is 40 lb per ft^2 (192 kg per m^2) and a roof has no slope, the builder must use lumber and other materials designed to withstand that snow load. As a roof's slope increases, the load diminishes because of the assumed diminution of snow accumulation (see Table 4-3).

Two regions on the map in Figure 4-19 stand out: one classed "90," cen-

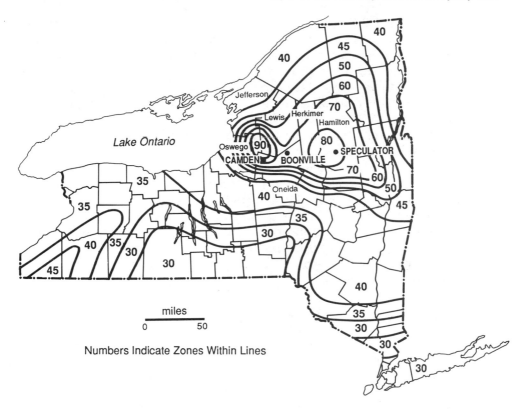

Figure 4-19   Snowfall in New York State. (From New York Division of Housing and Community Renewal, *New York State Uniform Fire Prevention and Building Code* [Albany and New York: Lenz and Riecher, 1984], p. 215.)

TABLE 4-3   SNOW LOAD IN NEW YORK STATE
(in pounds per square foot)

Zones (as shown in Figure 4-19)	Roof slope from horizontal*					
	0°	20°	30°	40°	50°	60° or more
30	30	27	17	9	3	0
35	35	31	20	10	4	0
40	40	35	23	12	4	0
45	45	40	25	13	5	0
50	50	44	28	15	5	0
60	60	53	34	18	6	0
70–90**						

Source: New York State Division of Housing and Community Renewal, *New York State Uniform Fire Prevention and Building Code* (Albany and New York: Lenz and Riecher, 1984) p. 214.
* For slopes between.
** For zones 70, 80, and 90 use same tabular values as for zone 60.

tered on the Oneida Lake-Boonville area; and one classed "80," centered on the Village of Speculator. These regions are textbook examples of how the "lake effect" and elevation influence snowfall. Lake Ontario is a source of relatively warm, moist air which, when added to colder air moving generally eastward over the lake, produces heavy snows on the eastern, or Adirondack, side of the lake. Forced to rise over the plateaus, the moist air cools to the dew point and thus becomes saturated, and the moisture evaporated from the lake is subli-mated (changed in state from water vapor to ice crystals which, in turn, form snowflakes). Although the lake effect could cause heavy precipitation around the entire perimeter of Lake Ontario, atmospheric pressures and resultant winds create a "snowbelt" to the east and southeast of the lake.[24] New York's snowbelts are the closest to the equator of all lowland snowbelts in the world.[25] The other snow-load zones in Figure 4-19 relate directly to latitude and elevation; the east-west banding of zones is interrupted only in instances where mountains impose rapid change over short map distances, as shown by a change in the isolines' direction to more nearly north-south trending and, in some places, by a closing of the space between isolines.

Degree-Days.   The degree-day method of estimating fuel consumption was devised about 60 years ago, and the heating industry in the United States has used it for about 40 years. Heating degrees for a given day are simply the number of degrees the average temperature falls below 65°F (18°C), the upper temperature at which heating is presumed necessary.[26] Summing daily heating degree-days over the entire year yields annual heating degree-days. As Figure 4-20 illustrates, normal annual heating degree-days vary widely across the United States. For example, Hawaii (not shown in Figure 4-20) has no heating degree-days since the temperature does not fall below 65°F (18°C), and central Florida has only 1,000 or fewer degree-days per year. At the other extreme, places on the Arctic slope of Alaska record 20,000 or more degree-days in a year. In the 48 contiguous states, the annual index rarely reaches 10,000 degree-days—except for northwestern Maine, northern parts of Minnesota, North Dakota, Montana, and some of the higher Rockies.

The difference in degree-days accumulated over a month or a year in a series of places is proportional to the difference in the amount of fuel needed to maintain equivalent temperatures. For example, heating a building in central Arkansas (3,000 degree-days) for one year would require about one-third the fuel needed to heat a building on the southern shore of Lake Superior or in the

[24] Based on the discussion in Bud Hedinger, *Bud Hedinger's Weather Guide* (Syracuse: WIXT Television, 1979), pp. 30–31.

[25] Douglas B. Carter, "Climate," in *Geography of New York State*, John H. Thompson (ed.) (Syracuse, N.Y.: Syracuse University Press, 1966), pp. 69–70.

[26] Cooling degree-days are defined as the number of degrees the average daily temperature exceeds 65°F (18°C). This discussion is based in part upon that found in John L. Baldwin, *Climates of the United States* (Washington, D.C.: U.S. Government Printing Office, 1974), pp. 19–20.

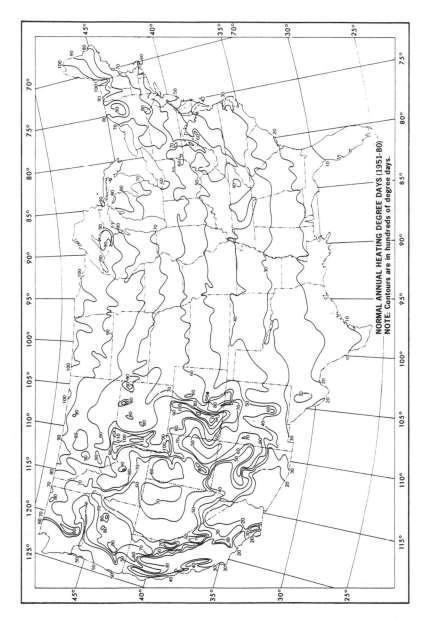

Figure 4-20 Normal annual heating degree-days in the United States, 1951–1980. Contours are in hundreds of degree-days. (From U.S. Department of Commerce, National Oceanic and Atmospheric Administration, National Environmental Satellite, Data, and Information Service, *Annual Average Climatic Maps of the United States,* Environmental Information Summaries C-21 [Asheville, N.C.: National Climatic Data Center, September 1983].)

Adirondacks of New York (9,000 degree-days). The practical value of this measure is thus of great importance to both consumers and suppliers of home-heating fuel, especially at the retail level. In the case of fuel oil, for example, subtracting the degree-days at the time of delivery from those at the last delivery and dividing the difference by the gallons of oil delivered indicates the degree-days per gallon, or the K-factor:

$$K = \frac{\sum \text{degree-days, current} - \sum \text{degree-days at last delivery}}{\text{gallons delivered}}$$

Consumers and suppliers can use this figure—which obviously varies with the space being heated, the temperature(s) at which the heating system is set, the degree to which the building is insulated, and the heating system's efficiency—to project two other figures, the date of the next delivery and the date when the supply will run out, both of which form the basis for the automatic delivery touted by oil dealers. Degree-day maps are worth consulting when one contemplates a move to a different region; they may lessen the shock of increased fuel or electric bills.

Insulation, R-Values, and Heating Zones.   The *R*-value is an insulation efficiency rating to be applied to the many types of insulating material used in construction.[27] The *R* refers to resistance to heat loss when the temperature inside a building is below the temperature outside and to heat gain when the situation is reversed in summer. Figure 4-21 relates heating zones to recommended *R*-values. Table 4-4 translates these zones into *R*-values for attics, walls, and ceilings, and relates the *R*-value to the thickness of selected insulation materials.

As the map and table suggest, Zone 1 is an area that includes most of the southern portion of the United States, from southern California to the North Carolina-Virginia coastal boundary. South of this zone lie two areas, one in south Texas and the other covering most of peninsular Florida, which require no insulation because of subtropical conditions. These "0" zone lines coincide with the 1,000-degree-day isoline shown in Figure 4-20. At the northern or most rigorous extreme in Figure 4-21, Zone 5 is restricted to North Dakota, the northern half of Minnesota, and a small area in northern Wisconsin and upper-peninsula Michigan, and is not far removed from the 9,000-degree-day line in Figure 4-20.

Since the problems with oil supplies arose in the early 1970s, when the developed nations found oil in short supply and at staggering prices, American homeowners have changed their habits—lowering thermostats, insulating more effectively, and taking advantage of federal tax credits. As many homeowners have found, with dismay, unless they exercise care in selecting insulating ma-

---

[27] U.S. Department of Energy, *Tips for Energy Savers*, DOE/CE-0049 (Washington, D.C.: U.S. Government Printing Office, 1983), p. 3.

Figure 4-21   Heating zones of the United States. See Table 4-4 for heating zone-insulation requirements. (From U.S. Department of Energy, *Tips for Energy Savers*, DOE/CE-0049 [Washington, D.C.: U.S. Government Printing Office, 1983], p. 15.)

terials and in installing insulation, little good is derived, and in some cases moisture problems arise and cause structural damage to the dwelling.

Solar Energy.   The price of fossil fuels, the development of technology, and the further financial incentive of tax credits have combined to make solar heating an increasingly popular option for homeowners. The costs of equipment and labor constitute almost all the financial outlay, since no fuel must be purchased—an attractive alternative, indeed. Because of the shape of the earth and the relationship between earth and sun, however, the amount of received insolation varies latitudinally and, given the axial inclination and revolution of the earth, seasonally. Moreover, local conditions such as topographic barriers, cloud cover, and pollution add to the inhibition of solar receipt at the surface. Figure 4-22, a three-map composite, illustrates mean annual total hours of sunshine (top), mean annual percentage of possible sunshine (center), and mean daily solar radiation (bottom) in January across the United States. The upper map illustrates the simple fact that arid, more nearly cloudless atmospheres at lower latitudes admit the most insolation, totaling as much as 4,000 hours in a year in the Yuma area of southwestern Arizona. This is an astounding figure when one considers that the year contains only 8,766 hours and half of those

TABLE 4-4   *R*-VALUES IN THE UNITED STATES

R-values recommended for heating zones			
Zones (as shown in Figure 4-21)	Attic floors	Exterior walls	Ceilings over unheated crawlspace or basement
1	R-26	For full walls,	R-11
2	R-26	range is R-11 to	R-13
3	R-30	R-13 and	R-19
4	R-33	depends on	R-22
5	R-38	materials used.	R-22

	R-values of selected materials				
	Batts or blankets		Loose fill		
R-values	Glass fiber	Rock wool	Glass fiber	Rock wool	Cellulose fiber
R-11	$3\frac{1}{2}''$–$4''$	$3''$	$5''$	$4''$	$3''$
R-13	$4''$	$4\frac{1}{2}''$	$6''$	$4\frac{1}{2}''$	$3\frac{1}{2}''$
R-19	$6''$–$6\frac{1}{2}''$	$5\frac{1}{4}''$	$8''$–$9''$	$6''$–$7''$	$5''$
R-22	$6\frac{1}{2}''$	$6''$	$10''$	$7''$–$8''$	$6''$
R-26	$8''$	$8\frac{1}{2}''$	$12''$	$9''$	$7''$–$7\frac{1}{2}''$
R-30	$9\frac{1}{2}''$–$10\frac{1}{2}''$	$9''$	$13''$–$14''$	$10''$–$11''$	$8''$
R-33	$11''$	$10''$	$15''$	$11''$–$12''$	$9''$
R-38	$12''$–$13''$	$10\frac{1}{2}''$	$17''$–$18''$	$13''$–$14''$	$10''$–$11''$

Source: U.S. Department of Energy, *Tips for Energy Savers*, DOE/CE-0049, Washington, D.C.: U.S. Government Printing Office, 1983, pp. 14–15.

are in darkness. Thus, as the center map in Figure 4-22 indicates, the Yuma region enjoys more than 90 percent of possible sunshine. Most of the remainder of the country pales in comparison, as parts of the Pacific Northwest and northern New England show 1,800 hours of sunshine annually and less than 50 percent of possible sunshine. The lower map in Figure 4-22, January's mean daily insolation, summarizes the regional variations nicely. Note that the range (in Langleys [units of insolation equal to 1 gram calorie per cm^2 of surface]) is from almost 350 in Miami and over 330 in Yuma to 67 in Seattle in the contiguous United States. Our tropical exclaves exceed 500 in places, as the insets show.

Figure 4-22   Mean annual total hours of sunshine (upper map), mean annual percentage of possible sunshine (center map), and mean daily solar radiation in January in Langleys (lower map) in the United States. (From U.S. Department of Commerce, Environmental Science Services Administration, Environmental Data Service, *Selected Climatic Maps of the United States* [Asheville, N.C.: National Climatic Data Center, March, 1980], pp. 24–26.)

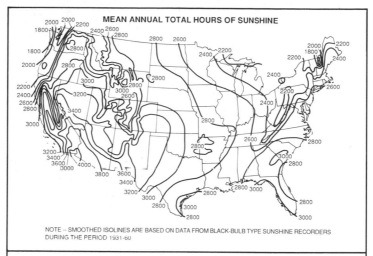

MEAN ANNUAL TOTAL HOURS OF SUNSHINE

NOTE -- SMOOTHED ISOLINES ARE BASED ON DATA FROM BLACK-BULB TYPE SUNSHINE RECORDERS DURING THE PERIOD 1931-60

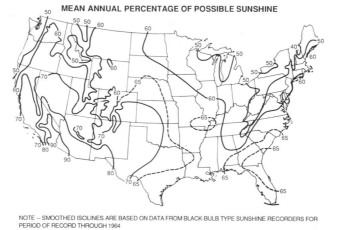

MEAN ANNUAL PERCENTAGE OF POSSIBLE SUNSHINE

NOTE -- SMOOTHED ISOLINES ARE BASED ON DATA FROM BLACK-BULB TYPE SUNSHINE RECORDERS FOR PERIOD OF RECORD THROUGH 1964

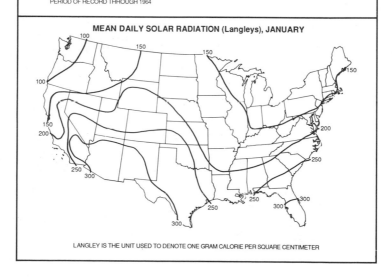

MEAN DAILY SOLAR RADIATION (Langleys), JANUARY

LANGLEY IS THE UNIT USED TO DENOTE ONE GRAM CALORIE PER SQUARE CENTIMETER

Thus, paradoxically, the regions that need heat have much less solar potential than those at lower latitudes that have less rigorous winters.[28]

Wind Chill and Heat Stress

Atmosphere may be hazardous to your health. This warning would be true were all pollution to magically disappear, because extreme temperatures have an impact that varies from causing discomfort to threatening life. A recent publication of the U.S. National Oceanic and Atmospheric Administration stated that, from 1936 to 1975, heat stress killed almost 20,000 people.[29] Indeed, without considering any element except temperature, Greenland Ranch, a location in Death Valley, California, holds the record for the highest officially observed temperature in the United States—134°F (57°C). At the other extreme, the official low for the contiguous 48 states was a temperature of −69.7°F (−57°C) recorded at Rogers Pass, Montana.[30] Temperature is not always a reliable indication of what we feel, however; wind, humidity, and insolation also play roles, as do an individual's metabolism and manner of dress. Two results of extreme atmospheric conditions, wind chill and heat stress, are antipodal effects of extreme temperatures on the human body.

Wind chill, simply put, is the lowering of body temperature by evaporation of perspiration or by the wind blowing on a person.[31] As Table 4-5 illustrates, temperature declines as wind speed increases: for example, a temperature of 20°F (about −7°C) is reduced to 16°F (about −10°C) when wind velocity is 5 mph (8 kph), and falls to −15°F (about −26°C) when wind attains a speed of 25 mph (40 kph). This effect is quite regular to about 45 mph (about 72 kph), when increased wind speed produces little additional chilling. Figure 4-23 shows wind chill isolines over the United States in January, expressed in kilogram calories per square meter per hour. As with other temperature-related indicators, the lines are essentially latitudinal; are influenced by topography; and differ over land and water, indicating the different heating and cooling properties of those two media. Given Americans' increased interest in winter sports, espe-

---

[28] For those interested in solar energy, particularly solar heating, a good source of data is U.S. National Oceanic and Atmospheric Administration, Environmental Data and Information Service, *Solar Radiation Data*, Environmental Information Summaries C-18 (Asheville, N.C.: National Climatic Center, June 1980). In addition, William F. Foster, *Build-It Book of Solar Heating Projects* (Blue Ridge Summit, Pa.: TAB Books, 1977) is a good practical guide to installing solar systems in the home.

[29] NOAA, *Heat Stress*, Environmental Information Summaries C-19 (Asheville, N.C.: National Climatic Center, October 1980), p. 1.

[30] NOAA, *Temperature Extremes in the United States*, Environmental Information Summaries C-5 (Asheville, N.C.: National Climatic Center, June 1979), pp. 1 and 5.

[31] John L. Baldwin, *Climates of the United States* (Washington, D.C.: U.S. Government Printing Office, 1974), p. 21.

TABLE 4.5 WIND-CHILL EQUIVALENT TEMPERATURES

Wind velocity (mph)	Dry bulb temperature (°F)*																		
	45	40	35	30	25	20	15	10	5	0	−5	−10	−15	−20	−25	−30	−35	−40	−45
0	45	40	35	30	25	20	15	10	5	0	−5	−10	−15	−20	−25	−30	−35	−40	−45
5	43	37	32	27	22	16	11	6	0	−5	−10	−15	−21	−26	−31	−36	−42	−47	−52
10	34	28	22	16	10	3	−3	−9	−15	−22	−27	−34	−40	−46	−52	−58	−64	−71	−77
15	29	23	16	9	2	−5	−11	−18	−25	−31	−38	−45	−51	−58	−65	−72	−78	−85	−92
20	26	19	12	4	−3	−10	−17	−24	−31	−39	−46	−53	−60	−67	−74	−81	−88	−95	−103
25	23	16	8	1	−7	−15	−22	−29	−36	−44	−51	−59	−66	−74	−81	−88	−96	−103	−110
30	21	13	6	−2	−10	−18	−25	−33	−41	−49	−56	−64	−71	−79	−86	−93	−101	−109	−116
35	20	12	4	−4	−12	−20	−27	−35	−43	−52	−58	−67	−74	−82	−89	−97	−105	−113	−120
40	19	11	3	−5	−13	−21	−29	−37	−45	−53	−60	−69	−76	−84	−92	−100	−107	−115	−123
45	18	10	2	−6	−14	−22	−30	−38	−46	−54	−62	−70	−78	−85	−93	−102	−109	−117	−125

Source: U.S. National Oceanic and Atmospheric Administration, Environmental Data Service, *Wind Chill (Equivalent Temperatures)*, Environmental Information Summaries C-3 (Asheville, N.C.: National Climatic Center, November 1981), p. 4.

* Dry bulb temperature is the temperature unchanged by evaporation, as is the case with "wet bulb temperature," in determining humidity from psychrometric tables.

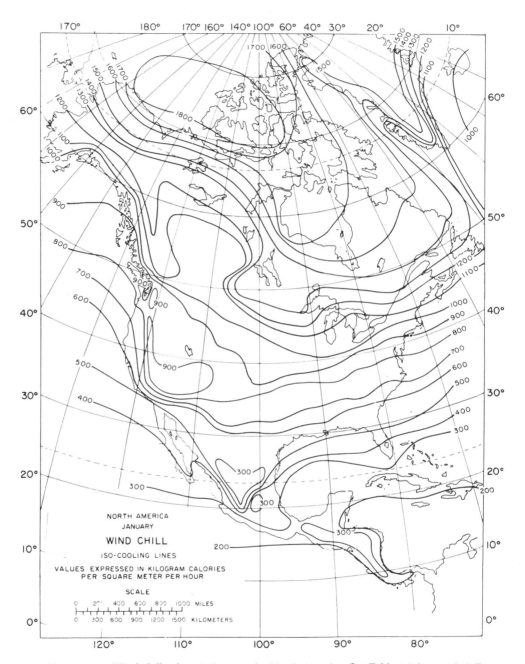

Figure 4-23 Wind chill values in January for North America. See Table 4-5 for wind-chill equivalent temperatures. (From U.S. Department of the Air Force, *Handbook of Geophysics* [New York: Macmillan, 1960], p. 2-44. Used with permission.)

cially skiing, it behooves us to understand the hazards of wind chill and the clothing and equipment available to reduce its effects.

At the higher extremes of temperature, heat stress may ensue from the combination of air temperature, humidity, wind, insolation, and a variety of factors related to attire, physiology and conditions at the place in question. Temperature and humidity are usually most important for determining human comfort. Recently, a study of "sultriness" served as the basis for a new temperature-humidity index: *apparent temperature* represents an attempt to measure sensible temperature, or what the atmosphere feels like to people at a variety of temperature-humidity combinations.[32] Figure 4-24 portrays the effects of July temperature and relative humidity, the leading components of apparent tem-

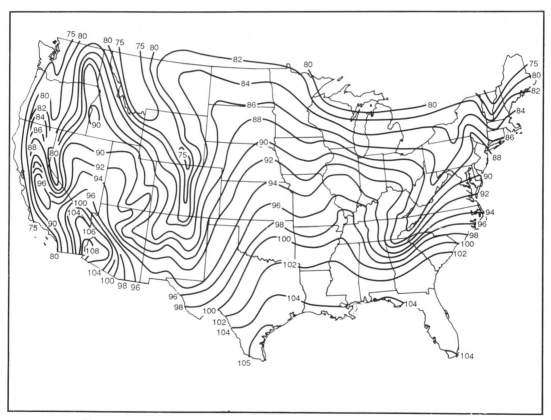

Figure 4-24   Average mid-summer noon apparent temperatures in the United States. Adjusted for relative humidity, wind, and insolation. (After R. G. Steadman, "The Assessment of Sultriness," *Journal of Applied Meteorology*, 18, no. 7, 1979, 861–84, with supplemental data added by the National Climatic Center: U.S. Department of Commerce, National Oceanic and Atmospheric Administration, Environmental Data and Information Service, *Heat Stress*, Environmental Information Summaries C-19 [Asheville, N.C.: National Climatic Center, 1980], p. 4.)

peratures, in the 48 contiguous states. Unsurprisingly, the tropical parts of the conterminous states, peninsular Florida and the Gulf Coast westward to Texas, are indexed at 104 and 105 in the apparent temperature scale, since this region is both hot and humid. In fact, one finds an index of 100 or more in most of the area south of 35°N and east of the 100th meridian. The remainder of the country has apparent temperatures of less than 100, except for the southern California-Arizona area centered roughly on Yuma, Arizona. Given relative humidity figures in July of not more than 40 percent on a mean daily basis, it is obvious that temperatures in excess of 100°F (38°C) (on a normal daily maximum basis for July), explain the high index that peaks for the country at 108 over Yuma. An apparent temperature of more than 130 is extremely dangerous to humans, making heatstroke or sunstroke likely. An index between 105 and 130 could bring on sunstroke or heat exhaustion, and heatstroke is possible. An index of 80 or more, in fact, is high enough to call for cautious behavior, especially by the aged and the ill.[33]

Given the variety, high quality, and availability of government-produced maps, it is surprising that they are not utilized to a much greater extent in helping us make some of the more important decisions in our lives. For example, having a sense of the type and frequency of atmospheric hazards—tornadoes, hurricanes, snow, wind, as well as the related difficulties such as floods and frozen roadways—might well assist one in deciding generally where he or she would like to settle. The conditions of the atmosphere are no minor contributor to the array of residential and recreational amenities that places have or lack. Indeed, the current penchant for physical fitness and recreation favors locales where one can pursue outdoor activities much of the year, if not year-round. Also, as fewer of us earn livelihoods by manual labor and as our leisure time increases, we seek more and better ways to occupy time, often in the outdoors.

FOR FURTHER READING

BALDWIN, JOHN L., *Climates of the United States*. Washington, D.C.: U.S. Government Printing Office, 1974.

CRITCHFIELD, HOWARD J., *General Climatology* (4th ed.). Englewood Cliffs, N.J.: Prentice-Hall, 1983.

DE LAUBENFELS, DAVID J., *Mapping the World's Vegetation: Regionalization of Formations and Flora*. Syracuse: Syracuse University Press, 1975.

[32] NOAA, *Heat Stress*, p. 1, which describes the work of Steadman. See R. G. Steadman, "The Assessment of Sultriness," part 1, "A Temperature-Humidity Index Based on Human Physiology and Clothing Science," and part 2, "Effects of Wind, Extra Radiation, and Barometric Pressure on Apparent Temperature," *Journal of Applied Meteorology* 18, no. 7 (1979), 861–84.

[33] NOAA, *Heat Stress*, p. 3, Figure 1.

LANDSBERG, HELMUT E., et al. *World Maps of Climatology* (2d ed.). Berlin and New York: Springer, 1965.

NAVARRA, JOHN GABRIEL, *Atmosphere, Weather and Climate: An Introduction to Meteorology.* Philadelphia, London, and Toronto: W. B. Saunders, 1979.

ROSS, HOWARD, and MICHAEL PERLEY, *Acid Rain: The Devastating Impact on North America.* New York: McGraw-Hill, 1982.

TREWARTHA, GLENN T., and LYLE H. HORN, *An Introduction to Climate.* New York: McGraw-Hill, 1980.

U.S. Department of Commerce, Environmental Science Services Administration, Environmental Data Service, *Selected Climatic Maps of the United States.* March 1980.

U.S. Environmental Data Service, *Weather Atlas of the United States* (2d ed.). Detroit: Gale Research, 1975.

U.S. National Oceanic and Atmospheric Administration, National Environmental Satellite, Data, and Information Service, *Environmental Information Summaries*, C-1 through C-25. Asheville, N.C.: National Climatic Data Center, various dates.

CHAPTER FIVE

Population Maps

In a democratic society, demographic maps—literally, "maps of people"—show the geography of power and the geography of weakness. Because people vote, purchase goods, require government services, commit crimes, and contract diseases, population maps attract the attention of politicians, marketing analysts, public administrators, police officials, and medical scientists. In a more exacting but no less urgent vein, demographic scholars use maps to explore population distribution and density variations; they study the geography of ascribed characteristics, such as age, sex, and race, as well as causal agents and achieved characteristics, such as income, educational attainment, and occupation. Concern with describing accurately, projecting, and improving the quality of life directs much of this cartographic effort toward the components of population change: fertility, mortality, and migration. Because they must portray counts, densities, rates of change, composition, and relationships between variables, population maps embrace a variety of cartographic symbols and thus are of particular interest to the map enthusiast.

Population maps lagged well behind maps of the physical environment, and examples before the mid–nineteenth century are rare. Very early demographic maps used numbers and words, rather than geometric or shaded symbols, to describe distribution and ethnicity.[1] The earliest symbolic population

[1] Arthur H. Robinson, *Early Thematic Mapping in the History of Cartography* (Chicago and London: University of Chicago Press, 1982), pp. 109–13.

map was a crude 1830 dot-distribution map of France, on which each dot represented 10,000 people. In 1833 a three-category world map of population density was published in London, and during the 1840s population maps became more common.[2] In the United States, a number of commercially prepared demographic maps published in the 1850s and 1860s used data from the decennial census, and in 1872 the official report for the U.S. Census of 1870 included statistical maps of population density, illiteracy, and ethnic origin.[3] The usefulness of these census maps encouraged the secretary of the interior to recommend approval of a refined and expanded collection of maps, which was published in 1874 as the *Statistical Atlas of the United States*.[4] Since then, population maps have been an important part of the publications program of the Bureau of the Census, which has produced graphic summaries of census tabulations, as well as a series of thematic maps.[5] Each census has yielded a center of population, such as that Figure 5-1 shows for 1900. This "median point" separates the northern half of the population from the southern half and the eastern half from the western half. Demographers conveniently summarize the settlement history of the United States by plotting the movement of this point westward and, in recent decades, to the southwest, as Figure 5-2 shows. The significance of demographic maps is underscored by the even more timely maps based on census data included in nationally prominent newspapers such as the *New York Times* and the *Christian Science Monitor*.[6]

After a brief examination of censuses and the areal units used in reporting population data, this chapter discusses the variety of cartographic symbols employed for demographic maps and explores some of the refinements used to enhance the map's accuracy, meaningfulness, and visual effect. A survey of the uses of population maps then examines the roles of atlases and supporting graphics and the cartographic needs of planners and marketing analysts. Careful study of the chapter's illustrations and caveats should promote an understand-

[2] Janusz J. Klawe, "Population Mapping," *Canadian Cartographer* 10, no. 1 (June 1973), 44–50.

[3] Fulmer Mood, "The Rise of Official Statistical Cartography in Austria, Prussia, and the United States, 1855–1872," *Agricultural History* 20, no. 4 (October 1946), 209–25.

[4] Herman R. Friis, "Statistical Cartography in the United States Prior to 1870 and the Role of Joseph C. G. Kennedy and the U.S. Census Office," *American Cartographer* 1, no. 2 (October 1974), 131–57.

[5] For a discussion of thematic mapping at the U.S. Bureau of the Census, see Robert C. Klove, "Statistical Cartography at the U.S. Bureau of the Census," *International Yearbook of Cartography* 7 (1967), 191–99; and Morton A. Meyer, Frederick R. Broome, and Richard H. Schweitzer, Jr., "Color Statistical Mapping by the U.S. Bureau of the Census," *American Cartographer* 2, no. 2 (October 1975), 100–117.

[6] See, for example, the map of population gains and losses, 1970–1980, among counties in the New York metropolitan area, accompanying Robert Hanley, "Census Suggests Boom Is Over in Suburbs Nearest New York," *New York Times*, October 7, 1980, pp. A1 and B4. *American Demographics*, a national magazine published monthly by Dow Jones and Company, uses several maps in every issue.

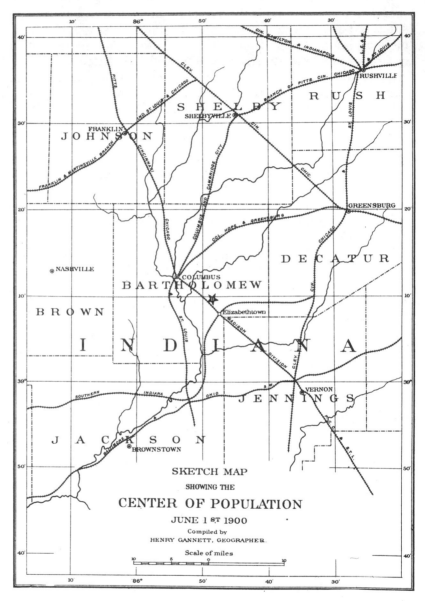

Figure 5-1 Map showing the center of population for the United States in 1900. (From *Twelfth Census of the United States, 1900,* vol. 1, Population, part 1 [Washington, D.C.: U.S. Census Office, 1901], plate 6; courtesy of E. S. Bird Library, Syracuse University.)

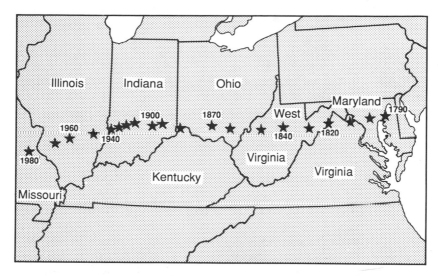

Figure 5-2 Movement westward of the center of population, United States, 1790–1980. (Adapted from map in U.S. Bureau of the Census, *Statistical Abstract of the United States: 1984*, 104th ed. [Washington, D.C.: U.S. Government Printing Office, 1983], p. 7.)

ing and appreciation of abstract but useful maps of population and other statistical data.

POPULATION DATA

Population information can be collected by census and noncensus methods, and by registration systems of vital events, marriages, divorces, and migration in and out of the country. Geographers' interest in noncensus methods—the use of visible evidence of settlement as a means of estimating numbers of inhabitants—goes with the discipline's long traditions in field work and empiricism. Interest in censuses and vital and other registries underscores geography's social science status. Indeed, in previous generations some would have argued that geographers' interest was not so much in the inhabitant, but in the residence inhabited: not so much in the worker, but in the factory, farm, or mine. The maps in early geography books tend to support this view. But today's more specialized population geographer is as concerned with the range of demographic elements and processes as are other disciplinarians who work with censuses and registries as primary sources of demographic data. Moreover, a wide variety of demographic workers find maps a necessary tool for exploring the spatial aspects of population.

Noncensus Methods

Whereas census methods involve counting heads of all inhabitants or a sample of the whole—for enumeration of a variety of characteristics and trends of the group—noncensus techniques often involve the counting of individual homes or groups of homes in a settlement. Demographers then expand this number to reflect some average occupancy and estimate the number of inhabitants in the place under study. Noncensus methods, while useful to anthropologists or geographers in less developed areas, are of marginal utility except as surrogates or fill-ins in the absence of census enumerations. Thus they are often applied to places without up-to-date censuses and, by necessity, involve comparatively small areas. An example of a study that employed aerial reconnaissance to supplement records is the work of Walter Deshler on the distribution of settlements in a county in Uganda.[7] A more recent project used aerial photographs to estimate Nigeria's urban population and to compensate for the costs and delays associated with a census. Based on the assumption that each land-use category might have a "characteristic" density of population, the study revealed that population density varied within a land-use class, particularly in "unplanned" residential areas.[8] Satellite imagery, the state of the art in noncensus enumeration, also uses indirect means in counting settlement artifacts and estimating settler numbers.[9] In the long run, however, it seems that remote sensing technology will have far more utility in maps for the intelligence and military communities than in maps for other users of population data.

Censuses

The major source of demographic data remains the census, a systematic way of collecting population information every decade or so, along with almost continuous analyses of the data collected and estimations of intercensal counts and trends. Such an undertaking by the government requires cooperation among different segments of society; a census is more effective when promoted by the business community acting in its enlightened self-interest. The census counts myriad traits as well as heads and thus yields the data for an almost infinite variety of maps. In the United States, aside from answering the constitutional requirement upon which the seats in the House of Representatives are apportioned, the census supplies the basic information needed to describe and analyze

---

[7] Walter Deshler, "Livestock Trypanosomiasis and Human Settlement in Northeastern Uganda," *Geographical Review* 50, no. 4 (October 1960), 543.

[8] Peter O. Adeniyi, "An Aerial Photographic Method for Estimating Urban Populations," *Photogrammetric Engineering and Remote Sensing* 49, no. 4 (April 1983), 545–60.

[9] See, for example, Joji Iisaka and Emoke Hegedus, "Population Estimates from Landsat Imagery," *Remote Sensing of Environment* 12, no. 4 (September 1982), 259–72.

TABLE 5-1   CHARACTERISTICS OF POPULATION IN THE 1980 U.S. CENSUS

Ascribed characteristics	Achieved characteristics	
	Social	Economic
Age	School enrollment	Employment status
Sex	Educational attainment	Hours worked
Race	Spanish/Hispanic origin or	Place of work
Color	descent	Travel time to work
	State or foreign country of birth	Means of transportation to work
	Citizenship or year of	Number in carpool
	immigration	Year last worked
	Current language and English	Industry
	proficiency	Occupation, type of
	Ancestry	employment
	Place of residence five years ago	Number of weeks worked, 1979
	Veteran status and period of	Usual hours worked weekly,
	service	1979
	Presence of disability or	Number of weeks seeking work,
	handicap	1979
	Marital status	Amount of income, 1979
	Children ever born	
	Marital history	
	Household relationship	

Source: Based upon list in U.S. Bureau of the Census, *1980 Census of Population and Housing: Tentative Publication and Computer Tape Program* (Washington, D.C.: U.S. Government Printing Office, August 1979), p. 5.

our demographic, social, and economic pulses, in ways that are easily summarized cartographically.

The U.S. Census of 1980 collected a broad array of information on ascribed and achieved characteristics—the former including biological traits of age, sex, race, and color, and the latter typically divided into social and economic characteristics. As Table 5-1 suggests, the census includes far more than enumerations at local levels and the aggregation of such counts into a variety of levels, up to and including national. Indeed, many of the characteristics listed here are combined with counts to yield vital information such as population change by age, race, and sex and the reporting of a variety of social and economic traits by age, race, and sex, all of which can be mapped. Although the U.S. Census omits religion and language is covered only by questions for the foreign born, Canada's census includes religion and treats language in detail, a reflection of the Canadian population's bilingualism and enduring roots in two European cultures.[10]

[10] See *1971 Census of Canada, Population: Religious Denominations* (Ottawa: Statistics Canada, September 1973); and Canada, Minister of Industry, Trade and Commerce, *Canada Year Book 1978–79* (Ottawa: Statistics Canada, 1978).

Registration Systems

Most governments maintain registration systems to record births, deaths, marriages, and divorces; immigration departments attempt to count new arrivals and cancelled citizenships. Because the numbers of births and deaths can be tabulated for intercensal periods, vital registries are particularly useful supplements to census enumerations. Both types of data can be used with the *demographic equation*, arranged as

$$\text{net migration} = \text{population change} - (\text{births} - \text{deaths})$$

to estimate net migration for areal units.

Several Eastern European countries, as well as Sweden and Norway, also maintain address registries and require all citizens to report any change in residence. In addition to having the most detailed migration data, showing origins and destinations of internal moves, these nations have highly accurate censuses and can readily tabulate population size between enumerations. Registration systems appear to work only in economically advanced socialist nations with homogeneous societies. The United States, with its permeable southern border and a traditional wariness about government controls, is not likely to adopt an address registry. Nonetheless, a variety of existing government records, such as the files of the Social Security Administration, are highly useful in estimating number of inhabitants for noncensus years.[11]

Areal Units

All census maps reflect data reported and aggregated by areal unit. In the United States, for instance, the lowest unit of aggregation in urban areas is the *block face*, usually the run of households on the same side of the street between two consecutive intersections. To guard against disclosing facts about individuals, the Census Bureau does not make block-face data available directly, but aggregates them to the *block*, which usually comprises several contiguous block faces bounded by linked streets. The block is the smallest unit for which Census reports provide information in print, on microfiche, and on magnetic tape. Because of the large number of blocks in metropolitan areas, relatively few variables are reported at the block level, and the Census Bureau itself does not map population distribution and characteristics at the block level. For convenience, the bureau groups socioeconomically similar and contiguous blocks together to form *census tracts*. More data are published at the tract level, some as maps.

---

[11] See Mary Kay Healy, "Introduction to Basic Procedures," in *Population Estimates: Methods for Small Area Analysis,* eds. Everett S. Lee and Harold F. Goldsmith (Beverly Hills, Calif.: Sage Publications, 1982), pp. 27–37.

For the 1970 census, for example, the bureau prepared urban atlases with color maps based on tract data for the nation's 65 largest metropolitan areas.[12]

Census tracts are restricted to that part of a metropolitan region that meets an elaborate minimum-density criterion.[13] This zone, which surrounds one or more central cities, is termed the *Urbanized Area*. Small units outside the Urbanized Area are called "county census divisions" or "minor civil divisions," although their names vary somewhat by state. New York's villages and towns are similar to New England's, whereas much of the country has townships, within which may be found a variety of urban places, including boroughs, towns, and villages, as well as unincorporated urban places (hamlets, for example) with 2,500 or more persons, for which the Census Bureau also tabulates population data. Maps at the minor-civil-division level are produced principally by county and state agencies.

The smallest unit most often employed in national maps of population is the *county* (the *parish* in Louisiana and the *election district* in Alaska). Throughout the United States over 3,000 counties make up this first level of state disaggregation. Other national maps are provided at the state level, and occasionally one finds maps that focus only on Metropolitan Statistical Areas (MSAs), which consist of one or more whole counties.

One problem with county-unit maps is the wide variation in county area: tiny counties tend to be populous and important, whereas very large counties that dominate the map often include settlements within very sparsely inhabited wastelands or forests. On a national map at 1:17,000,000, for instance, the 119 km² (46 mi²) of Hudson County, New Jersey, occupy a barely visible 0.0041 cm² (0.0006 in.²) whereas the 48,021 km² (18,155 mi.²) of Nye County, Nevada, receive a comparatively great 1.7-cm² (0.25-in.²) symbol. Yet in 1980, Hudson County had 557,000 residents, whereas Nye County had only 9,000. San Bernardino County, California, perhaps a classic illustration of nonuniform population distribution, has 51,966 km² (20,064 mi²) extending westward from the Nevada border to within 50 km (30 mi) of the Pacific Ocean, but over 90 percent of its 895,000 inhabitants recorded for 1980 were concentrated in the county's southwestern quarter. To address these problems, cartographers have developed a number of strategies, including the *demographic base map*, or *area cartogram*, in which mapped areal units are proportional in size to numbers of inhabitants, and hence to their demographic significance. National news magazines use cartograms widely in reporting forecasts and results for presidential elections.

Another solution to the problem of area variation is the *uniform grid*. Al-

---

[12] Meyer, Broome, and Schweitzer, "Color Statistical Mapping," pp. 109–16. A similar program, unfortunately, has not been funded for the 1980 Census.

[13] For detailed definitions of Urbanized Area and other statistical units used in the censuses of the United States and other nations, see Henry S. Shyrock et al., *The Methods and Materials of Demography*, vol. 1 (Washington, D.C.: U.S. Bureau of the Census, 1971), pp. 113–33.

though census maps in the United States are still tied to generally irregular political and administrative units, both Sweden and Britain have used grid-cell maps to advantage. A particularly significant cartographic product based upon

Figure 5-3   Inhabited square-km cells in England, Scotland, and Wales. Inset is for the Orkney and Shetland Islands, north of the tip of Scotland. (Modified from larger-scale color illustration in *People in Britain: A Census Atlas* [London: HMSO, 1980], p. 15; © Crown Copyright, 1980; reproduced with the permission of the Controller of Her Brittanic Majesty's Stationery Office.)

aggregation to square cells is *People in Britain: A Census Atlas*, for which census returns were aggregated to 147,685 one-km squares inhabited by at least one person.[14] Figure 5-3, in which only the inhabited cells are darkened, shows that the rugged interior is generally uninhabited, especially in Scotland, to the north. Except in the north, the coast is marked by a continuous border of "inhabited" cells. To enhance reliability, however, most of the maps in the atlas are symbolized only for the 67,543 squares with 25 or more inhabitants.

SYMBOLS FOR SMALL-SCALE MAPS

The symbols used for population maps are by no means unique to the mapping of human populations. Because geographers, social scientists, planners, and business people are concerned with a great variety of demographic phenomena, the general topic of population maps is a convenient vehicle for discussing a wide variety of cartographic treatments.

Dot-Distribution Maps

Perhaps the most straightforward portrayal of people on maps is a dot-distribution map on which one dot represents one person. In theory the user should be able to count the dots and estimate population size. In practice, however, the dot map serves mainly to portray geographic variation in population density: dense concentrations of dots represent relatively dense concentrations of people, and places on the map with few dots correspond to regions with comparatively few inhabitants. A good legend for a dot map includes examples of representative density values because it is difficult to interpret dot densities.

Most dot maps employ dot symbols that represent more than one person. On a small United States map measuring about 13 cm (5 in.) from left to right, the U.S. Bureau of the Census used dots about 0.25 mm (0.01 in.) in diameter to represent 10,000 persons.[15] Maps at smaller scales require either a larger dot value or a smaller dot; otherwise, dots might overlap and obscure density differences. Ideally the dots should barely coalesce in the region with the greatest density. Because very tiny dots are aesthetically unappealing, hard to see, and easily lost during reproduction, small-scale national and global dot maps require that each dot represent as many as a million persons, depending upon map scale and the crowding of the population represented.

Compiling and drafting a dot map is a complex task in geographic judgment and accounting in which the cartographer must consult related maps on terrain

[14] University of Durham, Department of Geography, Census Research Unit, *People in Britain: A Census Atlas* (London: Her Majesty's Stationery Office, 1980).

[15] The map described here appears in George A. Schnell and Mark Monmonier, *The Study of Population: Elements, Patterns, Processes* (Columbus, Ohio: Charles E. Merrill, 1983), p. 44.

and land use.[16] Since 1973, the U.S. Bureau of the Census has used a computer program and a computer-readable generalized land-use map to generate dot maps of not only population but also agriculture.[17] A dot, after all, can represent a population of 500 hogs or 100 tractors as logically as it might represent 1,000 people. Dots can also vary in size, value, and shape, as in the innovative "night-view" map in Figure 5-4. Here the Bureau of the Census shows the exact extent of Urbanized Areas. Three different types of dot represent three categories of other urban places, with larger dots for larger cities. For the rural population, dots representing places of 1,000 to 2,500 people are larger than dots for 500 rural residents. This map is a highly effective portrayal of the concentration of population in major metropolitan corridors and the relative paucity of people in deserts and remote mountainous regions.

Proportional Point Symbols

An obvious variation of the dot symbol assigns only one symbol to each place and scales each symbol so that its area represents numbers of inhabitants. The circular dot thus becomes the "graduated circle." In this way a single symbol can most clearly represent a single town, city, or metropolitan area. The map user is thus better able to judge which of two urban or metropolitan populations is larger. We must be careful, however, not to estimate the relative sizes of, say, different cities portrayed by graduated circles. If, for example, Baltimore and Philadelphia, with 1980 city populations of 0.8 and 1.7 million, respectively, are represented by circles of 1.0 and 2.1 cm², in the same proportion as their populations, most map users would estimate Philadelphia to have somewhat *less* than two times as many residents as Baltimore. Judging relative area is not easy—at least not without training. In a very rough sense, our eyes estimate ratios based on *both* area *and* diameter, so that symbols scaled on the basis of area tend to be underestimated when compared with smaller symbols on the map or in the legend.[18] Another limitation, particularly in population maps, is the overlap of adjacent symbols. Increasing the number of persons a square centimeter represents may reduce overlap, and breaking a larger circle where it intersects a smaller circle may make small amounts of overlap visually acceptable. In regions with tightly clustered municipalities, however, often the

---

[16] See, for example, David J. Cuff and Mark T. Mattson, *Thematic Maps: Their Design and Production* (New York and London: Methuen, 1982), pp. 31–35.

[17] For a brief description of the algorithm, see U.S. Bureau of the Census, *Census of Agriculture, 1969. Volume 5. Special Reports, Part 15. Graphic Summary* (Washington, D.C.: U.S. Government Printing Office, 1973), pp. 14–15.

[18] For discussion of the objectives and limitations of psychophysical rescaling applied to graduated-circle maps, see Kang-tsung Chang, "Circle Size Judgment and Map Design," *American Cartographer* 7, no. 2 (October 1980), 155–62; and J. S. Keates, *Understanding Maps* (New York: John Wiley & Sons, 1982), pp. 31–40.

Figure 5-4   Portion of the "night-view" dot map of the United States population. (From "Population Distribution Urban and Rural, in the United States: 1970," United States Maps, series GE-70, no. 1, U.S. Bureau of the Census, 1973.)

only solution to the overlap problem is an inset map at a larger scale so that the user can recognize individual symbols.

Circles can be used effectively with dots on the same map to represent highly concentrated urban populations and less dense, more widely scattered rural populations. Because of the clustered urban population, a dot in the left-hand map in Figure 5-5 must represent 1,000 persons; in the right-hand map, where graduated circles portray the urban population, dots representing only 500 people can provide a more detailed view of the distribution of the rural population. Proportional point symbols also can be segmented as one slices a pie to show not only magnitude but also porportion. In Figure 5-6, for example, graduated pie charts show that among the nine divisions of the United States used by the Bureau of the Census, the Mountain division has the smallest population, the black population is proportionately more numerous in the South Atlantic division, and the Pacific division has the highest proportion of Asians, Native Americans, and other racial groups. *Decagons*, regular polygons with 10

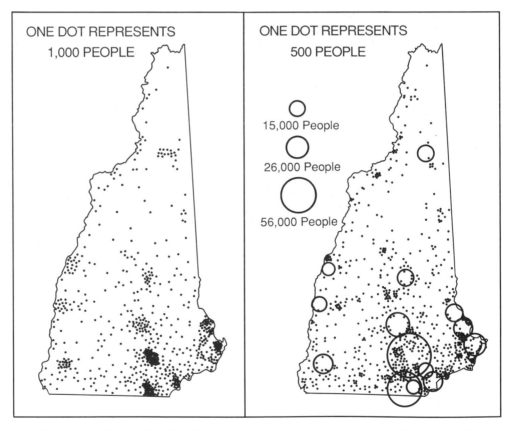

Figure 5-5 Maps of the New Hampshire population using only dots (left) and a combination of dots and graduated circles (right).

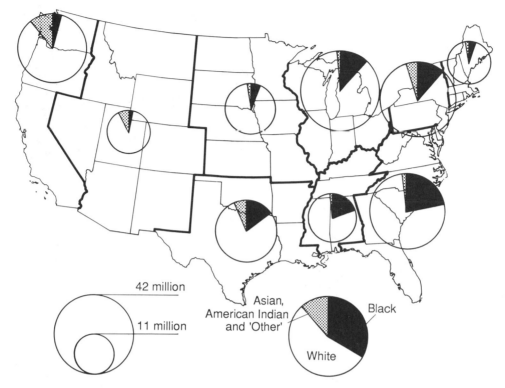

Figure 5-6 Population by census division and major racial group, United States, 1980.

sides that serve as visual cues for estimating percentages, have been proposed as a more perceptually appropriate substitute for the pie chart.[19]

Where population size varies greatly, as on a map that includes both villages and large urban centers, graduated spheres and cubes may be useful. These symbols are scaled so that volume, not area, represents magnitude; thus a symbol twice the height of another symbol can represent a population nine times as large. Because the eye-brain system cannot easily judge apparent volume, a legend with many representative symbols is needed if the map user is to estimate the populations these symbols represent. Moreover, users should be cautioned against attempting to estimate, for example, how many times one place's population exceeds that of another place—a task difficult even with circles, squares, and other symbols scaled according to area. Despite these difficulties in magnitude and ratio estimation, graduated spheres and cubes have been useful in a number of geographic studies, including Wilbur Zelinsky's examination of the

[19] See Olayinka Y. Balogun, "The Decagraph: A Substitute for the Pie Graph?" *Cartographic Journal* 15, no. 2 (December 1978), 78–85.

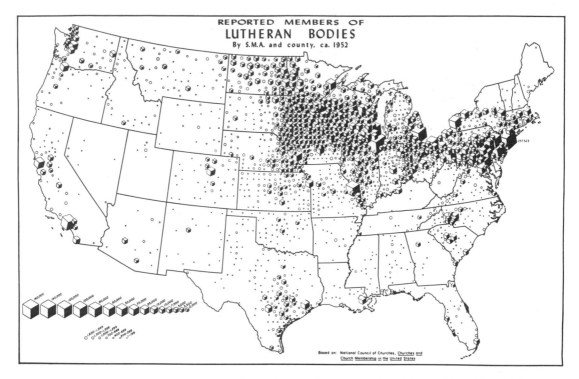

Figure 5-7 Lutheran church membership, by county, United States, 1952. (From Wilbur Zelinsky, "An Approach to the Religious Geography of the United States: Patterns of Church Membership in 1952," *Annals of the Association of American Geographers* 51, no. 2 [June 1961], 174; used with permission.)

religious geography of the United States, which uses such maps to advantage.[20] Had Zelinsky used graduated circles in his map of Lutherans (see Figure 5-7), detail in the South and the West would have been sacrificed to avoid excessive overlap of symbols in the Midwest and the East.

Another use of symbol-size variation to portray population is the *pillar map*, with vertical columns proportional in height to population size or some other demographic index. A series of maps illustrating results of the Canadian population census uses this symbolism quite effectively. A computer program designed by David Douglas plots pillar symbols and draws a base map of political boundaries that resembles a satellite view showing the earth's curvature (see Figure 5-8). Since most of Canada's population is concentrated along a comparatively narrow strip following the U.S. border, the pillars do not interfere

[20] Wilbur Zelinsky, "An Approach to the Religious Geography of the United States: Patterns of Church Membership in 1952," *Annals of the Association of American Geographers* 51, no. 2 (June 1961), 139–93.

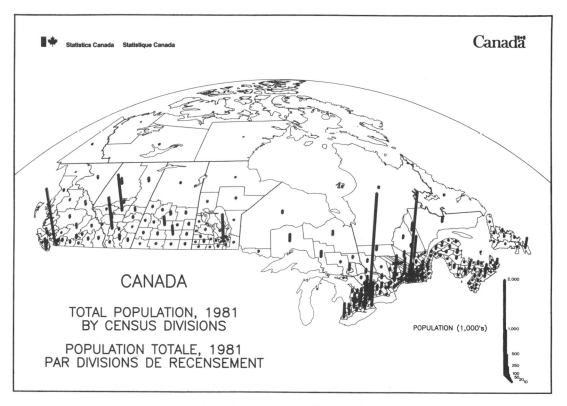

Figure 5-8   Pillar map of population by census division, Canada, 1981. (From a large-scale color map produced in 1983 by the Geocartographics Subdivision, Statistics Canada.)

graphically with each other. This oblique globular projection enhances the three-dimensional effect of the map and its symbols.

Choropleth Maps

Most population maps are *choropleth maps*, on which areal units are shaded with light tones to represent low densities, percentages, or ratios, with dark tones representing high values. The choropleth approach is widely used because printed base maps and printed toning patterns with self-adhesive backing have enabled map drafters to construct publishable versions of these maps far more rapidly than dot-distribution maps or other portrayals of population data. Usually a choropleth map groups the data into a limited number of classes, each representing a range of values and symbolized by a uniform shading pattern. Computer-driven pen plotters and mapping software have made the generation of choropleth maps easier still, as well as more rapid and less costly. Moreover, because area patterns can vary continuously on the gray scale from light to dark,

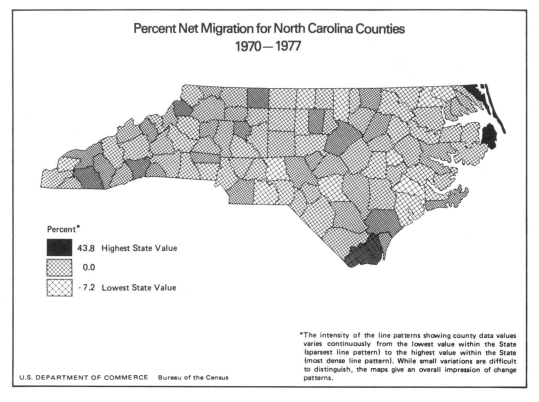

Figure 5-9   Continuous-tone, nonclassed choropleth map showing percent net migration, by county, North Carolina, 1970–1977. (From U.S. Bureau of the Census, *Current Population Reports*, series P-26, no. 77-33, September 1978, p. 9.)

classing is no longer needed: each place can have a pattern with a gray tone directly proportional to its density, percentage, or ratio.[21] Continuous-tone, non-classed choropleth maps, such as the population density map of North Carolina in Figure 5-9, can be plotted by computer to eliminate some of the uncertainty and loss of information inherent in classed choropleth maps. Yet classed maps seem likely to remain the dominant variety because of tradition, lack of appropriate computer software, or a preference for the distinct regions shown on maps generalized by classification of the data.

Because most choropleth maps are based upon a classification and a limited number of area tones, the map user should recognize the pitfalls of classing and selecting toning patterns. Many different map patterns can be generated from

[21] See W. R. Tobler, "Choropleth Maps Without Class Intervals?" *Geographical Analysis* 5, no. 3 (July 1973), 262–65; and Mark Monmonier, "Modelling the Effect of Reproduction Noise on Continuous-tone Area Symbols," *Cartographic Journal* 16, no. 2 (December 1979), 86–96.

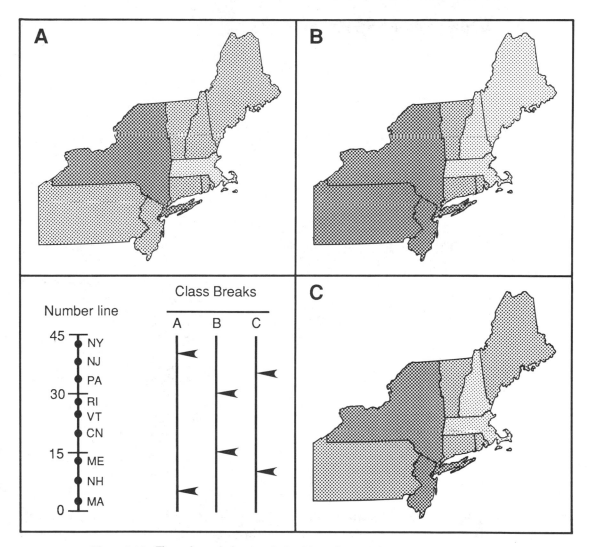

Figure 5-10 Three choropleth maps derived from the same data (lower left) using different class breaks yield distinctly dissimilar patterns.

the same data, after all, and as Figure 5-10 shows, these cartographic kinfolk can vary greatly in complexity and geographic pattern.[22] Users must be wary of the information lost—or distorted—through classification. They also must examine carefully the map legend and not be duped by sets of area symbols, such as those in Figure 5-11, that lack consistent, logical progression from light

---

[22] See Mark Monmonier, *Maps, Distortion, and Meaning* (Washington, D.C.: Association of American Geographers, Resource Paper no. 75-4, 1977), pp. 25–29.

Per Capita Personal Income, 1983

UNITED STATES $11,687
Southeast Region $10,215

$10,000-$12,999
$9,000- $9,999
$8,000- $8,999

Figure 5-11 Choropleth map of per capita income in a government report uses white to represent the intermediate category and two area shadings, similar in graytone but different in texture, for the high and low categories. This apparent attempt to highlight extremes requires frequent reference to the map key to avoid confusion. (From U.S. Department of Commerce, Bureau of Economic Analysis, *Local Area Personal Income, 1978–83,* vol. 6, Southeast Region [Washington, D.C.: June 1985], p. 1.)

to dark, and thus misrepresent geographic patterns. Color maps, produced with little effort or thought by uneducated "cartographers" with access to elaborate computer graphics systems, are among the worst offenders.

When maps portray demographic data such as birth and death rates, the map user must be concerned not only with whether the value for a place is high or low but also with whether a high or low rate is particularly meaningful. An area with only 100 inhabitants, for example, might by happenstance record 5 deaths in one year and merit a mortality rate of 50 per 1,000, high even by Third World standards. If registered by a far more populous place, this rate could not so easily be dismissed as a random, meaningless event. Similarly, a place with a small population might record no deaths or very few deaths for a single year, and thus garner the apparent but undeserved distinction of a healthful environment. To stabilize the mapped pattern, population geographers often av-

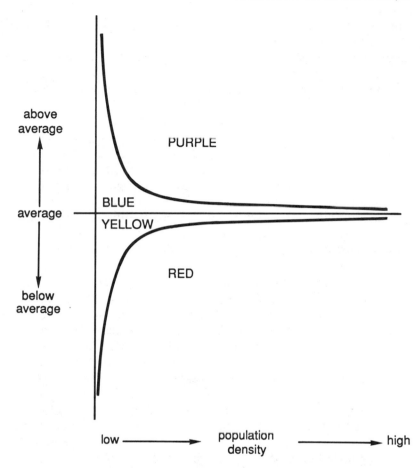

Figure 5-12 Thresholds for the signed chi-square criterion. (Adapted from diagram in *People in Britain: A Census Atlas* [London: Her Majesty's Stationery Office, 1980], p. 7.)

erage vital rates for a period of several years, over which these random effects tend to cancel one another.

The designers of *People in Britain*, the grid-cell based census atlas mentioned earlier, approached this problem with a four-way classification based upon probability theory.[23] Called the "signed chi-square criterion," this classification scheme differentiates places in two ways: as above or below the national average and according to population density. Figure 5-12 illustrates the threshold curve that requires larger deviations from the mean for more sparsely inhabited places. Color symbols are particularly useful in communicating the two-way classifi-

[23] See *People in Britain*, pp. 6–7, and M. Visvalingam, "The Signed Chi-square Measure for Mapping," *Cartographic Journal* 15, no. 2 (December 1978), 93–98.

cation: below-average cells are assigned warm colors (red or yellow), above-average cells receive cool colors (purple or blue), cells with rates significantly above or below the mean have bold colors (red or purple), and cells with rates that are average or of dubious significance have weak colors (blue or yellow). Most of the national and regional maps in the atlas were based on this concept.

REFINEMENTS

Cartographers have proposed a number of refinements to the simple and much abused choropleth map. As both consumers of geographic information and connoisseurs of cartographic art, astute map users should be aware of various strategies for producing more detailed or more meaningful maps of population.

Dasymetric Maps

As a refinement of the choropleth map, the *dasymetric map* addresses the problem of areal units with wide internal variations. Like the simple choropleth map, the dasymetric map employs gray-tone area shading patterns. It differs, however, in the network of boundaries that confine the gray tones: these boundaries are redrawn to approximate breaks or transition zones in the distribution.[24] Ideally, the areas within these boundaries represent comparatively homogeneous zones, and the resulting map pattern usually is more detailed than that of a simple choropleth map.

Sometimes dasymetric maps are based upon not only the distribution being portrayed but also maps of related distributions that might suggest the general locations of homogeneous areas and sharp transition zones. Figure 5-13, the classic illustration of the dasymetric approach, shows the pattern of population density for Cape Cod, Massachusetts. It was published in 1936 by John K. Wright, a cartographic scholar who later became director of the American Geographical Society.[25] Wright refined a township-level choropleth map of population by delineating uninhabited areas and using "calculated guesswork" and his knowledge of the area to adjust boundaries and densities.

Small-scale maps of world population, which must be highly generalized, are sometimes derived from detailed choropleth maps, but this generalization calls for not only a smooth image but also the geographer's knowledge of important regional patterns in terrain. In compiling a world map of population,

[24] See, for example, John Campbell, *Introductory Cartography* (Englewood Cliffs, N.J.: Prentice-Hall, 1984), pp. 316–19. The dasymetric technique was developed by Henry Drury Harness, a survey engineer who prepared a series of traffic flow and population maps for the Second Report of the Irish Railway Commissioners. See Arthur H. Robinson, "The 1837 Maps of Henry Drury Harness," *Geographical Journal* 121, pt. 4 (December 1955), 440–50.

[25] John K. Wright, "A Method of Mapping Densities of Population with Cape Cod As an Example," *Geographical Review* 26, no. 1 (January 1936), 103–10.

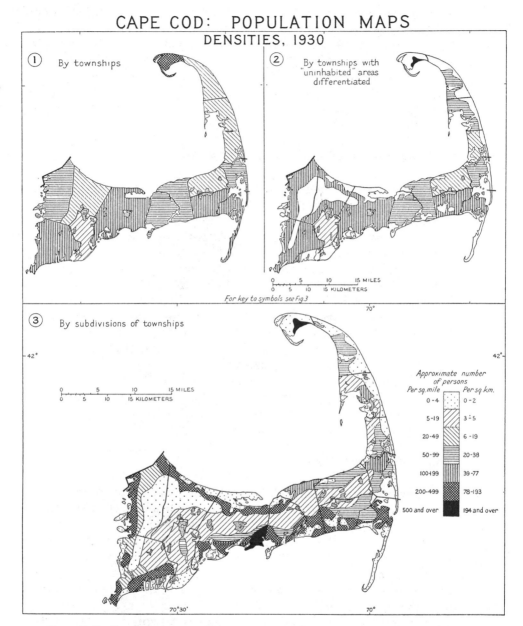

CAPE COD: POPULATION MAPS
DENSITIES, 1930

① By townships

② By townships with "uninhabited" areas differentiated

For key to symbols see Fig. 3

③ By subdivisions of townships

Approximate number of persons	
Per sq. mile	Per sq. km.
0 - 4	0 - 2
5 - 19	3 - 5
20 - 49	6 - 19
50 - 99	20 - 38
100 - 199	39 - 77
200 - 499	78 - 193
500 and over	194 and over

Figure 5-13 Population maps of Cape Cod, Massachusetts, based on (1) township census data, (2) refined by differentiating nonresidential areas, and (3) further refined to yield a dasymetric map. (From John K. Wright, "A Method of Mapping Densities of Population With Cape Cod As An Example," *Geographical Review* 26, no. 1 [January 1936], 105; reprinted with the permission of the American Geographical Society.)

for instance, a geographer aware of the concentration of Egypt's population in the Nile Valley would find the dasymetric concept useful in showing the abrupt transition along the valley's edge from population densities over 100 persons per km^2 to densities less than one person per km^2.[26] Although a world map based on small subnational areal units might yield the desired pattern, a dasymetric map based on considerations similar to those described for the Nile valley would be more accurate than a choropleth map if data were generally available only for national units.

Oblique Views of Statistical Surfaces

The advent of computer-assisted cartography and the wide availability of pen plotters prompted an increased use of maps that portray statistical surfaces such as population density as three-dimensional landscapes viewed from a point above the horizon (see Figure 10-20). As with topographic maps, statistical surfaces can also be displayed with contours or isolines, but the oblique three-dimensional view is far more effective in showing the equivalents in the "demographic landscape" of peaks, pits, ridges, troughs, gentle lowlands, and high plateaus. Figure 5-14, a series of views for the Ottawa-Hull metropolitan area on the Ontario-Quebec border, is a forceful illustration of the cleavage between English and French Canadians.[27] On the left, a view looking south from Hull shows a small English-speaking population on the Quebec (north) side of the Ottawa River and a large English-speaking group on the Ontario side. On the right, a view looking north from Ottawa shows that most persons speaking only French reside across the river in Hull. In the center, another view from the south shows bilingual Canadians, mostly of French background, as a slight majority in Hull but a distinct minority in Ottawa.

Age-Adjusted Rates

Another refinement, particularly useful in maps of birth and death rates, is age adjustment. This modification, which may be applied to choropleth, statistical surface, dasymetric, and other kinds of maps, alters the data values and not the areal units they represent. It is based upon the simple and obvious fact that young populations generally have higher birth rates and lower death rates than old populations. To compute an age-adjusted rate, we must have information about each area's age structure—that is, the number of persons in each age group, or cohort. We must also have a reference population: the entire United States for 1940 is a common standard to which local rates are adjusted.

---

[26] See, for example, the population map for Africa in Edward B. Espenshade, Jr., and Joel L. Morrison, eds., *Goode's World Atlas*, 16th ed. (Chicago: Rand McNally, 1982), p. 215.

[27] D. R. F. Taylor, "Graphic Perception of Language in Ottawa-Hull," *Canadian Cartographer* 14, no. 1 (June 1977), 24–34.

English-speaking   Bilingual   French-speaking

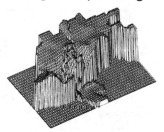
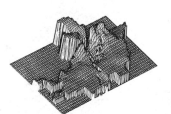

Figure 5-14 Oblique views of the Ottawa-Hull region using surface height to portray the bilingual population (center) and persons speaking only English (left) and only French (right). The left-hand view looks south from Hull, whereas the other views look north from Ottawa. (From D. R. F. Taylor, "Graphic Perception of Language in Ottawa-Hull," *Canadian Cartographer* 14, no. 1 [June 1977], 28–29; used with permission.)

We then estimate the number of deaths that would have occurred had the area in question been subject to the death experience of the reference population. We do this by multiplying the number of persons in each cohort by the death rate in that cohort for the reference population and then summing the numbers of deaths "expected" in each cohort. The total number of "expected deaths" is divided by the place's actual number of deaths to yield a *standardized mortality ratio*, which sometimes is multiplied by 100 and mapped directly. An *age-adjusted death rate* can be computed by multiplying the standardized mortality ratio by the crude death rate for the reference population.[28]

The cartographic effect of age adjustment can be marked, particularly where wide variations in age exist. In Figure 5-15, for instance, age-adjustment reverses the north-south pattern for Canadian death rates. The southern provinces, with relatively older populations, have higher crude death rates than do the Yukon and Northwest Territories, where few older Canadians choose to live. When age-adjustment is invoked, the northern territories receive the higher rates because the number of deaths there is high relative to the ages of the inhabitants. In the United States, age-adjustment produces a similar reversal for Florida and Alaska.

Demographic Base Maps

News magazines frequently employ *demographic base maps* (or *cartograms*) in their cartographic analyses of presidential elections. Each state is represented by a symbol proportional in area to the state's number of electors, which in turn

[28] The procedure described here is the *indirect method* of demographic standardization. The *direct method*, which requires age-specific rates for each cohort for each areal unit, is less commonly used. For further discussion of demographic standardization, see Ronald Pressat, *Statistical Demography*, trans. by Damien A. Courtney (New York: St. Martin's Press, 1978), pp. 48–54.

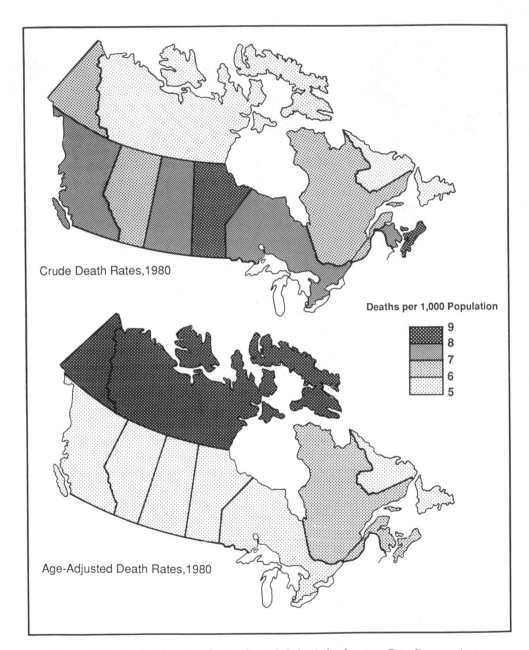

Figure 5-15 Crude (above) and age-adjusted (below) death rates, Canadian provinces, 1980. Reference population for age-adjustment is the 1956 Canadian population. (From *Vital Statistics*, vol. 1, *Births and Deaths, 1980* [Ottawa: Statistics Canada, 1982], pp. 46–47.)

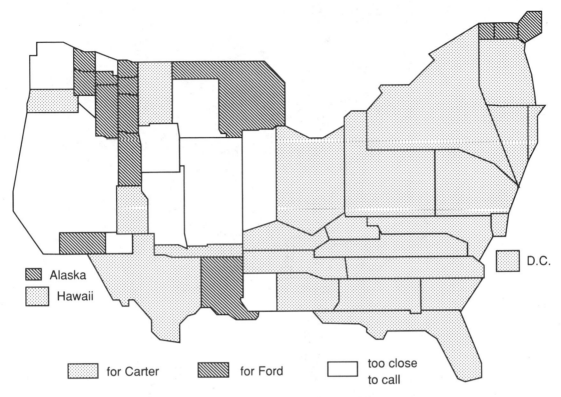

Figure 5-16 Forecast of the presidential contest between Gerald Ford and Jimmy Carter on a base map with area proportional to number of electoral votes. (Redrawn and adapted from a color five-category map in *Newsweek* 88, no. 18 [1 November 1976], 19. Journalistic cartographer Ib Ohlsson acknowledged use of base map from the Ohio Bureau of Employment Services.)

reflects the state's population. States small in area but large in population have greater visual impacts. For example, with almost six million inhabitants and 13 electors, Massachusetts's presence on the map far exceeds that of Montana, a state 18 times larger in area but with less than a million residents and only four electors. These adjustments are highly appropriate, given the tendency for states in the West to be larger in area, less dense in population, and more politically conservative than states in the Northeast.[29]

Figure 5-16 demonstrates this effect most vividly in a redrawn election forecast map published by *Newsweek* two weeks before the Ford-Carter presi-

---

[29] For a discussion of strategies in designing demographic base maps, see J. R. Eastman, W. Nelson, and G. Shields, "Production Considerations in Isodensity Mapping," *Cartographica* 18, no. 1 (Spring 1981), 24–30.

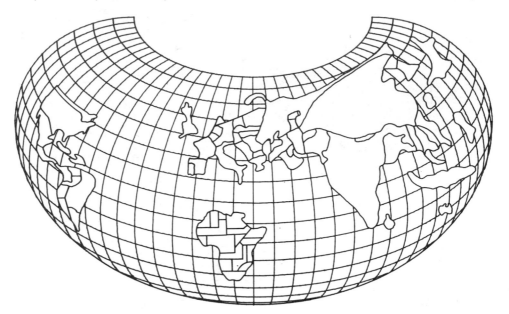

Figure 5-17 "World on a Torus" 1980 demographic base map. (Copyright 1982 by Mark Monmonier.)

dential election in 1976.[30] In addition to showing the geographic sources of the candidates' strengths, this map clearly depicts Jimmy Carter's projected lead, with 308 electoral votes, against 88 for Gerald Ford and 142 considered at the time "too close to call." A standard base map would have inflated visually the significance of these 230 electoral votes, mostly in large western states.

Area cartograms, as these maps are called, can be particularly effective on a small-scale world map, but they have their limitations. Several years ago we wrote a textbook on population geography that employed a demographic base map showing the world's major nations as well as residual areas, usually contiguous groups of countries with individual populations less than 10 million or so.[31] This base map, shown in Figure 5-17, was a 1980 refinement of a generally similar base map used to illustrate a 1953 Twentieth Century Fund report on world population pressures.[32] The pseudo-grid of the torus conveys the general impression of a world base map. The map sacrifices some information because

[30] Where a candidate's strength is overwhelming, as with Ronald Reagan in 1980 and 1984, almost any use of a map might seem like graphic overkill. For instance, a map of the results of the 1984 presidential election would have served merely to depict the political isolation or enlightenment, depending upon one's view, of Minnesota and the District of Columbia.

[31] Schnell and Monmonier, *Study of Population.*

[32] Wladimir S. Woytinsky and Emma Shadkhan Woytinsky, *World Population and Production: Trends and Outlook* (New York: Twentieth Century Fund, 1953), pp. 42–43.

it does not show relatively small countries—such as Ireland and Bolivia, with 3.5 and 5.6 million inhabitants, respectively—individually, but groups them with similar nearby nations. Numerical data by country were included in a large table in the book's appendix, however, so that the reader could find estimates of demographic counts and rates and related indexes for all nations, large and small. Page-size maps could thus focus attention on numerically significant parts of the geographic pattern, so that, for instance, the map shifts the reader's attention from Australia, Canada, and other sparsely inhabited but large areas to geographically small but populous nations such as Japan.

Animated Maps

Advances in computer graphics promise dynamic displays, including what might be termed *animated maps*. Many mapped demographic phenomena are dynamic rather than static, and a fuller appreciation of their geographic distribution requires cartographic treatment of the dynamics of their evolution. Unfortunately, the mapping of historical demographic data usually has been confined to individual maps showing rates of change and to series of cartographic snapshots, usually for successive censuses. Because of cost and their own inexperience, cartographers have virtually ignored proven, graphically powerful techniques of film animation.[33]

Advances in electronics, particularly in video computer graphics, promise to whet appetites for dynamic maps and bring highly effective action graphics into home and classroom. Most promising is the sophisticated image generation system used to produce efficiently the many frames needed for award-winning feature-length animated films.[34] Also important will be videotex systems (discussed in Chapter 10) that use telecommunications networks to deliver carefully composed sequenced graphics to television sets in subscribers' homes.[35] Pedagogically useful dynamic maps will also take advantage of split-screen techniques appropriate for illustrating the interaction of demographic, economic, cultural, and physical factors. Insofar as most places are the way they are because of population movements produced by human aspirations and stages in the life cycle, developments in dynamic cartography will be particularly beneficial to the study of migration.

[33] For two of the few cartographic discussions of film animation, see Norman J. W. Thrower, "Animated Cartography in the United States," *International Yearbook of Cartography* 1 (1961), 20–30; and W. R. Tobler, "A Computer Movie Simulating Urban Growth in the Detroit Region," *Economic Geography* 46, no. 2, supplement (June 1970), 234–40.

[34] See, for example, Don Miskowich, "Digital Technology and Motion Pictures," *Computer Graphics World* 5, no. 7 (July 1982), 50–62.

[35] See D. R. F. Taylor, "The Cartographic Potential of Telidon," *Cartographica* 19, nos. 3 and 4 (Autumn and Winter 1982), 18–30.

USES OF POPULATION MAPS

Constitutional requirements for maintaining proportional representation lead to redistricting, in which maps become legal instruments and the focus of debate (as discussed in Chapter 6). At the local level, however, busing has become a point of contention, as the issue of where children should go to school has often become one of race—with blacks believing that their educational opportunities are limited by attendance at neighborhood schools, populated mostly, if not entirely, by blacks and other ethnic minorities. The conflict centers on the differences in quality in education occasioned, some argue, by school officials and a public who either ignore the situation or take minority students less seriously than their white counterparts. Others argue that areas of school attendance traditionally have been an outgrowth of population distribution, and that until the racially and ethnically diverse populations of cities and other school districts with more than one school at various levels are integrated residentially, educational opportunity will continue to vary despite court decisions calling for school desegregation. It is interesting that, in his probing book on Hamilton, Ohio, Peter Davis points out the differences between the city's two high schools and the sad truth that the disparities are based in part on race and class.[36] Attendance maps, commonly constructed by school officials from maps of the school-age population, illustrate an important and far-reaching use of population maps. This section explores other applications and provides a variety of examples of the wide influence of maps of census and other demographic data.

Population Maps in Atlases

No educational medium surpasses the atlas for the cartographic communication of demographic information. *Goode's World Atlas*, a standard, widely used school atlas, treats population distribution and density almost from the outset, by including a variety of maps and aerial photographs that portray, among other things, settlement at a variety of scales.[37] Further, the very first map in the opening section, "World Thematic Maps," is a population cartogram in which the size of each country is proportional to the size of its population. This map also shows natural increase in population, using colors.[38] A two-page map in the same section which shows population density for the world, preceded a series of half-page maps showing world patterns in the birth rate, death rate, natural increase, urbanization, GNP per capita, literacy, language, and religion.[39] On a standard, equal-area base, these maps are followed by cartograms

---

[36] Peter Davis, *Hometown* (New York: Simon and Schuster, 1982), pp. 27–28, 32–34, and 41–47.

[37] Espenshade and Morrison, *Goode's World Atlas*, pp. vii–xv.

[38] Ibid., p. 1.

[39] Ibid., pp. 20–23.

portraying world patterns in calorie supply, protein consumption, physicians, and life expectancy.[40] In its regional sections, *Goode's* includes population density maps for North America, South America, Europe, Asia, Australia, and Africa.[41] These are in addition to population maps at subcontinental scale and a broad array of physical-political maps and city maps in which demographic phenomena are implicit.

Most developed nations have national atlases, and atlases have been prepared for many of the individual United States, Canadian provinces, and other subnational regions. The *Atlas of California*, a well-designed and skillfully executed portrayal of the important elements of one state's geography, illustrates how maps of population data contribute to a state or regional atlas. In addition to page after page of maps of myriad contemporary demographic elements and processes, the atlas includes a number of maps addressing the history of settlement in the state and the evolution of the present population pattern. In the first section of the atlas, for example, a map entitled "The Human Impact" traces Native American settlements from 1770 to 1970. Mission history is depicted cartographically, as is population change beginning in the mid–nineteenth century. The collection of maps spans the elements and processes of demography, and its presentation is compelling.[42]

Population is also the theme of a number of single-subject atlases. As an example, *The Changing Population of the Southeast*, a thematic atlas compiled by John Florin and Richard Kopec, geographers at the University of North Carolina, inventories demographic trends in that region and presents them in maps with commentary. Coverage ranges over distribution and density, growth, composition, and the components of change. An especially interesting map is their plot portraying "Decade of Maximum Population Growth," reprinted in Figure 5-18. As this map shows, counties that attained their maximum population in 1970, the most recent census used in the atlas, were concentrated in peninsular Florida, the Gulf Coast, the Piedmont, and the Great Valley. As Florin and Kopec state, "Only five counties with a significant coastline did not have a 1970 population maximum."[43] Counties with an earlier peak and subsequent decline are associated with economic trends, particularly the decline of coal and cotton. But then, as Florin and Kopec point out in noting the tendency toward concentration of the country's population, "a majority of all of the counties in the United States had a smaller population in 1970 than they had in some previous decade."[44]

[40] Ibid., pp. 26–27.

[41] Ibid., pp. 75, 135, 145, 182, 207, and 215.

[42] Michael W. Donley et al., *Atlas of California* (Culver City, Calif.: Pacific Book Center, 1979), pp. 8–51.

[43] John W. Florin and Richard J. Kopec, *The Changing Population of the Southeast* (Chapel Hill: University of North Carolina, Department of Geography, Studies in Geography no. 5, 1973), pp. 7–8.

[44] Ibid.

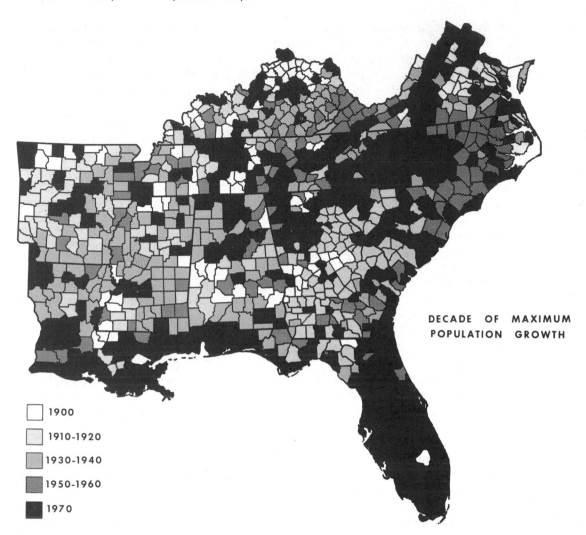

DECADE OF MAXIMUM
POPULATION GROWTH

1900
1910-1920
1930-1940
1950-1960
1970

Figure 5-18   Decade of maximum population growth in the southeastern United States. (From John W. Florin and Richard J. Kopec, *The Changing Population of the Southeast* [Chapel Hill: University of North Carolina, Department of Geography, Studies in Geography no. 5, 1973], p. 8; used with permission.)

This thought-provoking map, indeed the whole atlas, underscores the educational value of population mapping.

Supporting Graphics

Because demographic data often are rich in information about population characteristics and interrelationships, population maps are often accompanied by nonspatial graphics that add considerably to an understanding of demographic trends and processes and promote a more informed interpretation of geographic patterns. Supporting graphics are particularly useful for portraying the composition of a national population for which the map provides the geographic detail. Especially appropriate is the pie chart, a circle divided to illustrate a nation's population classified according to race, ethnic origin, educational attainment, occupational structure, or place of residence (rural or urban). The *National Atlas of Canada* used pie charts with dot-distribution maps to promote comparisons of the country's provinces.[45] Where the number of areal units is not large, individual graphs showing temporal trends can be juxtaposed to present historical data more efficiently than possible with maps alone. By convention, time is scaled along the horizontal axis, and the index in question is scaled along the vertical axis. Colored or patterned lines can portray trends for population subgroups. A single page in the Canadian national atlas provides a concise summary of population growth; individual graphs for the nation, its 10 provinces, and its two territories cover a 90-year period and illustrate trends for the total population and its urban, rural, rural non-farm, and farm components as well.[46] Although a similar portrayal for the 50 United States might be awkwardly large and visually overwhelming, arrays of graphs are often presented for the four "regions" or the nine "divisions" into which the country is customarily divided. Figure 5-19, based on the four regions, is effective in illustrating slackened population growth in the Northeast and North Central regions and more vigorous increases in the South and the West.

A uniquely demographic device is the *population pyramid*, used to portray age-sex composition. As Figure 5-20 illustrates, a pair of pyramids for Pennsylvania and the United States group the population in 5-year cohorts represented by bar graphs stacked vertically, from the youngest at the base to the oldest at the apex. The population is subdivided also by sex, with separate horizontal scales extending from the center to the right for females and to the left for males. Age pyramids usually taper toward the top, where the older cohorts have been reduced by death. A pyramid narrower at its base than at its middle reflects a declining birth rate. To promote comparisons, each age-sex cohort is represented by its percentage of the total population. It is thus obvious in this example that Pennsylvania in 1980 had proportionately fewer persons aged 40 to 54 than the nation as a whole. The constriction in the pyramid for middle-aged cohorts largely reflects the out-migration, years earlier, of young adults discouraged by limited opportunities for local employment.[47]

Supporting graphics are especially helpful in describing relationships be-

[45] *National Atlas of Canada*, 4th ed. (Toronto: Macmillan of Canada; Ottawa: Department of Energy, Mines and Resources; Ottawa: Information Canada, 1974), pp. 91–93.

[46] *National Atlas of Canada*, p. 94.

[47] See George A. Schnell, "Recent Trends in Pennsylvania's Dependency, Fertility, and Population Growth: A Graphic Summary," *Proceedings of the Pennsylvania Academy of Science* 57, no. 1 (1983), 88–92.

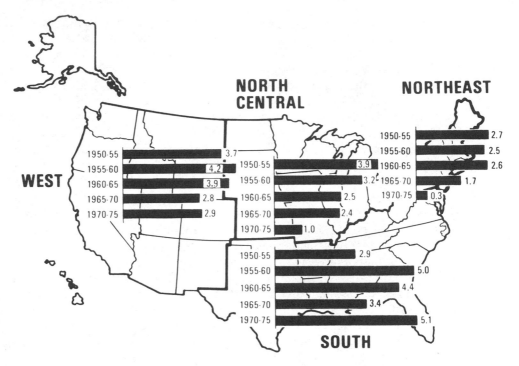

Figure 5-19   Cartographic diagram of population growth, by region. United States, 1950–1975. Numbers to right of bars indicate five-year population increase in millions. (From cover of U.S. Bureau of the Census, *Current Population Reports*, series P-25, no. 640, November 1976.)

tween two geographic distributions. Choropleth maps placed side-by-side or overlaid for visual comparison enable the viewer to examine the spatial correlation of the distributions. But the spatial correlation may be markedly stronger or weaker than the statistical correlation, which can be displayed graphically in a scatter diagram, as in the right side of Figure 5-21. For statistical correlations based on geographic data, areal units are treated as statistical-geographic equals, regardless of population size or land area, and are represented on a scatter diagram by uniform dots. Because political and other reporting units can vary greatly in land area, large places, often with comparatively small populations, can distort visual estimates of statistical correlation based on maps. The categories selected for choropleth maps further confound visual estimation: class intervals may even be deliberately manipulated to prove a point or to distort reality.[48] Nonetheless, map pairs and overlays can provide a useful supplement to the scatter diagram, which inherently ignores urban-suburban-exurban pat-

[48] For a discussion of the limitations of cartographic correlation, see Monmonier, *Maps, Distortion, and Meaning*, pp. 29–33.

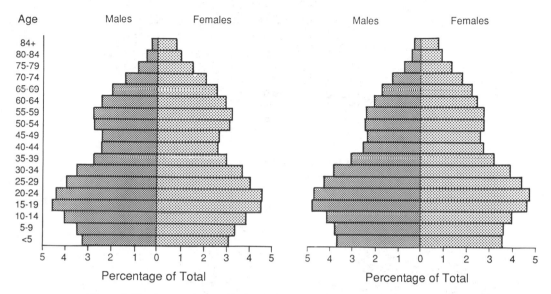

Figure 5-20   Age-sex pyramids for Pennsylvania (left) and the United States (right), 1980.

terns around cities, regional consistency, and similar meaningful geographic trends.

Maps and scatter diagrams, which are complementary, can be supplemented by a numerical index, the *product-moment correlation coefficient,* a summary measurement particularly useful when one must examine many possible pairwise relationships.[49] The correlation coefficient ranges from 1.0 for a perfect positive correlation, for which the points in a scatter diagram lie in a straight line sloping upward to the right, to −1.0 for a perfect negative correlation, for which the points lie in a line sloping downward to the right. A value of 0.0 would indicate no linear trend at all, merely a random scatter of points. Intermediate values indicate the direction and strength of the trend by their sign and magnitude, respectively. The relationship in Figure 5-22 portrays, for instance, a correlation of −0.25, indicating a weak negative linear relationship between education and poverty. Because the correlation coefficient measures only the *linear* trend in a scatter diagram, a perfect "curvilinear" pattern of points, lying on a line curving upward to the right, say, would yield a coefficient less than 1.0. When our understanding of a relationship between two variables must be

[49] For a discussion of the theory and formulas for the product-moment correlation coefficient, see David Unwin, *Introductory Spatial Analysis* (London and New York: Methuen, 1981), pp. 196–201.

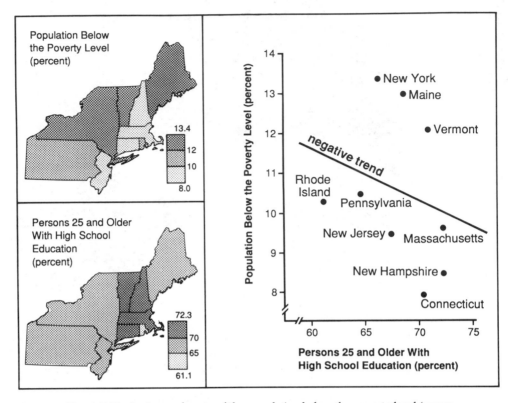

Figure 5-21   Juxtaposed maps of the population below the poverty level (upper left) and the adult population with a high school education (lower left) in the northeastern United States portray geographic association, whereas the scatter diagram (right) and trend line portray statistical association.

more thorough than possible with a single number, maps and scatter diagrams are convenient methods for exploring what the data might reveal.

A final caveat is needed: maps, scatter diagrams, and correlation coefficients based on areal-unit data tell nothing about the demographic behavior of individuals. We cannot interpret an analysis based on county data and showing a strong positive correlation between educational attainment and median per capita income, for example, to mean that persons with more education have above-average earnings. Only data for individuals can tell us that. Moreover, we must interpret census data aggregated by areal units only for the given level of aggregation: we thus should qualify our interpretation and say that "populations aggregated at the county level with high rates of educational attainment tend to have high per capita income." And we should be prepared to discover that the correlation might be notably different were the data to reflect state averages or a random sample of households. (Poorly educated millionaires can afford college-trained servants, after all.) To do otherwise would risk a serious

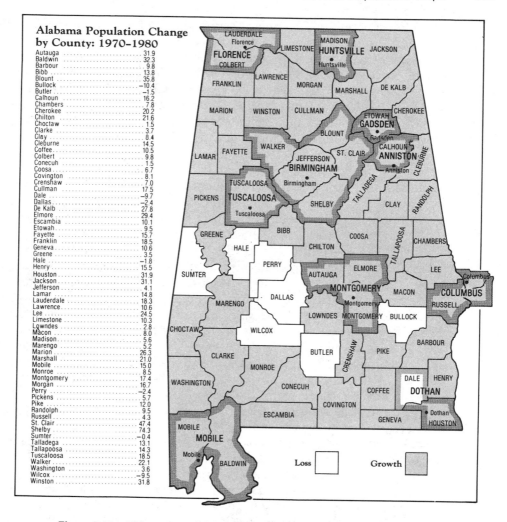

Alabama Population Change by County: 1970–1980

County	Change
Autauga	31.9
Baldwin	32.3
Barbour	9.8
Bibb	13.8
Blount	35.8
Bullock	−10.4
Butler	−1.5
Calhoun	16.2
Chambers	7.8
Cherokee	20.2
Chilton	21.6
Choctaw	1.5
Clarke	3.7
Clay	8.4
Cleburne	14.5
Coffee	10.5
Colbert	9.8
Conecuh	1.5
Coosa	6.7
Covington	8.1
Crenshaw	7.0
Cullman	17.5
Dale	−9.7
Dallas	−2.4
De Kalb	27.8
Elmore	29.4
Escambia	10.1
Etowah	9.5
Fayette	15.7
Franklin	18.5
Geneva	10.6
Greene	3.5
Hale	−1.8
Henry	15.5
Houston	31.9
Jackson	31.1
Jefferson	4.1
Lamar	14.8
Lauderdale	18.3
Lawrence	10.6
Lee	24.5
Limestone	10.3
Lowndes	2.8
Macon	8.0
Madison	5.6
Marengo	5.2
Marion	26.3
Marshall	21.0
Mobile	15.0
Monroe	8.5
Montgomery	17.4
Morgan	16.7
Perry	−2.4
Pickens	5.7
Pike	12.0
Randolph	9.5
Russell	4.3
St. Clair	47.4
Shelby	74.3
Sumter	−0.4
Talladega	13.1
Tallapoosa	14.3
Tuscaloosa	18.5
Walker	22.1
Washington	3.6
Wilcox	−9.5
Winston	31.8

Figure 5-22 Alabama population change by county, 1970–1980. (From Joseph J. Molnar and Sheila Carroll-Portis, "Close Up, Alabama," *American Demographics* 6, no. 8 [August 1984], 41; used with permission.)

conceptual error known to geographers and other social scientists as the "ecological fallacy."[50]

Demographics and Marketing

At the national, regional, and local levels, maps and graphics play indispensable roles in both the daily and the longer-range aspects of planning and development

[50] For a discussion of the ecological fallacy, see W. S. Robinson, "Ecological Correlations and the Behavior of Individuals," *American Sociological Review* 15, no. 3 (June 1950), 351–57.

of all fire, police, and emergency services, and of sanitary and water services as well. The usefulness of maps transcends public-private boundaries when applied in normally private-sector operations such as marketing and facilities siting. Since many of these cartographic subjects are discussed elsewhere—notably in Chapter 6, "Political Maps," and Chapter 7, "Maps of the Municipality"—the few examples treated here are largely demographic in focus.

"Demographics," the application of population data to marketing and its many strategies, is one of the most current terms in the use of demography generally and of population maps in particular. Approaches vary, obviously, depending upon the product line, and thus demand a breadth of understanding of the elements and components of population change. It seems obvious that size of the population, its composition, and its distribution—*the elements*—all play important roles in marketing. After all, the magnitude of the target population and its characteristics affect the manner in which the total population as well as a variety of subpopulations array themselves over the area under scrutiny. As for the components of change, fertility is important because infants, especially first-born, are prime targets for many manufacturers. Think about all those purchases—from nursery furniture and toys to pharmaceuticals and clothing, if diapers are properly classified as clothing. Mortality is important too, for death often occurs after extensive medical services have been provided and also demands an additional set that concerns funerals, cemetery plots, and monuments. Migration often places families and individuals in new residences (new to them, if not new in construction), in this case demanding an array of goods and services associated with "settling in."

In one of its series of "Close Ups," *American Demographics* describes Alabama as "a slow but steady participant in the Sunbelt's boom."[51] The magazine discusses regional trends among blacks, declines in the farm population, metropolitan-nonmetropolitan differences in patterns of growth, labor force changes, income, marriage, housing, and education, noting differences between blacks and whites in almost all cases. However, the single graphic, a map of population change by county for 1970 to 1980 (see Figure 5-22), has no caption and is not mentioned in the text, except by implication. In this single-state vignette, however, the map needs neither caption nor mention because its subject summarizes much of the article's content and stands alone quite well.

A periodical devoted to marketing, *Sales and Marketing Management*, has an annual issue, its "Survey of Buying Power," which is literally full of demographic data.[52] In addition to several feature articles, this special issue highlights metropolitan areas by population density, regional trends among the largest metropolitan areas, and retail sales and effective buying power for both leading and lagging metropolitan markets. It examines metropolitan areas with large

---

[51] Joseph J. Molnar and Sheila Carroll-Portis, "Close Up, Alabama," *American Demographics* 6, no. 8 (August 1984), 40–42.

[52] "1984 Survey of Buying Power," *Sales and Marketing Management* 133, no. 2 (July 23, 1984).

numbers of black and Hispanic consumers, and summarizes trends for house-holds of various size and for rural areas, as well as for the nation, the nine census divisions, and the states. Demographic tables in this periodical also survey buying power for metropolitan areas, counties and cities, organized by state and Canadian province. Maps portray the geographic patterns of metropolitan areas with the greatest population densities, large metropolitan areas with substantial population losses, states with significant Hispanic populations, metropolitan-nonmetropolitan differences in sales growth, and states leading the nation in growth in households.[53] Although few in number in comparison to the scores of pages devoted to tabular data, these simple, straightforward maps communicate with little chance of misunderstanding and supplement well the issue's text and data.

Emergency Management

Aside from the obvious life-and-death drama explicit in fertility and mortality, another area of population study and mapping literally deals with life and death—emergency management and planning. Under the aegis of the Federal Emergency Management Agency (FEMA), this field addresses hazards of natural and human origin at all levels. FEMA's operations are intended to insure that government continues to function and that resources are mobilized during national security emergencies; to support state and local governments in planning for, responding to, and recovering from emergencies; to develop practical applications of research in order to diminish the impact of disasters and emergencies; to coordinate civil defense preparedness in case of nuclear attack, as well as power plant or nuclear weapon accidents; to reduce losses from fire; and to administer flood insurance programs.[54]

Among the many activities of FEMA, those associated with nuclear attack and accident are widely publicized and sometimes controversial. For example, the U.S. General Accounting office and FEMA have disputed the latter's role in evacuation plans.[55] Indeed, the entire issue of evacuation of areas around nuclear power plants is controversial, as are many aspects of nuclear energy generally, and cartographic presentations are often used to argue one side or the other. In a study of survival after a hypothetical nuclear attack on Great Britain, for instance, geographers Stan Openshaw and Philip Steadman criticized estimates made by the British government's Home Office for being overly optimistic. Using the results of a hypothetical situation, these researchers plotted by county the population likely to survive the attack and concluded that "the

[53] Ibid., pp. A-8–A-9, A-52, A-54, and A-56.

[54] For a brief overview of the many responsibilities and operations of FEMA, see U.S. Federal Emergency Management Agency, *This is the Federal Emergency Management Agency*, L-135 (Washington, D.C., May 1983).

[55] Middletown, New York, *Times-Herald Record*, 24 August 1984, p. 28.

current 'stay put' policy may condemn a large portion of the urban population of Britain to an early death."[56] As for mapping survivorship in the United States, FEMA considered its earlier maps of high-risk areas out of date and embarked on a major revision in the 1980s.[57]

Heat and radiation are not the only hazards of a nuclear blast. A panel sponsored by the National Research Council (NRC) was not satisfied with how the military shields electronic equipment from the pulse of electromagnetic energy released in a high-altitude nuclear explosion. With no atmospheric tests by the United States or the Soviet Union for more than two decades, knowledge about these effects is uncertain. But knowledgeable scientists believe that an electromagnetic pulse (EMP) could disrupt communications, involuntarily fire missiles, cause radar-controlled aircraft to crash, and among a variety of civilian effects, create havoc in and around the home by destroying TV sets, damaging car ignitions, and disrupting local power. The impact on computers would be widespread, it is projected, eradicating the machines' memories. Aside from reporting suggested solutions to these disruptions, the NRC report summarized the impact of an electromagnetic pulse with a map showing how the area affected would vary with the height of detonation. The punch line of the study is that at a height of 480 km (300 mi) the blast would create a pulse felt across the entire 48 contiguous states, well into Canada, and deeply into Mexico and the Caribbean.[58]

Although it may not elicit emotions as strong as the fear of nuclear attack or accident, the flood hazard is an ever-present threat in many communities in the United States. Although the Flood Disaster Protection Act was passed in 1968, Hurricane Agnes, which four years later ravaged significant sections of the Northeast, gave the National Flood Insurance Program a new urgency. In exchange for the adoption by communities of flood-plain management to protect life and property, the National Flood Insurance Program covers property owners against flood damage. FEMA, which administers the program, also provides technical assistance in management of flood plains and encourages construction in areas above those that are flood prone. As of 1983, about 17,000 communities were in the program, and almost 2 million properties were covered.[59]

A central tool of the program is the Flood Insurance Rate Map, which provides an accurate rendering of the distribution of flood-prone areas. A typical hazard map, such as Figure 5-23, shows areas likely to be inundated by theoretical floods occurring every 100 and 500 years and, as the legend explains, a

---

[56] Stan Openshaw and Philip Steadman, "The Bomb: Where Will the Survivors Be?" *Geographical Magazine* 55, no. 6 (June 1983), 293–96.

[57] U.S. Federal Emergency Management Agency, *High Risk Areas for Civil Defense Planning Purposes*, TR-82 (Washington, D.C., September 1979).

[58] *New York Times*, 8 August 1984, p. A-12.

[59] FEMA, *This is the Federal Emergency Management Agency*.

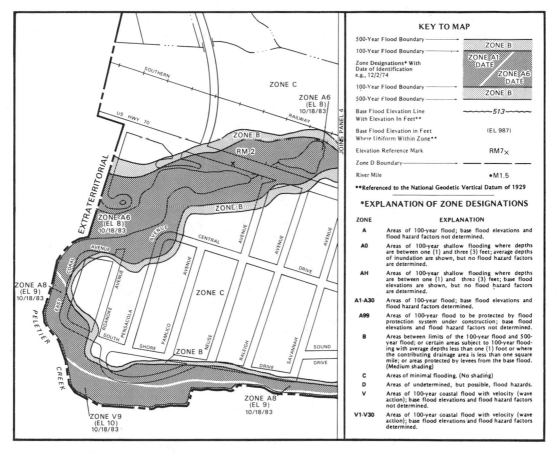

Figure 5-23   Part of Flood Insurance Rate Map, Town of Morehead City, North Carolina. (Photographically reduced. Courtesy of the Federal Emergency Management Agency.)

variety of areas between these extremes—those with minimal flooding and those with undetermined status. The map delineates likely flood zones, lists base floor elevations, dates the year each zone was identified, shows where coastal flooding occurs, and indicates the severity of wave action.

Figure 5-23 is taken from maps describing the details of flood hazard for Morehead City, North Carolina, a coastal area about 140 km (85 mi) northeast of Wilmington. The map is used essentially to determine which properties in the community are located within flood-prone areas and are thus eligible for enrollment in and coverage under the National Flood Insurance Program. The map shown is actually one of five for Morehead City, and repays careful study by offering detailed explanations of the symbols shown and the local likelihood of flood hazard. By its existence, this map is an effective control on land use, discouraging maldistribution of population by identifying not only flood hazard, but also the dangers of residing on such land and the problems of developing flood zones in general.

FOR FURTHER READING

FISHER, HOWARD T., *Mapping Information: The Graphic Display of Quantitative Information.* Cambridge, Mass.: Abt Books, 1982.

McEREDY, COLIN, and RICHARD JONES, *Atlas of World Population History.* London: Allen Lane, 1978.

MONKHOUSE, F. J., and H. R. WILKINSON, *Maps and Diagrams: Their Compilation and Construction* (3d ed.), pp. 312–95. London: Methuen, 1971.

RHIND, DAVID, ed., *A Census User's Handbook.* London: Methuen, 1983.

SCHNELL, GEORGE A., and MARK MONMONIER, *The Study of Population: Elements, Patterns, Processes.* Columbus, Ohio: Charles E. Merrill, 1983.

TUFTE, EDWARD, *The Visual Display of Quantitative Information.* Cheshire, Conn.: Graphics Press, 1983.

UNWIN, DAVID, *Introductory Spatial Analysis.* London and New York: Methuen, 1981.

CHAPTER SIX

Political Maps

A little knowledge can be dangerous, as the oft-quoted saying goes. "A little knowledge" probably contributes to the belief that geography is concerned largely with the physical environment, place names, and principal exports—and thus useful largely to Trivial Pursuit enthusiasts. A similar misconception surrounds the "political map," which many people believe is limited to mundane maps of boundaries. Although boundary maps are indeed important political maps, the variety of maps dealing with political sovereignty is much greater than suggested by the straightforward political maps found at the front of atlases and as frontispieces in textbooks about geography, history, and international relations.

Identification of the wider role of political maps requires understanding the terms *politics, political,* and *political geography.* Webster's simple definition of *politics* as "the art or science of government" requires a restricting elaboration: "political affairs or business; specif. competition between competing interest groups or individuals for power or leadership (as in government), political activities characterized by artful and often dishonest practices."[1] The word *political* relates to the making of government policy, as well as to the administration of such policy once it has been made. A pejorative connotation to these terms—

[1] *Webster's Ninth New Collegiate Dictionary* (Springfield, Mass.: Merriam-Webster, 1985), p. 911.

201

"often dishonest practices"—relates to the "competition between . . . groups or individuals for power and leadership."[2]

Political geography is concerned with political-spatial organizations, the geographical implications of political processes at all scales and levels of organization.[3] In dealing with politically organized areas, political geography is often concerned with these units' resources and areal extent. Yet, as a discipline, political geography focuses on the study of the state.[4] Geographic methodologist Richard Hartshorne viewed political geography as "the study of the variation of political phenomena from place to place in interconnection with variation in other features of the earth as the home of man" and included in these political phenomena features produced by political forces and the political ideas that generate these forces.[5] Traditional themes in political geography are "boundaries, capitals, growth of nation states, and national voting."[6]

This chapter is organized to cover themes usually associated with political geography, but to concentrate on those in which map use and appreciation are obvious and appropriate. One could easily quibble over what has been omitted, for the field is vast and our space is limited. Beginning with topics international in scope, the chapter examines the way in which maps and atlases conventionally have presented the world's nations. Discussion of projections, viewing directions, and traditional cartographic practices shows how many maps in our culture heighten the importance of Europe and of the Northern Hemisphere in general. Discussion of geopolitics, propaganda, and boundaries follows, with the latter highlighting change in boundaries and law of the sea. A national section looks at boundary types, land survey, and the cessions that combined to produce the 48 contiguous United States of America. Apportionment and electoral geography constitute the chapter's culminating sections.

HAVES AND HAVE-NOTS: MAPS AND NATIONAL STATUS

Map conventions have promoted misinformation through a kind of cartographic chauvinism. For example, the phrase "down south" connotes an inferior position below north. From this usage comes the fallacious notion that rivers *properly* flow from north to south (in the Northern Hemisphere, of course) and that those which do not are aberrant. Needless to say, many of the Soviet Union's rivers flow the "wrong way" in their Arctic quest, and even the little Wallkill

---

[2] Ibid., p. 910.

[3] W. A. Douglas Jackson and Edward F. Bergman, *A Geography of Politics* (Dubuque, Iowa: Wm. C. Brown, 1973), p. vii.

[4] Norman J. G. Pounds, *Political Geography*, 2d ed. (New York: McGraw-Hill, 1972), p. 1.

[5] Richard Hartshorne, "Political Geography in the Modern World," *Journal of Conflict Resolution* 4, no. 1 (March 1960), 52.

[6] Stanley D. Brunn, *Geography and Politics in America* (New York: Harper & Row, 1974), p. xii.

River flows north and east from New Jersey's highlands into New York's mid-Hudson region. Take a world map and turn it upside-down or east-side-up (180° longitude at the top): these are strange views of the world for those schooled on maps with north up and 60 percent or more of the mapped area shown being devoted to the Northern Hemisphere.

Peters's Projection versus Mercator's

In the early 1970s, a West German historian, Arno Peters, redrew the customary world map in an attempt to show countries of Africa, Asia, and Latin America in a manner more consistent with the late twentieth century, when Europe no longer dominates the world (see Figure 6-1). When many map projections now in use were developed, Europe was economically and politically dominant, of course. According to Peters, his "new" map is not only equal-area, with all places shown in a comparable way, but also "equal axis," with meridians extending north-south as straight, vertical lines so that "points can be seen in their precise directional relationship—northwest, southeast, northeast, or southwest." The projection is "equal position," showing all places equidistant from the equator on the same straight-line parallel, and "fair to all peoples," in its accurate portrayal of each country's size and location. Thus Peters claims that his map is superior to the familiar projection developed by Gerhardus Mercator because the latter portrays the "North" (North America, Greenland, Europe, the Soviet Union, and Japan) as larger than the "South," when in fact the North is less than half the area of the South. Mercator's map incorrectly shows two-thirds of the earth's land area lying north of the equator. Although Europe's area is about 9.9 million km^2 (3.8 million mi^2) and South America's area is roughly 18 million km^2 (approximately 6.9 million mi^2), Europe is larger in Mercator's map (Figure 6-1).[7]

Unfortunately, the map Peters selected for comparison, Mercator's, was designed for navigation: its conformal properties and grid are intended to show lines of constant compass direction as straight lines. The use of Mercator's map for other, general purposes (as a political map, say) merely reflects the woeful ignorance of many map users. Moreover, the qualities pointed out by Peters in touting his map projection are shared by many equal-area maps devised long before his "new" map appeared. Indeed, Johann Heinrich Lambert first described the Cylindrical Equal-Area Projection in 1772.[8] Further, cartographers who have examined Peters's map indicate generally that there is little new about it and that Peters's claims are, in the main, inaccurate. For example, since par-

---

[7] From marginal notes, "Why This New World Map?" on *World Map in Equal Area Presentation, Peters Projection* (New York: Friendship Press, undated).

[8] D. H. Maling, "Peters' Wunderwerk," *Kartographische Nachrichten* 24, no. 4 (August 1974), 153.

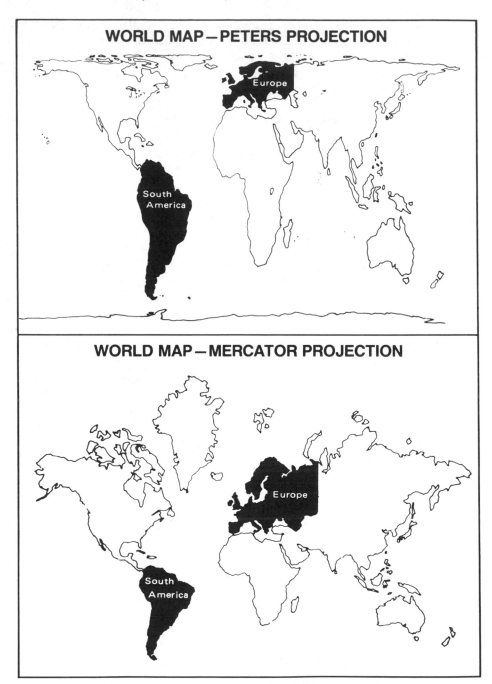

Figure 6-1 Peters's projection and Mercator's projection. (Courtesy Friendship Press, New York, undated; used with permission.)

allels become shorter north and south of the equator, how can a map on which *all* parallels are the same length be factual concerning distance?[9] Peters's objections to the Mercator map were not the first; an earlier generation of cartographers were concerned about Mercator's projective distortion of area, as the following statement made in the 1940s illustrates: "Mercator's projection for world maps should be abjured by authors and publishers for all purposes . . . the misconceptions it has engendered have done infinite harm. A map that makes Greenland look larger than South America, instead of smaller than Argentina, is not suited to portray world relationships. The Mercator is ideal only for navigation."[10]

Cartographic history notwithstanding, the National Council of Churches in the United States has been a ready adopter and vocal advocate of Peters's projection, which it has promoted as a cartographic messiah at press conferences and in its publications. Although the council's motives in promoting geopolitical fairness are beyond reproach, on cartographic grounds the projection itself is a questionable addition to the hundreds of extant equal-area projections. Perhaps the last word (here) on distortion and map projection comes from a writer who agrees that new maps can be enlightening: "if you want to free your mind from all the preconceived ideas and prejudices that flat world maps seem to generate . . . get a globe—and keep rolling it around."[11]

Atlases and National Pride

National atlases are the publication of officially collected geographic knowledge and, perhaps of greater and more lasting importance, symbols of national unity and pride. Christopher Saxton's *Atlas of England and Wales*, completed in 1579 and considered by some to be the first national atlas, not only provided useful information to the government of Elizabeth I, but also afforded an identity to local areas and counties by illustrating how they were a part of England. Not much later, *Le Theatre Francois* proved most useful in proclaiming the unity of France under Henry IV. *The Statistical Atlas of the United States*, compiled by Francis A. Walker and published in 1874, represents this country's first "national atlas." Indeed, maps of settlement and westward expansion, along with Walker's essay, have been cited as the kernel of the idea for historian Frederick Jackson Turner's frontier concept, the frontier as significant in American history. At a time when science was emerging as an institution, the iconic role of a

---

[9] Arthur H. Robinson described many problems with the projection in responding to "American Cartographers Vehemently Denounce German Historian's Projection" in "What they say," a feature of *ASCM Bulletin* no. 60 (February 1978), 27.

[10] S. W. Boggs, "Cartohypnosis," *Scientific Monthly* 64, no. 6 (June 1947), 474.

[11] "Upside Down, Inside Out," *Economist* 293, nos. 7373/7374 (December 22, 1984), 24.

national atlas as a scientific triumph fit well with its more overt information function.[12]

Much later, *The Atlas of Egypt*, published in 1928 by the Survey of Egypt, epitomized the postcolonial national atlas, with its title page proudly announcing that the atlas was produced "by command of his majesty, King Fouad I" and ignoring Egypt's status as a British protectorate from 1914 to 1922. Symbolic of Marxist thought, the *Bolshoi Sovietskiy Atlas Mira* (the Great Soviet Atlas of the World), which occupied 175 cartographers and was published in two volumes (1937 and 1939), presents a great number of economic themes. Although the Soviets suppressed distribution of the atlas in 1939, as World War II began, the U.S. War Department and Department of State had obtained copies, which provided the U.S. military with much needed geographical information. In fact, the U.S. Office of Strategic Services (forerunner of the C.I.A.) produced a facsimile edition in color in 1943, attesting to the value of the Great Atlas to our intelligence community. By 1980, many lesser developed countries had sought to detail their geography and proclaim their nationhood through a national atlas.[13]

On the subject of less-developed countries, the *Third World Atlas*, published in 1983, addresses three questions:

"What is the Third World?

How was it made?

What changes are taking place in the Third World today?"

The Atlas is organized in three sections that attempt to answer these questions with maps and text. Throughout the first section, all world maps delineate the Third World as the "South," or the area south of the Rio Grande in the Western Hemisphere and including Africa, "West Asia" (the Middle East), and Asia south of the USSR in the Eastern Hemisphere. Australia and New Zealand, of course, are in the "North."[14]

GEOPOLITICS AND PROPAGANDA

Global strategists of the nineteenth century and the first half of the twentieth argued for sea power or for the power associated with great land area, and eventually for air power. Yet much of what they had to say may have become

---

[12] Mark Monmonier, "The Rise of the National Atlas," draft of a paper presented at "Images of the World: The Atlas Through History," a symposium sponsored by the Center for the Book and the Geography and Map Division, Library of Congress, Washington, D.C., October 25 and 26, 1984.

[13] Ibid.

[14] Ben Crow and Alan Thomas, *Third World Atlas* (Milton Keynes, Eng., and Philadelphia, Pa.: Open University Press, 1983).

academic in August 1945, when one plane dropped one bomb and destroyed Hiroshima, Japan. Nonetheless, the evolution of geopolitical thought is an important topic in a book like this because maps were so important a part of geopolitics, both the ideas per se and their communication.

Heartland/Rimland

In a general history of Europe and North America from 1660 to 1783, from the age of sailing ships to the end of the American Revolution, Alfred Thayer Mahan focused upon sea power. In his opus, this American naval officer argued that "whoever rules the waves rules the world." Mahan based his thesis on six elements affecting sea power, the prowess of navies and merchant marines:

1. Geographical position with respect to sea lanes, coasts, and land boundaries
2. Physical conformation, such as harbors, inlets, and stream outlets
3. Extent of territory, specifically the length of coastline and the nature of harbors and their defense
4. Number of population, including the potential for building and manning both merchant and naval vessels
5. National character with regard to "aptitude for commercial pursuits," since sea power is "really based upon a peaceful and extensive commerce"
6. Character of the government in influencing development of sea power[15]

The elements in this list are familiar to geographers and others who adopt a geographic approach to politics.

Although Mahan's arguments were translated into realities in the United States—with the construction of a huge navy, the building of the Panama Canal, and the establishment of bases in Hawaii and the Caribbean—events occurring before his death soon diminished the impact of his arguments. The first and most obvious setback to a doctrine of naval supremacy was the Wright Brothers' flight at Kitty Hawk, North Carolina, in 1903. The second setback was the influential ideas of the English geographer Sir Halford J. Mackinder, who emphasized land power rather than sea power. Developed first in a paper, "The Geographical Pivot of History," presented to the Royal Geographical Society in 1904 and then in a book, *Democratic Ideals and Reality*, Mackinder's union of geography and political science influenced academics and world leaders alike in emphasizing "Euro-Asia" and Russia's potential for military and political

---

[15] Alfred Thayer Mahan, *The Influence of Sea Power Upon History, 1660–1783* (Boston: Little, Brown, 1890), pp. iii and 25–58.

The Natural Seats of Power

Pivot area: wholly continental
Outer crescent: wholly oceanic
Inner crescent: partly continental, partly oceanic

Figure 6-2   Mackinder's "Pivot Area." (From Halford J. Mackinder, "The Geographical Pivot of History," *Geographical Journal* 23, no. 4 [April 1904], 435.)

strength.[16] Mackinder's hypothesis was based on a series of three logically connected assertions:

"Who rules East Europe commands the Heartland.
Who rules the Heartland commands the World-Island.
Who rules the World-Island commands the world."[17]

These principles of Mackinder's "geopolitics"—a term coined by the Swedish political scientist Rudolf Kjellen—clearly placed the "Pivot Area" in czarist Russia, in the supreme strategic position, as Figure 6-2 illustrates. Mackinder viewed the "Pivot Area" as impregnable to attack by sea and thus capable of building a land power great enough to achieve world hegemony (leadership). In Mackinder's hypothesis, the "Heartland" is the "Pivot Area" modified somewhat to

[16] Halford J. Mackinder, "The Geographical Pivot of History," *Geographical Journal* 23, no. 4 (April 1904), 421–37; and *Democratic Ideals and Reality* (New York: Henry Holt, 1919 and 1942).

[17] Mackinder, *Democratic Ideals and Reality*, p. 150.

include the core of Eastern Europe, much of Russia, and their peripheries. The "World-Island" includes coastal Europe, all of Africa, Southern and Eastern Asia ("Monsoon Coastland"), and the Middle East (Arabia).[18] Figure 6-3 portrays the Heartland and the World-Island.

Mackinder considered "Europe and European history as subordinate to Asia and Asiatic history, for European civilization is . . . the outcome of the secular struggle against Asiatic invasions."[19] He remarked that the most noteworthy aspect of modern Europe's political map was Russia's vast area. Thus he portrayed Russia as capable of creating and maintaining land-based might of proportions that would permit world domination.

No mere academic theoretician, Mackinder injected his Heartland thesis into the 1919 Paris Peace Conference that followed World War I; he recommended buffer states in Eastern Europe to prevent any nation(s) from gaining control of the Heartland, especially through a German-Soviet alliance. The conference's subsequent creation of independent states from territories that had been parts of Austria-Hungary, Germany, or Russia varied little from Mackinder's proposal and included Estonia, Latvia, and Lithuania (along the Baltic Sea) and Poland, Czechoslovakia, and Yugoslavia (extending from the Baltic to the Adriatic) as Figure 6-4 shows.[20]

The German political geographer and military tactician Karl Haushofer borrowed much from Mackinder in framing what was to become the Nazi version of geopolitics. Haushofer's *Geopolitik* (in German) took on a more sinister aspect as it became associated almost completely with Nazi concepts of world domination and racial superiority. Haushofer also wrote of the need for *Lebensraum*—the German word for "living space"—a concept attractive to Nazi leaders, who preached that the German state needed room to grow and develop. Haushofer's fascination with the Heartland concept led to his calling for an alliance between the Soviet Union and Germany on the eve of World War II. The German-Soviet alliance of 1939 demonstrated Haushofer's support by the German military hierarchy and the realization of Mackinder's greatest fear. Fortunately for the Allies, the pact was short lived: Hitler soon opened the second front by attacking the Soviet Union in 1941.[21]

Writing almost 40 years after publication of "The Geographical Pivot of History," Mackinder concluded that "if the Soviet Union emerges from this war as conqueror of Germany, she must rank as the greatest land power on the globe. Moreover, she will be the Power in the strategically strongest defensive position. The Heartland is the greatest natural fortress on earth. For the first time in history it is manned by a garrison sufficient both in number and qual-

[18] Ibid., p. 7.

[19] Mackinder, "Geographical Pivot," p. 3.

[20] Andreas Dorpalen, *The World of General Haushofer: Geopolitics in Action* (New York and Toronto: Farrar & Rinehart, 1942), p. 70.

[21] Ibid., pp. 154–55.

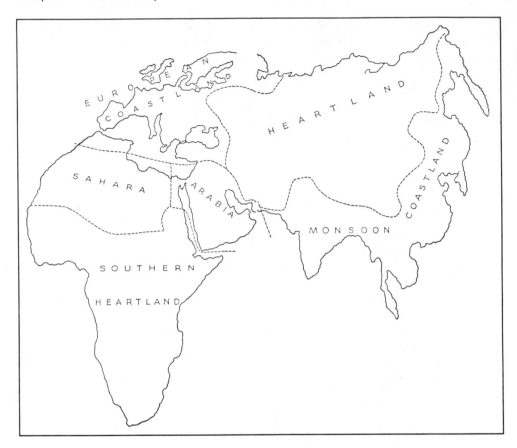

Figure 6-3 Mackinder's World-Island, divided into six natural regions with equal-area projection. (From Halford J. Mackinder, *Democratic Ideals and Reality* [New York: Henry Holt, 1919 and 1942]. Copyright © 1919, 1942 by Henry Holt and Company, Inc. Reprinted by permission of CBS College Publishing.)

ity."[22] Not surprisingly, Mackinder had "no hesitation in saying [the Heartland Concept] is more valid and useful today than it was twenty or forty years ago."[23]

In *The Geography of the Peace*, published in 1944, an American political scientist, Nicholas Spykman, maintained that "the Mackinder dictum . . . is false. If there is to be a slogan for the power politicians of the Old World, it must be 'Who controls the rimland rules Eurasia; who rules Eurasia controls the destinies of the world.'"[24] Figure 6-5 illustrates that Spykman's "rimland" is equivalent

[22] Halford J. Mackinder, "The Round World and the Winning of the Peace," *Foreign Affairs* 21, no. 4 (July 1943), 601 and 603.

[23] Ibid.

[24] Nicholas Spykman, *The Geography of the Peace* (New York: Harcourt, Brace, 1944), p. 43.

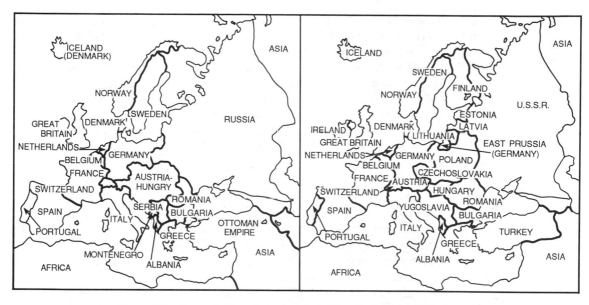

Figure 6-4 Europe's boundaries before (left) and after (right) World War I.

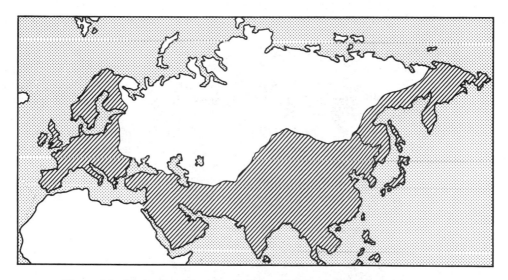

Figure 6-5 Rimland and heartland. (From Nicholas John Spykman, *The Geography of the Peace* [New York: Harcourt Brace, 1944], p. 52. Slightly adapted from *The Geography of the Peace* by Nicholas John Spykman, copyright 1944 by Harcourt Brace Jovanovich, Inc. Reproduced by permission of the publisher.)

to Mackinder's "Marginal Crescent," the area of Europe and mainland Asia minus the Heartland and plus the Arabian Peninsula. Spykman saw the rimland "as an intermediate region situated . . . between the heartland and the marginal seas. It functions as a vast buffer zone of conflict between sea power and land power. . . . Its amphibious nature lies at the basis of its security problems."[25] Spykman thus referred to the rimland's battles with both Russia (Mackinder's Heartland) and Great Britain and Japan (the sea power of offshore islands).

Perhaps Spykman's most legitimate argument favoring Rimland over Heartland was that, because of climate, western Russia and not the central region of Siberia was that country's focus of agriculture (and thus the Heartland's). Indeed, as Figure 6-6 shows, except for the narrow extension of the North European Plain into the Heartland, the cultivated lands of Eurasia are found mostly in the rimland.[26] In addition, Spykman cited the alliances of Eurasia as having mixed land and sea power with and against each other—rimland states with Great Britain against Russia with "rimlanders" as allies, or a rimland power against Russia and Great Britain. Thus he argued that a war between land powers and sea powers would never occur.[27]

Finally, Spykman cited Mackinder's last published work on the Heartland as demonstrating Mackinder's recognition of "the predominant importance of the rimland and the necessity of British-Russian-United States collaboration to prevent the growth of German power in the area."[28] Specifically, Spykman referred to Mackinder's statement in 1943 that the Heartland *now* excluded the area east of the Yenisei River because of its rugged terrian and sparse settlement, placing the Heartland in the Soviet's area of greatest population and development.[29] Geopolitical strategists relied upon a variety of maps for their "data."

Air Power and the Nuclear Age

In 1952, discussing previous generations of strategists, aviation pioneer Alexander de Seversky cited the "classic axiom of the art of war" as the "focusing of resources and effort in the crucial strategic dimensions, instead of frittering away strength on secondary objectives."[30] That is, nations at war had concentrated efforts on becoming invincible on land *or* at sea, and Americans accepted sea power as more important because of their nation's insular position. He viewed the earth's atmosphere as the truly efficient medium through which to attack, citing the development of air power since World War II as providing the

---

[25] Ibid., p. 41.

[26] Ibid., pp. 38–39.

[27] Ibid., p. 43.

[28] Ibid., p. 44.

[29] Mackinder, "Round World," pp. 598–99.

[30] Alexander P. de Seversky, *Air Power: Key to Survival* (London: Herbert Jenkins, 1952), p. 288.

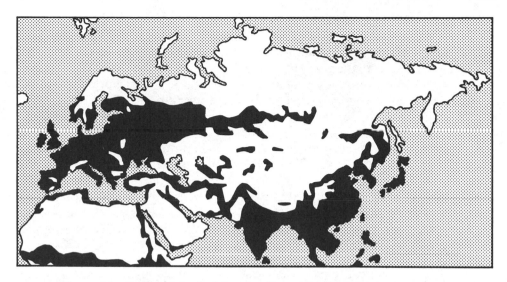

Figure 6-6 Cultivated land of Eurasia. (From Nicholas John Spykman, *The Geography of the Peace* [New York: Harcourt Brace, 1944]. Slightly adapted from *The Geography of the Peace* by Nicholas John Spykman, copyright 1944 by Harcourt Brace Jovanovich, Inc. Reproduced by permission of the publisher.)

wherewithal "to strike any target from [the] home base; to accept battle anywhere regardless of distance."[31] Control of the skies, he maintained, must be the highest priority of warring nations located on different continents, even at the expense of land and sea power.

Two decades later, political scientist Alan Henrikson asserted that "Air-Age Globalism" had been responsible for a sweeping change, beginning in the 1940s, in the way the people of the United States viewed and mapped the earth. The "Cold War," the attempt by the United States and the Soviet Union to contain each other, resulted, Henrikson says, in a shrinking earth that was to become a part of the work of geographers and cartographers.[32]

With a new "globalism" brought on by the United States being attacked and drawn into World War II, there was need for "a new way of representing the earth's geostrategic pattern graphically—a new cartography to complement the so-called 'new geography.'"[33] The cartographers of the 1940s tried to achieve "a geographical sense" according to Richard Edes Harrison, and in so doing called for the flexibility of cartographic presentation and of outlook in viewing the world that Henrickson termed "Air-Age Globalism."[34]

[31] Ibid., pp. 288–89.

[32] Alan K. Henrikson, "Maps, Globes, and the 'Cold War,'" *Special Libraries* 65, no. 10–11 (October/November 1974), 445.

[33] Ibid., pp. 446–48, 450–51, and 453.

[34] Ibid., pp. 446–48 and 450.

The new world image required that the round earth be recognized and that it replace the "flat-earth 'Mercator mind'" that placed Japan directly west of California rather than on an arc of a circle, a great circle at first sweeping poleward and then equatorward across the Pacific. With its recognition of a spherical earth, Air-Age Globalism also created a new world view of "continuity and unity." This new view of the earth was brought about, in part at least, by an increased use of airplanes, and the resultant "aerial perspective," a third distinctive feature of Air-Age Globalism. "Polar centrism," the use of the North Pole as the center of the world map, is the fourth and final characteristic of the new world view. Indeed, in 1942 de Seversky had touted the north polar region as the "area of decision" in *Victory Through Air Power*, since the United States's attention would be turned toward the Soviet Union as the Axis Powers became less threatening in World War II. As Figure 6-7 illustrates, the polar azimuthal projection, centered on the North Pole, shows a variety of shortest-distance routes or trajectories from the United States to the Soviet Union as straight lines through the pole. This view was fostered by the American-Soviet confrontation on a seemingly smaller planet without the distraction of other nations seriously vying for great-power status.[35]

Sea, land, or air power as described by the geopoliticians cited here pale in this nuclear-computer-space age. Although war or peace may continue to hinge upon a tenuous balance of power, the fact remains that humankind's destructive capability has never been more awesome. Indeed, perhaps as radical geographer Bill Bunge suggests, the contemporary political map might well show the border of the United States as a map covering the Soviet Union, and vice versa, with the two "super powers" jointly bordering the airspace of other nations.[36] But the geopolitical picture is made more complicated by satellite weapons and the "nuclear capability" of smaller powers such as India and Israel. Today's geopolitical strategist is likely to depend principally on large-scale satellite imagery to verify disarmament or to detect build-up, rather than on small-scale maps to promote or diminish theories.

Propaganda Maps

Discussion of propaganda and maps appropriately follows discussion of geopolitics, since Karl Haushofer turned German geography and cartography into propaganda tools—science without objectivity for the purpose of promoting German nationalism and territorial expansion. (Look, for an example, at the German map depicting Czechoslovakia as an air threat to Germany in Chapter 9, Figure 9-23.) In 1919, when General Haushofer became Professor Haushofer,

[35] Ibid.

[36] W. W. Bunge and R. Bordessa, *The Canadian Alternative: Survival, Expeditions, and Urban Change*, Geographical Monographs, no. 2 (Toronto: Department of Geography, York University, 1975), p. 401.

Figure 6-7   Polar azimuthal equidistant projection showing a polar route from the Soviet Union to the United States. The line is the shortest distance between the points, and the map is the type that became popular during the "Cold War."

he continued to tout his central themes: that, compared to other nations, Germany was cramped for living space (*Lebensraum*), and that Germany needed to educate its youth, the nation's future leaders, in world politics and geography, *Geopolitik*. Haushofer's goal was to persuade all Germans to think geopolitically and their leaders to act geopolitically. One of his greatest weapons was what he termed the "suggestive map," a map strong in support of a particular point of view that underplays or omits facts contrary to the favored opinion or argument. Haushofer's *Geopolitik* found its way into Hitler's vision for world conquest; even *Mein Kampf* incorporated Haushofer's ideas.[37] In fact, some have suggested that Haushofer believed he could use Hitler to advance his concepts. Figure 6-8, "A Study in Empires," effectively illustrates the ideas of insufficient living space and its corollary, the necessity of territorial expansion. The question on the left map is hardly necessary!

Although Swedish political scientist Rudolf Kjellen coined the term *geopolitics* to describe the intersection of geography and politics in interpreting world affairs, and the German geographer Frederick Ratzel was first to describe *Lebensraum*, Haushofer popularized these terms and reduced them to slogans of what might be called a pseudoscience at best. In differentiating between political geography and geopolitics, for example, he concluded that "political geography views the state from the standpoint of space, geopolitics views space from the standpoint of the state."[38]

There is more to cartography as applied to propaganda than *Geopolitik* and its application by regimes such as the Nazis. In "Magic Cartography," Hans Speier described the map as a tool of propaganda in a way which makes it clear that propagandists, not cartographers, misuse maps for purposes other than science and truthful communication. In order for cartographic propaganda to be successful, Speier said in 1941, the science of cartography must be well developed, reproduction capability must be available, and the target population must be unschooled in interpreting maps and their system of symbols. Speier pointed out that propagandists use quirks of shape—such as the fact that the map of Italy resembles a boot—and other map elements with scientific purposes—such as north being at the top of the globe, "higher" than south—to "turn geography into a kind of magic" that subordinates truth to the communication of an idea or viewpoint.[39] Thus geography and cartography become "subservient to the demands of effective symbol manipulation. . . . The propagandist who uses [maps] borrows the prestige of science" but violates its spirit.[40]

According to geographer John Ager, who recently discussed the main variables in propaganda maps, the prime goal of propagandists using maps is to go beyond believability by using visual impact to convince the viewer. The main map variables, he says, are essentially the same for the impartial cartographer and the propagandist; the difference is in how the cartographer and the propagandist manipulate the variables. Ager's list of variables manipulated by the propagandist includes *selection*, which means the choice of information to be shown so as to support the case being made—that is, the "pitch." *Symbols* go far in getting the desired message across, depending on which symbols are used and what size, tone, and design are chosen for them. All maps are distorted,

[37] Dorpalen, *World of General Haushofer*, pp. 16–17 and 19.
[38] Ibid., p. xxi.
[39] Hans Speier, "Magic Cartography," *Social Research* 8, no. 3 (September 1941), 313.
[40] Ibid., p. 330.

A STUDY IN EMPIRES

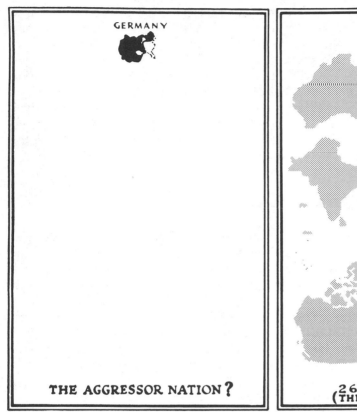

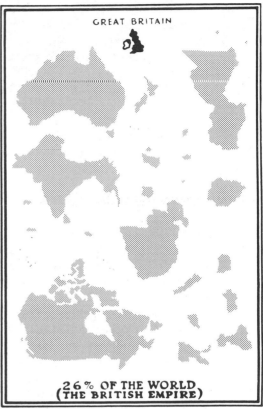

Figure 6-8 A study in empires. (From German Library of Information, *Facts in Review* 2, no. 5 [February 5, 1940], 33.)

but by judicious selection of the *projection* the propagandist can heighten misconceptions, especially when area or spatial relationships are distorted. *Color* and *shading* used in certain ways can increase the relative importance of a map region or, by contrast, render it less important; propagandists commonly use reds and yellows to indicate "us and them," the former color being associated with vitality, the latter with morbidity and cowardice. *Typography*, the lettering on maps, implies all sorts of messages by variation in its size, thickness of line, and style. *Statistics* provide the numerical fodder for graphic devices and are sometimes used to mislead by selection of class-intervals or symbol manipulation. *Combinations* of maps, as in Figure 6-8, can make words superfluous because of the clarity of the graphic message. Finally, the *artist* working on an advertisement or political cartoon may use a map as a part of a presentation, a subsidiary tool that assists in conveying the thought. Ager calls ads and cartoons "non-cartographic maps"; they appear on posters, for example, and are not the primary focus of the picture.[41]

The moral here is that the cartographer or the artist should be careful to communicate geographic data accurately and fairly by careful use of the map variables and, equally important, that the map user should maintain a healthy skepticism about maps and graphics generally. S. W. Boggs suggested that map users who wish not to be taken in should remember "that it is the actual situation on the earth that is significant; that maps have definite limitations as well as unique capabilities; and that map makers are human."[42] His latter point is well taken: not all cartographers have sinister objectives, but some do manage inadvertantly to deceive the map reader. Thus, such cartographers achieve the same end as propagandists. Be informed and be aware.

BOUNDARIES ON LAND AND AT SEA

The subject of boundaries is popular among political geographers—so popular this chapter discusses it twice, here and in a section on the United States. The focus here is on boundary changes and the manipulation of boundaries in power politics. The examples are the natural divisions of Europe viewed over hundreds of years and the case of the Balkans viewed over a 70-year period. Obviously the subject lends itself to cartographic description and analysis. Another topic discussed here is the boundary that defines a nation's seaward jurisdiction. Offshore boundaries lack landmarks, but often show the influence of coastal features. Discussion of the law of the sea thus concludes the section.

Europe's Boundaries: Constancy and Change

American students easily take international boundaries for granted. After all, how long has it been since the United States experienced a major change in the geographic extent of the contiguous 48 states? A look at a time series of European or African maps, however, shows that, on a global scale, change is the rule! Figure 6-9 illustrates the relative permanence of some boundaries between European states. On a continent of conquests and shifting alliances, lines over 400 years old are exceptional. Note that, from west to east, Portugal, The Netherlands, Switzerland, and a part of the Spanish-French boundary are ancient by American or, for that matter, Eastern European standards. In contrast, the political divisions throughout the Eastern European area from the Balkans to the Baltic present a plethora of changing states, as new were carved from old, op-

---

[41] John Ager, "Maps and Propaganda," *Bulletin of the Society of University Cartographers* 11, no. 1 (1977), 4–14.

[42] Boggs, "Cartohypnosis," p. 473.

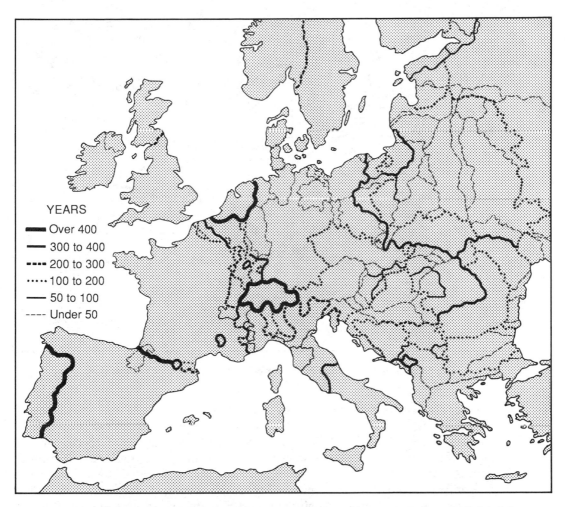

Figure 6-9 Duration of European boundaries. (From Norman J. G. Pounds, *Political Geography* [New York: McGraw-Hill, 1972], p. 37; and Columb S. Gilfillan, "European Political Boundaries," *Political Science Quarterly* 39, no. 3 [September 1924]; used with permission.)

posing sides divided and redivided another's territory, and annexations and political creations proceeded apace.

The Balkans present an especially interesting politico-cartographic example of change. The left half of Figure 6-10 illustrates the Balkan Peninsula before the First Balkan War, which began in late 1912. Bounded by the Black Sea to the east, the Adriatic and Ionian seas to the west, the Sava and Danube rivers to the north, and the Aegean and associated waterways to the south, the Balkan region is quite different on the present-day political map in the right part of

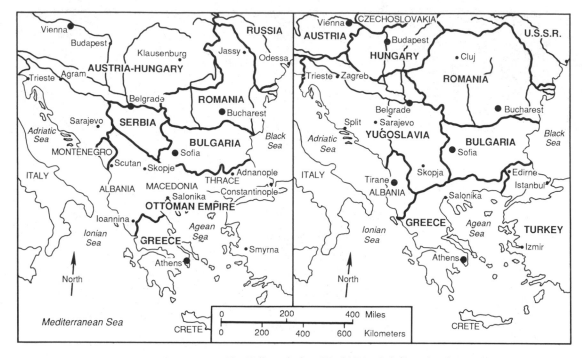

Figure 6-10   The Balkans before World War I (left) and today (right).

Figure 6-10. The earlier map depicts the strong influence of Turkey, since much of the southern area was within the Ottoman Empire. Bulgaria is shown to be a little smaller in 1912 than today, but is essentially in place, and Greece is shown as having once been limited to the southern part of its present lands. The area's geopolitical importance is attested to by its having been called the "Powder Keg of Europe" because of the number of wars that began there.

Briefly, after Roman domination and Slav appearance in the fifth century A.D., the area fell under the Ottoman Empire by 1400. During the period of rampant nationalism, the peoples of the Balkans sought independence from Turkey in the nineteenth century. Greece, Montenegro, Serbia, and Bulgaria eventually gained independence. The First Balkan War erupted as Montenegro fought Turkey; shortly thereafter, Turkey declared war on Serbia, and Bulgaria and Greece soon entered that conflict. Despite an armistice, Turkey fought on until May 1913 rather than relinquish European territory. At that time Serbia, Bulgaria, and Greece expanded at Turkey's expense. Albania became independent at that time and cut off Serbia from the sea. Following much intrigue, the Second Balkan War broke out in June 1913 as Bulgaria attacked Greece and Serbia. A treaty signed less than two months later cost Bulgaria much of the territory it gained in the First Balkan War. The two world wars split allegiances. Bulgaria and Turkey fought with the Kaiser in World War I, but in World War

II Bulgaria joined the facist regimes of Hitler and Mussolini, which controlled the Balkan Peninsula through much of the war, while Turkey remained neutral until early 1945, when it declared war on Germany. Greece and Turkey are NATO members today, and the other states are in the Eastern Bloc. These maps reflect a rich political-cartographic saga for so small a corner of Europe.

Law of the Sea

Until the early to mid-twentieth century, nations had been inclined to control waters adjoining their coasts but had allowed "freedom of the high seas" beyond the generally accepted limit of three mi (4.8 km). Freedom of the high seas, among other things, involves freedom to navigate, fish, lay submarine cable and pipelines, and fly over the area.[43] Consequently, on globes and world maps, international boundaries stopped at the coast.

According to political geographer Lewis Alexander, "The law of the sea may be defined as the specialized set of decisions dealing with the nature and extent of control exercised over the marine environment."[44] Alexander cites three aspects of special interest to geographers: the manner in which controls over the sea are distributed, the customs and laws that provide the bases for controls, and the way in which the controls influence the use of marine resources.

Given the importance of the world's oceans, seas, and other major water bodies existing between continents and islands and, therefore, between sovereign states which occupy the land, jurisdictional disputes are not surprising. Over the years, policies have varied from closed seas, in which sovereignty might be established over large marine areas, to the recognition that the sea should not be privately owned except for gulfs and other enclosed bodies of water. The "cannon-shot" principle, whereby some argued that effective maintenance of coastal waters could only occur if shorelines were adequately fortified, gave way to national zones of fixed breadth along coasts, within which sovereignty for the usual functions might be maintained. A three-mi (4.8-km) limit suggested in 1782 was held to be the maximum cannon range. At that time, an additional three-mi zone of neutrality was suggested to complement the three-mi sovereignty belt. Yet cannon range as late as 1814 was only about a mile, so the cannon-shot idea had little basis in fact.[45]

As Figure 6-11 illustrates, jurisdictional problems over offshore areas may include internal waters, the territorial sea, the contiguous zone, or the area beyond, in which claims over fishing rights may cause international debate. Such areas are often characterized as valuable fisheries located on the continental

---

[43] C. John Colombos, *The International Law of the Sea* (New York: David McKay, 1967), p. 65.

[44] Lewis M. Alexander, "Geography and the Law of the Sea" (Review Article), *Annals of the Association of American Geographers* 58, no. 1 (March 1968), 177.

[45] Lewis M. Alexander, *World Political Patterns*, 2d ed. (Chicago: Rand McNally, 1963), p. 72.

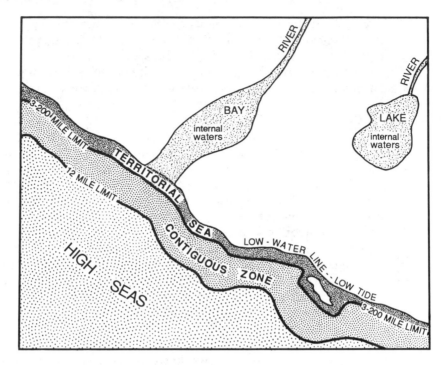

Figure 6-11   Coastal features as they relate to law of the sea.

shelf, where depths are not great. Controlled by the state with the adjacent coast, the territorial sea is an area within which innocent passage is granted to foreign ships except when such passage is a threat to national security. The contiguous zone permits the coastal state to control customs, sanitation, and immigration, among other measures, preventive and otherwise.[46] The breadth of the territorial sea varies from 3 mi (4.8 km) to 200 mi (322 km). Several coastal states, including the United States, the United Kingdom, and Australia, claim 3 mi, but for most nations 12 mi (19.3 km) is the rule. For 14 mostly African and Latin American states, however, the territorial sea stretches to 200 mi (322 km). Fishing limits vary, but are 200 mi from the baseline of the territorial sea for most nations.[47]

Issues of concern now necessitate mutual understanding among nations. These include, but are not limited to, ownership of natural resources, scientific research and exploration, pollution, and military uses.[48] There have been three

[46] Ibid., p. 73.

[47] John Paxton, ed., *The Statesman's Yearbook 1979–1980*, 116th ed. (New York: St. Martin's Press, 1979), pp. xxiv–xxvi.

[48] R. P. Barsten and Patricia Birnie, eds., *The Maritime Dimension* (Boston: George Allen & Unwin, 1980), pp. 1–3.

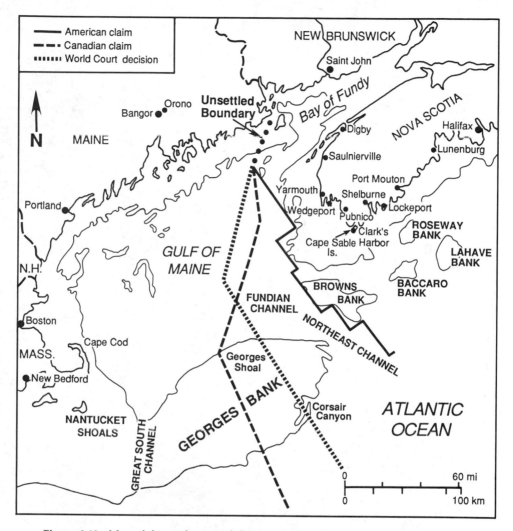

Figure 6-12 Map of the settlement of the American-Canadian fishing-rights dispute in Georges Bank. (From Ralph Surette, "Divvying Up the Fish," *Canadian Geographic* 105, no. 3 [June/July 1985], 38; used with permission of *Canadian Geographic* magazine.)

United Nations Conferences of the Law of the Sea (UNCLOS). At UNCLOS III in 1973, negotiations roamed widely, but participants generally agreed about definition of activities allowed in an exclusive economic zone of up to 200 mi (322 km) from the coast.[49]

A recent example of a dispute over United States-Canada fishing rights in Georges Bank illustrates the complexities of settling such issues. The Interna-

[49] Bernard Oxman et al., eds., *The Law of the Sea, U.S. Policy Dilemma* (San Francisco: Institute for Contemporary Studies Press, 1983), pp. 149–60.

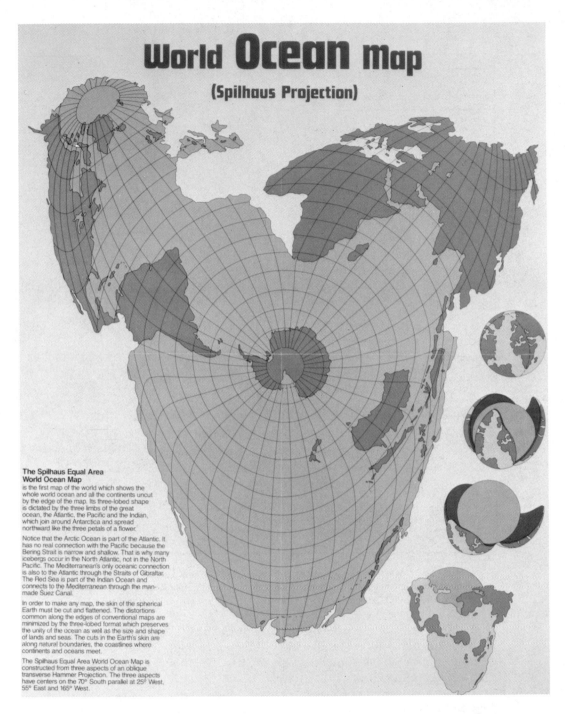

World **Ocean** map

(Spilhaus Projection)

The Spilhaus Equal Area World Ocean Map is the first map of the world which shows the whole world ocean and all the continents uncut by the edge of the map. Its three-lobed shape is dictated by the three limbs of the great ocean, the Atlantic, the Pacific and the Indian, which join around Antarctica and spread northward like the three petals of a flower.

Notice that the Arctic Ocean is part of the Atlantic. It has no real connection with the Pacific because the Bering Strait is narrow and shallow. That is why many icebergs occur in the North Atlantic, not in the North Pacific. The Mediterranean's only oceanic connection is also to the Atlantic through the Straits of Gibraltar. The Red Sea is part of the Indian Ocean and connects to the Mediterranean through the man-made Suez Canal.

In order to make any map, the skin of the spherical Earth must be cut and flattened. The distortions common along the edges of conventional maps are minimized by the three-lobed format which preserves the unity of the ocean as well as the size and shape of lands and seas. The cuts in the Earth's skin are along natural boundaries, the coastlines where continents and oceans meet.

The Spilhaus Equal Area World Ocean Map is constructed from three aspects of an oblique transverse Hammer Projection. The three aspects have centers on the 70° South parallel at 25° West, 55° East and 165° West.

Figure 6-13 "World Ocean Map," Spilhaus Projection, © Athelstan Spilhaus, 1983. Note that Antarctica is in the center and North America is in the periphery in the upper left. (Used with permission of the author.)

tional Court of Justice (the World Court at the Hague, The Netherlands) decided to divide about equally between the two countries the rich fishing area off the coast of Massachusetts, Maine, and Nova Scotia (see Figure 6-12). The prize, Georges Bank, happens to be where these nations' 200-mi fishing limits overlap. The line drawn on the map is fixed, but Canadian fishermen fear American tariffs on Canadian imports are a way to gain fishing access to the Canadian part of Georges Bank. Canadian claims to the World Court cited $100 million as the annual value of the catch, and stated that up to 5000 jobs would disappear were the American claim granted. Needless to say, claims of the United States on behalf of its fishermen were voluminous. In all, the World Court considered 9,600 pages of testimony and more than 300 maps. Ultimately, the criteria adopted by the Court in setting the line on the map "were geographical features which could not be altered by political, social or economic interpretations. Its guiding principle was equity—to draw a line 'which need only be stated to be seen as equitable.' . . . One of the guiding principles was the 'proportionality of coasts'—the relative size of the coasts facing the disputed zone."[50] Next, Canada will probably take on France, which is claiming a 200-mi zone around St. Pierre and Miquelon, tiny French possessions just south of Newfoundland. As for the American-Canadian dispute, the important issue concerns the wise use of Georges Bank, this "oceanic miracle."

Since we live on land, we almost always make maps that depict water bodies as afterthoughts, the spaces between the continents. Athelstan Spilhaus, an oceanographer, has addressed this oversight, reminding us that ours is indeed "a water planet, with a single great ocean covering nearly three-quarters of its surface."[51] His solution is shown as Figure 6-13, a map of the world's seas. An equal-area projection, Figure 6-13 is "the first world map showing the whole ocean and all the continents uncut by the edges of the map."[52]

NATIONAL BOUNDARIES: THE UNITED STATES

Growth and expansion of the United States provides a revealing illustration of change in both international and internal boundaries on political maps. This section also discusses land survey systems and disputed political boundaries.[53]

[50] Ralph Surette, "Divvying Up the Fish," *Canadian Geographic* 105, no. 3 (June/July 1985), 34–43.

[51] Athelstan Spilhaus, "To See the Oceans Slice Up the Land," *Smithsonian* 10, no. 8 (November 1979), 116.

[52] Athelstan Spilhaus, "World Ocean Maps: The Proper Places to Interrupt," *Proceedings of The American Philisophical Society* 127, no. 1 (January 1983), 58.

[53] For a different view of United States boundaries and an interesting treatment of cultural regions, see Joel Garreau, *The Nine Nations of North America* (Boston: Houghton Mifflin, 1981).

Expansion and Growth of the United States

Figure 6-14 shows the original 13 American colonies, which stretched along the Atlantic Coast from part of what is now Maine but was then a northern section of Massachusetts to the Spanish colonies of Florida in the South. The map portrays the coastal states from Maryland northward to Massachusetts essentially as they are today. These colonial boundaries, after all, were the outgrowth of grants and charters, such as the first Charter of Virginia (which consisted of lands granted by King James I of England in 1606) and the grant from Charles II of England to William Penn (which established the Province of Pennsylvania in 1681).[54]

Historians rely upon maps to illustrate the territorial conquest by the United States of the choicest parts of the North American continent. As Figure 6-15 shows, treaties with Great Britain following the successful Revolutionary War left the new nation with an area bounded by Spanish Florida to the south, Canada to the north, the Atlantic Ocean to the east, and the Mississippi River to the west. This original territory constitutes a mere third of the present area of the 48 contigous states. Comparison of Figures 6-14 and 6-15 shows that the land between the Mississippi and the 13 colonies was largely unoccupied. Seven colonies claimed parts of this territory, but these claims were often in conflict. The trans-Appalachian west eventually was apportioned to form all or part of Ohio, Indiana, Illinois, Michigan, Wisconsin, Minnesota, Alabama, and Mississippi. What remained was claimed by states as originally part of their land: Kentucky was part of Virginia, Tennessee a part of North Carolina, and so forth. Left unsettled at the ratification of both the Articles of Confederation and the Constitution, many of these claims were not adjudicated until years later by the U.S. Supreme Court. In a new country, such disputes are expected. Although many early maps portray mistakes that our present knowledge of the earth's surface would easily correct, some of the old maps are surprisingly accurate. Indeed, the "Map of the British and French dominions in North America," by John Mitchell (probably not actually published until after 1762, but nevertheless dated at 1755) was cited by John Adams as the map relied upon to mark the boundaries of the United States. This map, used in the negotiations in Paris between Great Britain and the United States in 1782–1783, has been identified as the most important map in American history.[55]

Figure 6-15 portrays a number of accessions, large and small, between 1803 and 1853. The Louisiana Purchase in 1803 filled in much of the area west of the Mississippi and north of Texas. The era ended with the Gadsden Purchase, in 1853, which transferred from Mexico the southernmost portions of present-day Arizona and New Mexico. Texas was annexed in 1845, the Oregon Territory's

---

[54] Franklin K. Van Zandt, *Boundaries of the United States and the Several States*, Geological Survey Bulletin 1212 (Washington, D.C.: U.S. Government Printing Office, 1966), pp. 124 and 143.

[55] Ibid., pp. 1–3.

Figure 6-14 The 13 American colonies.

title was established in 1846, and the southwest was ceded by Mexico in 1848. Not included here, of course, are the 1867 purchase of Alaska from Russia and the 1898 annexation of the Hawaiian Islands. The Alaska purchase added over 151.5 million hectares (375 million acres) to the United States, almost one-fifth the area of the 48 states at a cost of just $7 million or so.

Land Survey Systems

Good barriers make good boundaries, but ease of definition can be useful too. The most common boundaries are water (streams, lakes, or others), a ridge or divide between drainage basins, and a meridian or parallel.[56] Figure 6-16 illustrates state boundaries based upon ridges (above) and water (below), with the remaining boundaries, those not highlighted, being surveyed lines. The relatively few state lines defined by ridges include the western Maine-Canada line, much of the line separating Virginia from West Virginia and Kentucky, the North Carolina-Tennessee line, and the major part of the Montana-Idaho line as established along the Bitterroot Range of the Rocky Mountains. The Alaska panhandle is delimited by the summit of the Coast Mountains, which thus delineates

[56] Ibid., p. 5.

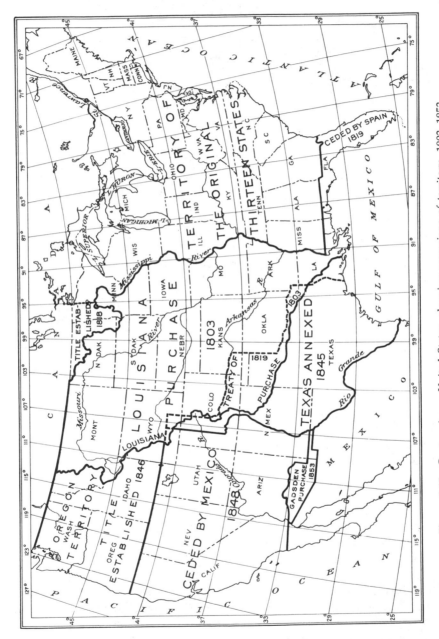

Figure 6-15 Conterminous United States, showing accessions of territory, 1803–1853. (From Franklin K. Van Zandt, *Boundaries of the United States and the Several States,* Geological Survey Bulletin 1212 [Washington, D.C.: U.S. Government Printing Office, 1966], p. 15.)

the United States-Canada boundary. Water boundaries obviously set the limits of the 48 contiguous states, along the Atlantic coast from Maine to Florida, along the Great Lakes and associated rivers from New York to Minnesota, along the Gulf of Mexico as far west as Texas, and along the Pacific from southern California through Washington. Hawaii is *in* the Pacific, and the southern, western, and northern boundaries of Alaska are set by oceans, seas, gulfs, and straits. Moreover, in the more humid eastern half of the country, many state lines are set by stream courses, as are a few in the west. (Examination of the United States-Canada border offers insight into the nature of over 6,400 km [3,986.5 mi] of international boundary.) Except where rivers have changed course, as has happened a few times to the Missouri, Mississippi, and the Rio Grande, these natural boundaries are remarkably stable.

State boundaries not highlighted in Figure 6-16 are a series of arcs, which appear as straight lines on some map projections and which surveyors had to mark on the earth. These surveyed lines arose from an absence of politically acceptable natural boundaries or boundaries that could not easily be determined at the time the territory was partitioned.

Land survey as a technique and a profession arose from the need to establish and mark boundaries for taxation and definition of ownership, and its practice is ancient indeed. The early civilization of Egypt, possessed of a population with the technical knowledge and skill to build the pyramids more than 7,000 years ago, surveyed and constantly resurveyed property lines along the Nile River, where annual floods obliterated property markers. Similarly, Babylonians set inscribed stones to mark boundaries more than 3,000 years ago, and threatened with numerous curses those who might move them. The Romans, the English, and the Incas, among others, are known to have carried on surveys of note in times past.[57]

Several people who performed surveys in colonial America, including George Washington and Thomas Jefferson, were destined for greatness. Generally the early surveys were carried out on an ad hoc basis, called *metes* and *bounds*, whereby distances and directions were unrelated to a regular system. This "nonsystem" was replaced in the late eighteenth century by the U.S. rectangular survey system, described as a "marvel of simplicity" and designed to mark one-mile square "sections" over all federal lands—that is, the lands outside the original thirteen colonies and their western territories (see Figure 6-15). Lest the reader be unaware of the importance of public lands, the federal government controls about one-third of the national area today. As Figure 6-17 shows, all states are involved, and the proportion of federal ownership ranges from highs in Alaska and Nevada, 95 percent and 85 percent, respectively, to just 0.3 percent

---

[57] The brief overview of land survey history and information on rectangular land survey presented here is based on U.S. Department of the Interior, Bureau of Land Management, *Surveying Our Public Lands* (Washington, D.C.: U.S. Government Printing Office, 1980), a booklet of 17 pages.

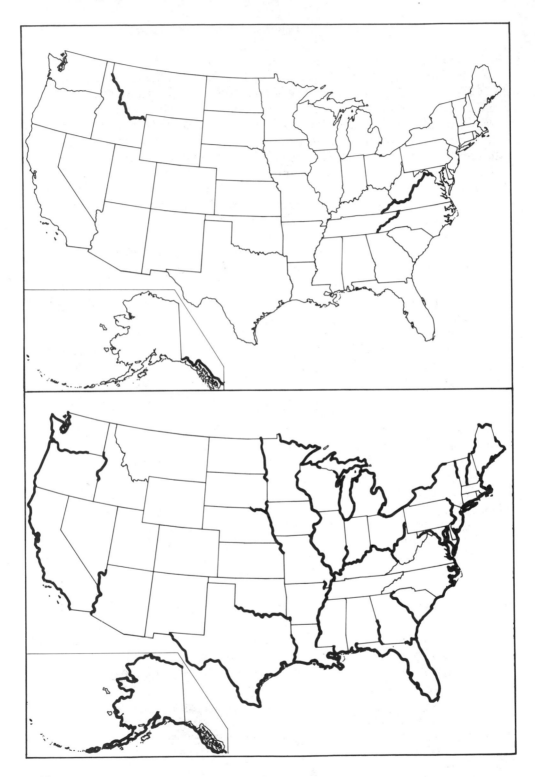

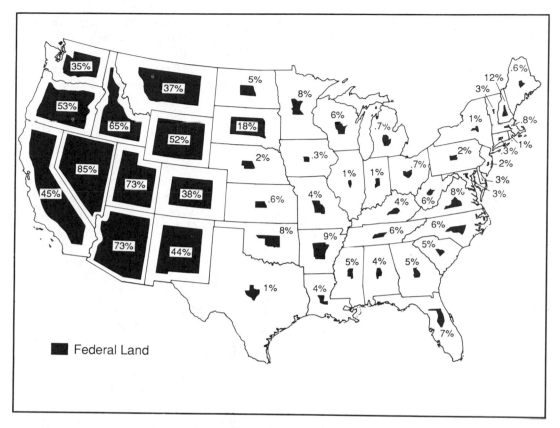

Figure 6-17   Federal ownership of land as a proportion of state area. (From Richard H. Jackson, *Land Use in America* [New York: V.H. Winston & Sons, John Wiley & Sons, 1981], p. 48; used with permission of Edward Arnold, Ltd.)

in Connecticut.[58] Since federal ownership limits development and the ability to tax, the map of federal land also is useful in suggesting a cause of negative attitudes in the West toward Washington. A chief target of some western con-servatives is the U.S. Bureau of Land Management (BLM), the agency in the Department of the Interior responsible for the largest extent of public lands. Indeed, the BLM manages minerals, oil and gas, forests, range, recreation, wild-life, soil, and water on more than 190 million hectares (470 million acres), more than half of which is in Alaska.[59]

[58] Richard H. Jackson, *Land Use in America* (New York: V. H. Winston & Sons, John Wiley & Sons, 1981), pp. 47–51.

[59] Ibid.

Figure 6-16   Ridges (upper map) and water bodies (lower map) as boundaries of the United States and of the several states.

The Continental Congress authorized the rectangular survey in the Land Ordinance of 1785. After much work and long debate, a committee chaired by Thomas Jefferson approved the system. The first survey under the ordinance was completed in Ohio along the Pennsylvania line; rectangular surveys were initiated in Indiana in 1805 and eventually extended all the way to the Pacific Ocean.

With the rectangular system came "survey before settlement," the first of three new theories of land management. The second was recognition of the need for a general plan, mathematically designed, to be followed throughout, and the third involved "the section," a newly created standard land unit uniform in shape and standard in area, whose boundaries were actually marked on the ground. Preceding any actual measurement, the new system demanded a series of known points from which principal meridians and base lines (parallels of latitude) could be established. Figure 6-18 portrays the principal meridians and base lines that govern public land survey in this nation. Although retaining the principles established in the 1785 Land Ordinance, the survey has been refined over the years, and is plotted as Figure 6-19 shows. To begin, public lands are divided into a square grid of "townships," each about 6 mi (9.7 km) on a side. Township corners are set from the principal meridians and base lines, and once they are established township location within the system is a simple matter except for one problem, curvature of the earth. Since the earth is nearly spherical, meridians converge at the poles and thus require an adjustment by running correction lines every 24 mi (38.5 km). Townships are further divided into 1-mi square sections, each with an area of 640 acres (2.59 km^2). Numbered in the snake-like pattern shown in Figure 6-19, "sections" are divided into 160-acre "quarter sections," the basic unit of the Homestead Act of 1862. "Half-quarter sections" (80 acres each) and "quarter-quarter sections" (40 acres) are further subdivisions, as the diagrams in Figure 6-19 illustrate. A necessary feature of the system is that each parcel have a unique identification, as in Figure 6-19, which identifies as T.2S, R.W3 the township two townships (east-west rows) south of the base line and three ranges (north-south columns) west of the principal meridian. The section shown (14) is described as sec. 14, T.2S, R.W3, with the principal meridian named to ensure precision. Within sections, quarters (known as "Aliquot parts") are described by using "northeast," "southeast" and so forth, and the quarters are divided as shown. The Land Ordinance thus created a system of survey and, in so doing, promoted growth of local government by establishing administrative areas.[60]

[60] The Land Ordinance also introduced the geographical, or nautical, mile, which is an important modification of linear measure. Thomas Jefferson defined the nautical mile—6,076 ft (or 1,852 m)—based on its length equalling one sixtieth of the length of a degree of latitude (an angular minute). Had it been accepted as the official or statute mile, it would have revised land measure so that a square mile would contain 1,000 "acres." Other land measures would have been simplified similarly. See William D. Pattison, "The Original Plan for an American Rectangular Land Survey," *Surveying and Mapping* 21, no. 3 (1961), 342 and 344.

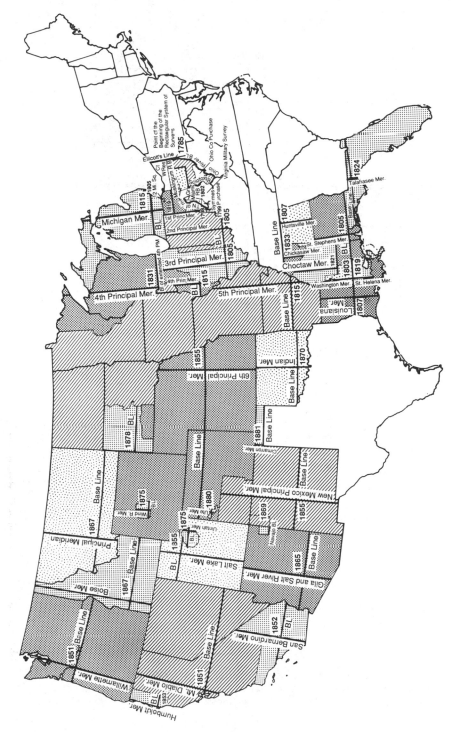

Figure 6-18 Principal meridians and base lines governing the United States public land survey. (From U.S. Department of the Interior, Bureau of Land Management, *Surveying our Public Lands* [Washington, D.C.: U.S. Government Printing Office, 1980], p. 8.)

TOWNSHIP GRID

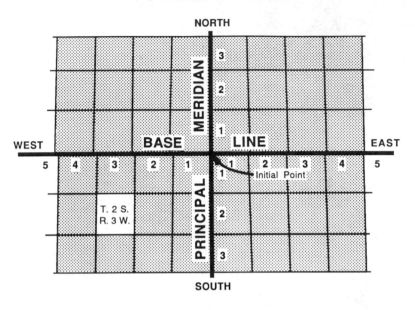

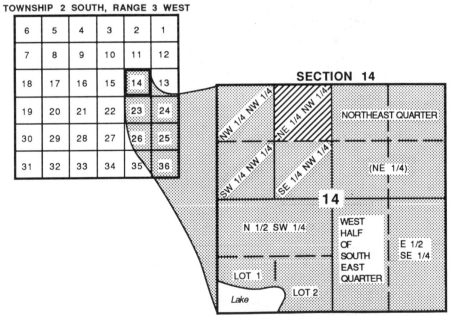

Figure 6-19 Township, section, and further divisions of the United States public land survey. (From U.S. Department of the Interior, Bureau of Land Management, *Surveying our Public Lands* [Washington, D.C.: U.S. Government Printing Office, 1980], p. 9.)

Boundary Problems

Lines drawn easily and simply on a paper map often obscure the effort or uncertainty of the field survey. International boundaries of the United States, as
well as states' boundaries, are the products of colonial charters, purchases, treaties, and Acts of Congress. Boundaries "on the ground" often are problematic
because of ignorance of the physical geography of the area, vaguely written
descriptions, and surveying errors. Like most new nations, the United States
tried to establish boundaries prior to very much exploration, so boundary problems are understandable in a nation so large at a time when few roads had been
built, Native Americans were hostile, and settlement was sparse: the job of
marking boundaries on the ground was monumental! Furthermore, vague word-
ing of documents fixing lines often caused disputes over interpretation of treaties. Obviously, courts at all levels of jurisdiction have long been busy on suits
over boundaries and ownership. Improved technology, better methods, and
higher standards have increased accuracy and rendered earlier work questionable. When disputes arise, the surveyor must find the line in question on the
ground rather than move the line to agree with the existing description in the
treaty or deed, since the line on the ground becomes the true line once accepted
by interested parties.[61]

The dispute between Great Britain and the United States over several parts
of the latter's northern boundary included Maine's northern line in the 1820s
(see Figure 6-20). Doubt about the course of the St. Croix River complicated
Maine's northeastern boundary. Although both countries agreed about the
longitude of the meridian, as shown, the British claim was well over 160 km
(100 mi) south of the American claim. Resolution of the dispute depended upon
establishing the true source of the St. Croix River. The King of the Netherlands,
selected in 1829 as the arbitrator, made his award in 1831. Maine protested,
however, and the U.S. Senate refused to accept the king's decision. For 11 years
the area was in dispute; some feared a war would ensue and, as a result, both
Maine and the Congress provided funds to defend the area. In 1842, a treaty
offered an amicable arrangement: although the United States received more of
the area in dispute than Canada did, the settlement granted this country almost
10 percent less than had the earlier decision by the Dutch monarch.[62]

Maps are definitely legal documents with clout when boundary disputes
go to court. Witness the arguments for Georgia and South Carolina before the
U.S. Supreme Court over the lower reaches and mouth of the Savannah River,
heard in 1981, with the bulk of the evidence taking the form of some 200 maps
depicting the area over a period of 200 years or so.[63] Experts called as witnesses

[61] Van Zandt, "Boundaries of the United States," pp. 2–4.

[62] Ibid, pp. 22–27.

[63] Louis De Vorsey, Jr., "Historical Maps Before the United States Supreme Court," *Map
Collector* no. 19 (June 1982), 24.

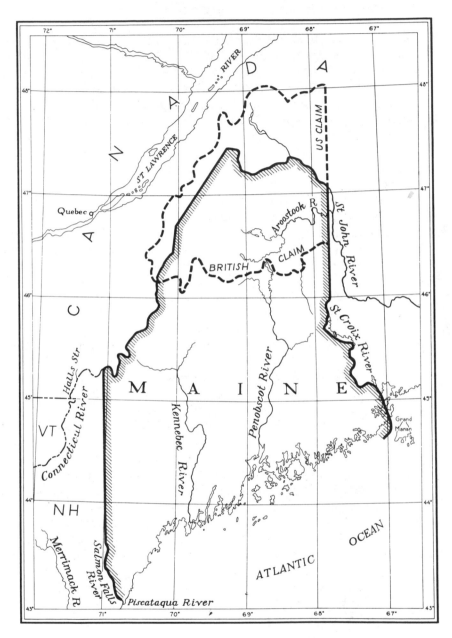

Figure 6-20 Maine, showing the claims of the United States and Great Britain in 1827 and the present boundary. (From Franklin K. Van Zandt, *Boundaries of the United States and the Several States,* Geological Survey Bulletin 1212 [Washington, D.C.: U.S. Government Printing Office, 1966], p. 23.)

included specialists in historical cartography. One of the experts, geography professor Louis De Vorsey, supported Georgia's claim and was countered by testimony from Arthur Robinson, a cartographic historian. "The best conclusion for this study comes in the form of a map overlay," wrote De Vorsey, "the 1855 U.S. Coast Survey chart of the lower Savannah River area on a 1976 National Ocean Survey chart of the same area. . . . The overlay represents a cartographic inventory of . . . landscape change . . . very useful when attempting to fix the correct location of the Georgia-South Carolina boundary."[64] Documenting landscape change and boundary shifts with old maps is a mixture of meticulous scholarship and high-stakes litigation.

MAPS AND CITIZENSHIP

Americans vote for elected officials at all levels of government and, in this way, exercise their constitutional right. The impact each citizen has on a given election varies with the office being contested, its spatial dimensions, and the size of the electorate. At the federal level, the Senate is composed of two individuals elected statewide from each state, and members of the House of Representatives are elected from districts within states in numbers based on state population. This principle is difficult to maintain when changes in population numbers and characteristics continually cause inequalities in apportionment. This section treats electoral geography and apportionment maps as tools of both description and analysis.

Apportionment

In 1787 the Constitutional Convention passed a resolution to create a bicameral national legislature, bringing to an end a policy of equal representation without regard to population size. This compromise between large and small states maintained equal representation in the Senate and established representation based on number of state inhabitants in the House. The convention further decided that a federal census would be taken every ten years to ensure that the House would be comprised of representatives at the rate of not more than one for every 30,000 citizens.[65]

Since colonial times, issues of area, population, and compactness have combined to distort the concept of equal representation. Population shifts and growth, coupled with the states' reluctance to reapportion and redistrict, have created pronounced problems, particularly in the 1920s with respect to urban-

[64] Louis De Vorsey, Jr., *The Georgia-South Carolina Boundary: A Problem in Historical Geography* (Athens, Ga.: University of Georgia Press, 1982), p. 163.

[65] Abner J. Mikra and Patti B. Saris, *The American Congress: The First Branch* (New York: Franklin Watts, 1983), p. 53.

rural differences, as cities became progressively underrepresented and the countryside progressively overrepresented. By 1946, noncompliance by states led to the first appeal to the Supreme Court.[66] In 1964, the court ruled that, within states, congressional districts had to have population counts as similar as possible by 1972 to reflect "one person-one vote." Despite the ruling, by 1980 population shifts had caused inequalities across the country in the size of congressional districts (CDs) and the need for reapportionment.[67] Other rules that affect district boundaries and the maps describing them require that all representatives be elected from their own districts; each state must draw only the number of districts allowed by federal apportionment formula; each district must be contiguous; and no district may cross state lines.[68]

The obvious problem here is that Americans are mobile and, in addition to reproductive change, create constant trends in number, distribution, and density of population through migration. Table 6-1 summarizes this problem nicely by listing the extremes of population density for the 98th Congress. Note that the density ratio from most dense (C.D. 15 in New York City, which is the southeastern part of Manhattan Borough/New York County and not more than 3.2 km [2 mi] wide and 13 km [8 mi] long) to least dense (the entire State of Alaska with one representative at large) is more than 100,000 to 1. Not surprisingly, all 10 most dense CDs are in the city of New York.[69] Figure 6-21 illustrates the great disparity in CD area across the nation, reflecting the equally great disparity in population density—very small, dense districts from Baltimore to Boston, compared to the wide open spaces of Alaska and the mountain states with their huge CDs. Table 6-2 lists the populations of the 10 largest and 10 smallest CDs in 1980. Note that the numbers, large and small, are a far cry from the original statement in the Constitution about 30,000 persons per CD, as those listed range upward from 460,000 to over 690,000. The average CD in 1980 represented 519,328 persons.

Finally, as Figure 6-22 illustrates, gerrymandering—the manipulation of the boundaries of election districts in order to give a party, interest group, or incumbent an advantage—is not solely a political relic of the nineteenth century. (See Figure 9-2 for a view of the original 1812 gerrymander.) As the text in Figure 6-22 confirms, the practice is alive and well throughout the country. At more local levels, as well, "politician-cartographers" strive to create districts favorable

[66] John S. Adams, ed., *Urban Policy Making and Metropolitan Dynamics: A Comparative Geographical Analysis*, Association of American Geographers, Comparative Metropolitan Analysis Project (Cambridge, Mass.: Ballinger, 1976), p. 540.

[67] Lynda McNeil, ed., *State Politics and Redistricting*, Part 1 (Washington, D.C.: Congressional Quarterly, Inc., 1982), Editor's note.

[68] Nelson W. Polsby, ed., *Reapportionment in the 1970s* (Berkeley, Calif.: University of California Press, 1971), pp. 251–53.

[69] U.S. Bureau of the Census, *Congressional District Atlas, Districts of the 98th Congress* (Washington, D.C.: U.S. Government Printing Office, 1983), unpaginated.

TABLE 6-1 POPULATION DENSITY IN CONGRESSIONAL DISTRICTS OF THE 98TH
CONGRESS, 10 HIGHEST AND 10 LOWEST OBSERVED VALUES

	Highest population			Lowest population	
CD	per km^2	per mi^2	CD	per km^2	per mi^2
N.Y. 15	28,476	73,773	Alaska*	0.3	0.7
N.Y. 16	24,917	64,551	Nev. 2	1.5	3.8
N.Y. 12	18,142	46,999	Mont. 2	1.6	4.2
N.Y. 18	15,384	39,854	Wyo.*	1.8	4.8
N.Y. 17	15,328	39,711	Mont. 1	2.8	7.3
N.Y. 11	13,334	34,544	Oreg. 2	2.9	7.5
N.Y. 13	11,721	30,524	N. Mex. 3	3.0	7.7
N.Y. 9	9,487	24,518	N. Mex. 2	3.0	7.9
N.Y. 7	9,105	23,589	Nebr. 3	3.4	8.8
N.Y. 10	8,612	22,310	Colo. 3	3.5	9.1

Source: U.S. Bureau of the Census, 1980 Census of Population, *Congressional District Profiles, 98th
Congress, Supplementary Report PC80-S1-11* (Washington, D.C.: U.S. Government Printing Office,
September 1983), p. 44.

* Unnumbered CDs indicate that the state has one representative at large.

to powerful or useful legislators and to the party in power, while equally determined "judge-cartographers" resist these efforts.

Electoral Geography

Inextricably related to the many geographic-cartographic aspects of apportionment is the subject of electoral geography. Voting analyses are appealing to
geographers primarily because of the utility of the map in such research: the
map, after all, is a most dramatic portrayal of election results. But the map's
principal value is as an analytical tool, for election maps depict the electorate's
differences in behavior at the polls based upon attitudes, perceptions, and
biases. The political geographer who attempts to explain these differences uses
maps to study elections varying from international votes on a world scale at,
say, the United Nations to those for nations, states, counties, and even minor
civil divisions.[70] Spatial differences in political behavior at all scales, as mani-
fested at the polls and portrayed on maps, thus provide a rich source of material
for electoral geography, as the following discussion attempts to illustrate.

One might think that the 1980 presidential election was dull—after all,
Ronald Reagan walked off with 489 electoral votes to Jimmy Carter's 49, almost
half of that 49 coming from the losing presidential and vice-presidential candidates' home states (Georgia, of course, and Fritz Mondale's Minnesota). The

[70] Robert E. Norris and L. Lloyd Haring, *Political Geography* (Columbus, Ohio: Charles E.
Merrill, 1980), pp. 275 and 276.

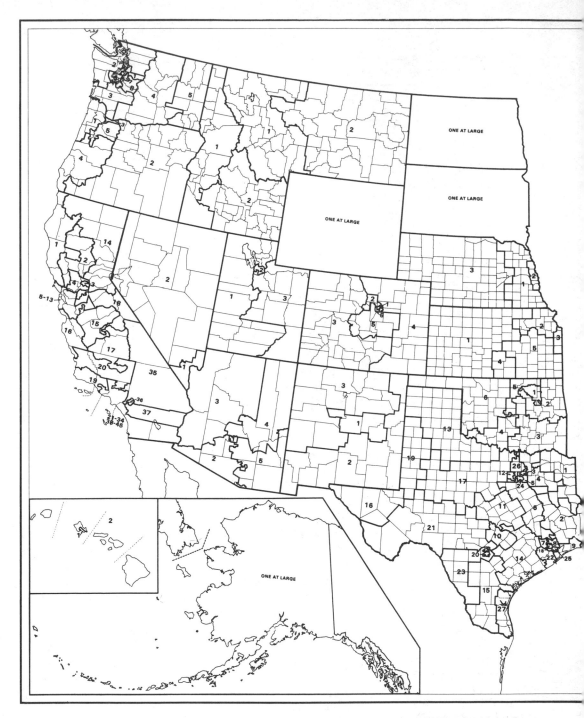

Figure 6-21 Congressional districts of the 98th Congress. (From U.S. Bureau of the Census, *1980 Census of Population, Congressional District Profiles, 98th Congress,* Supplementary Report PC80-S1-11 [Washington, D.C., September 1983], pp. IV–V.)

Figure 6-21 (*continued*)

TABLE 6-2 POPULATION OF THE 10 LARGEST AND 10 SMALLEST
CONGRESSIONAL DISTRICTS, 1980

Largest		Smallest	
District	Population	District	Population
S. Dak.*	690,768	Mont. 2	376,619
N. Dak.*	652,717	Nev. 2	399,857
Del.*	594,338	Nev. 1	400,636
Maine 1	581,185	Alaska*	401,851
Ark. 1	573,551	Mont. 1	410,071
Ark. 3	572,937	N. Mex. 3	432,492
Ark. 4	570,831	N. Mex. 1	434,191
Ark. 2	569,116	N. Mex. 2	436,261
Ala. 1	563,905	N.H. 2	459,747
Ala. 4	562,088	N.H. 1	460,863

Source: U.S. Bureau of the Census, 1980 Census of Population, *Congressional District Profiles, 98th Congress, Supplementary Report PC80-S1-11* (Washington, D.C.: U.S. Government Printing Office, September 1983), p. 2.

* Unnumbered CDs indicate that the state has one representative at large.

popular vote, however, as Figure 6-23 shows, was much closer, as Carter polled 41 percent and the third-party candidate, John Anderson, garnered about 7 percent. Recognizing Reagan's decisive win, the map concentrates on Carter, Anderson, and their "strongholds."

Carter won in the District of Columbia, Georgia, Hawaii, Maryland, Minnesota, Rhode Island, and West Virginia; as the map shows, he polled at least 45 percent of the popular vote in much of the South and in Minnesota. Support for "favorite sons" explains Democratic majorities in Georgia and Minnesota. The District of Columbia usually supports the incumbent, given the large number of federal employees among its residents, and West Virginia remains a Democratic stronghold. Yet the map reflects the strong support for Reagan in the West and, except for New England, the Northeast.

Anderson's greatest support, minor overall, was in New England, Colorado, Washington, and Hawaii. Why did these nine states' electorates each cast more than 10 percent of their popular vote for this third-party candidate? John Anderson, an Illinois Representative at the time, held positions on several issues that were quite different from those of other Republican candidates in the primaries. For instance, he gained media attention for his support of abortion and opposition to increased military spending. He proposed raising gasoline prices by increasing taxes on petroleum products and thereby inducing conservation; the "wrinkle" was that the taxpayer would pay less in Social Security payments and feel little or no net change in tax outlays. Indeed, he believed that the

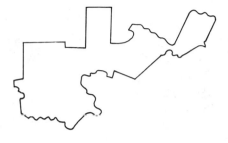

Both the Republican and Democratic parties still delight in creating gerrymanders but several recent court decisions promise a belated end to the practice. A three-judge federal court has ruled unconstitutional a 1966 North Carolina Democratic gerrymander, even though district populations were within acceptable limits. The court cited the "tortuous lines" that delineated district boundaries in its decision. An example was the 4th District created for Agriculture Committee Chairman Harold D. Cooley (D).

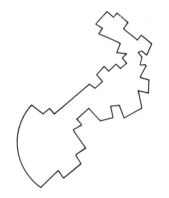

Not all gerrymandering has produced the intended results. New York Republicans in 1961 hoped to achieve a 25-16 party delegation balance in their favor. After the 1962 elections the party balance stood at only 21-20 in the GOP's favor. A good example of their ill-fated attempt was Brooklyn's 15th District.

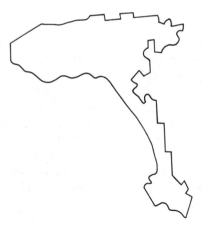

California Democrats, the same year, proved more skillful in gerrymandering. In the 1962 elections, California Democrats gained nine seats by drawing a number of oddly shaped districts such as the 28th, which runs along the Los Angeles coastline and concentrates the maximum number of heavily Republican areas, leaving surrounding districts to the Democrats.

Figure 6-22 The gerrymander lives on. (From *Representation and Apportionment* [Washington, D.C.: Congressional Quarterly Service, 1966], p. 58; used with permission.)

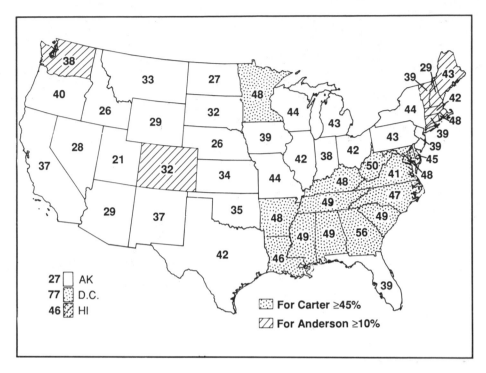

Figure 6-23 1980 presidential election showing percentage of popular vote cast for Jimmy Carter and states where Carter and John Anderson fared well relatively.

American oil supply was both limited and unreliable, based as it was on foreign as well as domestic sources. (Figure 9-18, "The World of Known Oil Reserves," a map showing the vast differences between the world's major consumers and major producers of oil, illustrates this point.) His position on energy during the Republican primary might well account for his national prominence at that time. On the matter of reallocating taxes, Reagan ridiculed Anderson's ideas as just another example of Big Government thinking it can spend public funds more wisely than the people do. Yet nearly 7 million people voted for Anderson and, in so doing, probably cast a vote of no-confidence for the candidates of the major parties as much as a vote in support of Anderson. Although Anderson's independent candidacy seems not to have given Reagan the edge by taking Carter votes, it did contribute to the wide margin.[71]

[71] Gerald M. Pomper et al., *The Election of 1980: Reports and Interpretations* (Chatham, N.J.: Chatham House, 1981), pp. 13, 15, 45–46, 84, and 158.

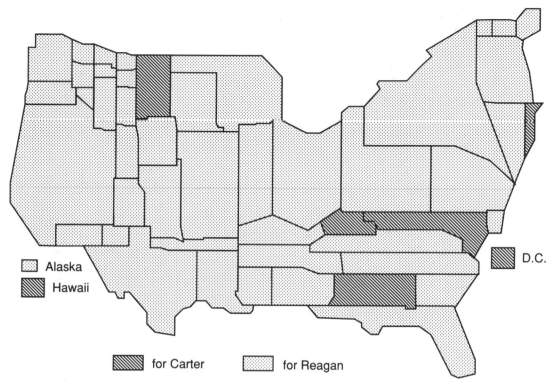

Figure 6-24   Area cartogram of the 1980 presidential election, in which area is proportional to electoral vote.

Presented on an area-cartogram base emphasizing electoral strength rather than land area, the Reagan victory is placed in a more accurate political-geographic perspective. Whereas the Republican standard-bearer did well in the West, strong support from trans-Mississippi states would have been insufficient for a Reagan win. Study Figure 6-24 and compare it to Figure 6-23, recalling that the latter is based on popular vote and the former on electoral ballots.

In their variety, the illustrations in this chapter show that the roles of the map in politics and political scholarship are as varied as the concerns of government itself and those who study it. Political maps demonstrate the effectiveness of the map both as an analytical tool and as a small-scale model of reality. Maps of boundaries represent either the resolution of or the potential for conflict. Maps from political propagandists demonstrate that cartographic viewpoints are inherently selective and subject to the probity of the map maker. The map is not reality, however, and we must never mislead ourselves into believing that changing a boundary is as easy as drawing a line or that a widely accepted cartographic solution will produce a lasting, peaceful political solution.

FOR FURTHER READING

BARRACLOUGH, GEOFFREY, ed., *The Times Atlas of the World*, rev. ed. London: Times Books; Maplewood, N.J.: Hammond, 1984.

CROW, BEN, and ALAN THOMAS, *Third World Atlas*. Milton Keynes, Eng., and Philadelphia: Open University Press, 1983.

DE VORSEY, LOUIS, and MEGAN C. DE VORSEY, "The World Court Decision in the Canada-United States Gulf of Maine Seaward Boundary Dispute: A Perspective From Historical Geography," *Journal of International Law* 18, no. 3 (1986), 415–42.

GARREAU, JOEL, *The Nine Nations of North America*. Boston: Houghton Mifflin, 1981.

GLASSNER, MARTIN I., and HARM J. DE BLIJ, *Systematic Political Geography*, 3d ed. New York: John Wiley & Sons, 1980.

HARDY, LEROY, et al., eds., *Reapportionment Politics: History of Redistricting in the 50 States*. Beverly Hills, Calif.: Sage Publications, 1981.

KIDRON, MICHAEL, and RONALD SEGAL, *State of the World Atlas*. New York: Simon & Schuster; London: Heinemann, 1981.

MORRILL, RICHARD L., *Political Redistricting and Geographical Theory*, Resource Publications in Geography. Washington, D.C.: Association of American Geographers, 1981.

POMPER, GERALD M., et al., *The Election of 1984, Reports and Interpretations*. Chatham, N.J.: Chatham House, 1985.

ROBINSON, ARTHUR H., "Arno Peters and His New Cartography," *The American Cartographer* 12, no. 2 (October 1985), 103–11.

SCHOYER, GEORGE, "The Coverage of Political Patterns and Elections in Some Selected State Atlases of the United States," Special Libraries Association, Geography and Map Division, *Bulletin* no. 117 (September 1979), 2–7.

SHELLEY, FRED M., et al., "Rednecks and Quiche Eaters: A Cartographic Analysis of Recent Third-Party Electoral Campaigns," *Journal of Geography* 83, no. 1 (January/February 1984), 7–12.

SPILHAUS, ATHELSTAN, "World Ocean Maps: The Proper Place to Interrupt," *Proceedings of the American Philosophical Society* 127, no. 1 (January 1983), 50–60.

TYNER, JUDITH A., "Persuasive Cartography," *Journal of Geography* 81, no. 4 (July/August 1982), 140–44.

CHAPTER SEVEN

Maps
of the Municipality

The administration of any city may teem with virtue, fidelity and honesty, but unless its endeavors rest upon basic facts showing conditions and indicating tendencies, it is likely to sink into oblivion—and deservedly so—for lack of efficiency . . . and as urban life grows more complicated and thereby forces to the front the necessity for practical city planning, the urgent need for fundamental facts in reference to every municipal activity will become greater. The time has passed when city administrations can decide questions of development and make changes in policy on guesses.

Every city has a map showing its boundaries, its streets and its trolley, water and sewer systems; a few have ward maps showing the location of individual real estate holdings. These for a long time have been regarded as absolutely necessary in every engineer's office. Except for these, however, it is impossible to find in the archives of most municipalities the other important maps that every administration should have spread before it at every meeting at which are discussed or made plans for some city improvement or development.[1]

So wrote an official of the New York State Conference of Mayors and Other City Officials in 1914, as that organization launched an effort to promote the advantages of cities using maps to compile basic information and assist in mu-

[1] William P. Capes, "Has Your City These Maps?" *American City* 10, no. 5 (May 1914), 460; used with permission.

nicipal problem solving and planning. In fact, an advisory committee prepared a map questionnaire and sent it to each mayor in the state. Beyond political maps, the survey inquired about maps of population growth, residential districts, house types, places of work, the surrounding area, topography, land use, trees, streets and walks, underground facilities, accidents, recreation, transportation, public buildings, and tuberculosis. This survey was years ahead of its time; statutes and local laws calling for such maps had yet to be enacted in an attempt to control land use, protect the environment, provide efficient public works, and generally safeguard city inhabitants' health and welfare. The writer of the comments quoted above extolled maps as sources of crucial municipal information, listing three basic advantages that would accrue to municipalities that prepared a set of maps.

1. Guesswork is replaced by more accurate planning and administration by city officials.
2. Problems are more easily related to other problems by means of map analysis and, ostensibly, solutions are facilitated.
3. It is easier to treat problems of one city area as part of the whole jurisdiction, which results in better planning through coordination of effort.[2]

Although more than 70 years old, these assertions are quite timely and relevant, serving well to introduce the subject of this chapter, maps used in municipalities and maps about municipalities. The chapter is organized so that the various kinds of municipalities are defined in part by maps that aid in describing them. The second section concerns maps and the provision of services. The culminating section treats the kinds of maps one would find in an average American city and discusses their sources.

THE MUNICIPALITY SPATIALLY DEFINED

A municipality, generally defined, is an incorporated urban place with the powers to govern itself. Defining the municipality in spatial terms, however, presents some problems and interesting cartographic situations. Boundaries delimit one municipality and thereby separate it from other political divisions. One may overstate a boundary's political importance and understate its physical, economic, and social implications, which combine to facilitate or inhibit interaction among the residents of different political divisions. Interaction includes trips to work, stores, schools, and recreation, as a city's inhabitants attempt to satisfy

[2] Ibid., p. 461.

wants and needs for a variety of goods and services.[3] This section examines municipal service districts and highlights some of the modern confusion about place. A variety of civil divisions, although not, strictly speaking, municipalities, nevertheless exist and require specific services that include the provision of maps.

Municipal Service Areas: Many Districts

Within minor civil divisions, political boundaries are but one expression of the unit's spatial extent. For example, as Figure 7-1 illustrates, New Paltz, New York, has an immediately obvious and possibly confusing dualism based on two jurisdictions: a town(ship) and, at its core, a village. The village is incorporated and thus functions as a political unit. The town, some 7,700 hectares (about 19 thousand acres) in area, surrounds the village and offers similar services to its residents as its influence extends into the village for taxation and the provision of police protection. As the political map shows, the fire district's boundaries coincide with the town line but is one of the few service areas that does. Even water and sewer services are less than townwide, as most nonvillage residents rely upon on-site services, wells and septic systems. For that matter, sewer lines are not yet provided throughout the village.

As Figure 7-1 further portrays, the area served by the branch of the U.S. Postal Service in New Paltz extends beyond the town line into five other jurisdictions. Yet on the northeastern edge of New Paltz, one area is served by the neighboring town's post office and has a zip code different from that of New Paltz.

The two remaining districts on Figure 7-1 are conspicuous because of their relatively great area. The county legislative district embraces all of New Paltz and extends southward and southwestward to include three other towns. The district encompasses what might be described as the south-central region of the county. Some would argue that New Paltz has little in common with two of these towns, but the district seems to function adequately. The school district includes almost all of New Paltz save a very small area along its eastern side, which is included in the neighboring district. Otherwise, the school district extends into five other towns. With all of this territory (the school district is about 10 or 11 km [6–7 mi] wide and some 32 km [20 mi] north to south), less than 1,900 students were enrolled in the local schools in the early 1980s, and the district was the second smallest in the county.

[3] Confusion over a municipality's geographic extent is neither confined to modern times nor to small municipal units. The small European kingdom of Macedonia, the home of Alexander the Great in the fourth century B.C., contained great ethnic diversity; its population represented at least 150 nationalities, living in roughly the same number of cities. Although Macedonia's general location was well established, no two authorities agreed on its exact boundaries. Henry Robert Wilkinson, *Maps and Politics: A Review of the Ethnographic Cartography of Macedonia* (Liverpool: University Press of Liverpool, 1951), p. 4.

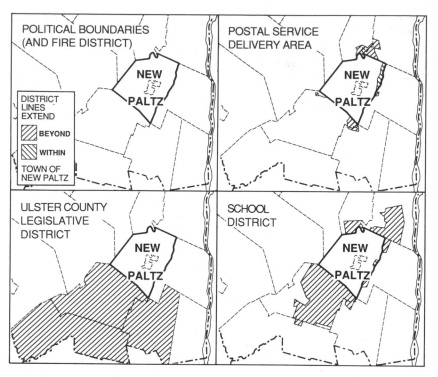

Figure 7-1   Selected district boundaries, Town and Village of New Paltz, New York.

Many other such administrative areas create confusion and, at times, consternation among citizens. For example, in counties with relatively small populations such as New Paltz's home County of Ulster, state assembly and state senate districts include large areas that cross both county lines and town lines. The 101st state assembly district, for instance, is partly in Ulster County, as are the 95th and 96th districts. The 39th and 40th state senatorial districts share Ulster County, but also extend beyond it. The state police have well-defined zones of operation, and several other divisions of the area include agricultural and election districts. The point of all this is that even in relatively rural, sparsely populated areas beyond the metropolitan fringe, people in most if not all states enjoy a range of services offered in ways that redefine "place" again and again.

The Many Municipalities: Maps of Urban Places

In the past, a profusion of civil divisions were subsumed under the words *city* and *town*.[4] Today, we have minor civil divisions such as hamlets, which may

---

[4] Defining the word *urban* presents problems in many places. For example, China had no clear definition of urban areas in its 1953 census. Basically, the Chinese defined as urban any set-

have a main street with a few stores, but which have no legal status beyond a post office and a zip code. Ranging upward, we find villages, boroughs, towns, urban townships, and cities among the places that may be considered municipalities. Beyond these, when we consider functional economic and social relationships, we can add to the litany the central city, the urbanized area, and the metropolitan statistical area.

In the United States the city is an exception to the spatial hierarchy. In general, a state is divided into counties—parishes in Louisiana and organized boroughs in Alaska. Each county, parish, or borough may be divided into townships—or towns in New England, New York, and Wisconsin. The city is the only type of area within a county that is not part of a township, and some cities even occupy parts of two or more counties. Baltimore and St. Louis are independent cities, not part of any county.[5] In general, however, a city is an incorporated urban place, politically independent from surrounding townships, with a relatively densely settled population pursuing a variety of economic and social activities.[6]

New York is a notable exception to the city as a county subdivision. As Figure 7-2 illustrates, the City of New York actually consists of five counties or, as is equally confusing, five "boroughs." The counties are Bronx, Kings, New York, Queens, and Richmond. Brooklyn Borough is spatially equivalent to Kings County, Manhattan Borough to New York County, and Staten Island to the County/Borough of Richmond. In the Bronx and Queens, the borough has the same name as the county. These counties/boroughs thus combine to form one of the largest and best-known cities in the world.

In contrast to New York, the City of Philadelphia simplified civil matters

---

tlement in which more than 2,500 persons resided and in which 50 percent of the labor force was engaged in nonagricultural pursuits. An exception overrode these criteria: any place that was a local seat of government was considered urban. Thus larger places with limited industry and agricultural places with small populations were not urban on functional grounds, but were urban as seats of government. See Leo A. Orleans and Ly Burnham, "The Enigma of China's Urban Population," *Asian Survey* 24, no. 7 (July 1984), 788–804.

[5] Los Angeles presents an almost unique case. Although the city proper is obviously definable in spatial terms, the area called Los Angeles has been described as a loose assemblage of urban places in search of a center. Literally scores of cities, 14 with populations in excess of 100,000, have coalesced to form this large agglomeration in Southern California that functions in many ways as a single entity. See Stephen S. Birdsall and John W. Florin, *Regional Landscapes of the United States and Canada* (New York: John Wiley & Sons, 1978), pp. 328–31.

[6] The U.S. Bureau of the Census is of some help here, defining the urban population in 1980 as consisting of all persons living in (1) places of 2,500 or more inhabitants incorporated as cities, villages, boroughs (except in Alaska and New York), and towns (except in New England, New York, and Wisconsin), but excluding those living in rural parts of extended cities; (2) census designated places of 2,500 or more; and (3) all territory in urbanized areas. See U.S. Bureau of the Census, *Census of Population, 1980, Vol. 1, Characteristics of the Population, Chapter A, Number of Inhabitants, Part 1, United States Summary* PC80-1-A (Washington, D.C.: U.S. Government Printing Office, 1983), p. A-2.

Figure 7-2   The City of New York, a combination of five counties/boroughs.

in 1854 by consolidating 29 political entities, all of which were in the County of Philadelphia. Thus the City and County of Philadelphia became one. As Figure 7-3 shows, the original city was located at the place where the Delaware and Schuylkill rivers are closest. Prior to consolidation, many problems existed because of the many jurisdictions within the county, but the issue that caused great concern was law enforcement or, more precisely, the lack thereof. Criminals often escaped arrest and prosecution by crossing the city line into one of the other 13 townships, 6 boroughs, or 9 districts within the county, where local authorities often failed to cooperate in apprehending the suspect. In addition to upgraded police protection, consolidation promoted better fire protection, and an expanded tax base moved the new city of some 400,000 into the metropolitan-age and better prepared it to cope with urban-industrial evolution.[7]

The "legal" city delimited on maps is often much smaller than the functional or "geographic" city. A large urban cluster complete with business and

_____

[7] Russell F. Weigley et al., eds., *Philadelphia: A 300-Year History* (New York: W. W. Norton, 1982), pp. 359–60.

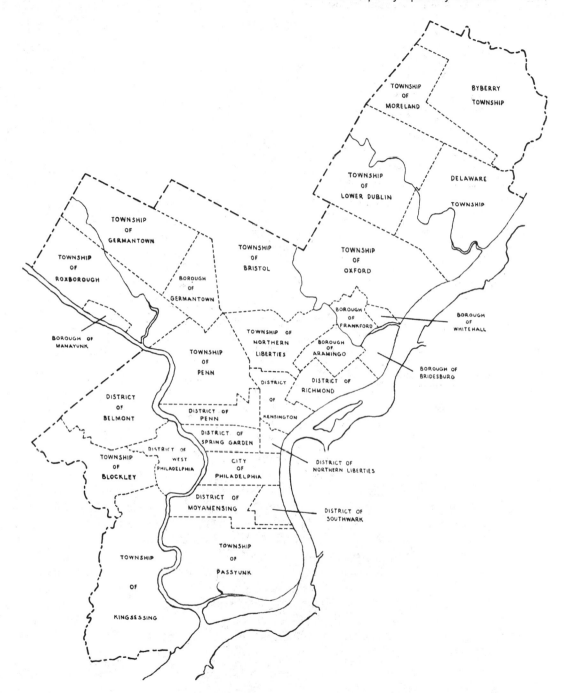

Figure 7-3 The City of Philadelphia at the time of consolidation in 1854. (Courtesy of the Philadelphia City Planning Commission.)

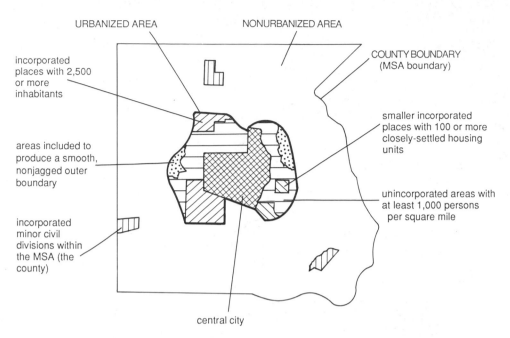

URBANIZED AREA

NONURBANIZED AREA

incorporated
places with 2,500
or more
inhabitants

COUNTY BOUNDARY
(MSA boundary)

smaller incorporated
places with 100 or more
closely-settled housing
units

areas included to
produce a smooth,
nonjagged outer
boundary

unincorporated areas with
at least 1,000 persons
per square mile

incorporated
minor civil
divisions within
the MSA (the
county)

central city

Figure 7-4   A model of a Metropolitan Statistical Area (MSA).

industry, the "legal" city is an "incorporation" sanctioned by state law. The "geographic" city is the area that better describes the total urban agglomeration—the corporate city and its environs extending outward to nonurban lands. Expanded a bit, the geographic or functional city idea leads nicely into the concept of metropolitan area, a term the U.S. Bureau of the Census has used, with almost continuous modification, since 1910, when the bureau introduced and mapped the Metropolitan District.[8] Figure 7-4 shows the components of the Metropolitan Statistical Area (MSA) in its current form. The underlying concept of the metropolitan area is based upon economic and social integration—the interdependency of central city (with its traditionally large nucleus of population and economic, social, and administrative functions), and surrounding townships, towns, boroughs, and villages. Some 35 years ago, the metropolitan area became a statistical unit in the census (of 1950), replacing the metropolitan district and allowing federal data to be presented on a common base as they describe metropolitan populations.[9] An area is designated as an MSA in one of two ways: it contains a city of 50,000 or more, or it contains an urbanized area of at least 50,000, together with a metropolitan population of at least 100,000

[8] Raymond E. Murphy, *The American City: An Urban Geography*, 2d ed. (New York: McGraw-Hill, 1974), pp. 12–15.

[9] Executive Office of the President, OMB-83-20, OMB Public Affairs Release, June 27, 1983, p. 2.

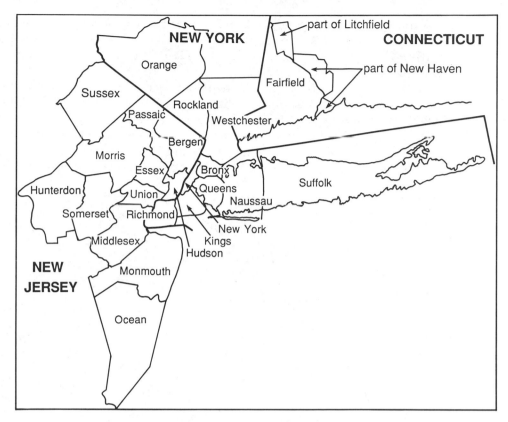

Figure 7-5 The New York–Northern New Jersey–Long Island, NY-NJ-CT Consolidated Metropolitan Statistical Area (CMSA).

(the latter referring usually to the county's total population). An MSA may contain more than one county, provided those other than the one in which the central city is located have strong social and economic ties with the central city.[10]

In the 1980s, two new designations joined the MSA. Whereas the MSA is not closely associated with other MSAs and is, therefore, surrounded by non-MSA territory, the Primary Metropolitan Statistical Area (PMSA) has a population exceeding one million and strong ties with other urbanized counties or groups of counties. Wherever PMSAs exist, they are aggregated upward to form Consolidated Metropolitan Statistical Areas (CMSAs). As of June 1983, 257 MSAs and 23 CMSAs, the latter consisting of 78 PMSAs, are recognized.[11]

Figure 7-5 illustrates the New York–Northern New Jersey–Long Island NY-NJ-CT CMSA, with New York City at its core and a very extensive area extending

[10] Ibid.
[11] Ibid.

well into New Jersey, up the Hudson River, and into southwestern Connecticut. It includes a total of 26 counties, 11 in New York, 12 in New Jersey, and 3 (in part) in Connecticut, housing some 18 million residents. Literally hundreds of governments function within this large and complex area, from the three majestic statehouses to village and town halls operating in frame houses in civil divisions of relatively insignificant size. Figure 7-6 represents the Philadelphia-Wilmington-Trenton PA-NJ-DE-MD CMSA, which, like New York's, is a multi-state spatial unit embracing a large area marked by equally large economic and social variations. Not municipalities by definition, these collections of municipalities, or metropolitan areas, have become ever more important as their in-

Figure 7-6 The Philadelphia-Wilmington-Trenton, PA-NJ-DE-MD Consolidated Metropolitan Statistical Area (CMSA).

habitants interact over the greater area in government, business, industry, education, recreation, and myriad other ways in seeking to satisfy wants and needs in late twentieth century America.

Given the number of administrative units and the wide-ranging services even many of the smaller, less populated places offer, maps become necessary descriptions of political jurisdictions and service areas. Although federal and state agencies (the Bureau of the Census and state departments of transportation, for example) are involved with mapping programs and charged with making many of their cartographic products available to the public, much of the cartographic effort devolves to the local communities and counties as they operate their areas day by day.

MAPS AND MUNICIPAL SERVICES

In the operation of the various departments of a political division, a surprisingly large array of maps is needed. Whether prepared in-house or contracted out, these maps serve to describe the streets and road patterns; the network of underground facilities—electric, gas, sewerage, or water lines; the location, ownership, allowed uses, and many other details about each lot or parcel of land, to mention but a few. Some maps serve as legal documents, whereas others are used with written descriptions to ascertain precisely the extent of districts, zones, subdivisions, lots, or whatever.

Municipal maps aid materially in improving our perceptions and comprehension of the area mapped. Chambers of commerce and state, county, and local public information agencies spend a great deal to show local residents and tourists where to ski, surf, skate, waterski, rock climb, swim, picnic, hunt, jog, fish, or visit historic sites, museums, wineries, orchards, dairy farms, and natural and humanly constructed oddities of all sorts. Business is brisk, so brisk that private firms now offer a wide variety of maps for sports enthusiasts.

This section focuses on some of the many maps municipalities use to better provide the array of services they offer. After looking at Sanborn sheets—fire insurance maps of thousands of places—we discuss a sequence of maps reflecting the needs of municipalities planning for, and ultimately experiencing development: planning, zoning, environmental protection, land subdivision, property survey, and tax mapping.

Fire Insurance Maps: Sanborn Sheets

Sanborn maps were a response to the need to improve a private-sector service to cities—fire insurance. Just as we discussed the recent mapping program taken on by thousands of jurisdictions in the United States in order to implement the federal flood insurance program (Chapter 5), the Sanborn Map Company produced a great number of maps of cities and towns dating from 1867. Offering detailed, accurate information about buildings and other structures, the maps show commercial, industrial, and residential land use in some 12,000 municipalities, mostly in the United States, but also in Canada and Mexico. Designed to assist in setting rates for fire insurance, these maps show size, shape, safety and pertinent construction features, street names and widths, property lines, building use, addresses, water mains, hydrants, and fire alarm boxes.[12]

The Library of Congress collection of Sanborn materials includes some 700,000 individual sheets in approximately 50,000 editions. This collection was enriched when, in 1967, a complete set of Sanborn maps was transferred from the Bureau of the Census; many of these were later editions than those acquired earlier, mostly through copyright deposit. The Census Bureau set in the Library of Congress is kept current by corrections supplied by the Sanborn Map Company.[13] Although we tend to associate the Bureau of the Census only with population, its functions include, among others, the collection and distribution of information on manufacturing, retail and wholesale trade, and services—basic information the Sanborn maps provide at a very large scale.

D. A. Sanborn, not surprisingly, was a surveyor (from Massachusetts) whose early work included an atlas of Boston (Insurance Maps of Boston, vol. 1, 1867), which is believed to be Sanborn's earliest publication. His work in Massachusetts and Tennessee convinced him of the market and he started the D. A. Sanborn National Insurance Diagram Bureau in New York City in 1867. Generally, credit for the first large-scale detailed fire insurance map is accorded George T. Hope, secretary of the Jefferson Insurance Company of New York, in about 1850. A committee of insurance officials was formed, hired an engineer to compile and map the information, and set the cartographic standards to be followed generally for a hundred years. The mapping of cities in this way was quite a business, probably as a result of the vast losses in New York brought about by a conflagration in 1835, when fire claims bankrupted many smaller insurance companies and led to the passage of statutes favoring large companies with greater reserves of funds. Given the broader service areas of these large companies, it became difficult, if not impossible, to inspect properties of applicants for insurance. The demand for maps showing detailed information on risk was assured.[14] Sanborn's coverage grew annually. Activity peaked in the 1930s, when maps in that period were available for some 13,000 municipalities.

An employee training manual describing Sanborn's maps as an easy and accurate reference on fire risk was published in 1905. The contents and tone of its introduction are instructive: "Sanborn maps are vastly different from all other publications, and the novice must start in with the idea that it is all new, though

---

[12] U.S. Library of Congress, Reference and Bibliography Section, Geography and Map Division, *Fire Insurance Maps in the Library of Congress,* with an Introduction by Walter W. Ristow (Washington, D.C.: Library of Congress, 1981), p. ix.

[13] Ibid.

[14] Ibid., pp. 3 and 6.

some former occupation, such as civil engineering and architectural work, should fit a man to readily grasp the primary principles. . . . Customers depend on the accuracy of our publications, and rely upon the information supplied, incurring large financial risks without making personal examinations of the properties."[15] The instructions encouraged Sanborn's employees to do the on-site work if records from courthouses or realtors were not easily obtainable.

The company prospered in building booms and weathered recessions, the Great Depression, and decades of scrutiny and attempts at creating competitors by the National Board of Fire Underwriters. During World War II, when construction was restricted, the company made maps for the military under contract. Postwar efforts to improve sales by using a smaller scale (from 1 in. = 50 ft to 1 in. = 100 or even 200 ft) might have helped had not the National Bureau of Fire Underwriters called into question the need for fire insurance maps of residential structures. (The bureau endorsed the need for commercial-industrial coverage, however.) Sanborn's market never really survived the war, as the 1950 vintage of their last catalog demonstrates.[16]

Fire insurance companies now use computer storage and retrieval of risk records, employ their own engineering departments to inspect where needed, and participate in improvements of construction, fire codes, and protection from fire. Modern risk management thus has limited interest in Sanborn Maps. In 1977 and 1978, however, the company copyrighted microfilm editions of several cities, corrected to 1975. At present, municipal governments provide 60 percent of the Sanborn market, and engineers and architects provide sales for the maps as well. Today about one-third of the collection is the basic large-scale, colored sheets; one-third is the smaller scale, colored maps of the 1950s; and one-third is small-scale, black-and-white photo-offset maps. Updated paste-on, photo-reproduction, and microimage services are available as well.[17] The Sanborn Fire Insurance Maps at the Library of Congress from 1867–1950 are available on high-quality microfilm (Chadwyck-Healey Inc., 623 Martense Ave., Teaneck, NJ 07666).

Nowhere can one find a better cartographic record of more than a century of urban growth and change in the United States than in the Sanborn materials. Figure 7-7 and Figure 7-8 show examples of these, representing Hannibal, Missouri, in 1924 and 1950. The greatest and most obvious change in that area over the years is the new highway extending across several blocks and leading to the railroad bridge, a development that resulted in the razing of several structures, as the maps show. Figure 7-9 is the Sanborn map legend for black-and-white editions and is included here to encourage the reader to use it to peruse the maps for the storehouse of information they show.

---

[15] From a *Surveyor's Manual for the Exclusive Use and Guidance of Employees*, published by the Sanborn Company in 1905, quoted in Ibid., p. 5.

[16] Ibid., pp. 6 and 8.

[17] Ibid., p. 9.

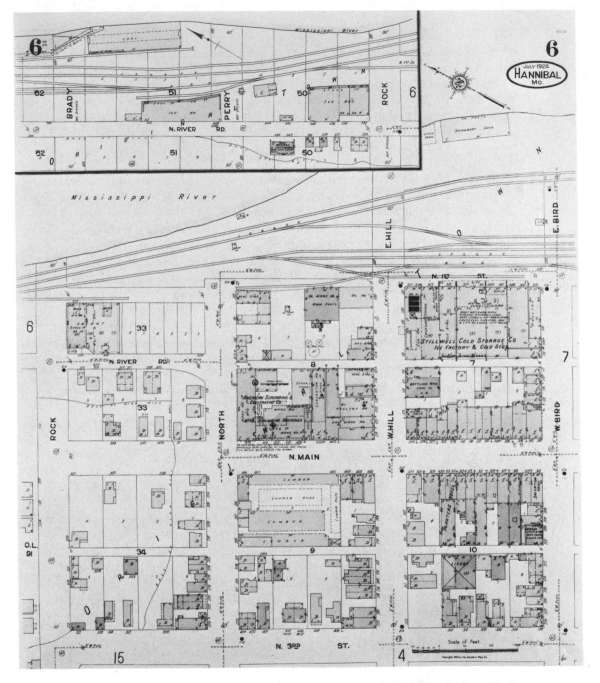

Figure 7-7 Sanborn map of Hannibal, Missouri, July 1924. The Sanborn Fire Insurance Maps at the Library of Congress are available on high-quality microfilm from: Chadwyck-Healey, Inc., 623 Martense Avenue, Teaneck, New Jersey 07666. (Used with permission of Chadwyck-Healey, Inc.)

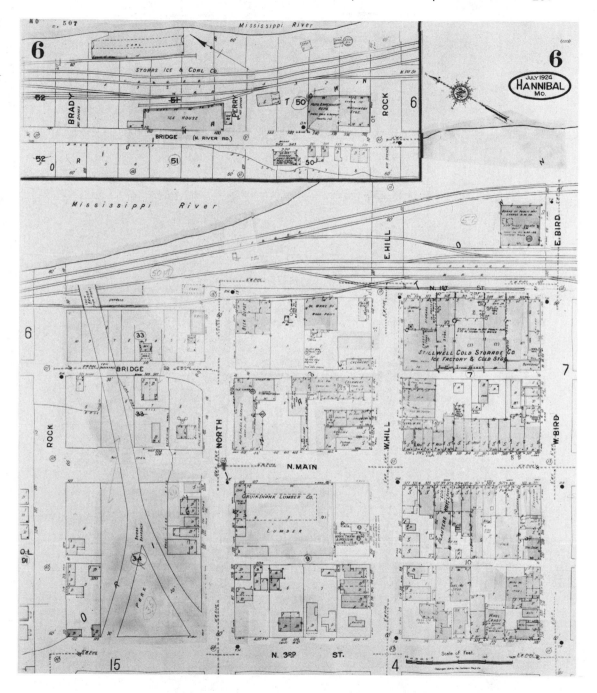

Figure 7-8 Sanborn map of Hannibal, Missouri, revised to 1950. (Used with permission of Chadwyck-Healey, Inc.)

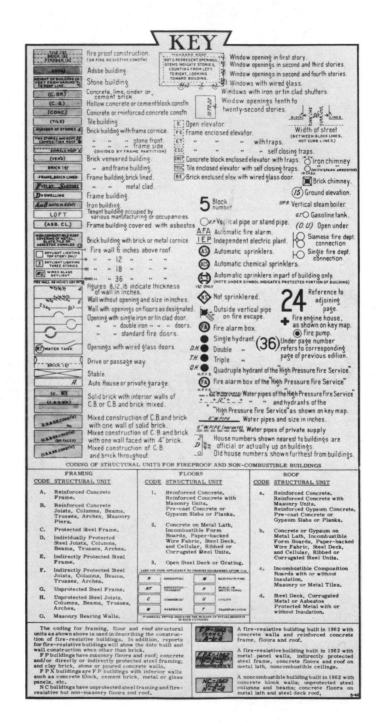

Figure 7-9 Key or legend for interpreting Sanborn fire insurance maps. (Used with permission of Chadwyck-Healey, Inc.)

Maps in Development

Whether by city, town(ship), or an incorporated minor civil division, oversight of development is accomplished essentially by regulation of land subdivision and land use through zoning. States and counties vary in their role in development, but the following account, based generally on New York statutes and town laws, illustrates the role of maps in this important municipal function.

Local elected officials establish the "official map" at the outset of planning to show existing streets and highways, drainage systems, and parks. All records pertaining to these facilities are considered part of the map. After the official map is drawn, the municipality must adopt a continuing process of changing the map to account for new, modified, or abandoned facilities.[18] Usually this task is the responsibility of the city, town, or village engineer—in large cities a full-time employee supervising a large staff, and in small municipalities usually a part-time consultant, who may serve several minor civil divisions.

Perhaps the ideal official map has been planned, if not achieved, in Irvine, California. Supposedly the largest master-planned urban place in the nation, Irvine was "born" in 1971 from a plan to develop a university community on 10,000 acres of the Irvine Ranch. Through a computer-aided system, the city is able to record changes in the built environment, the natural environment, and the human environment. The master map, it is hoped, will facilitate master planning so that individual site planning will yield to overall design, which provides a framework and an image of overall identity.[19]

Zoning.   Maps are an obvious and important component of the zoning law of municipalities countrywide, providing graphic expression of how the local code or ordinance is to be applied. The planning board, a group of appointed citizens, with the guidance and assistance of a professional planning consultant and legal counsel, prepares and modifies a comprehensive plan for the municipality. Such a development plan will show "desirable streets, bridges, and tunnels and the approaches thereto, viaducts, parks, public reservation . . . and such other features existing and proposed as will provide for the improvement of the city/town/village and its future growth, protection, and development, and will afford adequate facilities for the public housing, transportation, distribution, comfort, convenience, public health, safety and general welfare of its population."[20] Implicit in this statute is that the development plan will ordinarily contain a map or maps to "show" existing and proposed facilities. Figure 7-10, for example, portrays the master plan for what was a rural town(ship) in

---

[18] New York Department of State, *A Guide to the Planning and Zoning Laws of New York State*, rev. ed. (Albany, December 1981), pp. 16, 43, and 68.

[19] George A. Magnan, "Automating Land Use and Planning Graphics," *Design Graphics World* 9, no. 6 (June 1985), 20–23.

[20] New York, *Guide to Planning*, pp. 5, 25, and 51.

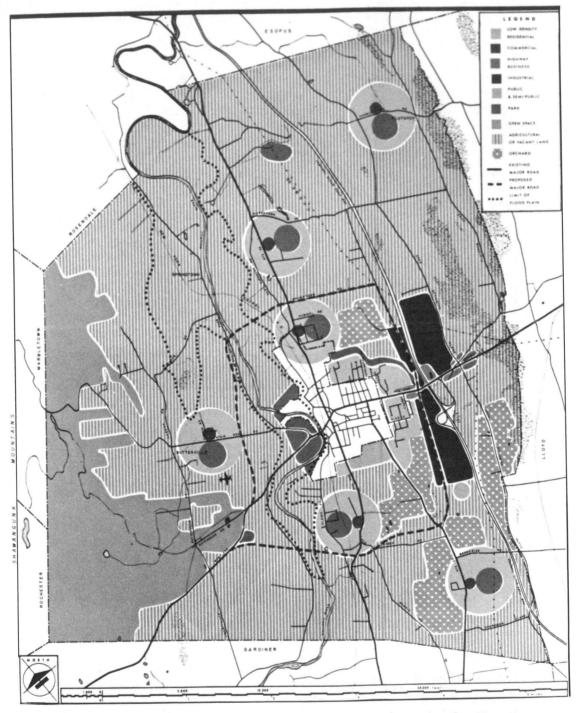

Figure 7-10 Development plan, Town of New Paltz, New York, 1966. (From Town of New Paltz Planning Study prepared by Brown and Anthony City Planners, April 1966.)

1966, the date the map was published. Note that the map includes the usual array of land-use designations—residential, agricultural, commercial, industrial—and attempts to meld physical capability by assigning density for some residential zones, open space, and vacant land, along the periphery of the flood plain.

Zoning refers to the specific application of powers and, in accordance with a comprehensive plan, is intended "to regulate and limit the height, bulk and location of buildings . . . to regulate and determine the area of yards, courts and other open spaces . . . to regulate the density of population . . . to divide the city into districts. . . . Such regulations shall . . . secure safety from fire, flood . . . and promote the public health and welfare . . . and shall be made with reasonable regard to the character of buildings . . . the value of land and the use to which it may be put . . . To regulate and restrict the location of buildings, designed for specified uses, and for such purposes to divide the city into districts and to prescribe for each such district the trades and industries that shall be excluded."[21] As broad and restrictive as the New York State law appears, its translation into local laws brings the powers of the state into the municipality.

Figure 7-11, a zoning map of the Town of New Paltz, New York, illustrates the several districts in which various uses are permitted. Residential uses dominate the area shown, as both residential and agricultural designations permit the construction of dwellings. Zones allow a variety of densities, with the number following the letter indicating the area in acres required per dwelling unit (R-1, A-1.5, A-3). The districts in which the variable residential designation is allowed promote clustering of housing to allow more open space. (This concept is discussed later, under "Subdivision of Land.") Business and light industry are allowed in certain sections along major highways and generally near the New York State Thruway in the case of industry. Although not explicit on the map, the local law contains lists of prohibited or excluded activities, those businesses and industries deemed to be dangerous or simply a nuisance. The open-space district Figure 7-11 shows is essentially the flood plain of the Wallkill River, where residences may be built provided federal flood insurance standards are met. (See Chapter 5, which discusses the Federal Flood Insurance Program.) Moreover, agriculture is permitted in the open-space zone. The Village of New Paltz, a political entity separate from the town, has its own zoning laws and is shown unzoned in Figure 7-11. Although the zone names and their specifications may vary, local laws such as these are in effect throughout the nation, attempting to temper change and development with concern for the residents and the environment.

It is interesting to compare the master plan for New Paltz in the 1960s with the recent zoning map. Although separated in time by almost 15 years, the

---

[21] Ibid. Although this statute applies to cities, those for towns and villages in New York are parallel, as are most such laws across the United States.

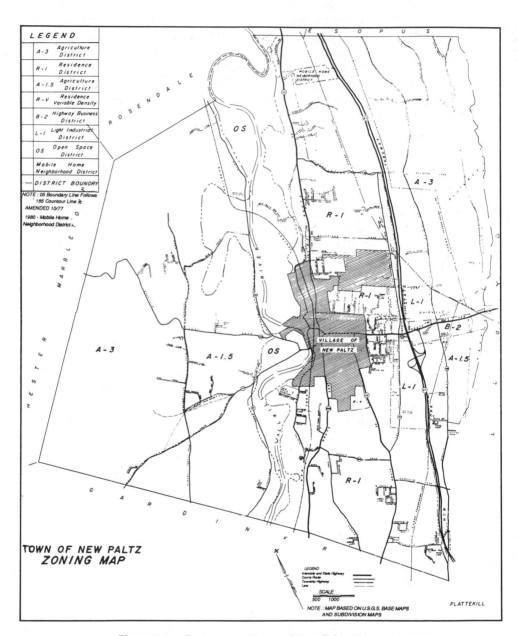

Figure 7-11 Zoning map, Town of New Paltz, New York, 1980.

general ideas of the earlier work are, more or less, shown in the later work. One sad reality is certainly apparent, however; in the areas where residential subdivisions have been built (note the southeastern periphery in Figure 7-11, where streets have been built and named), the use shown 15 years before on the development plan was orchard; thus apple orchards, productive agricultural lands, have been replaced by residences. The zoning map, it should be understood, represents a moment in an ever-changing series of events, occurring continuously as needs and desires evolve and priorities change.

Environmental Protection.   Given the growing concern for the manner in which development affects the physical environment, it is gratifying that federal and state authorities have provided municipalities with specific powers to demand an estimate of the environmental impact of any proposal and to deny or modify detrimental development plans. The National Environmental Policy Act (NEPA) of 1969 requires federal agencies to include environmental impact statements (EIS) in all development proposals when significant environmental impacts are projected.[22]

States followed the federal lead, since all levels of government, as well as the private sector, are involved in federal programs. New York's State Environmental Quality Review Act of 1975 (SEQR), for example, calls for all state and local government agencies to give complete consideration to environmental protection. SEQR's basic purpose is to ensure that environmental factors are considered at all levels and as early as possible in the process. SEQR requires all agencies to determine the extent to which actions they undertake directly, fund, or approve will affect the environment and, if the effect is deemed significant, to prepare or request an EIS. Climatic, hydrologic, and topographic aspects of the physical environment are specified in the law as worthy of consideration—the agency or the applicant must thus collect basic information and report on effects involving atmosphere, soils, surface drainage, and groundwater. Further aspects include geology, vegetation, land use, and wildlife, as well as social and economic factors and sites of historical significance. Cities and minor civil divisions are charged with the responsibility of completing natural resource inventories, mapping the results, providing the information to developers, and employing the inventories in the recommendations and decisions of elected and appointed officials.[23]

The municipalities of New York State have prepared maps, based generally upon soil surveys (maps and descriptions), to comply with the call for resource

[22] Elizabeth H. Haskell and Victoria S. Price, *State Environmental Management*, Praeger Special Studies in U.S. Economic, Social and Political Issues (New York: Praeger, 1973), pp. 265–67.

[23] New York Department of Environmental Conservation, *Natural Resource Inventory: A Guide to the Process* (Albany: Bureau of Community Assistance, Division of Educational Services, April 1980), pp. 3–18. For an excellent practical guide to the preparation and review of the EIS, see Michael Greenberg et al., *Environmental Impact Statements*, Resource Paper no. 78-3 (Washington, D.C.: Association of American Geographers, 1978).

inventories in SEQR. At a mapping unit of 2.4 hectares (6 acres) or more in which soil-determined areas of potential development are depicted, these maps are quite general. Nevertheless, they serve to alert the municipality and the applicant to environmentally sensitive areas and to cultural limitations on development. Figure 7-12, a four-map composite of some of the factors included in the inventory, provides several good examples of the information available when deciding about whether a project requires an EIS. Agricultural potential, mapped in the lower right of Figure 7-12, serves as a summary of the area's drainage, soil depth, and slope, the three other maps in the composite. These maps can be prepared for most parts of the country from soil survey reports and maps, prepared at the county level by the Soil Conservation Service of the U.S. Department of Agriculture.

Concern for the environment spurred the State of New York to enact the Freshwater Wetlands Act, designed to "preserve, protect and conserve freshwater wetlands, and benefits derived therefrom, to prevent the despoilation and destruction of freshwater wetlands, and to regulate use and development of such wetlands to secure the natural benefits."[24] What with the ever-increasing demands by residential and industrial users, and problems with purity and reliability of water supply, laws such as these are appropriate nationwide.

Freshwater wetlands are invaluable, providing flood protection, habitats for wildlife, and open space, not to mention the storage of water. As in other states, New York's law goes on to specify that all individual freshwater wetlands of at least 5 hectares (12.4 acres)—less if deemed of unusual local importance—shall be identified and mapped.[25] Figure 7-13 shows a part of the U.S. Geological Survey's 1:24,000 Middletown, New York, sheet as that area's freshwater wetlands map. Note that the map traces and identifies each wetland's extent. These maps, or more detailed versions, if required, become extremely important in municipalities when a designated wetland is within an area to be developed. According to the statute, a permit is required to conduct regulated activities on the wetlands as defined on the map. Such activities include, among others, draining, dredging, excavating, removal of soil or other material, dumping, filling, depositing, building structures or roads, causing any form of pollution, and carrying on any other activities that are inimical to the functions of freshwater wetlands.[26]

Subdivision of Land.   In subdividing land an owner may build houses and sell them, sell lots and let the buyers build, or build on some lots and sell others. In regulating land subdivision, the municipality must review proposed changes in the intensity of land uses. Although subdivision regulations might

[24] New York Department of Environmental Conservation, *Freshwater Wetlands*, Article 24 and Title 23 of Article 71 of the Environmental Conservation Law, October 1980, p. 1.

[25] Ibid., p. 5.

[26] Ibid., pp. 11 and 12.

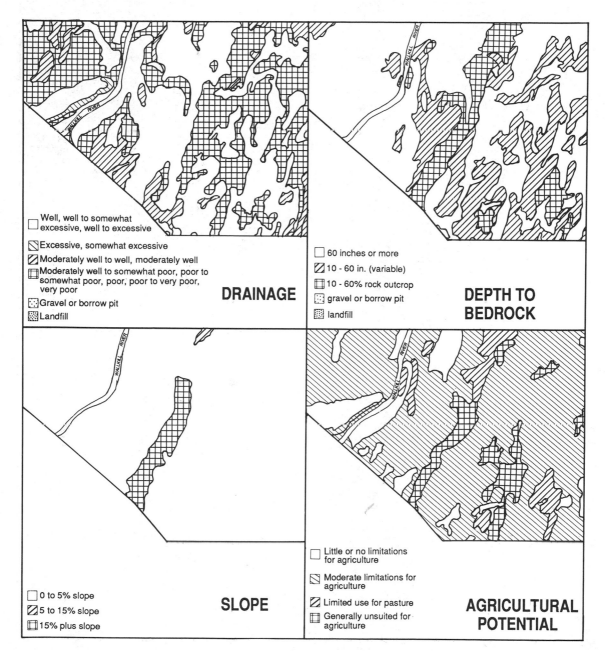

Figure 7-12 Examples of maps prepared as part of the natural resource inventory, Town of New Paltz, Environmental Conservation Commission, various dates.

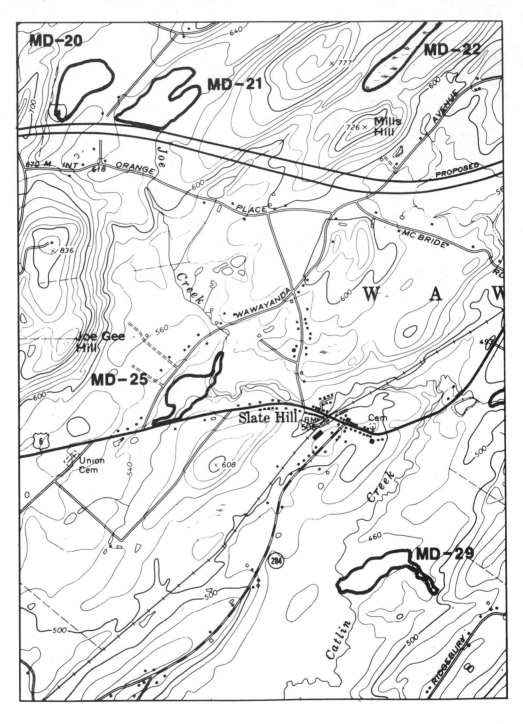

seem overly restrictive, they are the key to local control of land use. The open-space subdivision as an alternative to the conventional subdivision (shown in Figure 7-14) points up the kinds of opportunities afforded the municipality—by injecting some imagination into the subdivision of land and preserving open space at the same time. As the maps depict, both plans yield the same number of building lots. Yet the conventional plan uses all 108 acres for single-family, detached homes, whereas the open-space alternative has just 72 single-family detached lots and adds 36 single-family attached lots. Average lot size obviously would be smaller for the open-space plan, but compared to just 10 percent of land left in open space in the conventional scheme, the open-space design allows half the land to remain open. With this, the developer would need less road and sewerage footage and would experience cost savings. Perhaps most important, the open space preserved would yield recreational areas and many more trees, ponds, and other natural amenities.[27]

Figure 7-15 illustrates a subdivision map and accompanying notes. Notice that the lot lines show bearings and lengths (explained later and shown in Figures 7-17 and 7-18). The map also shows the roads and 2-foot contours. Although based on statutes and provisions found in local laws, the subdivision map also reflects discussion between the applicant and the planning board, with both parties attempting to divide the land in a fashion that yields a fair profit to the owner and has a minimal impact on existing residences and the area in general. This concern is perhaps best expressed in the notes accompanying Figure 7-15, listing in some detail the requirements to be observed, which the building inspector and others will watch for and insist upon before the site can be occupied. Although not illustrated here, the maps submitted in a subdivision application must include details about drainage and the provision for removal of, or on-site treatment of, effluent—septic tank, tile trench, leaching field—and the water supply. These sections and detailed drawings, reviewed by an engineer and the county board of health in addition to planning boards at local and county levels, illustrate the concern for the supply and purity of water and the proper disposition of sewage. Comparing small, less densely settled communities, such as New Paltz, with highly urbanized places reveals that both have major problems. Which, if either, is more easily managed is difficult to say, since, in cities, the water and sanitary systems are public, whereas many residents in more nearly rural communities depend upon wells and septic systems on their property. It seems that municipality-wide water services should be less subject to vagaries of supply and purity, but even this remains to be seen.

---

[27] New York Office of Planning Services, *The Open Space Subdivision*, Local Planning Guide Series (Albany, June 1972), pp. 8–9.

Figure 7-13   Freshwater wetlands map (part of Middletown, New York, map). Map base is the U.S. Geological Survey 1:24,000, 7.5-minute quadrangle map. (Courtesy of the New York State Department of Environmental Conservation, Region III Headquarters, New Paltz.)

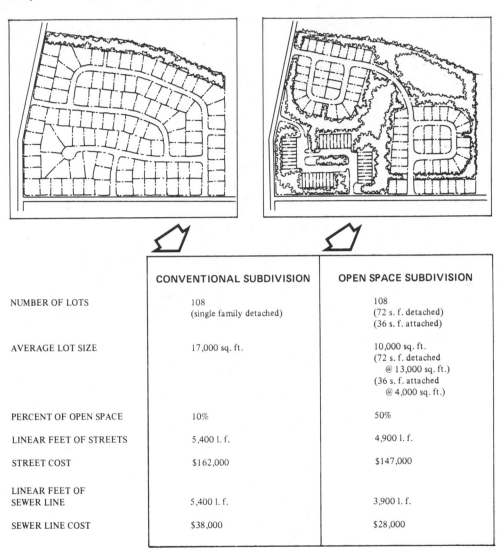

	CONVENTIONAL SUBDIVISION	OPEN SPACE SUBDIVISION
NUMBER OF LOTS	108 (single family detached)	108 (72 s. f. detached) (36 s. f. attached)

AVERAGE LOT SIZE	17,000 sq. ft.	10,000 sq. ft.
		(72 s. f. detached
		   @ 13,000 sq. ft.)
		(36 s. f. attached
		   @ 4,000 sq. ft.)

PERCENT OF OPEN SPACE	10%	50%
LINEAR FEET OF STREETS	5,400 l. f.	4,900 l. f.
STREET COST	$162,000	$147,000
LINEAR FEET OF SEWER LINE	5,400 l. f.	3,900 l. f.
SEWER LINE COST	$38,000	$28,000

Figure 7-14 Examples of open space and conventional subdivisions. (From New York Office of Planning Services, *Local Planning Guide Series: The Open Space Subdivision* [Albany, June 1972], pp. 8–9.)

Where Not To Dig: Maps of Underground Facilities. Aesthetics enter development in many ways, and rightly so, as local laws increasingly express concern for visual impact. For instance, in many communities new subdivisions of a given minimum number of lots must include the installation of electric service underground. Who could argue that such a requirement reduces the trappings of development by omitting from view the profusion of wires strung on the omnipresent poles lining the roadside. The burying of electric lines means that this service joins gas mains and laterals, along with water pipes, sewer lines, and storm drains, as invisible but extremely important parts of the infrastructure. Having such expensive hardware and equipment out of sight is fine, but how are repairs or changes accomplished? Also, whenever excavation for whatever purpose becomes necessary, how does the equipment operator avoid causing power outages, water main breaks, and other calamities of urban-suburban America? Maps provide the answer by showing in great detail where the various pipes and wires and conduits lie. Figure 7-16, a map of gas lines in a small urban place, was prepared by the local gas and electric company and is made available to those who need to know where not to dig. In some metropolitan areas, several utilities pool their efforts in an underground facilities protective organization that maintains a single master map and uses radio and newspaper ads with the plea: "Call before you dig."

Property Surveys.   Perhaps the one aspect of land survey with which most Americans are familiar is the survey prepared for a real estate transaction. Such surveys are often made if there is litigation over land; in the case of subdivision of land, the survey becomes an essential legal and administrative document. In all surveys, the licensed surveyor ensures that the parcel conforms to the legal description and that the map illustrates all physical features as they relate to the property lines, shows easements and rights-of-way, and illustrates any encroachments on or over the property line.

Among the most basic of land surveys is a *location* or *boundary survey* prepared to illustrate lines and buildings to a lending institution or title company so that the prospective buyer can borrow money for a mortgage and prove clear title. At a later date, the same surveyor might make an *updated survey* to show improvements or title conditions. A *subdivision survey* results in a map showing how the property has been divided for any purpose (see Figure 7-15). Finally, a *topographic survey*, often at a very small contour interval (say, two feet), shows the elevations of the land, along with roads and other improvements.[28]

Figure 7-17 presents a survey prepared to instruct surveying students. Most of the information it shows is straightforward; the actual description of the lot lines might require more detailed explanation, however, as offered in Figure 7-18. To plot the description of the building lot (Figure 7-17) requires a protractor, a sheet of graph paper, and a pencil. For example, beginning at the railroad spike "set" (which means the surveyor placed it there to mark the point), the description says, in part, "thence from said point of beginning and along lands reputedly of Small S 34° 30' 00" W 122.35 feet to an iron pin set." Place the protractor on the point representing the "railroad spike set," the north-south line parallel to the north arrow shown, and measure the bearing from south by

---

[28] Delaware and Hudson Land Surveyors Association, Inc., *Why a Survey is Necessary!* (Goshen, N.Y., 1980).

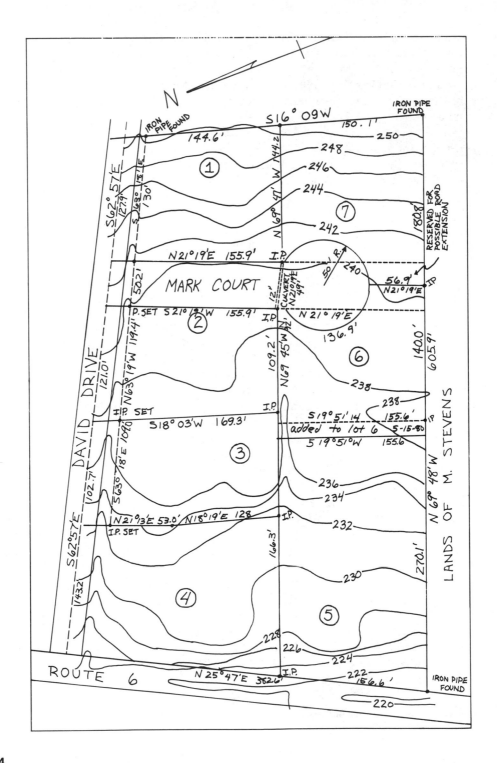

NOTES

① FILL SHALL BE PLACED ON UNDISTURBED VIRGIN SOIL AND ALLOWED TO SET FOR 30 DAYS BEFORE CONSTRUCTION IS STARTED.

② FILL MATERIAL SHALL BE APPROVED BY THE ULSTER COUNTY DEPT. OF HEALTH BEFORE BEING PLACED.

③ ALL FILL AREAS SHALL BE LOCATED AS TO ALLOW FOR A MINIMUM OF 36" OF FILL BELOW THE DISTRIBUTORS.

④ TILE SHALL BE PLACED WITH A MAXIMUM SLOPE OF 1/16 INCH PER FOOT. MINIMUM SLOPE OF 1/32 INCH PER FOOT.

⑤ THE ENDS OF THE TILE LINES SHALL BE TIED TOGETHER.

⑥ THE TILE LINES SHALL BE KEPT 8 TO 10 FEET FROM THE EDGES OF THE BED SURFACE OF THE FIELD.

⑦ PERFORATED PIPE MAY BE USED INSTEAD OF TILE PIPE. (PERFORATIONS DOWN)

⑧ A DISTRIBUTION BOX SHALL BE USED WITH TIGHT JOINT PIPE DISTRIBUTORS FROM THE BOX TO THE TILE LINES.

⑨ GRAVEL OR BROKEN STONE, 3/4" TO 1 1/2" SHALL BE PLACED 6" BELOW THE TILE PIPE, AROUND THE PIPE AND 2" ABOVE THE PIPE.

⑩ INSTALLATION AND MAINTENANCE OF SEPTIC SYSTEMS SHALL FOLLOW THE ULSTER COUNTY DEPT. OF HEALTH BULLETIN "RECOMMENDATIONS FOR SMALL SEWAGE DISPOSAL SYSTEM" AND THE NEW YORK STATE DEPARTMENT OF ENVIRONMENTAL CONSERVATION BULLETIN "STANDARDS FOR WASTE TREATMENT WORKS, 1970" AS AMENDED.

⑪ NO LOT MAY BE FURTHER SUBDIVIDED

⑫ ALL LOTS SHALL UTILIZE ABOVE-GROUND FILL SYSTEMS.

⑬ NO MORE THAN ONE SINGLE-FAMILY DWELLING PER LOT.

⑭ NO ROOF, CELLAR OR FOOTING DRAINS TO BE DISCHARGED INTO THE SEWAGE DISPOSAL SYSTEM.

⑮ ALL TREES MUST BE CUT FROM THE TILE FIELD AREAS.

⑯ NO BASEMENT FIXTURES ARE PERMITED WITHOUT SPECIAL SEWAGE DESIGN.

⑰ NO DRIVEWAYS, ROADWAYS OR PARKING AREAS SHALL BE CONSTRUCTED OVER ANY PORTION OF THE SANITARY DISPOSAL SYSTEM.

Figure 7-15 Example of a residential subdivision map and accompanying notes.

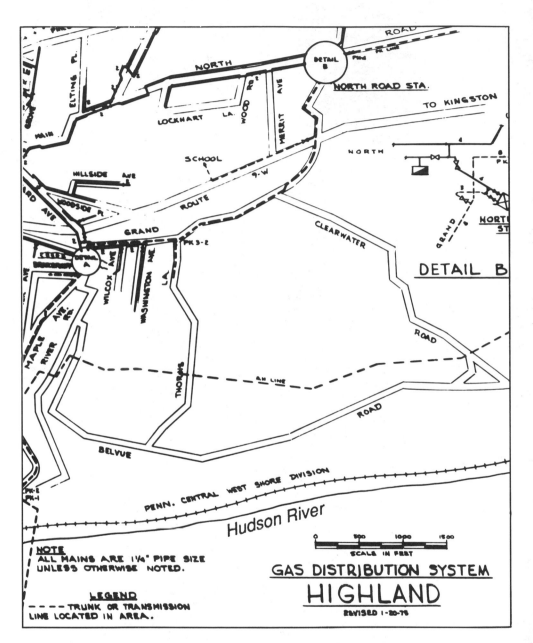

Figure 7-16 Map of a gas distribution system, underground gas lines. (Courtesy of Central Hudson Gas and Electric Company, Poughkeepsie, N.Y.)

finding the point on the arc 34°30′ west of south. Then scale the length of the line, 122.35 ft, and locate the next point ("iron pipe set"). Invert the protractor and center it on the "iron pipe set." From north, mark the bearing along the arc (the perimeter of the protractor). By proceeding through the description, the final bearing should take one back to the starting point and thus "close" the survey. (Chapter 6 also discusses land survey; see Figures 6-18 and 6-19.)

Tax Mapping.   For purposes of accuracy in property tax assessment, states have initiated tax-mapping programs, county by county. Aside from assessment capability, the maps provide an invaluable aid to those involved in property transfer: sale of land has become much less ambiguous, especially along minor civil division and county lines. Although specifics may vary, the purposes of the programs are clearly similar. Vermont's mapping program is well defined, and its goals were stated succinctly in 1974, as follows:

> The genesis of Vermont's total-concept mapping program is the need for accurate property maps for assessment purposes. However, the long range benefits to be derived from orthophoto base maps for the entire State of Vermont will be far-reaching in general planning, the environmental and agricultural fields, and a host of other disciplines. The property overlays will be the first use made of the ortho-photo base maps and will in themselves be long-needed tools, not only for property assessment but for planning and other purposes.
>
> The broadest and most exciting single purpose of the entire program is to provide state and local governments, as well as the private sector, with an accurate photo description of the State of Vermont. This will increase the ability of all to analyze problems and reach important decisions based on a real understanding of the facts.[29]

Figure 7-19 illustrates well the scales and area designations of the Vermont tax-mapping program. Notice the plane-coordinate system portrayed along the diagram's left and top, yielding the designation for the various sheets. Several scales are available. The sheet number refers to the lower left-hand corner of the sheet. Sheets differing in scale but sharing the same reference corner will have the same sheet number and must be differentiated by their scale. For example, the corner with grid coordinates East 144,000 and North 72,000 is shared by maps at 1:10,000, 1:5,000, 1:2,500, 1:1,250, and 1:625—all with sheet number 144072; but the next 1:10,000-scale sheet to the east is number 148072, whereas the next 1:2,500-scale sheet is number 145072. The system culminates in a sheet at a scale of 1:625, shown on the extreme southwestern corner of the index and designated sheet number 14450725, meaning that the mapping unit

---

[29] This statement, by then Governor Thomas P. Salmon, appeared in Vermont Agency of Administration, Department of Taxes, *Vermont Property Tax Program: Index to Base Mapping Sheets* (Montpelier, 1974).

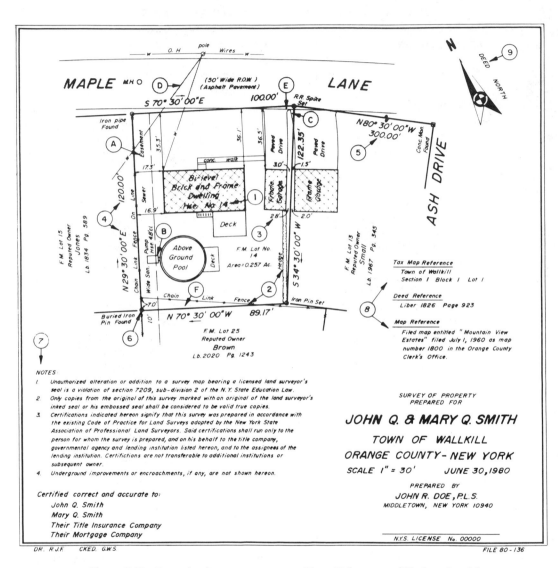

Figure 7-17   Example of a property survey. (From Delaware and Hudson Land Surveyors Association, Inc., *Why a Survey is Necessary!* [Goshen, N.Y., 1980]; used with permission.)

THE FOLLOWING ARE <u>SOME</u> OF THE POTENTIAL PROBLEMS WHICH A SURVEY COULD POINT OUT. YOU SHOULD CONSULT YOUR <u>ATTORNEY CONCERNING THEM.</u>

(A) The land within this easement probably has limited usability.

(B) This pump house is built within the bounds of an easement. This is a potential problem which might be unacceptable.

(C) The adjoiner's drive is built partly on the property. This could be an encroachment or an easement.

(D) The wires servicing the adjoiner are encroaching. This could indicate an easement.

(E) Part of the street pavement is encroaching. A potential problem which may not be correctable.

(F) This land between the fence and the property line appears to be part of the adjoiner's property, BUT is actually part of this lot.

THIS IS <u>SOME</u> OF THE INFORMATION <u>THAT A SURVEY MAP WILL PROVIDE.</u>

(1) This number is the street address of the property.

(2) The map shows various improvements on the property and their relationship to the property lines.

(3) This distance is called an offset. It shows the shortest distance from an improvement to the property line. It is useful for planning improvements and checking zoning requirements.

(4) These numbers are called bearings and distances. They define the shape of the property.

(5) This distance is called a tie. It shows the distance from closest street intersection to the beginning of the property.

(6) These points which were found indicate some of the field evidence which the surveyor used to locate the property.

(7) These notes are your assurance the survey was prepared according to accepted standards of work.

(8) These references serve to define the property's location.

(9) North arrow shows reference used.

<u>DESCRIPTION OF FILED MAP LOT 14</u>

All that certain lot, piece or parcel of land situate, lying and being in the Town of Wallkill, County of Orange, State of New York and being more accurately bounded and described as follows:

Beginning at a railroad spike set in the southerly line of Maple Lane, said railroad spike also being N 80°-30'-00" W 300.00 feet from the intersection of the southerly line of Maple Lane and the westerly line of Ash Drive, thence from said point of beginning and along lands reputedly of Small S 34°-30'-00" W 122.35 feet to an iron pin set, thence along lands reputedly of Brown N 70°-30'-00" W 89.17 feet to a buried iron pin found, thence along lands reputedly of Jones N 29°-30'-00" E 120.0 feet to an iron pipe found in the southerly line of Maple Lane, thence along said southerly line S 70°-30'-00" E 100.0' feet to the point of beginning and containing 0.257 acres of land, more or less as surveyed by John R. Doe P.L.S. on June 30, 1980.

Figure 7-17   (*continued*)

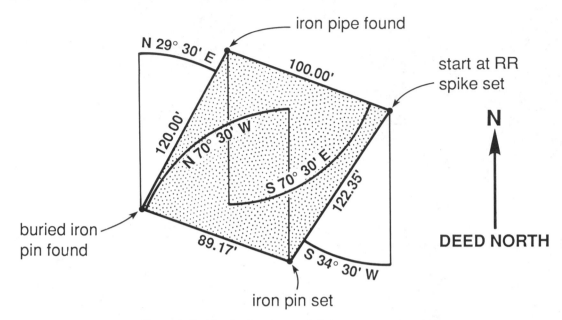

Figure 7-18 Plotting bearings and distances on a property survey.

is 500 m² at a coordinate value of E 144,500 m, N 072,500 m. Large-scale sheets cover smaller areas in greater detail and are presented only for places where greater spatial resolution is required. The scales shift from 1:10,000 (smallest) to 1:5,000, with selected village enlargements at 1:2,500. Maps are planned, as well, in urban areas at 1:1,250, with central business district enlargements at 1:625. Finally, the linear distances each scale will cover along the sheets' dimensions are shown as ranging from 0.5 km for central business districts to 8.0 km for area maps at 1:10,000. In English units, these cover from 1,640 ft to 26,246 ft (almost 5 mi) on a side.[30]

The State of New York Tax Mapping System is likewise based upon maps photogrammetrically prepared, with final maps at scales ranging from 1:4,800 (1 in. represents 400 ft) for rural areas to 1:600 (1 in. represents 50 ft) for densely inhabited areas. Intermediate scales are 1:2,400 (1 in. represents 200 ft) for semi-rural areas, and 1:1,200 (1 in. represents 100 ft) for incorporated places—cities and villages.[31] The specifications for these scales range from towns with less

---

[30] Ibid.

[31] In this discussion of New York's tax mapping specifications, no attempt has been made to show both metric and British measures because the latter units are legal and traditional, and unlikely to be discarded in favor of metric units.

Figure 7-19 Scales and areas of the Vermont Property Tax Program. (From Vermont Agency of Administration, Department of Taxes, *Vermont Property Tax Program, Index to Base Mapping Sheets* [Montpelier, September 1974].)

Boundaries of sheets of the Vermont Property Mapping Program are based on metric equivalents of the Vermont Plane Coordinate System.

Orthophotomaps are planned at scales of 1:10,000 and 1:5000 with enlargement of selected village areas to 1:2500. Line-and-symbol maps are planned in urban areas at scales of 1:1250 with enlargement of the central business district areas to 1:625.

The map on the facing page shows sheet boundaries of the 1:10,000- and 1:5000-scale orthophotomaps superimposed over the county and town outline map with the Vermont Coordinate System (VCS) values in metres around the perimeter.

The diagram below shows the coverage in English and metric linear units of one sheet at each of the various scales.

The sheet number 144072 in example below is derived from the Vermont Coordinate System value in thousands of metres (kilometres) of the southwest (lower left) corner of the sheet. (The coordinate value is E144,000m, N072,000m). The various scales will be indicated by a series number placed immediately beneath the sheet number, together with the date of applicable photography.

In the case of 1:625-scale sheets, the sheet dimension is 500 metres and therefore it is necessary to show the sheet number in hundreds of metres e.g. the number of the sheet below at the 1:625-scale is 14450725. (The coordinate value is E144,500m, N072,500m).

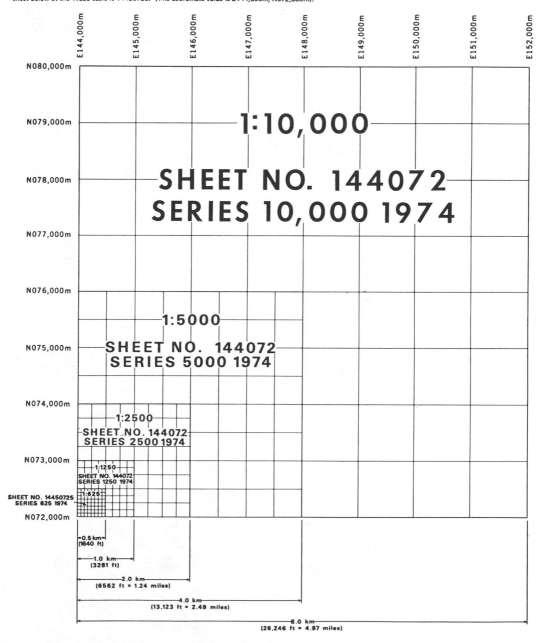

Figure 7-20 Example of a tax map.

than 100 acres per parcel and more than half of the parcels average one acre or more (rural, sparsely inhabited areas) to "dense areas," where parcels having frontages of 40 ft or less comprise 20 percent or more of the area.[32]

Figure 7-20, part of a New York State tax map at a scale of 1:2,400, illustrates the features depicted for a semirural area. Using as an example lot number 12, owned by Smith, the information shown includes all streets, named and with right-of-way width shown (Joalyn Road, 40 ft wide); the individual parcel's frontage in feet (152 ft); the owner's name (Smith); the lot number (12); the New York State plane-coordinate-system designation (East 57043-North 63555 at the visual lot center); area in acres (1.1 acres); and account number (107130.000). As property is subdivided, transferred, or otherwise modified or improved, all changes are recorded for the parcels affected by the county Real Property Tax Services Agency. Translated, this means in most cases an increase in property tax assessment and an increased tax bill!

Tax maps provide an accurate and up-to-date recording system of land ownership, parcel by parcel. In most parts of the country, as in New York, less effort is devoted to aesthetics than to geographic precision. Aside from the benefits accruing to the tax assessment capability of the municipality, the maps are invaluable for planning and development purposes. After all, land already occupied can hardly be re-developed without razing existing structures.

MAPS OF THE LOCAL AREA

Municipalities have a surprising number of maps, as the subjects treated thus far in this chapter attest. Federal, state, regional, county, and municipal agencies are most often responsible for the compilation, production, and distribution of maps, although the private sector provides maps too. This subject is indeed vast, and beyond the often parallel series produced by federal and state agencies, each community is to some extent idiosyncratic in the volume and variety of maps available. For purposes of discussion, we have elected to illustrate the point with a well-known, not-too-large city and the county in which it is located—Syracuse, New York, and Onondaga County.[33]

[32] New York Board of Equalization and Assessment, *Model Technical Specifications for Tax Mapping in New York State*, 2d rev. ed. (Albany, October 1975), p. 1.

[33] Syracuse and its environs provide an appropriate choice because of population size, ethnic mix, and socioeconomic characteristics, viewed by marketing firms and analysts as representative of the national scene. Indeed, the city was the subject of a news story that cited it as an "All-American kind of place," one "demographically representative," a "mini-America." *New York Times*, 22 February 1984, B1 and 2. In addition, a survey of maps on Syracuse and Onondaga County was completed in 1984 and provides a ready reference for much of the materials used here. Thus, except where indicated otherwise, the source of the material for this section is an unpublished guide to maps of Onondaga County, New York, prepared at Syracuse University by Ben Baldanza, Kevin Gadra, James Galvin, Jr., Robert Harmon, Leslie Nixon, Randy Sands, and Gregory Speich, under the direction of Mark Monmonier.

Table 7-1, a list of categories of maps found for the Syracuse area, illustrates the breadth of municipal-level mapping and includes several topics to which whole chapters or parts of this book are devoted: historical maps; topographic maps; planning, administration, and environmental maps; and aerial photographs and satellite images. Therefore this section will treat "locator" maps briefly and then turn to sources of local holdings.

Locator Maps

Locator maps are essentially guides to the local area, showing places, boundaries, routes, and points of interest. Street maps of cities are perhaps the most widely used maps of this type. An example of such a map is the planimetric map of Syracuse from the New York State Department of Transportation. Updated every five years or so, this map is a primary locator map for the city/county, showing all streets, highways, railroads, large buildings, and institutions at a scale of 1:24,000. Figure 7-21 is a section of the Syracuse West quadrangle showing part of the City of Syracuse. Prominent on the map are interstate route 81—running north-south from lower right to upper left in an intricate junction of expressways—several downtown churches, and an array of large public buildings.

Another kind of locator map, a popular example, is the park or recreation area map. Figure 7-22, a map of Highland Forest, near Syracuse, portrays roads and hiking trails, tenting areas, streams and ponds, forests, shelters, and trail symbols. It is a large-scale map and provides those interested in using the facilities with an essential tool, one of great help in enjoying the site safely. Often chambers of commerce, real estate offices, restaurants, and gasoline stations provide a variety of brochures, most of which contain a locator map showing the location of and routes to tourist attractions, such as amusement parks, mu-

TABLE 7-1   AVAILABLE MAPS OF ONONDAGA COUNTY
AND SYRACUSE

Subject
Historical maps
Topographic and planimetric map series
General locator maps
Planning, administrative, and environmental maps
Aerial photographs and satellite images
Cartographic bibliographies ⎱ Supplements to local holdings
Catalog of copyright entries ⎰
Newspapers as a cartographic source
Theses, dissertations, and atlases

Source: Ben Baldanza et al., unpublished, untitled survey of maps of Onondaga County and Syracuse, N.Y., 1984.

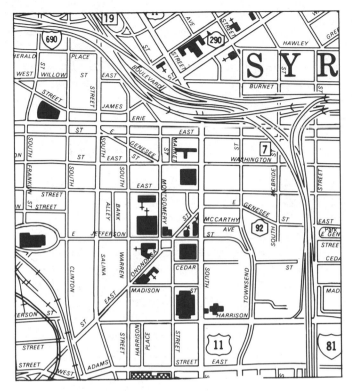

Figure 7-21 Portion of Syracuse West (south sheet) 1:9,600-scale planimetric map, produced in a series for urban areas in the state by the Mapping Services Bureau of the New York State Department of Transportation, in cooperation with the Federal Highway Administration.

seums, gardens, antique shops, and myriad other places of interest, such as discount factory stores, a popular tourist attraction spreading across the land.

Sources of Local Holdings

Maps found in general books, histories and geographies, public agencies such as the U.S. Geological Survey, local agencies, boards, and commissions are treated elsewhere in this book. Maps of the local area found in cartographic bibliographies, catalogs of copyright entries, newspapers, atlases, and theses and dissertations are treated here.

Cartographic Bibliographies.   Although rarely complete, bibliographies of maps are essential if one is to compile a useful list of maps of the local area. Aside from searching for map bibliographies, the map researcher should consult the map librarian or, in smaller libraries with small staffs, the librarian in charge of maps for checklists of holdings and of cartobibliographies. The following list illustrates a few typical cartobibliographies:

The Bibliographic Guide to Maps and Atlases, Supplement to the New York Public Library Dictionary Catalog of the Maps Division. Boston: G. K. Hall. Volumes by year.

Geographical Bibliography for American Libraries. Chauncy D. Harris, editor-in-chief. Washington, D.C.: Association of American Geographers and National Geographic Society, 1985. See especially the sections in part 1 on atlases, map guides, and geography and map librarianship.

The International Bibliography of Vegetation Maps of North America, vol. 1. August W. Kuchler, ed. Lawrence, Kans.: University of Kansas Libraries, 1965.

Maps and Charts Published in American Before 1800: A Bibliography. James C. Wheat and Christian F. Brum. New Haven, Conn.: Yale University Press, 1969.

The New York Public Library, Astor, Lenox and Tildon Foundations, the Research Libraries Dictionary Catalog of the Maps Division. Boston: G. K. Hall, 1971.

Panoramic Maps of Anglo-American Cities: A Checklist of the Maps in the Collections of the Library of Congress, Geography and Map Division. John R. Herbert, comp. Washington, D.C.: Library of Congress, 1974.

Union List of Sanborn Fire Insurance Maps Held by Institutions in the United States and Canada. Vol. 1, R. Philip Hoehn. Vol. 2, William S. Peterson-Hunt and Evelyn Woodruff. Santa Cruz, Calif.: Western Association of Map Libraries, 1976.

Copyright Entries.   In applying for copyright protection, a map publisher sends two copies of each map to the Copyright Office at the Library of Congress, which in turn publishes a list of copyrighted maps.[34] An examination of these copyright entries reveals two points of importance: that the private sector has played a major role in local mapping and that the subjects of maps have evolved over the years. For example, in Pennsylvania, the most frequent copyrights in the early 1870s were issued for county atlases, as such works were published and copyrighted for 57 of that state's 67 counties. By the 1920s, fire insurance maps, such as the Sanborn sheets, accounted for almost 60 percent of the copyright entries for Pennsylvania, and road maps were gaining popularity. The entry into the business of map production by the U.S. Geological Survey and other government agencies in the 1880s probably reduced the demand for county atlases and other commercial maps of the local area. As Table 7-2 illustrates, in the early 1970s copyright entries involved Pennsylvania's streets, roads, and

[34] U.S. Library of Congress, *The Catalog of Copyright Entries of the Library of Congress*, Washington, D.C.

Figure 7-22 Example of a locator map, Highland Forest, near Syracuse, New York.

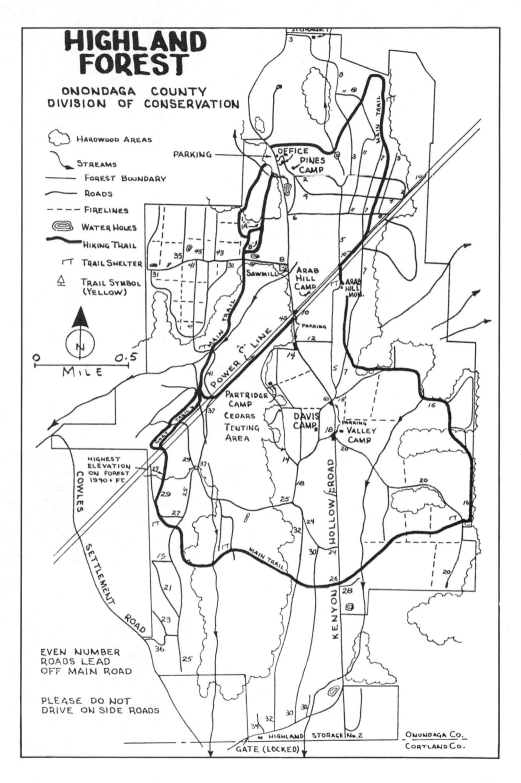

TABLE 7-2 COPYRIGHT ENTRIES FOR PENNSYLVANIA MAPS, BY TYPE, 1970–1974

Type of map	Number of copyright registrations	Percentage of copyright registrations
Urban area street[1]	87 (90)	55.8 (52.6)[2]
State road[1]	19 (19)	12.2 (11.1)
Tourist	7 (7)	4.5 (4.1)
Regional road	7 (7)	4.5 (4.1)
County road	6 (11)	3.8 (6.4)
Recreational	6 (8)	3.8 (4.7)
Utility and railroad (facilities)	6 (6)	3.8 (3.5)
Advertising market area	4 (4)	2.6 (2.3)
Local engineering/planning	2 (2)	1.3 (1.2)
Historical	2 (2)	1.3 (1.2)
Urban transportation routes	2 (2)	1.3 (1.2)
Aeronautical chart/airport guide	0 (5)	0.0 (2.9)
Other	8 (8)	5.1 (4.7)

Source: Mark Monmonier, "Private-Sector Mapping of Pennsylvania: A Selective Cartographic History for 1870 to 1974," *Proceedings of the Pennsylvania Academy of Science* 55 (1981), 71. Used with permission of the *Proceedings of the Pennsylvania Academy of Science.*

[1] Street maps commonly show and label all streets, whereas road maps show only major roads.

[2] Values in parentheses include 15 maps registered by Pennsylvania.

transportation more than eight times in ten.[35] (The first column in the table lists the number of copyright registrations for each category and the second column expresses that number as a percentage of the total number of copyright registrations for the state.) Commercial map publishers often use topographic and other government maps to serve as their base. Fortunately, these maps are usually available free-of-charge from advertisers and provide valuable assistance to sales and service people and others who travel extensively within a community.

Newspapers.   Chapter 9 discusses the fact that newspapers in Syracuse, New York, devote most of their cartographic efforts to international events, yet provide some local coverage. Subjects mapped in Syracuse newspapers in recent years include

ground redevelopment/reconstruction,

community services/concern,

business redevelopment/reconstruction, and

natural phenomena/history.

[35] Mark Monmonier, "Private-Sector Mapping of Pennsylvania: A Selective Cartographic History for 1870 to 1974," *Proceedings of the Pennsylvania Academy of Science* 55 (1981), 69–74.

Local maps in newspapers are common in cities where newspapers have editorial art departments or at least one staff artist working directly for the news editor. But since even small newspapers can reproduce local planning and zoning maps, it is perhaps equally important that a news editor see the need for maps to illustrate stories with a geographical component.[36]

Atlases.   Atlases of local areas have two important features: they are often available in libraries, and they are usually in relatively good condition. Several atlases are extant for Syracuse, New York, ranging in age from a *New Topographical Atlas and Gazetteer of New York,* published by Asher and Adams of New York in 1871, and (Homer De Lois) *Sweet's New Atlas of Onondaga County*, published by Walker Brothers and Company of New York in 1874, to those published in the 1970s and 1980s. The latter include Charles W. Collins's *Atlas of New York,* published by the American Printing Company of Madison, Wisconsin, in 1978, part of which is devoted to Onondaga County and Syracuse. Other parts of the country seem equally well covered. The atlas collection at the Library of Congress lists, in addition to state atlases, atlases focusing on cities, towns, or counties. In the mid-1970s, the U. S. Bureau of the Census published a brief, large-format atlas for the Syracuse SMSA (and over 60 other SMSAs as well).

Theses and Dissertations.   Large universities with diversified graduate programs are fertile grounds for finding the theses and dissertations of master's and doctoral candidates. Universities maintain copies of theses and dissertations by those who complete graduate programs, often both in the library and in the candidate's major department. As expected, in the survey in Syracuse, manuscripts in different fields were found to vary widely in the quantity of maps contained, ranging from a simple locator map or two, to tens of highly detailed maps. Geography, geology, and history theses often contain various maps of Onondaga County, Syracuse, and other places within the county. For maps in dissertations, the best general source is *Dissertation Abstracts International*, published monthly by University Microfilms International and available in college libraries and larger public libraries. For a list of "Recent Geography Dissertations Completed," see *The Professional Geographer*, the forum and journal of the Association of American Geographers. The first number (February) of each volume contains this list. Most studies included are available through interlibrary loan or can be purchased from University Microfilms International or the National Library of Canada.

---

[36] A sample survey of maps published in the *New York Times* from 1860 to 1980 indicated that, over the years, map themes diversified and maps appeared more frequently. Specifically, maps of crime, war, and accidents/disasters, the early themes of note, were supplemented by maps about local issues, tourism, recreation, sports, political and legal matters, development and transportation issues, science and the environment in more recent years. See Mark Monmonier, "Maps in the New York Times, 1860–1980: A Study in the History of Journalistic Cartography," *Proceedings of the Pennsylvania Academy of Science* 58 (1984), 79–83.

In general, finding maps is little different from searching for a bibliography of readings on any subject. The more one knows about the subject, the sources (agencies and the like), and the range of cartographic material that may be available, the more efficient and successful one's search will be. In any case, a sure place to begin with substantive questions about federal mapping is the National Cartographic Information Center. You may call the center at 1-800-USA-MAPS—a fitting telephone number.

FOR FURTHER READING

ADAMS, JOHN S., and RONALD ABLER, *A Comparative Atlas of America's Great Cities: Twenty Metropolitan Regions*, Association of American Geographers Comparative Metropolitan Project, vol. 3. Minneapolis: Association of American Geographers and the University of Minnesota Press, 1976.

BLACHUT, TEODOR J., et al. *Urban Surveying and Mapping.* New York, Heidelberg, Berlin: Springer-Verlag, 1979.

CATANESE, ANTHONY J., and JAMES C. SNYDER, eds., *Introduction to Urban Planning.* New York: McGraw-Hill, 1979.

DOWNS, ROGER M., and DAVID STEA, *Maps in Minds: Reflections on Cognitive Mapping.* New York: Harper & Row, 1977 (especially chapters 5 and 7).

MOORE, PATRICIA A., ed., *Computer Mapping Applications in Urban, State, and Federal Government.* Cambridge, Mass.: Harvard University, Laboratory for Computer Graphics and Spatial Analysis, 1981.

MURPHY, RAYMOND, *The American City: An Urban Geography*, 2d ed. New York: McGraw-Hill, 1974.

PALM, RISA, *The Geography of American Cities.* New York and Oxford: Oxford University Press, 1981.

SCHAEFER, JOHN E., "Computerized Municipal Utility System Mapping," *Journal of Surveying Engineering* 110, no. 1 (March 1984), 8–20.

THOMPSON, MORRIS, *Maps for America: Cartographic Products of the U.S. Geological Survey.* Washington, D.C.: U.S. Department of the Interior, Geological Survey, 1979.

U.S. National Research Council, Commission on Physical Sciences, Mathematics, and Resources, Committee on Geodesy, Panel on a Multipurpose Cadastre, *Procedures and Standards for a Multipurpose Cadestre.* Washington, D.C.: National Academy Press, 1983.

CHAPTER EIGHT

Old Maps

Old maps can be fascinating, and so can the study of the people who produced them and the techniques they used. Cartography has a long and rich history, extending back at least to the twentieth century B.C., when the Babylonians made property maps on clay tablets to assist in the assessment and collection of taxes. The cartographic record documents the growth of knowledge about the earth's surface, as explorers discovered new lands and seas, and of knowledge about human settlement and spatial behavior, as government officials and social scientists discerned patterns in human activity. Maps can teach us much about past nations—their governments, social life, and trade with other nations. Maps also record the evolution of measurement and graphic techniques for the systematic acquisition and presentation of geographic information. It should surprise no one that the accumulated writings of historians of cartography exceed in volume the modern scientific and technical literature on map production and map use, and that rare maps traded by collectors exceed in value all but the most extensive digital data bases (and the most confidential military plans!).

No textbook on map appreciation would be complete without an introduction to map collecting and the history of cartography. Because the richness and vastness of the history of mapping limits topics discussed here to a fraction of the whole, we focus on scholars' approaches to the study of the history of cartography, the literature resources available, and a limited number of selected significant milestones and periods in the development of cartographic knowledge and technology. We also devote considerable attention to map collecting, particularly of common yet interesting maps now widely available but likely to become rare and more appreciated in the near future.

THE STUDY OF THE HISTORY OF CARTOGRAPHY

Cartographers often distinguish "historical cartography" from the "history of cartography." This distinction is important: persons who use maps to interpret or explain wars, colonial expansion, cultural diffusion, and similar themes in the history of peoples and nations generally have objectives different from persons who seek a fuller understanding of the evolution of the theory and technology of mapping. The *historical cartographer*, for example, might produce a map to explain the loss of several thousand lives late in the American Civil War at the bloody but indecisive Battle of the Wilderness (see Figure 8-1), or study a 1943 U.S. Office of Strategic Services map of railroads and German administrative regions in captured Russian territory to understand better the American decision to send Lend-Lease aid in support of Soviet counterthrusts against Axis positions (see Figure 8-2). In contrast, the *cartographic historian* would be more interested in the techniques and procedures of military surveying and mapping and the role of militarism in stimulating cartographic innovation. Although historical geographers occasionally develop a strong interest in the history of cartography and cartographic historians develop a general understanding of the social, political, economic, and intellectual history of any era whose maps they intend to investigate, these groups of scholars, be they professors, archivists, or amateurs, for the most part do not interact.

Literature Resources

When most people think of a "history" they think of a narrative relating the development of a country, event, career, or idea from its origin to its conclusion or some other convenient stopping point. The more extensive the phenomenon in time or space, the more likely that its written history will be a collection of vignettes focusing on what scholars perceive to be major events. This loosely woven literary fabric is characteristic of the several seemingly comprehensive and so-called "popular" cartographic histories now available. Perhaps the most widely read of these is Lloyd Brown's *The Story of Maps* (1949). Aptly and honestly named, this book was well received as a text by university teachers and recently was reprinted in a paperback edition.[1] Other noteworthy representatives of the narrative genre are *The Mapmakers* (1981), by John Noble Wilford, a

---

[1] Lloyd A. Brown, *The Story of Maps* (Boston: Little, Brown, 1949). In addition to the paperback edition issued in 1979 by Dover Publications of New York, Vintage Books published a reprint hardbound edition in 1980.

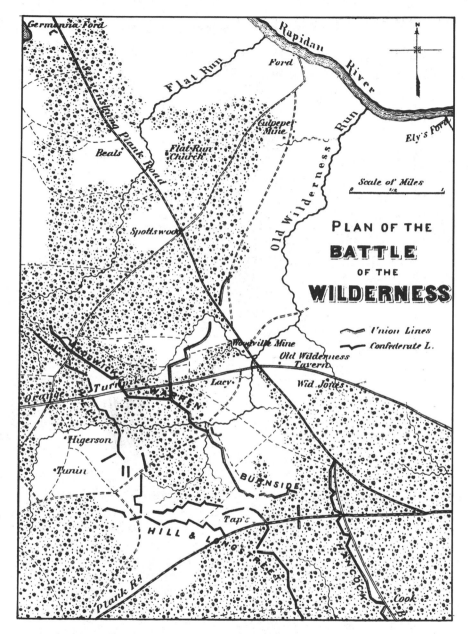

Figure 8-1 Map showing Union and Confederate troop positions on May 5, 1864, in the Battle of the Wilderness, in which Robert E. Lee's army inflicted 2,000 casualties on Ulysses S. Grant's forces, but suffered proportionately greater losses. (From William Swinton, *The Twelve Decisive Battles of the War: A History of the Eastern and Western Campaigns in Relation to the Actions That Decided Their Issue* [New York: Dick and Fitzgerald, 1873], plate facing p. 63; courtesy of E. S. Bird Library, Syracuse University.)

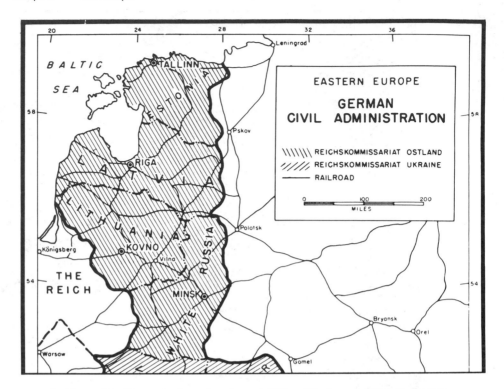

Figure 8-2 Upper portion of an August 1943 political map of Eastern Europe, produced by the Office of Strategic Services, forerunner of the Central Intelligence Agency. (Photographically reduced about 72 percent from Map No. 2594, Provisional Edition, 31 August 1943, R and A, OSS; courtesy of E. S. Bird Library, Syracuse University.)

science correspondent for *The New York Times*; *Maps and Their Makers* (first edition in 1953; fifth edition in 1978) by the late Gerald Crone, librarian and map curator at the Royal Geographical Society from 1934 to 1966; and *Understanding Maps* (1981) by Alan Hodgkiss, an academic cartographer at the University of Liverpool.[2] As might be expected from their titles, the books by Wilford and Crone highlight notable explorers and innovators, whereas Hodgkiss attempts a more systematic treatment, with chapters organized around, for example, cartographic language, cartographic vocabulary, and route maps. All these books are good introductions to cartographic history.

Whereas the neophyte may delight in the anecdotes and generally lucid

[2] John Noble Wilford, *The Mapmakers* (New York: Alfred A. Knopf, 1981); G. R. Crone, *Maps and Their Makers*, 5th ed. (Folkestone, Eng.: William Dawson & Sons; Hamden, Conn.: Archon Books, 1978); and Alan G. Hodgkiss, *Understanding Maps: A Systematic History of Their Use and Development* (Folkestone, Eng.: William Dawson & Sons, 1981). Random House issued a paperback edition of Wilford's book in 1982.

language of these narrative histories, the scholar is likely to point out their defects and omissions and to recommend either the more ponderous and recently reprinted *History of Cartography* (first edition in 1944, in German; revised edition in 1964), written by the Russian scholar Leo Bagrow and revised and expanded by the late R. A. Skelton, superintendent of the Map Room at the British Museum from 1950 to 1967; or a more focused, and thus inherently more complete, study, such as *Early Thematic Mapping in the History of Cartography* (1981) by Arthur H. Robinson, professor emeritus of geography and cartography at the University of Wisconsin.[3] But the Bagrow-Skelton book neglects nineteenth and twentieth-century cartography and treats American and Asian developments with short chapters that seem little more than afterthoughts; and monographs similar in depth to Robinson's cover few of the many significant events, epochs, institutions, and personalities in the history of mapping.

A prominent recent development may fill many of these gaps in the historical record, as well as evaluate and tie together in a consistent format facts and interpretations scattered over hundreds of books and thousands of journal articles. In the late 1970s Brian Harley and David Woodward, academic geographers at the University of Exeter and the University of Wisconsin, respectively, began work on a six-volume general survey of the history of cartography to be published by the University of Chicago Press.[4] The U.S. National Endowment for the Humanities has provided major funding for the project, and the National Geographic Society and a number of wealthy benefactors also have contributed. Many scholars are involved, including over 100 authors and an editorial board with representatives from more than 20 countries. Several section advisors guide the development of each volume of approximately 250,000 words, which will include carefully selected supporting illustrations, as well as reference maps compiled using digital cartographic data bases and lists of place names extracted on a word processor from the written text (see Figure 8-3). Originally the History was to consist of five volumes, but when some areas proved richer and more significant than first thought, Woodward and Harley added an additional volume to accommodate fuller treatments of Asian cartography and the twentieth century. Themes of the six volumes are

1. Prehistoric, Ancient and Medieval Europe and the Mediterranean;
2. The Traditional Asian Societies;
3. Renaissance and Discovery, 1470–1640;

---

[3] Leo Bagrow, *History of Cartography*, revised and enlarged by R. A. Skelton (Cambridge, Mass.: Harvard University Press, 1964); and Arthur H. Robinson, *Early Thematic Mapping in the History of Cartography* (Chicago: University of Chicago Press, 1982). Precedent Publishing Company of Chicago, Illinois, published a reprint, second edition of Bagrow's *History of Cartography* in 1985.

[4] For a description of the "History of Cartography" project see J. B. Harley and David Woodward, "The History of Cartography Project: A Note on Its Origin and Assumptions," *Technical Papers*, 43rd Annual Meeting, American Congress on Surveying and Mapping, 1983, pp. 580–89.

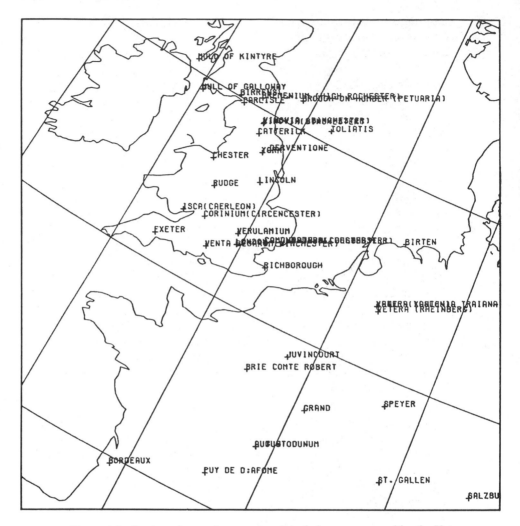

Figure 8-3 Portion of a rough computer plot of place names used by the University of Wisconsin Cartographic Laboratory to prepare fine-drawn locator maps for the six-volume *General History of Cartography* edited by J. B. Harley and David Woodward. Someday these crude machine-drawn maps will themselves be objects of study by historians of cartography. (Courtesy of David Woodward.)

4. Science, Enlightenment, and Expansion, 1640–1800;

5. The Nineteenth Century;

6. The Twentieth Century.

The University of Chicago Press published volume 1 in 1987 and has scheduled publication of the final volume for the mid-1990s.

The History is designed more as a "universal and balanced synthesis of the substance of the history of cartography" than as a definitive, encyclopedic compilation.[5] It is intended, of course, to document progress in map making, to survey and evaluate the findings and interpretations of earlier scholars, and to extend systematic coverage to such comparatively neglected areas as prehistoric and twentieth-century cartography. But its originators also have designed it to establish both an historical background and a humanistic perspective for the study of cartographic history. A deliberately broad definition of "map" will include images of celestial bodies and imaginary landscapes, as well as maps that are cosmological rather than terrestrial. Moreover, the History will treat maps both as artifacts and as expressions of a visual language. Its framework is geographic as well as chronological, and will emphasize centers of cartographic development, such as sixteenth-century Venice, which developed numerous innovations in map printing and cartographic representation, including Bernardus Sylvanus's low-distortion cordiform projection (see Figure 8-4). Some authors will attempt to trace the transfer of cartographic knowledge and to establish the preconditions for cartographic innovation. In addition to collecting, evaluating, and organizing existing scholarship, the History is stimulating considerable new research directed toward significant but neglected themes.

Other literature that serves the student of cartographic history includes *Imago Mundi*, a yearbook of scholarly articles, announcements, and book reviews published as the journal of the International Society for the History of Cartography, and the *Map Collector*, a quarterly magazine of particular interest to collectors of rare maps.[6]

Bibliographic guides are often useful for locating articles in these and the hundreds of other periodicals that sometimes carry articles on the history of cartography. *Bibliographica Cartographica*, which has been published annually since 1974 by the German publisher K. G. Saur, and which is marketed in the United States by the Shoe String Press, lists entries for articles and books contributed by bibliographers in over 40 countries.[7] The *Bibliography of Cartography*, compiled by the Geography and Map Division of the U.S. Library of Congress and published in five volumes in 1973, with a two-volume supplement issued in 1980, is especially valuable for identifying English-language material pub-

---

[5] Ibid., p. 583.

[6] *Imago Mundi*, which began with volume one in 1935, is published by Imago Mundi, Ltd., c/o Lympne Castle, Kent, England. Members of the International Society for the History of Cartography receive *Imago Mundi* in return for their annual dues. Interested collectors may write to the Membership Secretary, ISHC, Lympne Castle, Kent, England. The *Map Collector*, which began with issue no. 1 in 1977, is published by Map Collector Publications, Ltd., Church Square, 48 High Street, Tring, Hertfordshire HP23 5BH, England.

[7] *Bibliographica Cartographica* may be ordered from Shoe String Press, P.O. Box 4327, Hamden, CT 06514. A predecessor, *Bibliotheca Cartographica*, was published in Germany between 1957 and 1972 and is available at many research libraries.

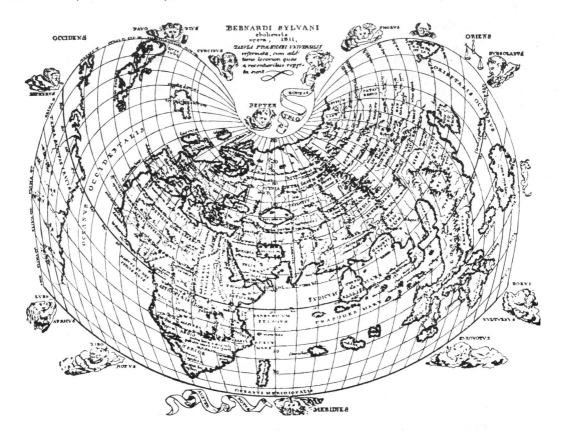

Figure 8-4 Reduced picture of Bernardus Sylvanus's ornate world map of 1511, on a cordiform, or heart-shaped, projection, which minimized distortion. This map, which illustrated a version of Claudius Ptolemy's *Geography* published in Venice, was one of the first world maps to show parts of North America. (From C. P. Daly, "On the Early History of Cartography, or What We Know of Maps and Map-Making, Before the Time of Mercator," *Journal of the American Geographical Society of New York* 11 [1879], 1–40, example from plate near p. 32; courtesy of E. S. Bird Library, Syracuse University.)

lished before 1973.[8] Available in print and microfilm editions, the *Bibliography* is a photofacsimile of the Library of Congress's catalog of books, articles, pamphlets, and other literature on the history and technology of mapping. The Geography and Map Division also publishes specialized bibiliographies and lists of historically significant maps in its collection.[9]

---

[8] The *Bibliography of Cartography*, published in September 1973 by G. K. Hall and Company, of Boston, is a photographic reproduction of approximately 100,000 index cards in the Geography and Map Division catalog. The first supplement, in two volumes, was issued in 1980, and additional supplements are likely. Microfilm editions are available. The staff of the division monitors 275 serials on a regular basis and records all articles on maps, mapping, and related topics.

[9] Recent publications of the division include John R. Sellers and Patricia Molen Van Ee, *Maps*

Approaches

Scholars have adopted a variety of strategies for studying and writing about the history of cartography. Aside from the general narrative "histories" such as Brown's *The Story of Maps*, most books by individual scholars address a single nation and a single period. Because of limitations on length, journal articles also tend to address specific times and countries. Michael Blakemore and Brian Harley, coauthors of a stimulating essay on research strategies in the history of cartography, have compiled data showing that the most common foci have been Europe and the sixteenth century.[10] They examined the first 30 volumes of *Imago Mundi*, published between 1935 and 1978, and identified the chronological and geographic patterns that Figures 8-5 and 8-6 portray. According to Figure 8-5, cartographic historians have expressed little concern for the maps of preliterate peoples, in contrast to considerable work on advances in map publishing following Johann Gutenberg's invention of movable type and other printing innovations of the fifteenth century and on the effects upon cartography of navigators and explorers, such as Ferdinand Magellan and James Cook, who discovered new places, refined geography, and generated a demand for more accurate maps. Although the comparative neglect of mapping from preliterate times through A.D. 1000 may be attributed to a scanty historical record, the minimal attention accorded the post-1800 period—which includes major advances in surveying and map reproduction, as well as the growth of national mapping agencies and the thematic map—is astonishing, particularly when compared to the careful attention economic and social historians devote to the nineteenth and twentieth centuries. The chronological pattern in Figure 8-5 underlies the regional and subject distribution of articles in *Imago Mundi*, shown in Figure 8-6. Seventy-nine percent of all map makers studied were European, and over 27 percent of all maps studied portrayed places in Europe. This limited agreement between the map maker's country and the area mapped underscores the cartographic historian's traditional interest in exploration.

Traditional chronological and regional studies in the history of cartography usually reflect one of three dominant concepts, or *paradigms*, according to Blakemore and Harley.[11] The *Darwinian paradigm*, named after the proponent of the

---

and *Charts of North America and the West Indies, 1750–1789* (Washington, D.C.: Library of Congress, 1981); Library of Congress, Staff of the Geography and Map Division, *Fire Insurance Maps in the Library of Congress* (Washington, D.C.: Library of Congress, 1981); and Andrew M. Modelski, *Railroad Maps of North America: The First Hundred Years* (Washington, D.C.: Library of Congress, 1984). For a list of publications, write to the Geography and Map Division, Library of Congress, Washington, DC 20540.

[10] See M. J. Blakemore and J. B. Harley, *Concepts in the History of Cartography: A Review and Perspective* (Toronto: University of Toronto Press, 1980), issued as *Cartographica* 17, no. 4 (Winter 1980), 15–17.

[11] Ibid., pp. 17–32.

Articles

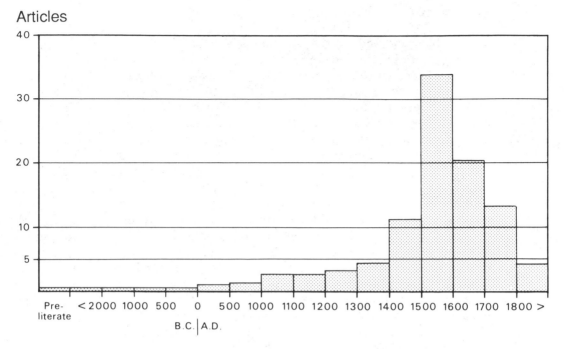

Figure 8-5 Chronological pattern of subjects of articles in *Imago Mundi*, 1935–1978. (Prepared from table in M. J. Blakemore and J. B. Harley, *Concepts in the History of Cartography: Review and Perspective* [Toronto: University of Toronto Press, 1980], p. 16.)

theory of natural selection in organic evolution, is an evolutionary view of map history in which maps improve in content and design as civilization and geographic knowledge advance. More an attitude or premise than a strategy for research, the Darwinian paradigm seems to have influenced most writers of one-volume narrative histories, such as Brown and Wilford. Whereas the facts often support this premise, there is the obvious danger that, in assuming progress to be inevitable, the historian will ignore evidence to the contrary. Other approaches that might compromise the objectivity of the historian are the *"old is beautiful" paradigm*, which reverently views old maps as rare treasures and tends in its most extreme to regard modern maps as uncreative works devoid of craftsmanship, and the *nationalist paradigm*, which perhaps too conveniently limits the scope of a scholar's endeavors and in so doing risks ignoring intellectual links with other countries. Any paradigm, in fact, blinds its practitioners somewhat; the wary reader must fathom the author's underlying premise and assess its possible effects on thoroughness and interpretation.

The life and work of a single map maker has provided the focus for several illuminating searches for events, individuals, and experiences that might explain the map maker's creativity or extent of influence on map making and geography.

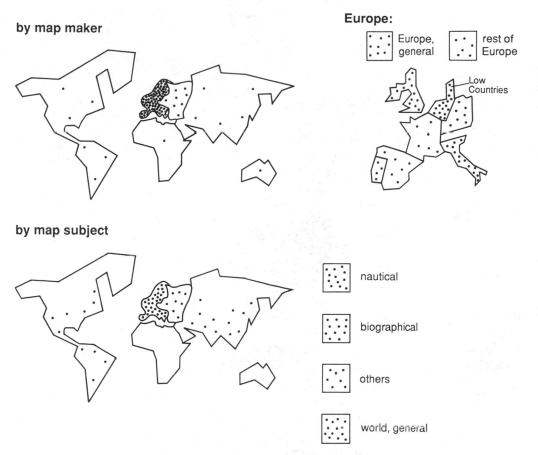

by map maker

Europe:

| Europe, general | rest of Europe |

Low Countries

by map subject

nautical

biographical

others

world, general

Figure 8-6 Spatial and topical trends, by map maker and mapped subject, for articles in *Imago Mundi*, 1935–1978. One dot represents 1 percent of all articles in volumes 1 through 30. (Prepared from tables in M. J. Blakemore and J. B. Harley, *Concepts in the History of Cartography: Review and Perspective* [Toronto: University of Toronto Press, 1980], p. 17.)

A good example of the biographical approach to the history of cartography is Ifor M. Evans and Heather Lawrence's study of Christopher Saxton, the sixteenth-century British surveyor who in 1579 published a detailed set of maps for the counties of England and Wales (see Figure 8-7).[12] Biographical studies also have addressed institutions rather than individuals; particularly noteworthy is W. A. Seymour's comprehensive history of Britain's Ordnance Survey, which

[12] Ifor M. Evans and Heather Lawrence, *Christopher Saxton, Elizabethan Map-Maker* (Wakefield, West Yorkshire: Wakefield Historical Publications; London: Holland Press, 1979). Saxton is regarded as the "Father of English Cartography." Also see J. B. Harley, "Christopher Saxton and the First Atlas of England and Wales, 1579–1979," *Map Collector* no. 8 (September 1979), 2–11.

Figure 8-7 Photographic reduction of map of Kent, Surrey, and Sussex in Christopher Saxton's 1579 *Atlas of England and Wales*, generally regarded as the first national atlas of Britain. (Courtesy of U.S. Library of Congress.)

began in the late eighteenth century as a military geodetic survey unit and evolved into one of England's best-known civilian institutions.[13]

Bibliographic studies, which provide much basic data for biographical explorations, attempt to inventory the cartographic record. Cartobibliographers have compiled extensive lists of printed and manuscript maps in order to document as fully as possible the cartographic record. These lists sometimes are based on a single extensive collection, such as the 10-volume catalog of the Map Division of the New York Public Library.[14]

[13] W. A. Seymour, ed., *A History of the Ordnance Survey* (Folkestone, Eng.: William Dawson & Sons, 1980).

[14] New York City, Public Library, Map Division, *Dictionary Catalog of the Map Division* (Boston: G. K. Hall, 1971). This photographic reproduction of 165,000 cards in the New York Public Library's Map Division catalog includes references to 6,000 atlases and 11,000 articles and books on cartography, mapping, and the history of cartography.

Cartographic historians and map collectors occasionally publish carefully selected collections of facsimile maps, usually reproduced from rare original copies. Perhaps the most notable and easily accessible facsimile collection of early maps is A. E. Nordenskiöld's *Facsimile-Atlas to the Early History of Cartography, with Reproductions of the Most Important Maps Printed in the XV and XVI Centuries* (first English-language edition, 1889; reprint edition, 1973), which includes over 70 full-size reproductions of maps printed in Europe between 1480 and 1600.[15] Facsimiles in Nordenskiöld's compilation include impressive innovations such as Bernardus Sylvanus's cordiform projection (see Figure 8-4), as well as comparatively primitive representations such as Zacharias Lilius's fifteenth-century schematic portrayal of the known world and its continents (see Figure 8-8). These so-called *mappaemundi*, Latin for "maps of the world," often placed Jerusalem near the center and east at the top, with Asia in the upper half, separated from Europe at the lower left by the Don River and from Africa at the lower right by the River Nile, with the Mediterranean Sea extending downward from the center to form a T-in-O pattern with the two rivers and the circular circumference. Although cartographic historians believe that this arrangement represents a medieval view of the earth as a flat disk with Jerusalem at the center, early mappaemundi do not support this interpretation. These maps originated in pagan Rome, and the Judeo-Christian bias that put Jerusalem at the center in the thirteenth and fourteenth centuries is reflected only in the more recent, more numerous survivors.[16]

More functional, particularly for navigators, was the *portolan chart*, of which Willem Barentszoon's sixteenth-century map of the sea to the west of the Straits of Gibraltar is typical (see Figure 8-9). *Rhumb lines* connect prominent points and show sailing directions, which can be read with the aid of the map's ornate compass roses. Mercator's projection, named after the prominent sixteenth-century Flemish map and atlas publisher, Gerhardus Mercator, was a more refined navigational aid, on which the parallels are drawn progressively farther apart with increasing distance from the equator, so that any straight line is a rhumb line whose bearing can be measured with a protractor relative to a meridian (see Figure 1-12 and pages 22–23).

While confined generally to the more abundant cartographic record that followed fifteenth-century advances in printing, facsimile collections are by no means restricted to Europe and the Renaissance. Many collections of facsimile maps have a regional focus, for example, the 35 maps reproduced in *The Shaping*

[15] A. E. Nordenskiöld, *Facsimile-Atlas to the Early History of Cartography with Reproductions of the Most Important Maps Printed in the XV and XVI Centuries* (Stockholm: P. A. Norstedt and Sons, 1889; New York: Dover, 1973). The Dover Publications facsimile edition includes a short essay about Nordenskiöld, an arctic explorer who lived from 1832 to 1901, by J. B. Post, head of the map collection at the Free Library of Philadelphia.

[16] For a discussion of T-in-O maps, see David Woodward, "Reality, Symbolism, Time, and Space in Medieval World Maps," *Annals of the Association of American Geographers* 75, no. 4 (December 1985), 510–21.

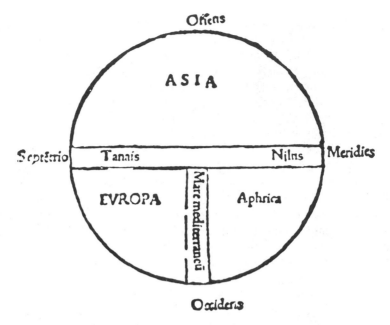

Figure 8-8 A crude T-in-O map included in *Orbis Breviarium*, published in Florence in 1493 by Italian geographer Zacharias Lilius. (From A. E. Nordenskiöld, *Facsimile-Atlas to the Early History of Cartography With Reproductions of the Most Important Maps Printed in the XV and XVI Centuries* [Stockholm: P. A. Norstedt and Sons, 1889], p. 38.)

of Vermont: From Wilderness to the Centennial: 1749–1877, by the curator of the Vermontiana collection in the University of Vermont library.[17] A facsimile collection may also have a systematic focus, such as the reproductions of over 300 eighteenth- and nineteenth-century city plans and oblique views published by Historic Urban Plans, of Ithaca, New York.[18] Intended for collectors as well as local historians and others who may, for whatever reason, appreciate old maps of particular places, these lithographic prints on heavy paper are highly suitable as wall decorations (see Figure 8-10). A catalog lists maps of most large cities in the United States and Canada, as well as of several interesting and representative

[17] J. Kevin Graffagnino, *The Shaping of Vermont: From the Wilderness to the Centennial: 1749–1877* (Rutland, Vt.: Vermont Heritage Press, 1983).

[18] Collectors may write to Historic Urban Plans, Box 276, Ithaca, NY 14850.

Figure 8-9 Portion of a portolan chart published in Amsterdam in 1594 by hydrographer and explorer Willem Barentszoon (Barents). (From A. E. Nordenskiöld, *Facsimile-Atlas to the Early History of Cartography With Reproductions of the Most Important Maps Printed in the XV and XVI Centuries* [Stockholm: P. A. Norstedt and Sons, 1889], p. 41.)

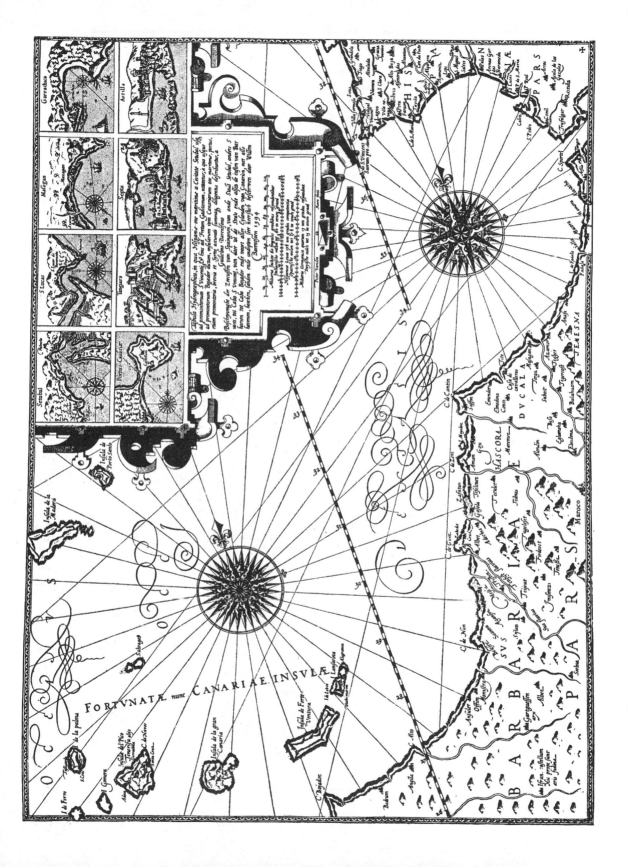

FORTVNATÆ nunc CANARIAE INSVLÆ

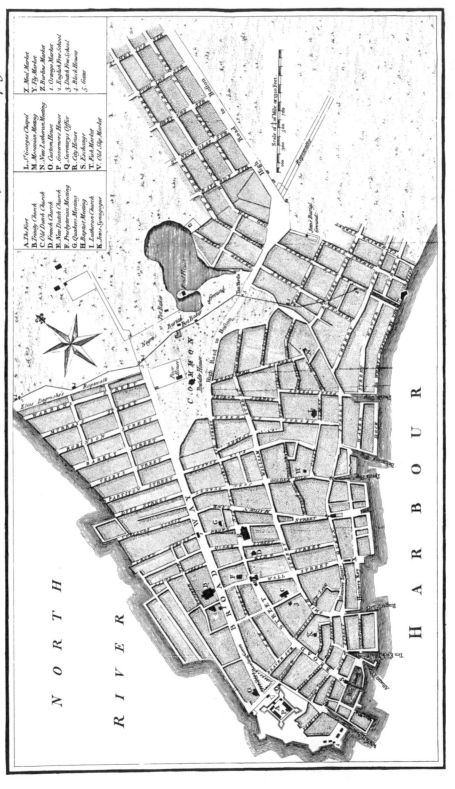

Figure 8-10 A 1763 plan of New York City, reduced photographically from a 24-by-40-cm (9.5-by-15.7-in.) facsimile available from Historic Urban Plans. (Used with permission of Olin Library, Cornell University.)

A PLAN of the CITY of NEW-YORK, *REDUCED FROM AN ACTUAL SURVEY, By* T. Maerfchalckm, 1763.

A. The Fort
B. Trinity Church
C. Old Dutch Church
D. French Church
E. New Dutch Church
F. Presbyterian Meeting
G. Quaker Meeting
H. Baptist Meeting
I. Lutheran Church
K. Jews Synagogue

L. St George's Chapel
M. Moravian Meeting
N. New Lutheran Meeting
O. Custom House
P. Governours House
Q. Secretarys Office
R. City House
S. Exchange
T. Fish Market
V. Old Slip Market

X. Meal Market
Y. Fly Market
Z. Burling Market
1. Oswego Market
2. English Free School
3. Dutch Free School
4. Block Houses
5. Gates

Scale of 1 of a Mile or 1300 Feet.

N O R T H   R I V E R

H A R B O U R

smaller cities, and of selected major cities elsewhere in the world. The firm is an outgrowth of the research of planning historian John Reps, author of several books on plans, bird's-eye views, and panoramic maps of American cities and towns.[19]

In addition to providing information about the geography of the past, cartographic artwork serves the map historian as an artifact with physical properties and graphic details useful in reconstructing the development of obsolete technologies of map production. David Woodward's study of wax engraving, a technique used principally in late nineteenth-century and early twentieth-century America for creating artwork easily transferred to a printing plate, provides an interesting illustration of how the analysis of graphic detail can be useful in tracing the spread of an innovation.[20] Wax engraving, used widely for transportation maps and school atlases, yielded detailed, economically reproduced maps with somewhat stiff linework and labels (see Figure 8-11). The technique, successfully adapted for cartography by Sidney Edwards Morse, brother of the inventor of the telegraph, involved drawing the linework and stamping point symbols and text in a thin coating of wax on a metal plate. Rand McNally used wax engraving for railroad maps and atlases as late as the 1960s. In addition to documenting the development of printing and engraving techniques, maps examined as artifacts have much to reveal about map publishing, the map trade, and the evolution of map symbols as a graphic language for communicating geographic data and ideas.

Map symbols have still another role in the study of the history of cartography: their positions provide a record of progress in geodesy and surveying. Map making, after all, depends upon accurate measurements of location—horizontal location relative to the grid of meridians and parallels, and vertical location relative to a convenient *datum*, such as mean sea level—and an accurate inventory of terrain features, such as roads, landmarks, and prominent boundaries. Because precise, efficient techniques for measuring elevation differences were not in widespread use until the nineteenth century, when most national survey organizations were established, very few topographic maps published before 1860 represent the terrain with elevation contours. And even by 1946, after almost two decades of photogrammetric surveying, the U.S. Department of the Interior noted that

> . . . topographic mapping in the United States was proceeding at such a slow pace that only a relatively small part of the country may be considered sufficiently well

[19] See, for example, John W. Reps, *The Making of Urban America: A History of City Planning in the United States* (Princeton, N.J.: Princeton University Press, 1965); *Town Planning in Frontier America* (Columbia, Mo.: University of Missouri Press, 1980); and *Views and Viewmakers of Urban America: Lithographs of Towns and Cities in the United States* (Columbia, Mo.: University of Missouri Press, 1984). Reps has published several other books on the history of urban plans and urban planning.

[20] David Woodward, *The All-American Map: Wax Engraving and Its Influence on Cartography* (Chicago: University of Chicago Press, 1977).

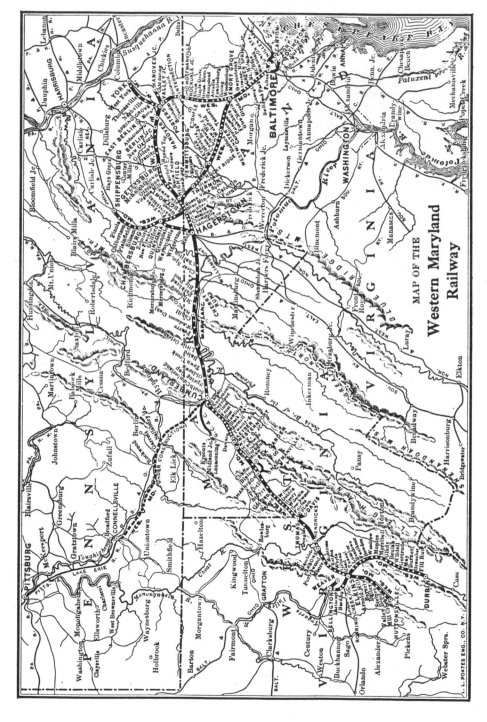

Figure 8-11 A wax-engraved map of the Western Maryland Railway. Note the crowded, mechanical type, produced with straight or curved type holders, or *stamping sticks*. (From *Poates Wax Engraving Superiority* [New York: L. L. Poates Engraving Company, 1913], p. 31; courtesy of David Woodward.)

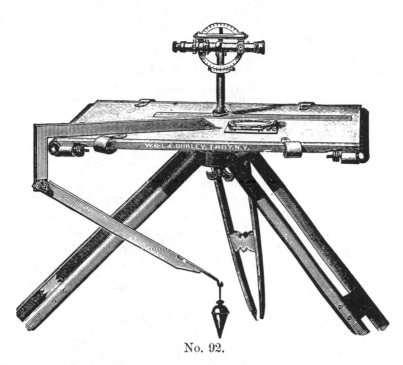

No. 92.

No. 92.—Plane Table, board 24 × 30 inches, mounted on large tripod, with
    leveling socket and clamp, and with plumbing bar, plummet and
    clamps for paper $45 00
Combined compass and levels 15 00
Alidade with telescope 9 inches long, power 20 diameters, with
    stadia. vertical circle to 1 minute, level on telescope, and clamp
    and tangent, mounted on column as in engraving.... .... 70 00
              Price as shown, total........................... $130 00

Figure 8-12 Engraving of a plane table advertised in a 1891 catalog of surveyors'
instruments. The alidade with a telescopic sight could be used to measure elevation angles or to draw horizontal lines used in positioning distant objects
through triangulation. (From *A Manual of the Principal Instruments Used in American Engineering and Surveying, Manufactured by W. and L. E. Gurley,* 29th ed. [Troy,
N.Y.: W. and L. E. Gurley, 1891], p. 209; courtesy of Science and Technology
Library, Syracuse University.)

mapped to meet present-day standards. Half of the nation is without topographic
maps; of the maps available for the other half, some are considered adequate for
present-day requirements, but others are of too low quality to meet the varied
needs. . . . Although about 48 percent of the country is topographically mapped
in some manner, much of the older work was accomplished by rapid reconnaissance
methods.[21]

Because U.S. Geological Survey topographers used comparatively crude
plane-table methods (see Figure 8-12) until the 1930s, most early quadrangle

[21] See U.S. Department of the Interior, *Annual Report of the Secretary of the Interior for the Fiscal
Year Ended June 30, 1946* (Washington, D.C.: U.S. Government Printing Office, 1946), pp. 200–201.

maps contain at least a few areas where the mapped landscape differs in both form and elevation from its more modern portrayal (see Figure 8-13). Although present-day maps, based upon highly precise, reliable, and efficient electronic surveying instruments, often reveal startling inadequacies in their earlier counterparts, the generally accurate representation of the landscape on early maps is in many ways surprising in view of the comparatively crude measuring devices available.

Early maps commonly omit the grid of parallels and meridians found on most modern reference maps. Even when the graticule is included, the latitude and longitude values typically differ from the values on more contemporary maps. Discrepancies in longitude are particularly likely, and antique maps provide a graphic account of the related problems of measuring longitude and of establishing a single, worldwide reference meridian. Early estimates of longi-

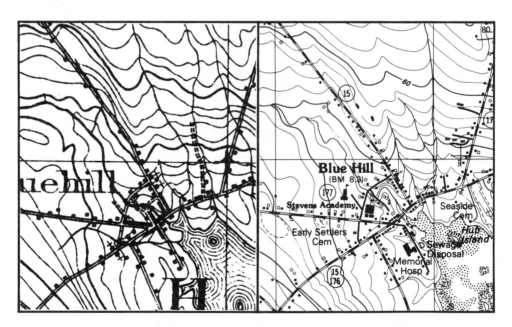

Figure 8-13 Corresponding portions of a 1904 topographic map (left) and its modern counterpart (right). On the older map, enlarged from 1:62,500 to 1:24,000, contours at a 20-ft interval show elevation above sea level and the grid lines are a meridian and a parallel. On the newer map, contours are spaced at a 6-m interval and grid lines refer to UTM coordinates. (See pages 25–28.) Note the change in level of development, which reflects three quarters of a century of growth, and the differences in the mapped shape of the terrain, which probably reflect improved mapping technology more than erosion. (From Blue Hill, Maine, U.S. Geological Survey 15-minute quadrangle map, 1:62,500, edition of Feb. 1904; and Blue Hill, Maine, U.S. Geological Survey 7.5-minute quadrangle map, 1:24,000, 1981.)

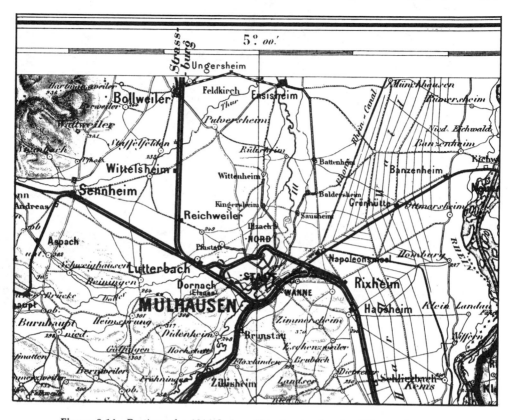

Figure 8-14 Portion of a 1916 Swiss railroad map showing 5°E meridian referenced to a principal meridian through Paris. Corresponding Greenwich longitude, used on modern maps, is approximately 7°20′E. (From *Eisenbahnkarte der Schweiz*, 1:250,000, 1916; courtesy of E. S. Bird Library, Syracuse University.)

tude, based upon observations of the heavens, were unwieldy for the navigator on the rocking deck of a vessel at sea, as well as time-consuming and inconvenient for the surveyor waiting for the night sky to clear. Before the invention of accurate chronometers in the eighteenth century, estimates often were in error by 10 degrees or more. And not until almost a quarter century after the International Meridian Conference, held in Washington in 1884, did most major trading nations accept the reference meridian at Greenwich, England, the site of the Royal Observatory.[22] "Prime meridians" on the maps of various nations once passed through Paris, Cadiz, Naples, Stockholm, and other nationally important origins. The 1916 Swiss railroad map shown in Figure 8-14, for example,

[22] See Derek Howse, *Greenwich Time and the Discovery of the Longitude* (Oxford, Eng.: Oxford University Press, 1980), pp. 138–55.

Figure 8-15 The llamas shown on this portion of a 1540 map of the Americas by Alonso de Santa Cruz may represent the first time this relative of the camel was depicted for a European audience. (From Wilma George, *Animals and Maps* [Berkeley and Los Angeles: University of California Press, 1969], pp. 64–65; used with permission.)

reports longitude relative to a reference meridian through Paris, 2° and 20′ east of Greenwich. Although the meridian on this map is labeled 5°, nowhere in Switzerland is the Greenwich longitude less than 6° East. Longitude estimated from an old map may not be reliable unless corrected for an obsolete prime meridian.

Other approaches to map history are the iconographic strategy, which explores the cultural, or poetic, meanings of map forms and symbols, and the linguistic model, which views maps as an efficient, useful and distinctively graphic language.[23] Iconographic studies are concerned in particular with a map's latent meaning, which might, like the T-in-O map in Figure 8-8, reinforce religious, political, mythological, or other symbolic values. As demonstrated in Wilma George's *Animals and Maps*, a study of the decorative figures of animals that embellish many medieval maps, symbols we might consider superfluous often are meaningful on several levels.[24] The llamas on Alonzo de Santa Cruz's 1540 map of America (Figure 8-15), for example, are among the earliest depictions

[23] Blakemore and Harley, *Concepts*, pp. 76–106.

[24] Wilma George, *Animals and Maps* (Berkeley: University of California Press, 1969). George demonstrated that the decorations on many medieval maps contain useful zoological data.

of this Andean pack animal. The linguistic model, another promising but little used strategy for studying early maps, is based on the premise that maps are a formal method for communicating spatial knowledge—knowledge that might be lost through poor design, ignorance, or deliberate distortion. Although several studies have invoked linguistic concepts in exploring such topics as the loss of information in map portrayals and the evolution of map images of a region as geographic knowledge expands, a clearly distinct linguistic strategy has yet to emerge.[25] Linguistic theory may be useful principally in prompting the historian of cartography to look carefully at the constructive role of cartographic distortion.

MAP COLLECTING

Collecting old maps can be a pleasant pastime for the antiquarian, an intriguing secondary interest for the cartographer or historian, a profitable business for the astute map trader, and a stimulating but often frustrating part of the occupational duties of the map librarian and the archivist. Among recognized hobbies, map collecting is new, but maps surely have had their enthusiasts and collectors since before the invention of printing, when copies were made by hand only for the wealthy, the soldier, and the navigator. But whether the interest is professional or amateur, and the financial resources lavish or limited, every map collector should define a goal, choose new acquisitions with care, organize the collection to promote retrieval and identify gaps, and protect the maps against the harmful effects of heat, light, moisture, acidic paper, and other agents of physical deterioration.

The Theme

Every map collection needs a theme, be it the representativeness and balance of an exhibit of evolutionary changes in cartographic symbolization or geographic knowledge, or a narrow, more manageable focus on the maps of a particular locality, map maker, time period, technique, or type of subject matter. For most collectors, limited in both money and available time, the focused approach is not only practicable but also highly fascinating, especially if the collection is intended to support an interest, say, in the local community, the Civil War, the hazards of sailing along the Maine coast, or the growth of railways in the nineteenth century. Collections that relate to both the past and the present can be equally valuable but markedly less expensive than those rooted only in the distant past. A collection of transportation maps, for instance, might include examples showing the development of canals and railroads as well as their

---

[25] For a review of studies treating early maps as a form of language, see Blakemore and Harley, *Concepts*, pp. 87–106.

decline.[26] Collectors ought not shun themes largely or solely within the twentieth century, such as aeronautical charts, oil company road maps, or satellite images. What is commonplace now will be rarer and less easily collected in the decades ahead: most very old maps in today's collections exist only because someone at a time when they too were more common appreciated their beauty, utility, or historic value.

Prospective collectors should not neglect two seemingly pedestrian yet important, highly personal foci—maps of places visited and maps that, for one reason or another, they find fascinating or particularly beautiful. Like an album of snapshots, a map collection with a focus on family vacations can increase the psychic value of travel, for we can gain as much satisfaction from reminiscing about a trip as from the travel itself. With foresight, we may even obtain maps of places to be visited before we travel in order to savor another of recreational travel's pleasures, anticipation. As for maps that merely catch our fancy, we can always acquire these as an adjunct to a more focused collection, or we may collect for several years without a specific strategy and then examine what we have acquired in hope of identifying either a possible theme or a strategy for making our eclectic collection more balanced.

Research and Acquisition

A specific theme permits the collector to concentrate on developing the background necessary to appreciate the range of maps that might be acquired, the circumstances of their compilation, design, and production, their scholarly value as historic or scientific documents, and their monetary value as art objects priced according to scarcity and demand. The conscientious collector will want to read up on the relevant periods in cartographic history and on other subjects peculiar to his collection. A general narrative history of cartography slanted toward map collecting is *Maps and Mapmakers* by Ronald V. Tooley, a prominent British map collector and dealer and a prolific author on these topics as well.[27] Also useful is R. A. Skelton's *Maps: A Historical Survey of Their Study and Collecting*, which combines concise surveys of the history of cartography and the history of the history of cartography (You read it correctly!) with a lively yet scholarly essay on map collecting and preservation.[28] The collector may also want to subscribe to the quarterly journal *The Map Collector*, which publishes short articles on map

---

[26] Maps represent perhaps the ultimate in model railroading, at a scale sufficiently small so that several sheets of paper can hold a meaningfully large "layout," with scenery in many ways more realistic than on an HO- or N-gauge model railway laboriously constructed in a hobbyist's basement. Moreover, because of widespread abandonment of railroad lines, maps permit the railroad enthusiast to collect highly detailed replicas of extinct branch lines.

[27] R. V. Tooley, *Maps and Mapmakers*, 6th ed. (London: B. T. Batsford, 1978). Also useful is Raymond Lister's *Old Maps and Globes* (London: Bell & Hyman, 1979).

[28] R. A. Skelton, *Maps: A Historical Survey of Their Study and Collecting* (Chicago: University of Chicago Press, 1972).

collecting and the history of cartography, lists dealers and auctions, and reports the sale prices of important items sold at auction; and he or she may want to join the International Map Collectors Society, which holds an annual symposium, map fair, and exhibition.[29] Collectors with an eye to early maps as a possible hedge against inflation might consult Douglas Gohm's *Maps and Prints for Pleasure and Investment*.[30] Even the collector pursuing the hobby on a modest budget will be fascinated by the prospect, albeit unlikely, of acquiring a rare find at a bargain price. More important, though, is the knowledge to be gained through background reading about working with dealers, evaluating the quality of a printed map, and caring for the collection.

A collector interested in maps of his or her local region may find most useful the services of a map reference library, possibly at the county historical society or a nearby university library. In addition to a number of books on the history, study, and collecting of old maps, the reference shelf of the map library probably will include a checklist of early maps of the region. Even if there is little hope of acquiring originals of the very early, rare maps found in private, state, university, or historical society collections, the collector surely will want to know what maps have been produced for the area and what cartographic information might have been available to early map makers.

For some purposes, however, photographic copies are useful substitutes for originals. Historical society collections, for example, commonly contain not only originals donated by wealthy benefactors but also whatever photographic copies may be needed to make a collection as complete and useful as possible. At a large library with a photographic or copy services section, the local collector may arrange to have copies made of original or noncopyrighted facsimile materials in the collection. Although the fees may seem high, the U.S. Library of Congress can supply reproduction-quality black-and-white prints of most maps ever produced for places within the United States.[31] In order to minimize wear, some libraries permit users to handle only microfiche copies, with which the researcher can conveniently examine the details of an enlarged image on the screen of a large-screen microfiche reader. To stimulate interest and raise funds, museums and historical societies sometimes sell facsimile lithographs of particularly intriguing examples of early local maps.

Collectors interested in maps of places in the United States may find a

---

[29] For the address of the publisher of *Map Collector*, see fn. 6. For information on the International Map Collectors Society, write to the IMCoS Membership Secretary, 83 Marylebone High Street, London W1M 4AL, England.

[30] D. C. Gohm, *Maps and Prints for Pleasure and Investment*, 2d ed. (London: John Gifford, 1978).

[31] One may order black-and-white glossy photographic prints and microfilm copies of maps and plates in atlases from the library's Photoduplication Service, subject to copyright restrictions. For information, write to the Library of Congress, Photoduplication Service, Washington, DC 20540. Color prints and color microfilm are not available, but the library can supply color transparencies as large as 20 by 25 cm (8 by 10 in.).

number of government agencies helpful. The Geography and Map Division of the Library of Congress (Washington, DC 20540), with over four million maps and almost 50,000 atlases in its collection, is perhaps the best single source of early American maps. A free booklet describing the division and its operations and activities is available, as is a publications list. A visit should be most enlightening. Staff members are helpful, and collectors can order photographic prints. The National Cartographic Information Center of the U.S. Geological Survey (507 National Center, Reston, VA 22092) can provide photographic reproductions of topographic maps dating back to 1884.[32] A full-size, 44-by-53-cm (17-by-21-in.) black-and-white photographic print of a late-nineteenth century topographic map costs less than $10. The National Archives (8th and Pennsylvania Avenue, N.W., Washington, DC 20408) is a useful source of information about special collections of historic maps—for example, maps from the Civil War. Most college map libraries will have a copy of the *Guide to Cartographic Records in the National Archives*, which describes the organization of its map collections.[33] The Center for Cartographic and Architectural Archives at the National Archives has an extensive collection of 1930s aerial photography taken for federal agencies and covering about 80 percent of the land area of the contiguous 48 states, and the Still Picture Branch has a rich collection of even earlier aerial views, some oblique and some taken from balloons. Collectors providing a detailed, specific description of the place and era of interest can receive a research report and price list for prints of available images.[34]

If not content to wait patiently—and often fruitlessly—for a "find," the collector must canvass dealers, advertise in collectors periodicals or local journals, and seek whatever assistance museums, public agencies, and other institutions may provide. Dealers' lists may be especially useful to collectors of maps sufficiently old, scarce, and treasured to command a dealer's attention. In the United States dealers carry maps as recent as World War II propaganda, military,

---

[32] Collectors interested in a photographic reproduction of a particular map should describe the map as completely as possible, preferably with the quadrangle name, state name, quadrangle series (7.5-minute, 15-minute, 30-minute, and so on), and publication date. The U.S. Geological Survey also sells unsprocketed 35-mm microfilm rolls with about 500 frames (but no more than a single state) per roll. This collection, which consists of over 120,000 maps of the Geological Survey, includes 15-minute quadrangle maps compiled by the U.S. Army Corps of Engineers, as well as selected maps from the National Park Service and the Federal Highway Administration. Libraries and historical societies that lack a complete collection of topographic maps for their state or region will find this USGS microfilm collection a most useful supplement to their own holdings. Paper copies of the index to the microfilm rolls are also available.

[33] U.S. National Archives, *Guide to Cartographic Records in the National Archives* (Washington, D.C.: General Services Administration, 1971). Collectors can order the guide from the Superintendent of Documents, U.S. Government Printing Office, Washington, DC 20402. When inquiring about the current price, specify the stock number 2202-0032. The National Archives will respond to requests for a free leaflet, *Cartographic Records in the National Archives*.

[34] Each inquiry should include your name, address, and a telephone number at which you may be reached during the day.

and intelligence maps. *The Map Collector* lists and carries advertisements for dealers to whom the collector may write for a catalog, and, like the Sunday *New York Times*, occasionally carries ads announcing the sale at auction of especially rare maps. Usually an ad includes an address, so that the collector may order a catalog and submit a mail bid.

Dealing with a map dealer is not as mysterious as it might seem to the neophyte, even if the dealer is in a foreign country.[35] A catalog describes each map and lists its price in the dealer's local currency. The table of foreign exchange rates published in the financial section of most large daily newspapers may be useful in estimating the cost in dollars of a map offered for sale in, say, British pounds. The buyer may charge the map to a major credit card account in order to avoid the often exorbitant charges for a bank draft in foreign currency. Most reputable dealers will sell maps on approval, so that the dissatisfied customer may return an item within a reasonable time for a full refund. Because dealers seldom have multiple copies of a rare map, the collector should respond rapidly, perhaps by telephone. A list a month or so old may be useful principally as a guide to prices asked for maps already sold, and dealers charge a nominal fee for their catalogs, which they send by first-class mail and, to overseas clients, by air.

Collectors with a theme that embraces the present as well as the past may reduce the expense of collecting by obtaining as much relevant current material now, before it goes out of print. Government agencies, private firms, trade associations, and other suppliers can advise the collector about maps now in print and how they dispose of obsolete material. A few replies might even include complimentary samples sent in empathy. Collectors interested in topographic maps should examine carefully the index maps and publication lists of the U.S. Geological Survey and state agencies that produce similar materials. For some areas, maps from the early 1900s may still be the most recent sheets available—but for how long? When a new edition is available, this older "stock" may be discarded as scrap or recycled. For example, when the Geological Survey prints a new edition of a quadrangle map, it often makes remaining copies of the previous edition into note tablets and envelopes.

Organization and Preservation

A collection of maps is distinguished from a mere hoard by its organization, documentation, and careful storage. Maps should be filed in a convenient order for easy retrieval, and this order should allow for the ready addition of an unspecified number of new maps and for retrieval with minimal handling of items not needed. University map libraries, whose collections for the most part include useful but not rare maps, rely largely upon horizontal map cases with

[35] See Clifford Stephenson, "The Mechanics of Map Collecting," *Map Collector* no. 22 (March 1983), 24–28, and "Do-It-Yourself Framing," *Map Collector* no. 24 (September 1983), 26–30.

10 to 30 large, shallow drawers, each holding 25 to 100 maps.[36] Folded maps, such as highway and city street maps, commonly are kept in a *vertical file* in standard or lateral filing cabinets. Small flat maps in a personal collection, at home or in the office, might conveniently be stored in individual, carefully labeled folders in a similar filing cabinet. Collectors of expensive, rare maps may want to frame some specimens to hang on the wall for fuller enjoyment and to mount others in *overlay mounts*, to permit handling and inspection without touching the paper. As Figure 8-16 shows, the top of the map is attached to a stiff card backing covered by a frame cut to fit the map. A clear plastic window covers the map so that one can inspect interior portions without touching the paper. The mount may also extend outward at the top so that it can be suspended in a large-sheet vertical map storage cabinet (see Figure 8-17).

Paper is not a permanent information-storage medium because over time it gradually oxidizes, turning yellow or brown and disintegrating. Papers manufactured after about 1860, when wood pulp replaced rags as the principal raw material, are acidic and deteriorate more rapidly than older papers.[37] Although maps printed on relatively stable, high-quality papers with comparatively low acidity will decay more slowly than most books and magazines, storing these maps in acidic file folders or next to maps printed on more highly acidic paper will nonetheless hasten deterioration. Map libraries address these problems with folders of plastic or acid-free paper, *encapsulation* of individual maps between layers of thin polyester film (at a cost of about $10 or more per map), or a somewhat complex chemical treatment to neutralize whatever acid the paper contains.[38] Other measures needed to inhibit decay include keeping the maps away from direct sunlight, radiators, and other sources of heat, and from insects and rodents. Ideally, collectors should keep maps in a fireproof area with a constant temperature between 16° and 20°C (60–68°F) and moderately low relative humidity, between 30 and 60 percent.[39]

[36] For a discussion of storage cabinets for a map collection, see Harold Nichols, *Map Librarianship*, 2d ed. (London: Clive Bingley, 1982), pp. 87–104. For the collector's more meticulous view, see Clifford Stephenson, "Storing Your Maps," *Map Collector* no. 23 (June 1983), 24–26.

[37] For a discussion of the deterioration of paper maps, see Richard Daniel Smith, "Maps, Their Deterioration and Preservation," *Special Libraries* 63, no. 2 (February 1972), 59–68. Also see Bob Akers, "History of Paper-Making," *Map Collector* no. 5 (December 1978), 11–15.

[38] For a discussion of polyester film encapsulation, see Peter Waters, "Polyester Film Encapsulation," *Information Bulletin, Western Association of Map Libraries* 10, no. 2 (March 1979), 117–27; and Paul N. Banks, "The Conservation of Maps and Atlases," *AB Bookman's Yearbook* n.v. (1976), part 1, 53–62. For a discussion of methods for the repair and preservation of old maps, see Robert C. Akers, "The Cleaning and Restoration of Maps," *Map Collector* no. 10 (March 1980), 19–23; and Betty Kidd, "Preventive Conservation in Map Libraries," *Special Libraries* 71, no. 12 (December 1980), 529–38.

[39] For a discussion of environmental factors that hasten the deterioration of maps see Mary Larsgaard, *Map Librarianship: An Introduction* (Littleton, Colo.: Libraries Unlimited, 1978), pp. 159–63. Also see Bob Akers, "Care and Handling of a Map Collection," *Map Collector* no. 4 (September 1978), 2–5.

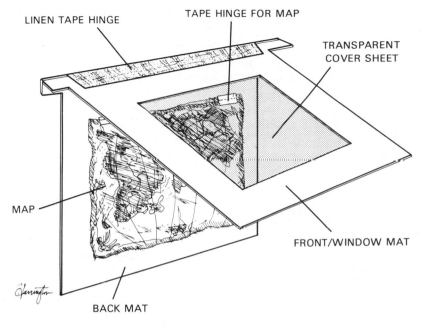

LINEN TAPE HINGE

TAPE HINGE FOR MAP

TRANSPARENT
COVER SHEET

MAP

FRONT/WINDOW MAT

BACK MAT

Figure 8-16 An overlay mount for rare-map storage that both protects the map and permits use and enjoyment. The top of the map is attached to the back of the mount, hinged at the top to a frame with a transparent window, through which the image is exposed. A stiff tab, protruding from both sides near the hinged joint at the top, may be used to support the mount in the vertical file shown in Figure 8-17. (Adapted from illustrations in Clifford Stephenson, ''Storing Your Maps,'' *Map Collector* no. 23 [June 1983], 24–26.)

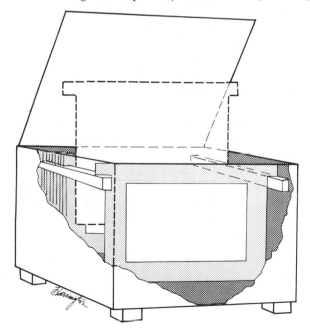

Figure 8-17 A vertical file used to store maps protected in overlay mounts. (Adapted from illustrations in Clifford Stephenson, ''Storing Your Maps,'' *Map Collector* no. 23 [June 1983], 24–26.)

Because most map sheets bear only minimal information about their publisher and symbols, the collector will want to keep on file whatever additional facts he or she has learned about each map's compilation, publication, distribution, and intended use. This file, on large index cards or the pages of a loose-leaf notebook, will serve as the collection's catalog. It should tell when and where each map was obtained, and at what price, and indicate the map drawer or folder in which the map is stored, perhaps with a unique identification number lightly penciled on the margin. The catalog might list books or journal articles that mention the map or the phenomenon portrayed. The collector might want to note related maps, particularly earlier or later editions of the same map. Notes on special features can indicate how the map contributes to the theme of the collection. The collector also will want to acquire copies of whatever related written material might be useful in interpreting the content and history of the map. Indeed, a collection of *just maps* might be considered as incomplete as a scholarly book without endnotes or footnotes.

MAPS AND LOCAL HISTORY

The variety of maps showing the geography of an area at various times in the past is amazingly large, particularly when one considers engineering, administrative, and utilities maps that might be stored in company or government basements, as well as maps that include not only the city or village in question but also its neighbors or its transport links to other centers. The list grows even larger for the collector prepared to examine clipping files and microfilm records of local newspapers—although maps in newspapers were comparatively rare until the early 1900s, when photographic processes simplified the production of a printing block from pen-and-ink artwork.[40] Despite the minimal use of local maps in most daily papers, the conscientious researcher occasionally finds intriguing locally significant maps, such as the 1886 map of a 200-acre farm offered to the city of Syracuse, New York, for a park (see Figure 8-18). Because xerographic and even photographic copies made from microfilm are seldom sharp, at least partly the result of a poor-quality newsprint image, transcribing the information onto a clearer reproduction of a city base map of the same era may be a useful means of capturing the map's geographic details for further study. Newspaper maps may also suggest places to look for otherwise obscure maps. At the local historical society, for example, a file on the county parks commission might contain a planning or zoning map described by a reporter but unacknowledged in the society's files under "Maps—Parks." Small maps bound into

[40] See, for example, Mark Monmonier, "Maps in the *New York Times*, 1860–1980: A Study in the History of Journalistic Cartography," *Proceedings of the Pennsylvania Academy of Science* 58, no. 1 (1984), 79–83.

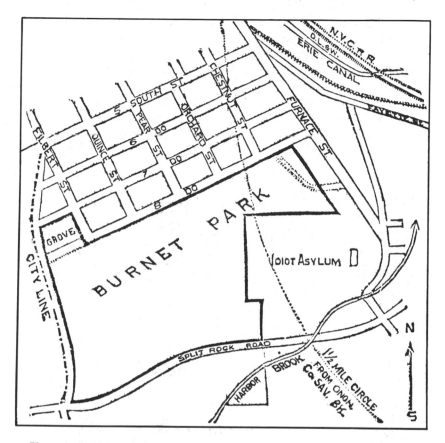

Figure 8-18   "Map of Burnet Park, the Pleasure Ground That We Have a Chance of Enjoying," published in Syracuse, New York, in the June 20, 1886, edition of the *Syracuse Sunday Herald*. (Courtesy of Onondaga Historical Association.)

the pages of a planning commission report, a local history, or the history of a locally prominent person or institution can easily escape the attention of the cartographic historian who looks only in the map cases.

The earliest maps available for an area are one of the first concerns of the collector. For many places the earliest detailed maps will show the boundaries of original land grants or the layout of the first settlement. Present-day Onondaga County, New York, for example, is in the part of upstate New York called the Military Tract and set aside for Revolutionary War veterans, many of whom sold their allotments to land developers. For a while, part of the tract was reserved for the Onondaga Indians, who still occupy a substantially reduced part of the original Onondaga Reservation. Syracuse did not exist in 1793, when Simeon DeWitt surveyed central New York, but the "Salt Spring" shown on

DeWitt's map (see Figure 8-19) later became the village of Salina, incorporated in 1824, a year before its neighbor, the village of Syracuse. Both villages manufactured salt by evaporating salt water in large vats, housed in sheds with movable roofs that could be opened to admit sunlight or closed to keep out rain and snow. Salt manufacture is a prominent feature on the 1836 map in Figure 8-20, which shows both Syracuse and Salina. Syracuse was a port on the Erie Canal, completed in 1825, and when the villages of Salina, Syracuse, and Lodi incorporated as a city in 1848, the merged metropolis took the name Syracuse. In another 25 years a well-developed downtown Syracuse was laced by the Erie

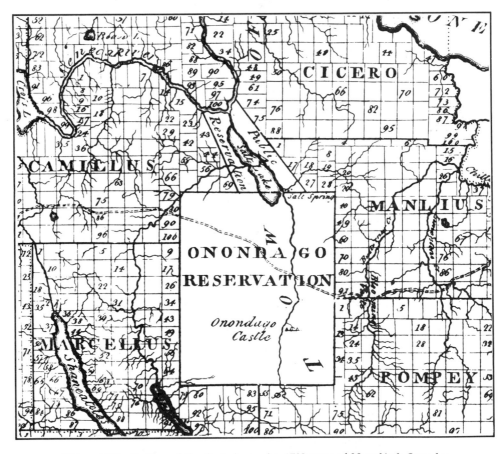

Figure 8-19   Portion of the first sheet of a 1793 map of New York State by surveyor Simeon DeWitt. Syracuse, New York, developed during the early nineteenth century at the southeast end of Onondaga Lake, called "Salt Lake" on DeWitt's map. Only a small part of the Onondaga Reservation still belongs to the Native American tribe that gave the county its name. (Courtesy of Onondaga Historical Association.)

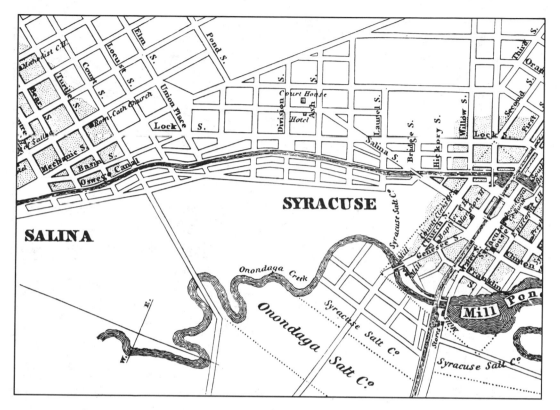

Figure 8-20   Portion of a 1836 map of Syracuse and Salina, New York, from *Gordon's Gazetteer*, published in Philadelphia by Thomas F. Gordon under the title *Gazetteer of the State of New York: comprehending its colonial history; general geography, geology, and internal improvements; its political state; a minute description of its several counties, towns, and villages.* . . . Unlike other Syracuse maps in this series of examples, north is to the left, not toward the top. (Courtesy of Onondaga Historical Association.)

and Oswego Canals, several steam railways, and a number of horse-car routes, as shown in the map prepared to accompany an 1873 city directory (see Figure 8-21).

   In 1874, when Walker Brothers of New York City published *Sweet's Atlas of Onondaga County, New York*, Syracuse already extended outward several miles from the city center, as indicated by the portion in Figure 8-22 of a plate covering the area to the west of downtown. Publishers of "subscription" atlases generally sold copies in advance, often before the county was surveyed and the maps were compiled, to patrons whose names were listed or whose residences were among those noted on the maps, as in Figure 8-23, the inset for Skaneateles Junction, a hamlet west of Syracuse. Flattering engravings of homes or businesses sometimes recognized the support of particularly generous subscribers,

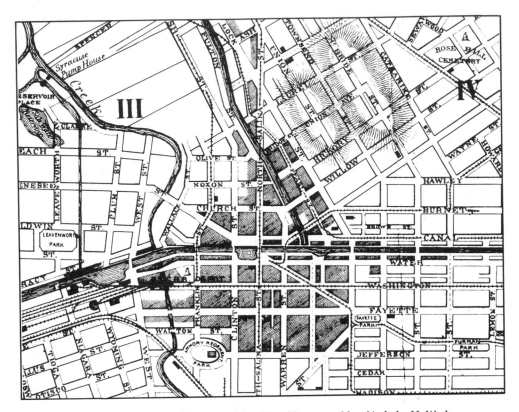

Figure 8-21   Portion of the map of the City of Syracuse, New York, by H. Wadsworth Clarke, local surveyor and civil engineer, published in 1873 to accompany Andrew Boyd's *Syracuse City Directory*. Note the hachures used to represent two adjoining drumlins (long, low hills) to the northeast of the city center and the route of the Erie Canal from east to west through downtown. (Courtesy of E. S. Bird Library, Syracuse University.)

for whom the atlas was as much a medium for proclaiming success and affluence as it was a geographic reference. With development costs favorably "picked up on the front end" through advance sales, commercial atlas publishers produced atlases for most of the counties in the Midwest and Northeast between 1860 and 1910, and sold numerous city atlases and county, city, town and village wall maps as well.[41] Students of local history, who value the county atlas's detailed

[41] See Norman J. W. Thrower, "The County Atlas in the United States," *Surveying and Mapping* 21, no. 3 (September 1961), 365–73; "Cadastral Survey and County Atlases of the United States," *The Cartographic Journal* 9, no. 1 (June 1972), 43–51; and Michael P. Conzen, "The County Land-ownership Map in America: Its Commerical Development and Social Transformation, 1814–1939," *Imago Mundi* 36 (1984), 9–31.

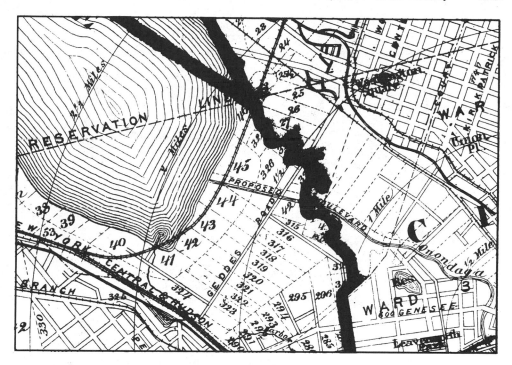

Figure 8-22 Portion of the map "Towns of Geddes and Salina and City of Syracuse" in an 1874 atlas of Onondaga County, New York. Circles show distance from the city center. Numbers identify the larger lots, and names identify individual householders in more rural areas. (From Homer D. L. Sweet, *Sweet's New Atlas of Onondaga County, New York* [New York: Walker Brothers and Co., 1874], p. 57; courtesy of E. S. Bird Library, Syracuse University.)

portrayal of neighborhoods and business districts, still can purchase many of these atlases from present-day publishers of facsimile editions.[42]

Two even more detailed references for the historical geographer are real estate and fire insurance atlases. Real-estate atlases showed all buildings and most lot lines, as in Figure 8-24, and used color to differentiate among wood-frame, brick, and stone buildings. Fire insurance atlases were even more detailed, providing the insurance underwriter with a general description of each building's dimensions, number of stories, and type of construction. The Sanborn Map Company and a few lesser publishers produced insurance maps and atlases

[42] Homer D.L. Sweet's atlas, from which Figures 8-22 and 8-23 are taken, has been published in a facsimile edition by Martin Wehle, 46 Stottle Road, Churchville, NY 14428. The Geography and Map Division of the Library of Congress occasionally publishes a list of facsimile maps and atlases that can be ordered from historical societies, private publishers, and public agencies. See Barbara R. Noe, *Facsimiles of Maps and Atlases* (Washington, D.C.: U.S. Government Printing Office, stock no. 030-004-00019-1, 1980).

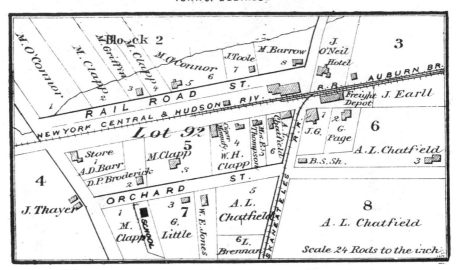

Figure 8-23   Inset map for the hamlet of Skaneateles Junction, west of Syracuse, New York, in an 1874 county atlas. (From Homer D. L. Sweet, *Sweet's New Atlas of Onondaga County, New York* [New York: Walker Brothers and Co., 1874], p. 39; courtesy of E. S. Bird Library, Syracuse University.)

for most American cities, villages, and other built-up areas, starting in the late eighteenth century, but mainly in the late nineteenth and early twentieth centuries.[43] Sanborn revised the maps every few years in most medium-sized and large cities, and urban planners also found them useful. Most municipalities had a set, and the planning commission, rather than the historical society, still might store and occasionally use the most recent edition. Sanborn had a specialized product with a limited market: in later years its biggest customer group was local government, and its lithographically printed editions seldom numbered more than 100 copies. Local collections may benefit from photographic copies ordered from the Library of Congress.[44]

Few parts of the United States have topographic map coverage more than 100 years old. The U.S. Geological Survey (USGS), established in 1879, did not publish its first standard topographic map until 1884, and as indicated in Figure

[43] See Walter W. Ristow, "United States Fire Insurance and Underwriters Maps, 1852–1968," *Quarterly Journal of the Library of Congress* 25, no. 3 (July 1968), 194–218. Sanborn maps commonly were at a scale of 1:600.

[44] For an extensive list of the 700,000 Sanborn maps in the collection of the Library of Congress, see U.S. Library of Congress, Geography and Map Division, *Fire Insurance Maps in the Library of Congress: Plans of North American Cities and Towns Produced by the Sanborn Map Company* (Washington, D.C.: Library of Congress, 1981). See fn. 31 for the address of the Photoduplication Service, from which prints may be ordered.

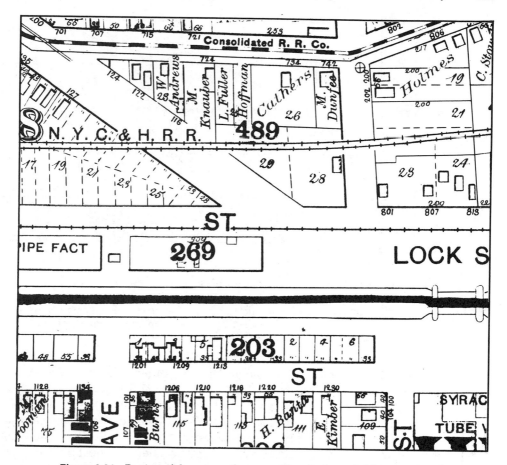

Figure 8-24   Portion of downtown Syracuse, New York, copied from a colored plate in an 1892 real-estate atlas by J. W. Vose. (From *Atlas of the City of Syracuse, Onondaga County, New York* [New York: J. W. Vose and Co., 1892], section 5; courtesy of E. S. Bird Library, Syracuse University.)

8-25, a plot of the cumulative portion of the contiguous 48 states surveyed for USGS large-scale (generally 1:62,500) topographic maps, the national topographic survey did not cover half the country until about 1940.[45] Syracuse, New York, was comparatively fortunate: the Geological Survey surveyed the area in the mid-1890s and published a 15-minute quadrangle map at 1:62,500 in 1898. In the late 1930s USGS resurveyed the area and divided the 15-minute quadrangle into four 7.5-minute quadrangles. One of these was the Syracuse West

[45] Data for Figure 8-25 are from the annual reports of the director of the U.S. Geological Survey for the years through 1932 and from the annual reports of the U.S. Department of the Interior for the years thereafter.

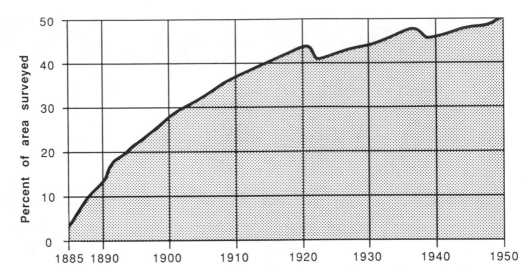

Figure 8-25   Percentage of the 48 contiguous United States surveyed for large-scale topographic mapping, 1885–1950. Apparent reductions in 1922 and 1938 represent adoption of more strict standards of accuracy that rendered some older surveys unacceptable. (Compiled by authors from annual reports of the U.S. Geological Survey and the U.S. Department of the Interior.)

quadrangle, for which the Geological Survey published a 1:31,680-scale map in 1942 and 1947. USGS published an updated 1:24,000-scale map of the area in 1953, with revisions once or twice each decade thereafter. As Figure 8-26 shows, these editions record a number of significant changes in the urban landscape, including the decline of the local salt industry and the penetration of freeways into the urban core. The Geological Survey has mapped most built-up areas with notable change several times during the past 40 years.

Despite the typical cartographic coverage of much of the country by subscription atlases, fire insurance maps, and USGS topographic maps, most places will have a unique cartographic history, perhaps because of special geographic features that attracted attention from afar or because of a small, idiosyncratic, and probably unsuccessful local map publisher.[46] Exploring and interpreting a place's cartographic history can be a challenging pastime, to be enjoyed privately or shared socially and intellectually with others. Perhaps the strongest testament to the lure of map lore is the establishment in the United States of the Chicago Map Society in 1976 and the development since then of other map societies in British Columbia, California, the Delaware Valley (near Philadelphia), Michigan,

---

[46] At various times between 1946 and 1977 27 firms and individuals covering but a single city registered copyrights for street maps of 11 of Pennsylvania's 14 major cities. See Mark Monmonier, "The Geography of Urban Street Mapping in Pennsylvania: Recent Cartographic History," *Proceedings of the Pennsylvania Academy of Science* 54 (1980), 73–77.

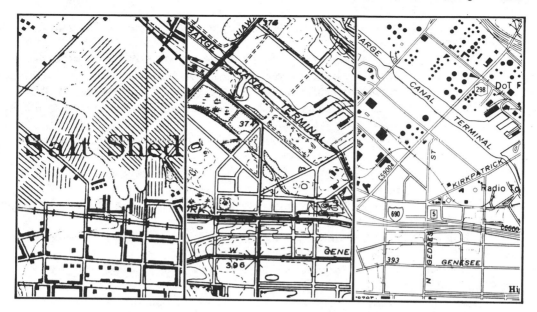

Figure 8-26 Change in the urban landscape of Syracuse, New York, as shown on topographic maps from 1898 (left), 1947 (center), and 1978 (right). Note the Salt Sheds on the early map, the Barge Canal Terminal on the 1940s map, and the freeway that replaced a multiple-track railway on the most recent map. (From Syracuse, N.Y., U.S. Geological Survey 15-minute quadrangle map, 1:62,500, edition of 1898, reprinted 1937 [enlarged to 1:24,000]; Syracuse West, N.Y., U.S. Geological Survey 7.5-minute quadrangle map, 1:31,680, edition of 1947, surveyed 1939 [enlarged to 1:24,000]; and Syracuse West, N.Y., New York State Department of Transportation 7.5-minute planimetric map with topography, 1:24,000, 1978, based on 1973 U.S. Geological Survey map at 1:24,000.)

New York City, Ottawa, and Washington, D.C.[47] The list is likely to grow as collectors and enthusiasts discover the advantages of periodic meetings.

FOR FURTHER READING

BAGROW, LEO, *History of Cartography* (2d ed.), revised and enlarged by R. A. Skelton. Chicago: Precedent Publishing, 1985.

BLAKEMORE, M. J., and J. B. HARLEY, *Concepts in the History of Cartography: A Review and*

[47] See David Woodward, "Activities in the History of Cartography: An Overview of Recent Events," in *U.S. National Report to ICA, 1984*, Judy M. Olson, ed. (Falls Church, Va.: American Congress on Surveying and Mapping, 1984), pp. 79–81. News of map societies and other activities of interest to map enthusiasts is carried regularly in *Mapline*, a quarterly newsletter published by the Hermon Dunlap Smith Center for the History of Cartography at the Newberry Library, 60 West Walton Street, Chicago, IL 60610.

Perspective. Toronto: University of Toronto Press, 1980; issued as *Cartographica* 17, no. 4 (1980).

BROWN, LLOYD A., *The Story of Maps*. Boston: Little, Brown, 1949; New York: Dover, 1979.

CARRINGTON, DAVID K., and RICHARD W. STEPHENSON, *Map Collections in the United States and Canada: A Directory* (3d ed.). New York: Special Libraries Association, 1978.

CRONE, G. R., *Maps and Their Makers* (5th ed.). Folkestone, Eng.: William Dawson & Sons; Hamden, Conn.: Archon Books, 1978.

HODGKISS, ALAN G., *Understanding Maps: A Systematic History of Their Use and Development*. Folkestone, Eng.: William Dawson & Sons, 1981.

MONMONIER, MARK, *Technological Transition in Cartography*. Madison: University of Wisconsin Press, 1985.

MORELAND, CARL, and DAVID BANNISTER, *Antique Maps: A Collector's Handbook*. London and New York: Longman, 1983.

RISTOW, WALTER W., *American Maps and Mapmakers: Commercial Cartography in the Nineteenth Century*. Detroit: Wayne State University Press, 1985.

ROBINSON, ARTHUR H., *Early Thematic Mapping in the History of Cartography*. Chicago: University of Chicago Press, 1982.

SCHWARTZ, SEYMOUR I., and RALPH E. EHRENBERG, *The Mapping of America*. New York: Harry N. Abrams, 1980.

SKELTON, R. A., *Maps: A Historical Survey of Their Study and Collecting*. Chicago: University of Chicago Press, 1972.

THROWER, NORMAN J. W., *Maps and Man: An Examination of Cartography in Relation to Culture and Civilization*. Englewood Cliffs, N.J.: Prentice-Hall, 1972.

TOOLEY, R. V., *Maps and Mapmakers* (6th ed.). London: B. T. Batsford, 1978.

TOOLEY, R. V., *The Mapping of America*. London: Holland Press; New York: Richard B. Arkway, 1980.

VAN DE GOHM, RICHARD, *Antique Maps for the Collector*. New York: Macmillan, 1973.

WILFORD, JOHN NOBLE, *The Mapmakers*. New York: Alfred A. Knopf, 1981.

WOODWARD, DAVID, ed., *Cartography and Art: Six Historical Essays*. Chicago: University of Chicago Press, 1987.

WOODWARD, DAVID, ed., *Five Centuries of Map Printing*. Chicago: University of Chicago Press, 1975.

CHAPTER NINE

Dramatic Effects with Maps

Maps can be dramatic. From the complex, aesthetically uninspired archives of property boundaries or sewer lines to the highly focused map telling a story or advocating a political or corporate position, maps play a diverse range of roles. This chapter addresses maps that in various contexts attempt to illustrate and heighten interest in a newspaper story or television program, to attract a buyer's attention toward an advertisement and sell a product, or to convince a viewer or reader of the rightness or worthiness of an idea or cause. Not drawn mechanically according to rigid rules, these maps often have a unique message, toward which the designer must direct the selection of scale, content, projection, and symbols. These maps are also intended for a wide and probably not cartographically astute audience; they must have visual impact for a general audience and not confuse the viewer with complex, distracting details.

Dramatic maps thus present a design challenge not found in other forms of cartographic display. Offered often and with flare in newspapers and magazines, they provide rich fodder for the collector, who might easily concentrate on amassing maps addressing conservative causes, liberal causes, transportation advertising, marketing humor, religious causes, and information graphics. Often drawn by aesthetically talented graphic artists lacking cartographic discipline, dramatic maps range from the truly brilliant and inspired to the blatantly deceptive and misguided—and some are even a bit of both! When drawn by artists in the news business, dramatic maps usually are less artsy than advertising maps and less shrill than propaganda maps. But, subject to the often inflexible deadlines of competing media outlets, journalistic cartography suffers a handicap uncommon to other forms of mapping. News maps thus reflect the truth of the moment, while often, as a result, being historically incomplete or inaccurate. They also are prone to conceptual or design error, as when the projection is inappropriate or the base map poorly centered, cluttered with irrelevant details, or lacking important features. Verbal accounts, of course, can be similarly afflicted by the rush to print or telecast, but map symbols seem strangely more convincing and factual than mere words, which are more common as well as more commonly shown to be vulnerable to distortion. Thus this chapter has a two-fold function: to make the reader appreciate the style and talent that can be brought to cartographic illustration and realize the distortion of geographic reality that can occur when the map message has been misshaped by exuberance, ignorance, inattention, greed, or malice.

MAPS IN JOURNALISM

Because of technical differences in printing words and printing pictures, maps were uncommon in newspapers until the nineteenth century and relatively infrequent until well into the twentieth century. In the eighteenth century printing was slow and primitive by modern standards. Printers selected type letter by letter and placed it in a *composing stick* to form a line, which they then added to a column resting in a frame called a *chase*. The chase might hold two or more columns of type separated by vertical lines, or *rules*. Letter areas on the type were raised, to receive ink; the inked type was pressed into a sheet of paper— hence the term "letterpress." Early hand-operated flat-bed presses were capable of only about 300 impressions per hour, and each side of the sheet had to be printed separately.[1] Printing an illustration was even slower, for the nonprinting areas on a block of wood had to be carved out carefully, leaving untouched the parts of the image intended to receive ink. Yet when newspaper circulations rose in the late nineteenth century, with multiplate cylinders that carried eight pages at a time revolving 200 times a minute on steam-driven rotary presses, the larger newspapers were able and eager to hire staffs of skilled engravers to make "cuts" of portraits, landscapes, and on occasion, maps.[2]

Stereotyping, a process for engraving curved metal plates for rotary presses, was another important technical advance. A papier-mâché *mat* was pressed into the chase to receive the image of type and artwork. Hot metal then was poured onto the mat; when the metal cooled, the durable metal press plate held the

[1] Anthony Smith, *The Newspaper: An International History* (London: Thames & Hudson, 1979), p. 21.

[2] John L. Given, *Making a Newspaper* (New York: Henry Holt, 1907), p. 300.

same image as the chase. Because several plates could be engraved from the same mat, stereotyping promoted the large circulations possible with multiple presses.[3]

The 1960s and 1970s occasioned a further revolution in newspaper production: "cold type" produced by electronic, computerized typesetting machines replaced the "hot type" with raised characters set by mechanical composing machines using molten metal. Page layout, or *make-up*, no longer required positioning type and engraved blocks in a chase. Now a printer could paste a page onto a "dummy" sheet of paper from which a press plate could be made photographically, without hot-metal stereotyping. Maps, halftone photographs, and other graphics now could easily be added to the page during "stick-up" without costly, time-consuming engraving.[4]

The lure of dramatic maps is at least as old as woodblock engraving, which predated stereotyping. Figure 9-1, the primitive "snake device" drawn by colonial editor Benjamin Franklin, was printed in Franklin's *Pennsylvania Gazette* on May 9, 1754. Franklin, who supported a "Plan of Union" for the American colonies, is credited with the first American political cartoon.[5] In a sense he might also be acclaimed for the first American newspaper map. Other colonial newspapers copied this striking design, which was revived on at least two later occasions calling for colonial unity.

Franklin was not the only journalist to dramatize a political point with a map. Perhaps the most famous example of this genre is the prototypical "gerrymander," shown in the right half of Figure 9-2. Unlike Franklin's snake, the gerrymander was itself suggested by a more conventional map, printed three weeks earlier in another newspaper and shown in the left half of Figure 9-2. In 1812, the Democrats in control of the Massachusetts legislature passed an apportionment law that redistricted the state and aroused the ire of the opposing Federalists. To favor their own candidates for the state senate, the Democrats split Essex County into two parts, one of which suggested a salamander to a Federalist journalist. But, as the story goes, his editor exclaimed, "No! It's a Gerrymander," invoking the name of Democratic governor Elbridge Gerry, who declined to veto the bill. The governor thus received a much larger place in history than Elkanah Tisdale, the artist who drew the cartoon. The unfortunate Gerry, a signer of the Declaration of Independence and the person who proposed

---

[3] For discussion of stereotyping and other printing and engraving processes historically important in the newspaper industry, see W. Turner Berry, "Printing and Related Trades," in *A History of Technology*, vol. 5, *The Late Nineteenth Century*, eds. Charles Singer et al. (Oxford, Eng.: Clarendon Press, 1958), pp. 683–715.

[4] See Ernest C. Hynds, *American Newspapers in the 1970s* (New York: Hastings House, 1975), pp. 234–42.

[5] Stephen Hess and Milton Kaplan, *The Ungentlemanly Art: A History of American Political Cartoons* (New York: Macmillan, 1968), pp. 51–53.

Figure 9-1 Benjamin Franklin's cartoon-map printed in the *Pennsylvania Gazette* on May 9, 1754. From head to tail, the parts of the snake are labeled with initials to indicate New England, New York, New Jersey, Pennsylvania, Maryland, Virginia, North Carolina, and South Carolina. Apparently no room was left for Georgia. (From Albert Matthews, "The Snake Devices, 1754–1776, and the Constitutional Courant, 1765," *Publications of the Colonial Society of Massachusetts* 11 [1906–1907], 409–53, plate 1, opposite p. 416.)

what is now the Library of Congress, is remembered principally for his largely passive role in manipulating election districts.[6]

The American press owes much of its tradition to the British press, including the use of maps to illustrate the news. Figure 9-3 portrays the growth of journalistic cartography through a graph of the average daily number of maps in five elite English, Canadian, and American newspapers.[7] Founded in 1785, Britain's most prestigious newspaper, the *Times* of London, published its first illustration in 1806: as Figure 9-4 shows, the artist and wood engraver used both an oblique view and a planimetric map to illustrate with dotted lines the movements of the murderers of Isaac Blight, a wealthy Thames resident. In 1875, the *Times* printed the first daily weather map regularly published by any newspaper.[8] Around 1900, when photo-engraving replaced the slow, tedious process of woodblock engraving, less than an hour was required to make a printing plate from the rapidly drawn pen-and-ink sketch or map. The *Times*, like other newspapers, included a number of maps to explain Britain's early losses to Dutch settlers of South Africa in the Boer War (1899–1902). But the first great upsurge in newspaper cartography was World War I (1914–1918), for which the *Times* occasionally was moved to include three or four maps in a single issue.[9]

[6] John Ward Dean, "The Gerrymander," *The New England Historical and Genealogical Register* 46, no. 184 (October 1892), 374–83; and Elmer C. Griffith, *The Rise and Development of the Gerrymander* (Chicago: Scott, Foresman, 1907).

[7] Mark Monmonier, "The Rise of Map Use by Elite Newspapers in England, Canada, and the United States," *Imago Mundi*, 38 (1986), 46–60.

[8] W. Turner Berry and H. Edmund Poole, *Annals of Printing: A Chronological Encyclopedia from Earliest Times to 1950* (London: Blandford Press, 1966), p. 201; and "The 'Times' Weather Chart," *Nature* 11, no. 285 (15 April 1875), 473–74.

[9] For example, on Sunday, August 2, 1914, the *Times* marked the onset of World War I with maps bearing the titles "Seat of the War in Serb States," "The Invasion of Luxemburg," "The European Theatre of War," "Russian Frontier of the Alliance," and "The War of the Lower Danube."

In wartime journalism, the map is not only a convenient tool for posting gains and losses and explaining complex maneuvers, but also a welcome substitute for the more dramatic but missing, delayed, or censored action photo. Figure 9-3 reveals the importance of military engagements and geopolitics as a stimulant for journalistic cartography. With some newspapers, in fact, the defeat of the German and Japanese armies in World War II occasioned a decline in map use. During the Korean War (1950–1953), however, numerous American and Canadian papers, including the *New York Times* and the *Toronto Globe and Mail*, printed a war map almost daily. For many newspaper readers, the steady advance southward of the Red Army was a daily cartographic drama that in many ways had a cliffhanger ending akin to fictional thrillers. Bold arrows were ominous, threatening symbols, as in Figure 9-5, which shows Communist pressure against U.S. and South Korean defenses in July 1950. With photo-engraving, war maps could be placed in the newspaper far more easily than during the American Civil War, when the *New York Herald* could meet its deadlines only by employing twenty wood engravers working on twenty different parts of half-page war maps.[10]

War maps sometimes can seem graphically straightforward and relatively mundane alongside large headlines providing whatever shrillness the editors deem appropriate for the story. But war maps also can be highly dramatic in their own right, as witnessed by the visually intriguing hemisphere maps cartographer Richard Edes Harrison drew during World War II for *Fortune*, *Time*, and *Life* magazines. The viewer saw visually effective, exaggerated terrain from an apparent vantage point well above the earth, an effect heightened by carefully plotted curved meridians and parallels and a visible horizon.[11] Harrison also introduced a number of innovative hemispherical, global views with purposeful orientations, the essential elements of which Figure 9-6 shows, together with their provocative captions.[12] Also, to show the area covered on his perspective maps of regional terrain, Harrison used small inset globes similar in concept to

See Ian Williams, ed., *Dateline World War 1: Facsimile Reproductions of Major Stories from Newspapers of the Day* (London: David & Charles, 1970).

[10] Alfred McClung Lee, *The Daily Newspaper in America: The Evolution of a Social Instrument* (New York: Octagon Books, 1973), p. 129.

[11] Harrison's technique is described in "Perspective Maps," *Life* 16, no. 9 (28 February 1944), 56–61. The large formats and color reproduction of *Life* and *Fortune* gave Harrison more creative space than did the smaller, monochrome pages of *Time*. Also, the deadlines of a weekly magazine did not permit the planning, research, and detailed artwork possible with *Fortune*, a monthly. Unfortunately, black-and-white printing and a relatively small page in this book cannot do justice to Harrison's skillful cartographic artwork.

[12] Political scientist Alan Henrikson noted that the cartographic world views of Harrison preceded and encouraged the political world view of the "Air-Age Globalists" of postwar America. Awareness of the "shrunken planet" inhabited by two fiercely competitive great powers was, according to Henrikson, a principal cause of the "Cold War" of the late 1940s and 1950s. See Alan K. Henrikson, "Maps, Globes, and the Cold War," *Special Libraries* 65, nos. 10/11 (October/November 1974), 445–54.

Figure 9-2 The map of Essex County, Massachusetts (left), printed on March 6, 1812 in the *Boston Weekly Messenger*, inspired the famous gerrymander map-cartoon (right), published on March 26, 1812 in the *Boston Gazette*. Parallel lines on the left-hand map show boundaries of the proposed senatorial districts; the right-hand map also includes remaining towns in Essex County. (Map at left from Elmer C. Griffith, *The Rise and Development of the Gerrymander* [Chicago: Scott, Foresman, 1907], p. 69. Map at right from James Parton, *Caricature and Other Comic Art* [New York: Harper & Brothers, 1877], p. 316.)

Figure 9-2 (*continued*)

the globe insets on foreign-area maps that the influential *Washington Post* uses today.

Modern warfare is not always as simple as the thrusts and fronts of World War I and World War II that newspaper maps conveniently portrayed. Recent military conflicts have tended to be either short and decisive, as when the Israelis crushed the Egyptians and the Syrians in the Six Days' War of June 1967, or protracted and indecisive, as in Vietnam during the 1960s and 1970s and in Lebanon in the 1980s. American strategists in Vietnam attempted unsuccessfully to control the countryside by controlling population centers. They relied heavily on aerial bombing and "search and destroy" missions, rather than on broad frontal attacks. Enemy guerillas, in Vietnam as elsewhere, specialized in isolated, surprise "hit-and-run" attacks that were not suited to dramatic cartographic portrayal unless particularly bloody and in an obscure, remote place, for which the foreign editor might deem a simple locator map appropriate.

Guerilla warfare, often practiced in cities and against civilians, may produce devastating results that demand a report more thorough than a body count, gory photograph, and routine locator map. Terrorists are vicious, sometimes

Figure 9-3 Average daily mean number of maps, 1870–1980, for five elite newspapers.

suicidal, and often armed with explosives of sufficient power to collapse large buildings. Favored targets include embassies, military barracks, transportation terminals, and other areas where large numbers of people gather. A map can be particularly helpful to a news story by organizing spatially whatever facts might be available, as in Figure 9-7, which shows an AWOL Marine corporal's destructive 3-week trek through the Southeast.

Detailed larger-scale local maps are useful for satisfying the reader's curiosity about the locations of armed robberies, murders, and sexual assaults. Crime maps can be particularly useful to citizens in developing a mental picture of hazardous and safe parts of their city. The *New York Times*, which in 1870 used a crude wood-engraved map to portray the floor plan of the home of a

Mr. BLIGHT's HOUSE.

Ground Plan of Mr. BLIGHT's House.

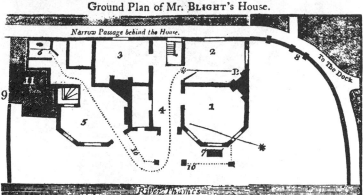

Figure 9-4   In discussing the trial of Richard Patch, the April 7, 1806, issue of the *Times* of London included these oblique and plan views of the house of Isaac Blight, a murder victim. (From facsimile published in the *Times Higher Education Supplement*, no. 645, 15 March 1985, p. 9; used by permission of Times Newspapers Limited.)

murdered stockbroker, in the 1970s and 1980s devoted about 3 percent of its maps to crime stories.[13]

Newspaper maps can be classified according to the theme of the article they illustrate, as in Table 9-1, which summarizes maps found in a sample for January and July 1985 of the *New York Times* and of the *Syracuse* (N.Y.) *Herald-Journal*.[14] Many newspaper maps serve principally to locate sensational events,

[13] This 3-percent estimate is based tentatively on an examination of all issues published during January and July for the years 1970 and 1980. See Mark Monmonier, "Maps in the *New York Times*, 1860–1980: A Study in the History of Journalistic Cartography," *Proceedings of the Pennsylvania Academy of Science* 58, no. 1 (1984), 79–83.

[14] The Sunday *Herald-American* is included with the weekday *Herald-Journal* to obtain the Syracuse estimates. The Newhouse Newspapers group owns both papers.

Figure 9-5 AP Wirephoto map showing North Korean and Chinese pressure (black arrows) against South Korean and U.S. defense line and threat to supply port at Pusan. (From the *Syracuse Herald-Journal*, 29 July 1950, p. 1; used with permission of the Associated Press.)

such as accidents, disasters, battles, riots, and terrorist attacks, local and domestic as well as foreign. But many other maps, particularly in the feature-rich Sunday edition of the *New York Times*, illustrate travel and other recreation-related stories. Still other maps explain zoning plans, flood hazards, crop failures, and other political, social, and physical phenomena. Many editors consider a two-column explanatory map well worth the space it consumes, and more efficient than the several hundred words that might have been required even to attempt a purely verbal explanation.

Bigger newspapers can afford not only a staff of foreign correspondents but also a map department. In 1985 the *New York Times*, which then had a weekday nationwide circulation around one million, but with principal distri-

THE U.S.: its geographical isolation is more seeming than real

ICELAND: kingpin of the North Atlantic

ARGENTINA: a dagger pointed at the heart of Antarctica

AUSTRALIA: island continent to which distances are great

Figure 9-6 Four global views designed by Richard Edes Harrison. The original drawings were in color, more fully labeled, neatly airbrushed to suggest a sphere, and printed with a diameter of almost 12 cm (4.5 in.). (Generalized from Richard Edes Harrison, *Look at the World: The Fortune Atlas for World Strategy* [New York: Alfred A. Knopf, 1944], pp. 52–53.)

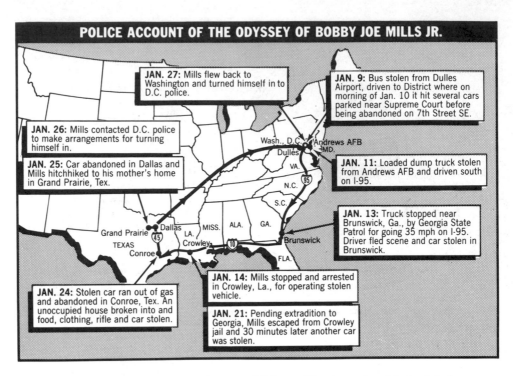

Figure 9-7 Map accompanying story "18 Days of Pandemonium; Marine Jailed After Multistate Chase." (Drawn by Larry Fogel; photographically reduced from the *Washington Post*, 30 January 1985, p. B1; used with permission.)

TABLE 9-1 THEMES IN A SAMPLE OF MAPPED ARTICLES IN THE *NEW YORK TIMES* AND THE *SYRACUSE HERALD-JOURNAL*

Theme	New York Times		Syracuse Herald-Journal	
	Number	Percentage	Number	Percentage
Crime	4	1.6	3	5.6
Public works, planning, and neighborhoods	38	14.9	10	18.5
Tourism, travel, recreation, and sports	71	27.8	3	5.6
Politics, elections, legal affairs	14	5.5	7	13.0
International relations, war, and defense	51	20.0	18	33.3
Economics, business, and transport	29	11.4	7	13.0
Accidents, disasters	12	4.7	4	7.4
Science, exploration, and environmental hazards	26	10.2	1	1.9
Education: history, demography, health, and so forth	10	3.9	1	1.9

Source: Tabulated by authors from 255 nonweather mapped articles in the *New York Times* and 54 nonweather mapped articles in the *Herald-Journal* and Sunday *Herald-American*, published in 62 daily and Sunday issues of each newspaper, January and July 1985.

bution in the city's metropolitan area and the Northeast Corridor, had 10 artists drawing all the maps and charts printed. In contrast, the Syracuse evening newspaper shared its six artists with the morning paper; moreover, they were responsible not only for maps and diagrams but also for feature-page artwork. The *Herald-Journal* thus relied on the Associated Press for all its weather maps and 28 percent of the nonweather maps in the sample. Nine and 36 percent of its maps came from United Press International and the Chicago Tribune Media Graphics syndicate, respectively. As Table 9-1 shows, the smaller number of maps in the Syracuse paper tended to focus upon planning, geopolitical, and sensational themes to a greater degree than did the larger number of maps in the *New York Times*.

Even a newspaper too small to afford an art staff can have an abundance of maps. In addition to local and state agencies that provide planning and other reproducible maps related to stories on zoning laws and industrial development, a number of news syndicates offer sets of locator maps and press-on symbols with which the resourceful news editor or clerk can consult an atlas and make a presentable map in a quarter of an hour or less. Chicago Tribune Media Graphics, for instance, supplies clients with base maps, symbols, and type with which to construct simple, good-looking locator maps on deadline. The map in Figure 9-8 of a hypothetical attack in Botswana was put together in less than 10 minutes using scissors, paste, and the base map sheet shown at its left.

More timely and influential as sources of cartographic illustration are the wire services, which now, of course, serve their clients largely by communications satellite and dish antenna, rather than through a network of copper wires. Newspapers subscribe to one or more wire services, which provide most of their nonlocal stories. The larger wire services also operate a "photowire," a separate system for news and sports photos, maps, financial charts, and other graphics. The Associated Press (AP) initiated its Wirephoto service in 1935 and now provides a variety of news graphics and timely locator maps from its headquarters in New York City.[15] United Press International (UPI), the AP's principal competitor, reorganized its faltering business in the mid-1980s around a few key services, one of which was news graphics.[16] Both AP and UPI now employ graphic designers who are also journalists. In addition to locator maps and separate daily weather maps for morning and afternoon papers, these wire services also offer such timely explanatory maps as Figure 9-9, which shows the path of a TWA jetliner forced by terrorists to make two round trips between Algiers and Beirut. When a more generous lead time permits, a wire service can send ahead by mail anticipatory maps such as Figure 9-10, portraying the marathon route in the 1984 Olympics.

[15] See, for example, "A.P. Wirephotos Flash Across Nation," *Editor and Publisher* 67, no. 34 (5 January 1935), 7; and "(AP)," *Fortune* 15, no. 2 (February 1937), 88–92 and 148–62.

[16] See, for example, "UPI Expands Graphics Dept.," *Editor and Publisher* 117, no. 33 (18 August 1984), 10 and 35.

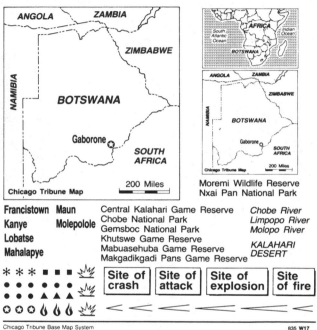

Figure 9-8   Chicago Tribune Graphics Service's base map sheet for Botswana (left) was used to produce a map (right) of a hypothetical attack. (Base map sheet reduced photographically from image 18 cm [7 in.] wide. Reprinted by permission: Tribune Media Services.)

Wire service cartography has been plagued by less than ideal image transmission and by the inability to control the size at which the client newspaper prints a map. One newspaper will enlarge a map to double-column width and blast the reader with type large enough for a small headline, whereas another will shrink the same maps to column width on an eight-column page and induce eye strain. Size reduction has been inadvertently encouraged not only by a shortage of space in the "news hole" for the day, but also by large, bold type intended to survive photowire transmission. Wire service pictures are transmitted as closely spaced lines of tiny black or white dots, packed 400 or more

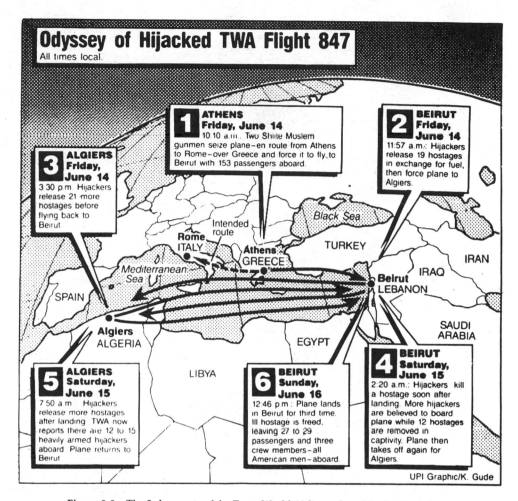

Odyssey of Hijacked TWA Flight 847
All times local.

1 ATHENS
Friday, June 14
10.10 a.m. Two Shiite Moslem gunmen seize plane–en route from Athens to Rome–over Greece and force it to fly to Beirut with 153 passengers aboard.

2 BEIRUT
Friday, June 14
11:57 a.m.: Hijackers release 19 hostages in exchange for fuel, then force plane to Algiers.

3 ALGIERS
Friday, June 14
3:30 p.m. Hijackers release 21 more hostages before flying back to Beirut

4 BEIRUT
Saturday, June 15
2:20 a.m.: Hijackers kill a hostage soon after landing. More hijackers are believed to board plane while 12 hostages are removed in captivity. Plane then takes off again for Algiers.

5 ALGIERS
Saturday, June 15
7:50 a.m. Hijackers release more hostages after landing. TWA now reports there are 12 to 15 heavily armed hijackers aboard. Plane returns to Beirut

6 BEIRUT
Sunday, June 16
12:46 p.m.: Plane lands in Beirut for third time. Ill hostage is freed, leaving 27 to 29 passengers and three crew members–all American men–aboard.

Intended route

Black Sea

Rome ITALY   Athens GREECE   TURKEY   IRAN

Mediterranean Sea   IRAQ

SPAIN   Beirut LEBANON   SAUDI ARABIA

Algiers ALGERIA   EGYPT

LIBYA

UPI Graphic/K. Gude

Figure 9-9 The 3-day route of the Trans World Airlines plane hijacked in Athens on June 14, 1985, and sent by United Press International to clients for use on June 17. (Photographically reduced; used with permission.)

per cm (160 or more per in.).[17] Finer resolution would require either a more expensive, "wider-band" transmission system or a reduction in the number of pictures "moved" throughout the day; about 7 minutes is required to transmit a photo or map. Fortunately, satellite communications can avoid some of the limitations on channel capacity inherent in copper wires. Moreover, increased interest in news graphics may lead to a separate graphics network with images

[17] See, for example, Gerald B. Healey, "Photo Transmission Hit by Production Managers," *Editor and Publisher* 110, no. 37 (10 September 1977), 26 and 50.

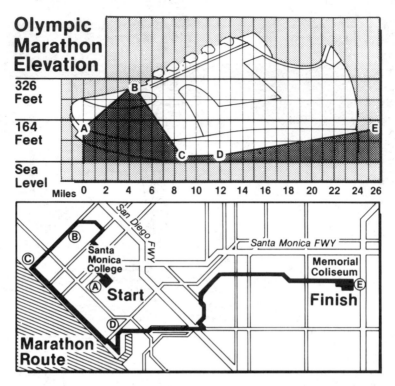

Figure 9-10   Route of the Olympic Marathon, summer 1984, distributed in advance by the Associated Press. (Photographically reduced; used with permission of the Associated Press.)

received not at a facsimile photoprinter, but at a microcomputer-typesetter, so that the newspaper can generate aesthetically pleasing type and symbols consistent with the overall design of the newspaper. Trends toward full-page, computer-assisted make-up system suggest that wire service clients eventually will be able to manipulate photos and graphics more easily and adapt them to their own style guidelines.

Concern about design and aesthetics in the newspaper industry is responsible for much of the recent increase in newspaper maps. Since the 1960s, newspapers have become more graphic, in part as a response to competition from television. This graphic revolution has affected not only photographs, typography, page layout, and the use of color, but also maps and diagrams, collectively called "information graphics." Map use has grown as newspapers have incorporated more feature stories—a phenomenon particularly obvious in the Sunday paper, where maps contribute to foreign and national news summaries, an elaborately illustrated travel section, and local-interest stories on neighborhoods, nature walks, house-and-garden tours, and jogging marathons. Maps are also incorporated into a newspaper's basic design, principally in "standing sigs" used to identify various parts of the paper with local, regional, statewide, national, and foreign stories (see Figure 9-11). The contemporary newspaper must be "reader-friendly" to the "scanner," who seeks only articles of special interest and who values a well-organized paper in which particular types of news or features are easy to locate.[18] Although the influence of packaging and "product context" upon news content disturbs many verbally oriented journalistic purists, the design revolution is enhancing the likelihood that a map will be used where words alone would fail to provide a satisfactory explanation for a story with an important geographic component.

MAKING A PITCH: MAPS IN ADVERTISING

Newspapers and magazines carry not only the most common map, the news map, but also the second most common map, the map used in advertising. Like news maps, not all advertising maps are dramatic. Some are crude boundary descriptions of properties offered at public auction, and others are bland displays of routes leading to an appliance discounter or furniture showroom. But advertising cartography has produced many highly imaginative, clever maps, carefully designed and painstakingly tested to catch the buyer's eye and present the seller's message. In making a pitch, the advertiser may make full use not only of the enigmatic attraction of information-rich cartographic artwork, but also of the ease with which features can be emphasized or suppressed and distances compressed or stretched. In combining cartographic license with aesthetic license, the huckster artist with a marketing mandate has exploited more fully than any other map maker the manipulatability and power of map symbols.

Distortion of Spatial Relationships

All small-scale maps distort distances, and so must advertising maps. But the alert art director surely cannot ignore the opportunity to have the inherent distortion of space serve the agency's client. Spatial distortions are particularly common when the advertiser is selling travel. After all, transport companies prefer their routes to look direct and efficient, and tourist bureaus want their playgrounds to seem convenient and accessible.

Railroads were among the earliest beneficiaries of carefully manipulated spatial distortions on advertising maps, printed on timetables and handbills as well as in newspapers and magazines. Prospective travelers needed to know

---

[18] For informative and insightful essays on the recent and continuing revolution in newspaper design, see Belden Associates, "Trends in Newspaper Editing and Design," *Design—The Journal of the Society of Newspaper Design* no. 16 (Summer 1984), 16–17 and 22–23; and Mario Garcia, *Contemporary Newspaper Design*, 2d ed. (Englewood Cliffs, N.J.: Prentice-Hall, 1987), pp. 150–56.

State taxpayer reporting revised

State tax officials say they are getting a large number of telephone calls from senior citizens who are confused about the new law exempting Social Security and Railroad Retirement income from Maryland's income tax.

while 7,483 players won $42 each for picking 4 of 6 numbers.

The winning numbers Saturday were 1, 15, 16, 30, 31 and 39.

Cat bill to be reconsidered

Legislation requiring cat owners to license their pets, which narrowly failed to win approval by the City Council last week, will be reconsidered by the council at next Monday's session.

Last night, Councilman Anthony J. Ambridge, D-2nd, first won council approval for reconsideration of the cat license bill, and then won a postponement of any vote on it and two companion measures until next week.

Northeast Journal

*Making money on a park,
on telephones to nobody,
on small town's refuse,
and saving on honors.*

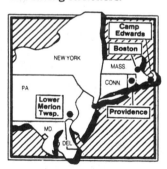

Direct Connection To Nowhere

IT is even more difficult than might
be expected, several studies suggest, to "reach out and touch someone" in Boston City Hall and the Mas-

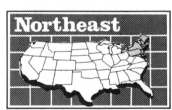

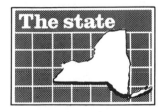

Figure 9-11 Cartographic icons used as "standing sigs" to identify the "Northeast Journal" in the Sunday edition of the *New York Times* (left); state and city news briefs in the *Baltimore Evening Sun* (above); and world, Northeastern, and state news briefs in the *Syracuse Herald-Journal* (right). (Left: © 1985 The New York Times Company. Reprinted by permission. Above: Courtesy of the *Baltimore Evening Sun*. Right: Courtesy of the Syracuse Newspapers, Inc.)

not only directions and endpoints of routes but also connections and intermediate stations. Perhaps understandably, these route maps were constructed
around the client's own railway, with lines following irregular terrain and mean-
dering rivers rendered as straight lines as much for graphic clarity and ease of
engraving and lettering as for a favorable comparison with competing routes.
Figure 9-12 shows one of the more extreme examples of route smoothing: the
gentle curve (left) of the Lehigh Valley Railroad between Pittston and Sayre,
Pennsylvania, contrasts strongly with the recurring curves of the right-of-way's
less generalized portrayal (right). Distortion was selective, however, and whatever competing lines were included on a railroad's map usually had more curvy,
less direct delineations.

Moreover, in focusing on a particular system, railway route maps tended
to distort the geography of outlying areas, included because of important origins
and destinations of "off-line" traffic, but compressed to fit the space available
without diminishing the more significant detail shown for "on-line" places.
Note, as an illustration, the severely expanded east-west extent of Vermont in
Figure 9-13, part of a map advertising to shippers a small independent railway
in northern Vermont. New Hampshire and southern Vermont are unimportant
to the map's goal of showing the "Direct Bridge Route between Maine, New
York State and the Midwest." Stretching tends to be parallel to the orientation
of the route the map promotes, as Figure 9-14 demonstrates again, with the north-

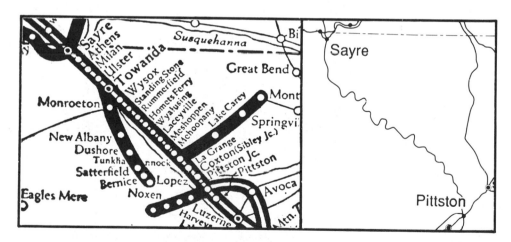

Figure 9-12   The relatively straight route (left) of the Lehigh Valley Railroad is
a convenient generalization of what is a markedly more winding route (right).
(Left-hand part enlarged from map of the Lehigh Valley Railroad in *The Official
Guide of the Railways* 84, no. 9 [February 1952], 154. © Copyright by NATIONAL
RAILWAY PUBLICATION COMPANY. Used with permission. Right-hand part
from "Railroads in New York State and Their Principal Connections," New York
State Department of Transportation, September 1974.)

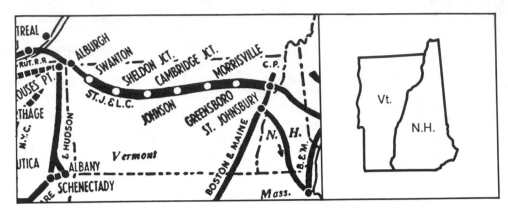

Figure 9-13 Severe east-west expansion of Vermont in the map (left) of the St. Johnsbury and Lamoille County Railroad is contrasted with a more planimetrically correct portrayal (right) of state boundaries. (Left-hand artwork enlarged from *The Official Guide of the Railways* 84, no. 9 [February 1952], 111. © Copyright by NATIONAL RAILWAY PUBLICATION COMPANY. Used with permission.)

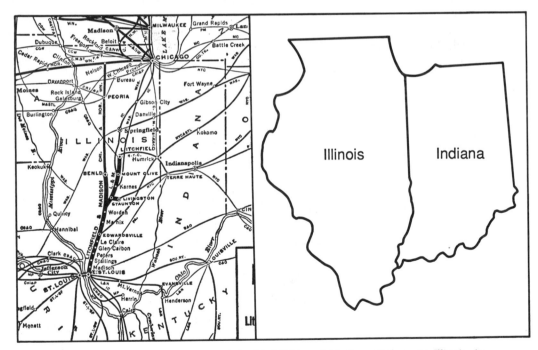

Figure 9-14 Indiana, to the east of the Litchfield and Madison Railway in Illinois, is compressed in an east-west direction so that the map (left) for "The St. Louis Gateway Route" can include Ohio and part of Pennsylvania (farther east, not shown here). The less-generalized map (right) shows Indiana as notably shorter but not so much thinner than Illinois. (Left-hand artwork from *The Official Guide of the Railways* 84, no. 9 [February 1952], 792. © Copyright by NATIONAL RAILWAY PUBLICATION COMPANY. Used with permission.)

south trending Litchfield and Madison Railway in central Illinois resulting in an emaciated-looking Indiana.

Railroad maps often seek business from industries by calling the traffic manager's attention to connections with other railways and other places. A particularly dramatic example is Figure 9-15, a map of a strategically positioned, 187-km (116-mi) "bridge line" linking Washington, D.C., with the South. The

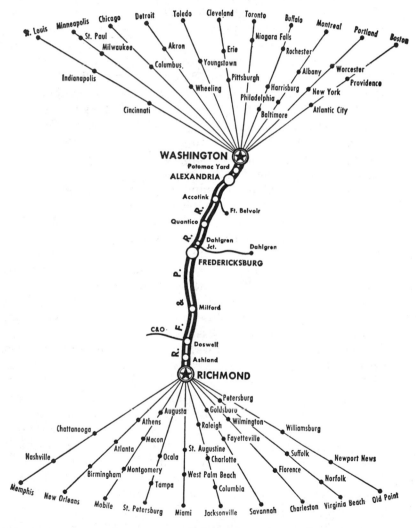

Figure 9-15 Map of the Richmond, Fredericksburg, and Potomac Railroad emphasizes the railroad's role as a "bridge line" between north and south. (From *The Official Guide of the Railways* 84, no. 9 [February 1952], 595. © Copyright by NATIONAL RAILWAY PUBLICATION COMPANY. Used with permission.)

map clearly shows that traffic originated or terminated on-line is less important than freight moved over the entire route between points north and south.

Route straightening and distance compression are particularly common in the maps of rapid transit systems, which compete not with rival high-speed rail carriers but with the private car, the public bus, and the alternative of staying at home. In many metropolitan areas several routes converge at a large and complex business district, served by more than a single junction point. Transit-system maps thus require more cartographic space for the city center than for the periphery, where stations to which the commuter can drive or travel by bus are much farther apart. On the map of the London subway system shown in Figure 9-16, the scale for central London is much greater than for outlying boroughs, for which a relatively close spacing of symbols hides greater distances between consecutive stations. More schematic still are the strip maps posted on elongated panels above car doors; these maps show the train's particular route as a straight line punctuated by evenly spaced station symbols and short color-coded intersecting segments for connecting lines.

Geographer Douglas Fleming believes that advertisers choose these seemingly self-serving spatial distortions to "lead rather than mislead."[19] And leading often involves capitalizing on existing knowledge or bias. Fleming, who examined the projections of maps in airline advertisements, notes a tendency among some global carriers to rely on the familiar, equatorially-centered, north-at-the-top Mercator world view—an ingrained perspective he regards as a "subconscious part of Western literacy." Other carriers, he points out, have abandoned this tradition for an azimuthal perspective that shows great-circle routes as "straight-line short-cuts." Fleming notes further that since the late 1950s and 1960s, when spacecraft and the news media promoted azimuthal views of the earth from space, this type of global projection has gained a familiarity among a more cartographically astute public, and thus provides another responsive chord for the advertiser's message.

Yet another incentive for the use of an azimuthal, or quasi-azimuthal, perspective in airline maps is the recent popularity of the hub-and-spoke network, with a single carrier operating many planes that several times a day converge on a hub airport to exchange passengers. In this way the carrier can offer economical service between many more pairs of points than could be served with direct flights. Typical of this new type of airline cartography is Piedmont Airlines's map of connections available through its hub at Charlotte, North Carolina, shown in Figure 9-17. Run in the *Chicago Tribune*, this ad emphasizes the convenience the hub affords passengers bound from Chicago for any of 16 airports in North Carolina and South Carolina.

Another type of projection advertisers use is the *area cartogram*, which systematically alters the relative areas of countries, states, and other recognizable

---

[19] Douglas K. Fleming, "Cartographic Strategies for Airline Advertising," *Geographical Review* 74, no. 1 (January 1984), 76–93.

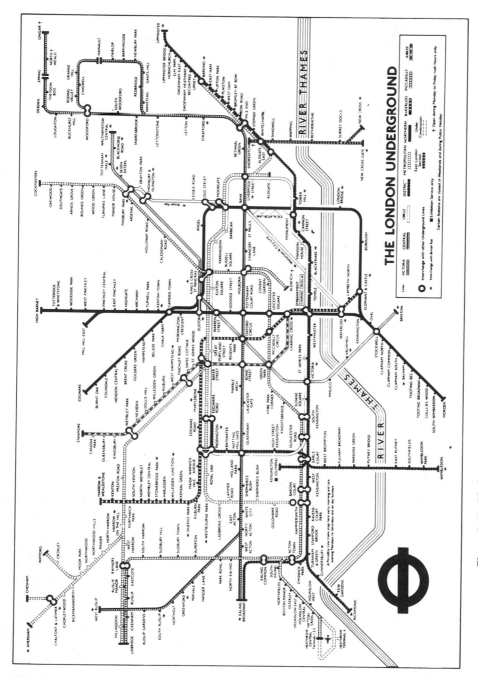

Figure 9-16 Black-and-white version of the London Underground map, designed by Paul E. Garbutt. (Used with permission of the London Transport Executive. Copyright London Transport Executive.)

Figure 9-17 Advertisement for Piedmont Airlines. (From *Chicago Tribune*, 28 May 1985, section 2, p. 2; used with the permission of Piedmont Aviation, Inc.)

units to portray the geographic distribution of something other than land area. A familiar tool of cartographers portraying demographic phenomena and electoral geography, the area cartogram can so radically distort a familiar pattern of boundaries and sizes that what might be called "map shock" causes the reader to pause, reflect, and register a more lasting impression than with a conventional portrayal. In an eight-page public-information advertisement run in national news magazines in the mid-1970s to explain both the increased difficulties of petroleum exploration and the need to develop a more diverse array of energy sources, the Exxon Corporation employed a colorful, air-brushed double-page version of the area cartogram to dramatize the concentration of known oil reserves in the Middle East and North Africa (see Figure 9-18). Already conditioned to prices at the pump well above the once familiar 30 cents per gallon, but recently having experienced long lines at gasoline stations, the American motorist was given a refined knowledge of the new importance of some lesser developed parts of the globe by this map of the "World of Known Oil Reserves."

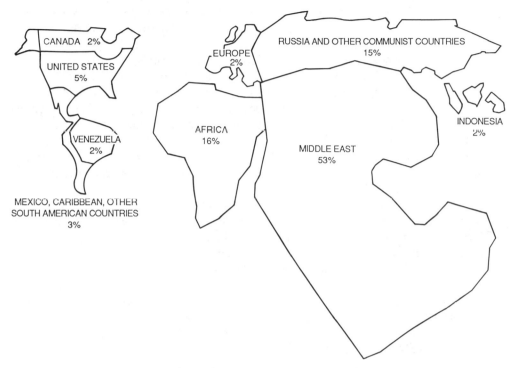

Figure 9-18   "The World of Known Oil Reserves," an advertisement for Exxon Corporation. (Redrawn at a smaller size from *Newsweek* 82, no. 23 [3 December 1973], 62–63.)

Alluring, Catchy, and Flattering Symbols

Advertisers have devised many manipulations of the map to catch the reader's eye and make a favorable impression for a particular product or service. Mere catchiness, in fact, is the main goal of many ads that seek to promote "name recognition," and even a map without a specific pitch can attract more than a casual glance from the reader scanning through a newspaper or magazine. Advertisements more commonly invoke the map as a visual concept than as a device to portray spatial relationships. Familiar country or state outlines often are the only geographic parts of catchy artwork designed to please or amuse as well as introduce the copywriter's verbal proposition. Paul McDermott, who observed a substantial increase after World War II in the use of cartographic motifs in advertising graphics, noted two minor varieties, the caricature and the jigsaw-puzzle map.[20] He was particularly attracted to the nondrafted, map-like shapes

[20] Paul D. McDermott, "Cartography in Advertising," *Canadian Cartographer* 6, no. 2 (December 1969), 149–55.

of a peach pie and a colorful collage of freshly washed clothing, both in the shape of the United States—the former to advertise an airline and the latter to promote a laundry detergent.

Catchiness need not require quaint, artsy, or obviously innovative symbols. Mere crudeness of linework can be catchy, as can intriguing accompanying text, or "copy." The viewer of Pan American's ad in Figure 9-19 is surprised and captivated by the pair of similar rough outlines, one relatively full of city symbols and names and the other comparatively empty. Separate maps for cities served by nonstop and one-stop flights provide a two-stage example of the where-we-can-serve-you theme many advertising maps develop. Somewhat similar are maps with the where-our-clients-are motif, a geographic version of the product testimonial by a celebrity.

Many advertising maps employ a somewhat different where-we-serve theme to promote the corporate image by flattering regions or neighborhoods. Place names abound on this type of map, which exploits the geographic variant of the pleasure people experience upon seeing their name in print. Cheery, humorous symbols contribute to the graphic celebration, as in the map in Figure 9-20, which appeared in national news magazines in 1979, shortly after the onset of the second American energy crisis. This map attempts to instill in the public a favorable, friendly image of the Consolidated Natural Gas Company, which was concerned about the enmity that was accompanying higher gas prices passed along to homeowners.

Helpful Way-Finders

A very different use of maps in advertising is the give-away highway or street map, on which the advertiser's logo or message is a mere appendage to a cartographic product useful in its own right. Advertiser-subsidized cartography is at least as old as the free oil company road map, pioneered in 1914, when the Gulf Refining Company gave away maps to announce its first service station in Pittsburgh.[21] Although the coin-operated vending machine and reduced competition in the retail gasoline business have largely abolished free general-purpose highway maps, most state governments still give away road maps in their efforts to attract tourists. Moreover, banks and real-estate firms often promote good will with free urban street maps, ordered in bulk at a unit-cost well below the price for the same product sold without an advertising panel in a drugstore or supermarket.[22] Many different local advertisers may support free or low-cost local area maps, paying for a short message in a frame of patrons' acknowledgments surrounding the cartographic artwork. The "Vermont Vacation Map,"

[21] Walter W. Ristow, "A Half Century of Oil Company Road Maps," *Surveying and Mapping* 24, no. 4 (December 1964), 617–34.

[22] See Mark Monmonier, "The Geography of Urban Street Mapping in Pennsylvania: Recent Cartographic History," *Proceedings of the Pennsylvania Academy of Science* 54, no. 1 (1980), 73–78.

Pan Am's the only airline that can get you to Tokyo from New York and Los Angeles without stopping. We also fly non-stop from San Francisco. So from just about any place (there are cities listed above) in the country, you can hop a flight to those gateway cities on a domestic airline and get to the Orient with only one stop. From Seattle, you can grab a Pan Am flight that makes only one stop. In a very nice place to stop: Hawaii.

(Pan Am's non-stop 747 service to Tokyo begins April 25 from Los Angeles. and April 26 from New York.)

Figure 9-19   Advertisement for Pan American Airlines flights from Tokyo to the United States. (Photographically reduced from *Newsweek* 87, no. 13 [29 March 1976], 77; used with permission of Pan American World Airways.)

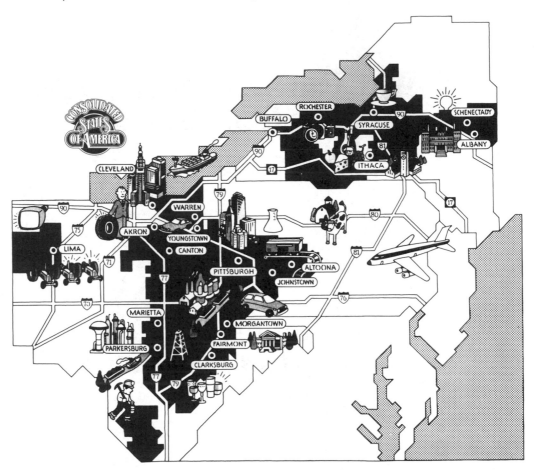

Figure 9-20 "The Consolidated States of America: Abundant in Energy; Rich in Markets,"
an advertisement for the Consolidated Natural Gas Company. (Photographically reduced
from *USAir Magazine,* September 1979, 96; used with permission of the Consolidated Natural Gas Company.)

a portion of which Figure 9-21 shows, uses knife-and-fork symbols to point out
villages with restaurants that are keyed to more complete descriptions printed
on the back. On maps distributed by some other local tourist agencies, the
locations of contributing attractions, shops, motels, and restaurants are identified directly on the map. And noncontributing sites, unless publicly owned or
nonprofit, generally remain cartographically anonymous.

Occasionally a single firm will undertake, as a good-will gesture, a map
of local or regional tourist attractions, parks, and fishing areas. In addition to
stand-alone flyers and newspaper ads, these public-service maps and their spon-
sors' logos also adorn placemats—perhaps the ultimate association of cartog-

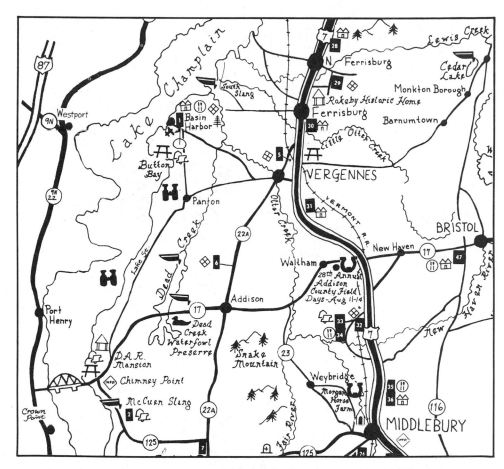

Figure 9-21 Portion of the "Vermont Vacation Map," focusing on west central Vermont. (Photographically reduced; used with permission of the Addison County Chamber of Commerce.)

raphy with the paper products industry. Well-designed advertising maps of this type and others serve also to enhance the public appreciation of all maps.

MAKING A CASE: MAPS THAT PERSUADE OR ADVOCATE

Although we discuss propaganda more completely in Chapter 6, "Political Maps," its inclusion here is justified because the use of maps to persuade is often based upon their dramatic effect. Propaganda, the attempt to influence the ideas and actions of others, comes from the Latin phrase *Congregatio de*

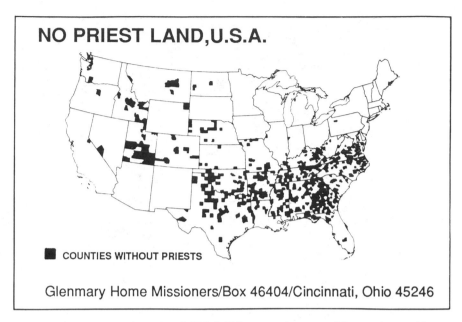

NO PRIEST LAND,U.S.A.

■ COUNTIES WITHOUT PRIESTS

Glenmary Home Missioners/Box 46404/Cincinnati, Ohio 45246

Figure 9-22   "No Priest Land, U.S.A." illustrates the parts of the contiguous 48 states, by county, that lack Roman Catholic priests. (Used with permission of Glenmary Home Missioners.)

Propaganda Fide—the Congregation for the Propagation of the Faith, a committee of the Roman Catholic Church charged with missionary tasks. It is fitting, therefore, to include here Figure 9-22, "No Priest Land, U.S.A.," a map printed on one side of the prayer card distributed by a Catholic missionary group. The map's message could not be more to the point: the South from the Texas-Oklahoma border eastward, including much of the area along the Atlantic coast from northern Florida to Virginia, as well as the states in the western and northern interior, is fertile ground for missionary activity.

In provoking a population, a propaganda map sometimes distorts an idea, as illustrated in Figure 9-23, a map with directional lines and symbols for aircraft to portray the "threat" to Germany Czechoslovakia supposedly posed after Germany had occupied Austria and surrounded much of western Czechoslovakia in the 1930s. Nazi geopoliticians depicted this small, outmanned country not as a state besieged, but as a power whose military might was pointed directly at the heart of Germany. The uninitiated viewer might overlook the possibility that the airplane symbols could easily be turned around to illustrate the threat of German air attack, a much more probable forecast in the late 1930s, given Hitler's lust for *Lebensraum*, or "living space."[23]

[23] Hans W. Weigert et al., *Principles of Political Geography* (New York: Appleton-Century-Crofts, 1957), pp. 76–77.

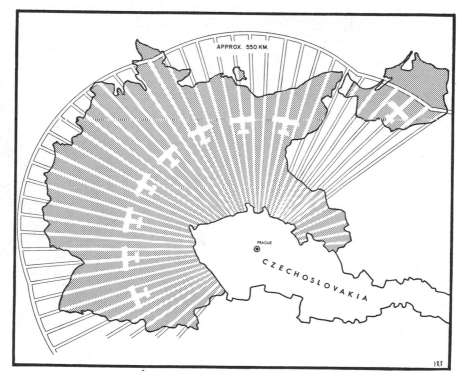

Figure 9-23 The map as a weapon of geopolitics: Czechoslovakia, a "threat" to Nazi Germany. (From Hans W. Weigert et al., *Principles of Political Geography* [New York: Appleton-Century-Crofts, 1957], p 77 Reproduced with permission of the authors.)

Figure 9-24, "Nuclear Weapons 'Accidents' and 'Incidents' in the United States," certainly qualifies as a map with a message. Its symbols cannot fail to gain the reader's attention, quicken the pulse, and convey the message that nuclear weapons are dangerous even if not fired at an enemy. The number of states involved among the contiguous 48, as well as Alaska and Hawaii, further communicates the notion that few areas are unaffected by the danger. Yet nuclear proponents might counter this assertion with maps showing the overwhelming hazards, to date, of fire, motor-vehicle collision, and other types of accident.

We are often very gullible, believing the silliest claims and statements just because they appear in print—blithely ignoring that they are part of a scheme to persuade or advocate. Add a map and the idea not only sounds good but looks good too. Often the idea and the accompanying map are not wrong; indeed, what they say and illustrate may be quite true—but the problem might lie in the more important truth that the point made is by no means unique to

Nuclear Weapons "Accidents" and "Incidents"

Figure 9-24 "Nuclear weapons 'accidents and incidents' in the United States." The map's original caption reads—

Ever since the world entered the nuclear age, accidents involving atomic weapons have threatened our country and others with the specter of nuclear holocaust. These accidents have occurred in isolated as well as populated areas—but, had there been a radioactive cloud travelling at the whim of the wind, large numbers of people could have been affected whenever an explosion occurred.

Each of the three service branches of the US military defines accidents and incidents somewhat differently. Basically, though, an "accident" involves an unplanned loss or destruction of, or serious damage to, nuclear weapons or their pertinent components, which results in an actual or potential hazard to life or property. An "incident" is an unexpected event involving damage to nuclear weapons or components which: (1) diminishes the safety of the nuclear weapons system, (2) requires immediate action in the interest of public safety, or (3) possibly could result in adverse public reaction. The military code names for these two events are 'Broken Arrow' and 'Bent Spear,' respectively.

The number of known nuclear accidents and incidents is only a fraction of the total, because it is the policy of our government, like others, *not* to report these occurrences unless obvious circumstances force them to do so.

(From National Action/Research on the Military Industrial Complex (NARMIC), Map Series, *The Military-Industrial Atlas of the United States.* The map originally appeared in *Win* magazine, 2 February 1978. © 1978 by NARMIC. Used with permission.)

the place in question. Take, for example, the "dodge" of showing a series of concentric circles on a map centered on the propagandist's industrial development site. The pitch is simple: "Look at us. We're in the midst of an area teeming with people and everything else you might need. Examine the distances, and you'll see that, in any direction, hundreds of thousands of customers are found, and the transportation system is in place to serve them." All this is quite accurate for the area of northern New Jersey shown in Figure 9-25. But

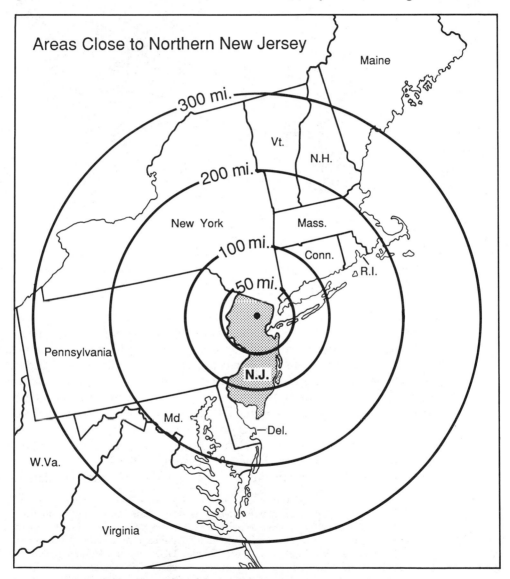

Figure 9-25   Northern New Jersey is near everything! Concentric circles illustrate the distances, up to 300 miles, from northern New Jersey.

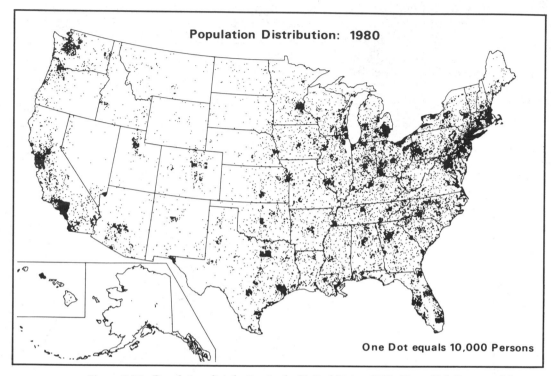

Figure 9-26   Population distribution in the United States, 1980. (From U.S. Bureau of the Census.)

what part of the greater area shown, say, between Boston, Portsmouth, or even Portland in the Northeast and southward at least as far as Washington, D.C., would not also possess a good location accessible to the interstate highway network and a large, densely settled population? As Figure 9-26 indicates, the area just described is indeed the largest, most densely settled section of the United States, and locational advantages, if there are any, must be found beyond mere geometric centrality—perhaps in tax advantages, moving subsidies, and other inducements, or in travel time. Indeed, travel time is rarely a matter of straight-line, as-the-crow-flies distance. Some places are difficult to get into and out of, whereas others are relatively accessible.

Figure 9-27 is a composite of three maps addressing population density

Figure 9-27   Top: Sparsely populated areas of the United States, by county unit. Middle: Geographic isolation as defined by distance from an interstate highway. Bottom: Geographic isolation as defined by distance from the core of a Standard Metropolitan Statistical Area. (From Stanley D. Brunn and Donald J. Zeigler, "Human Settlements in Sparsely Populated Areas: A Conceptual Overview, with Specific Reference to the U.S.," in *Settlement Systems in Sparsely Populated Regions of the U.S. and Australia*, R. E. Lonsdale and J. H. Holmes, eds. [New York: Pergamon Press, 1981], pp. 16–17. © Pergamon Press. Used with permission.)

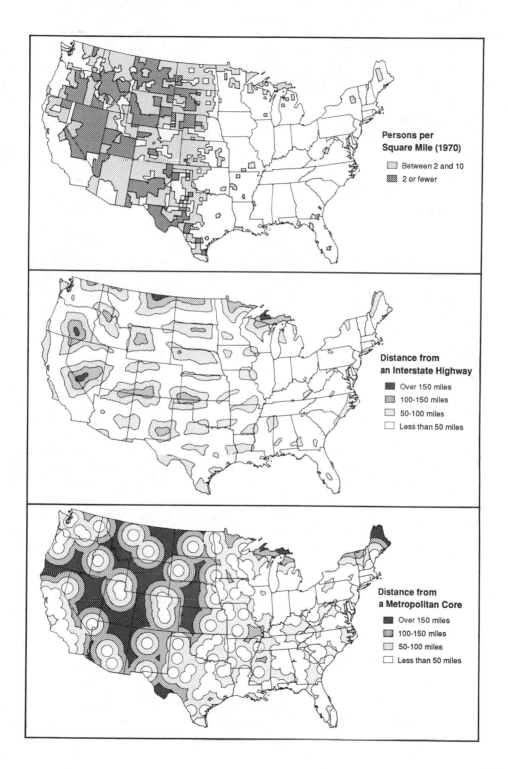

Persons per Square Mile (1970)

- Between 2 and 10
- 2 or fewer

Distance from an Interstate Highway

- Over 150 miles
- 100-150 miles
- 50-100 miles
- Less than 50 miles

Distance from a Metropolitan Core

- Over 150 miles
- 100-150 miles
- 50-100 miles
- Less than 50 miles

and accessibility. The upper map portrays sparsely populated counties by omitting those with more than 10 persons per mi^2 (4 per km^2). The middle and lower maps illustrate geographic isolation by distances from an interstate highway and by distance from the core of a Metropolitan Statistical Area, respectively. In all three maps the East is omitted from consideration far more than the West, and with few exceptions the Northeast is shown as neither sparsely inhabited nor remote from the interstate system or a metropolitan area. Rather, it is clearly the most urban-metropolitan part of the country, with many regionally advantageous industrial sites throughout.

In her summary to an illuminating article, "Persuasive Cartography," Judith Tyner offers guidelines to help us identify persuasive maps. Her list includes clues such as the highly generalized nature of the map, the absence of a scale, an unidentified map projection, the absence of a grid on a small-scale map, symbols with high emotional impact, the use of color to elicit emotion rather than to communicate, and limited text.[24] The viewer must guard against graphic seduction by a persuasive map that attempts to substitute a carefully selected array of symbols for a complicated, many-faceted reality.

MAPS IN FICTION: PORTRAYING PLACES REAL AND IMAGINED

Fiction often thrives on fictitious places, embellished by the rich imagery of a skilled storyteller's fertile imagination. The author who is not merely a "word person" will use a map to enrich the reader's experience. Indeed, imaginary places and the maps discribing them can take on a life of their own, to inspire not just one, but a series of novels. William Faulkner, for instance, created and mapped Yoknapatawpha County, Mississippi, which was the stage for 12 books and over 30 short stories.[25] Yet not all maps in fiction describe fictitious places, for the map is equally adept in adding believability to fictitious events staged in real places. Real or imaginary, the map is an important dramatic prop that can help the author describe places and their inhabitants and narrate the movements of characters.

Perhaps the most famous book about an imaginary place is Robert Louis Stevenson's *Treasure Island*, a well-known story that has a map as a central part of its plot. Figure 9-28 is that map, which illustrates Stevenson's spatial imagery.

[24] Judith A. Tyner, "Persuasive Cartography," *Journal of Geography* 81, no. 4 (July-August 1982), 144.

[25] Phillip C. Muehrcke and Juliana O. Muehrcke, "Maps in Literature," *Geographical Review* 64, no. 3 (July 1974), 317. For a collection of facsimiles of maps of imaginary places used in fiction, see J. B. Post, *An Atlas of Fantasy* (New York: Ballantine, 1979).

As the reader might recall, near the book's exciting climax, the end to a search for £700,000 in gold, Jim, the protagonist, says, "As we pulled over, there was some discussion of the chart. The red cross was, of course, far too large to be a guide; and the terms of the note on the back . . . They ran . . . thus:

'Tall tree, Spy-glass Shoulder, bearing to a point to
the N. of N.N.E.
'Skeleton Island E.S.E. and by E.
'Ten feet.'"

After deciding that a tall tree was the principal mark, and finding a human skeleton, which, Long John Silver decided, served as a directional signal, the plot twists to reveal that someone had found and removed the treasure.[26] The map thus plays a central role in the plot and aids greatly in the build-up of suspense.

Aspiring authors are advised not to overlook the value of a map. In an article in *Writer's Digest*, "Mapping Out Successful Fiction," two novelists describe the importance and function of maps in the fiction writer's road to success.[27] Roy Sorrels and Megan Daniel point out that maps improve stories written about places other than one's home area or about times other than the present. Maps refresh a writer's memory for places actually visited and afford a "feel" for places never visited, improving the author's accuracy of description and helping the author develop a sense of place, no matter how remote. Indeed, for the novelist writing about periods of old, maps from or about the particular period provide valuable insights into the layout of the place and how its inhabitants functioned. For imaginary places Sorrels and Daniel tout maps as providing a novel's setting with "an inner reality and consistency." No armchair geographers, Sorrels and Daniel cite the importance of getting out to see what the maps describe and recommend that the aspiring writer of fiction "become a compulsive map collector." Indeed, maps can be vital in suggesting plots and twists, and should not be consulted only as an afterthought. "Study the maps carefully," the two novelists note, "and soon you will be able to spot, among their many features, the road to fiction success."[28]

Among the basic modes of communication, graphicacy—the use of the visual-spatial aspect of human intelligence—is not only least recognized but

[26] Robert Louis Stevenson, *Treasure Island* (London: J. M. Dent and Sons; New York: Dutton, 1925), pp. 156, 158, and 164.

[27] Roy Sorrels and Megan Daniel, "Mapping Out Successful Fiction," *Writer's Digest* 61, no. 12 (December 1981), 32–34 and 54.

[28] Ibid., p. 54.

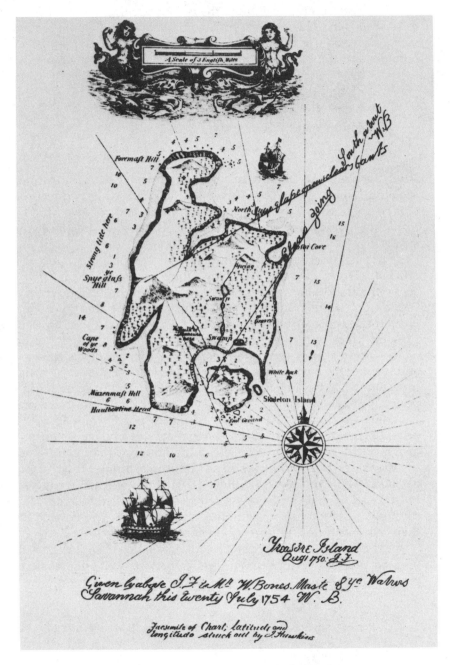

Figure 9-28   The map of *Treasure Island*. (From Robert Louis Stevenson, *Treasure Island* [New York: Charles Scribner's Sons, 1896], frontispiece.)

receives little attention in educational curricula at all levels.[29] Little, that is, compared to the traditional importance assigned to reading, writing, oral communication, and the use of numbers and their manipulation. It is not surprising, therefore, that maps, along with myriad graphic devices, are popular tools for those who want to sell products or ideas—for those who want to persuade or advocate.

FOR FURTHER READING

EVANS, HAROLD, *Pictures on a Page: Photojournalism and Picture Editing*. Belmont, Calif.: Wadsworth, 1978, 287–322.

HOLMES, NIGEL, *Designer's Guide to Creating Charts and Diagrams*. New York: Watson-Guptill, 1984.

HUTT, ALLEN, *The Changing Newspaper: Typographic Trends in Britain and America, 1622–1972*. London: Gordon Fraser, 1973.

MONMONIER, MARK, *Maps, Distortion, and Meaning*. Washington, D.C.: Association of American Geographers, 1977.

MUEHRCKE, PHILLIP C., and JULIANA C. MUEHRCKE, "Maps in Literature," *Geographical Review* 64, no. 3 (July 1974), 317–38.

POST, J. B., *An Atlas of Fantasy*. New York: Ballantine, 1979.

RISTOW, WALTER W., "Journalistic Cartography," *Surveying and Mapping* 17, no. 4 (October 1957), 369–90.

SOUTHWORTH, MICHAEL, and SUSAN SOUTHWORTH, *Maps: A Visual Survey and Design Guide*. Boston: Little, Brown, 1982.

TUFTE, EDWARD R., *The Visual Display of Quantitative Information*. Cheshire, Conn.: Graphics Press, 1983.

TYNER, JUDITH A., "Persuasive Cartography," *Journal of Geography* 81, no. 4 (July/August 1982), 140–44.

[29] The basic modes of communication are literacy, articulacy, numeracy, and graphicacy. See W. Balchin, "Graphicacy," *American Cartographer* 3, no. 1 (April 1976), 33–38.

CHAPTER TEN

Computer Maps

That the digital computer is changing both the form and the utility of maps should surprise no one. Most maps used by the general public are, after all, products of a manufacturing process; the computer has increased efficiency in most manufacturing industries and, in many instances, significantly reshaped the products as well. The computer has had a particularly strong effect upon map making, most notably by extending to consumers the opportunity to be the cartographer. In most North American and Western European universities, for example, geography students can, in a couple of hours, generate a multitude of maps by computer to explore spatial relationships or to illustrate a report. Some computer maps are ephemeral trial designs or exploratory views, whereas others are fine-drawn maps—or nearly so.

As a new technology, computer cartography is not without growing pains stemming from inadequate theory, unsophisticated software, and an overly tolerant response from overwhelmed, cartographically unaware users. Another decade may be required for this "gee-whiz!" fog to dissipate; for the more esthetically sensitive, cartographically educated customer to demand and get more graphically rational software; and for computer technology to become so pervasive that "computer map" seems as redundant as "printing-press map" does today.

Perhaps the single most significant result of computerization in cartography is an increased appreciation of the map as information, rather than as only a physical object. This change in attitude is obvious when cartographers now talk of the "map graphic," on which you can view spatial relationships with your eyes, and the "digital map," which is stored as a pattern of electronic signals. Although a map graphic can be derived from a digital map and either printed or displayed on an electronic screen, digital cartographic data can be used without ever having to create a visible map image. As pure information, the digital map may exist to be read, analyzed, and interpreted by computer and to be transmitted through a telecommunications network.

This chapter attempts to help the reader prepare for a future in which maps surely will be more numerous and more useful than they are now and in which they may even be better. The first section explains how the computer can make a map and store it for display and analysis. The next section describes the rapid rise of the computer map and discusses a variety of traditional cartographic products affected by automation. Then follows an examination of several new products and services brought about through advances in computing and telecommunications. The chapter concludes with discussion of some potential advantages and disadvantages of computerization and several educational and policy challenges faced by those engaged in digital cartography.

HOW COMPUTERS MAKE MAPS

Because the map may be described as a two-dimensional representation of the fabric of a geographic region, the Jacquard loom provides an historically convenient starting point for an introduction to computer cartography.[1] In 1801, Joseph Marie Jacquard, a French silk weaver, built a loom with which a complex pattern could be woven exactly, again and again. The relevant connection with computer-assisted cartography is that punched cards provided a step-by-step set of instructions, or *program*, for driving a machine that produced a graphically intricate product (see Figure 10-1). Jacquard's loom, which revolutionized the European textile industry, was the forerunner of modern process-control equipment. Powered by its operator's hands and feet, the loom was readily adapted to steam and water power for even more efficient operation.

An important related event was the development of computing machines for arithmetic and other data processing tasks. In 1832, Charles Babbage, a professor of mathematics at Cambridge University in England, designed an "analytical engine" theoretically able to perform rapidly and accurately a variety of complex mathematical calculations. Although widely recognized as the first computing machine, Babbage's computer received little enthusiasm and was never built, except as a simple but troublesome model his son constructed 18 years

---

[1] Although his application to weaving was original, Jacquard's idea for using a pattern of punched holes to control a machine was not unprecedented. See James Burke, *Connections* (Boston: Little, Brown, 1978), p. 111.

Figure 10-1 Engraving of a handloom with Jacquard action and chain of punched cards (at right) to control pattern. (From Alfred Barlow, *The History and Principles of Weaving by Hand and Power* [London: Sampson Low, Marston, Searle & Rivington, 1878], plate facing p. 158; courtesy of E. S. Bird Library, Syracuse University.)

after his death.[2] Yet Babbage's concept and Jacquard's punched card seem to have inspired Herman Hollerith, an engineer working for the Surgeon General of the United States, who designed and supervised the construction of a computer used in tabulating the 1880 U.S. census. A hole punched in a card the size of a dollar bill represented a digit between 0 and 9, and holes in successive adjoining columns represented the units—tens, hundreds, thousands, and higher digits (see Figure 10-2). A group of columns, called a *field*, was assigned to each item of data, and one card was prepared for each census return. Hollerith's "tabulating machine" could read these cards rapidly, sensing the holes mechanically and using electric circuits to increment the counter for the appropriate item of data. Its effect was equally noteworthy: Hollerith's machine is estimated to have cut by one-half the time otherwise needed to process returns from the census of 1890, and to have saved half a million dollars.[3]

[2] Anthony Hyman, *Charles Babbage: Pioneer of the Computer* (Princeton, N.J.: Princeton University Press, 1982), pp. 253–54.

[3] Burke, *Connections*, pp. 112–13.

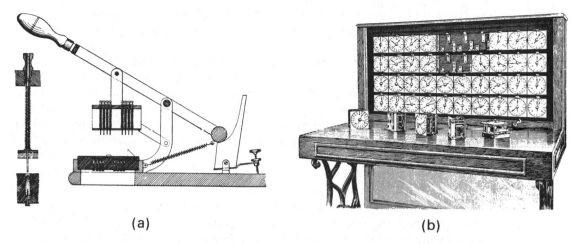

     (a)   (b)

Figure 10-2 Engravings of the (a) circuit closing press and (b) counters of the Hollerith tabulating machine used to count the 1890 U.S. Census. In the card press a pin is positioned above a cup partly filled with mercury. A punched card placed in the press will block the pin where a hole has not been punched and allow the pin to complete a circuit where a hole has been punched. When the circuit is completed, the corresponding counter will be incremented. (From Committee on Science and the Arts, "The Hollerith Electric Tabulating System," *Journal of the Franklin Institute* 79, no. 4 [April 1890], 302 and 304; courtesy of Science and Technology Library, Syracuse University.)

    Work on an electronic computing machine lagged well behind more readily applied inventions such as the telegraph, the telephone, the radio, and even the television, a prototype of which was demonstrated in 1926. Historians of technology recognize as the first large electronic digital computer the ENIAC (Electronic Numerical Integrator and Calculator), which a team of physicists and electrical engineers at the University of Pennsylvania built in 1945.[4] The significant advance this machine offered was an all-electronic control and logic system that manipulated numbers and program instructions represented by a series of two-state electronic signals transmitted as voltage pulses and stored as the polarity of tiny magnetic fields. Computer scientists refer to these signals as *bits*, short for *binary digits*. A binary code can represent a number by appropriate 0 or 1 values in the successive ones, twos, fours, eights, and higher places of the binary number system, which is based on powers of 2. Thus 26, which is the sum of 16, 8, and 2, may be written algebraically as $1(16) + 1(8) + 0(4) + 1(2) + 0(1)$, which is coded in binary as 11010. Standardized binary codes can represent alphabetic characters, punctuation marks, and special symbols such as the $ and @ for manipulation by computer.[5] Moreover, programs that specify

[4] Herman Heine Goldstine, *The Computer from Pascal to Von Neumann* (Princeton, N.J.: Princeton University Press, 1972), pp. 148–66.

[5] A character is usually represented by a group of eight bits called a *byte*. A set of numeric

the steps to be followed by the computer also can be coded in binary and stored on punch cards, magnetic tape, floppy disk, or another electronic storage medium.

Because electrons can be moved about and halted much more readily than wooden or metal parts, even the early computers of the 1940s and 1950s—which processed binary-coded data by controlling the flow of electrons through bulky vacuum tubes—could add, subtract, divide, search a list for the largest number, sort a list of names, and perform many more complex operations hundreds of times faster than their primitive mechanical counterparts. Modern miniaturized circuitry, with which thousands of bits of information can be stored on a silicon chip smaller than a child's fingernail, permits computers to be far more compact than the ENIAC's 19,000 vacuum tubes, which filled a large room. A modern microcomputer the size of a small suitcase can contain a million or more electronic components, which if no more miniaturized than the ENIAC, would require as much space as a football field.[6] Furthermore, with integrated-circuit technology, the microcomputer is also faster than earlier computers because electronic signals need not travel as far from where they are stored to where they are manipulated. Calculations that in the 1960s took several minutes now require less than a second.

To understand computer-produced maps and the potential of computer cartography one need not understand the workings of a computer, the solid-state technology that underlies chips and magnetic data storage, and the jargon of the computer scientist.[7] Yet the map user should appreciate how a graphic display device can be linked to and controlled by a computer. The simplest graphic display, and probably the basis for the earliest computer-produced maps, is the electronic typewriter, which provided the principal means of communication, input and output, between early computers and their users.[8] The computer thus could type an array of alphanumeric characters that resembled a map, as Figure 10-3 shows.

Before the digital computer, no self-respecting cartographer would have produced such a crude, esthetically unappealing graphic. What it lacked in eye appeal the computer made up for in speed, particularly when linked to a line

codes is then needed to relate numbers to special symbols and letters. Various standard codes have been developed for this purpose. See, for example, Frank J. Gallard, *Dictionary of Computing* (Chichester, Eng.: John Wiley & Sons, 1982), pp. 40–42.

[6] Christopher Evans, *The Making of the Micro: A History of the Computer* (New York: Van Nostrand Reinhold, 1981), pp. 103–4.

[7] For a readable, concise introduction to the most common computer jargon, see John Prenis, *Running Press Glossary of Computer Terms* (Philadelphia: Running Press, 1977); or Anthony Chandor, *The Penguin Dictionary of Microprocessors* (Harmondsworth, Eng.: Penguin Books, 1981). Terms more specifically concerned with graphic display can be found in Stuart W. Hubbard, *The Computer Graphics Glossary* (Phoenix, Ariz.: Oryx Press, 1983).

[8] See Waldo R. Tobler, "Automation and Cartography," *Geographical Review* 49, no. 4 (October 1959), 526–34.

```
MOVERS (1975 - 1980) AS PERCENTAGE OF POPULATION

CLASS 1 SYMBOL -    LIMITS 17 TO 20
CLASS 2 SYMBOL 0    LIMITS 20 TO 25
CLASS 3 SYMBOL #    LIMITS 25 TO 27.2
```

Figure 10-3 Photographically reduced image of a typewriter map of New Hampshire counties on an area-cartogram base.

printer able to print several hundred lines per minute on continuous strips of "fan-fold" paper 132 alphanumeric characters wide. Moreover, printing one line on top of another, called *overprinting*, provided a wider range of graytones and enhanced contrast among area symbols, as Figure 10-4 demonstrates.

A more recent development of the line-printer concept, the dot-matrix printer, provides some of the speed of the high-speed line printer but with more flexibility in placing small dots. It is called a matrix printer because it plots alphanumeric characters as an array of dots with, say, 8 rows and 5 columns, elongated vertically to provide characters taller than they are wide. Slightly more expensive printers use larger dot matrixes to provide more detail and to allow for the descenders on letters such as *j* and *g*. Such printers can also draw line symbols (see Figure 10-5), although smooth curves appear noticeably jagged. Individual dots may be darkened by heating a minute spot on a sheet or roll of thermally sensitive paper; by striking an inked ribbon with a small, rapid, electronically activated plunger; or by placing on the paper a small charge that then attracts particles of a fine powder, or *toner*.[9] In this third approach, called *elec-*

[9] See A. D. Moore, "Electrostatics," *Scientific American* 226, no. 3 (March 1972), 46–58; and Richard E. Groop and Richard M. Smith, "Matrix Line Printer Maps," *American Cartographer* 9, no. 1 (April 1982), 19–24.

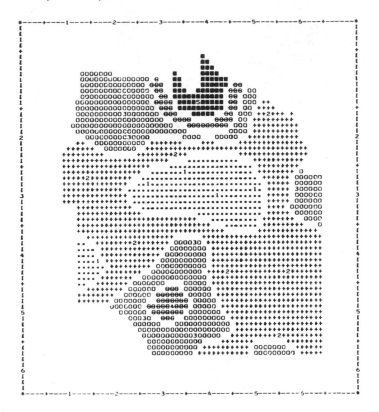

Figure 10-4   Line-printer map with dark symbols produced by overprinting several lines of type. Darkest symbol is formed by overprinting A, W, H, and I, and the next lightest symbol by overprinting 0 and -. Isoline map of Onondaga County, N.Y., portraying percentage change, 1970–1980, in housing units shows minimal increase in the city of Syracuse, near the center of the map, and substantial increase in the northern suburbs.

trostatic printing, the paper is then heated to strengthen its bond with the toner. Specially designed graphics printers can produce intermediate-quality images of fine dots packed to densities of 40 or more per running cm (100 or more per in.) in a grid of rows and columns. But electrostatic printers need not be bound to a grid of small matrix elements: high-speed electrostatic printers with a row of over 8,000 or more electric nibs spanning a roll of paper 107 cm (42 in.) wide can generate 800 rows of dots per minute and complete a large table- or poster-size drawing in 8 minutes or less.[10] As Figure 10-6 shows, the lettering and the geographic detail can be acceptable for planning applications, and even for publication. Color electrostatic printers use several toners—one set each for black,

[10] For a review of color dot printers and other hard-copy display hardware, see "Advances in Color Hard-copy Technology," *Computer Graphics World* 7, no. 1 (January 1984), 25–37.

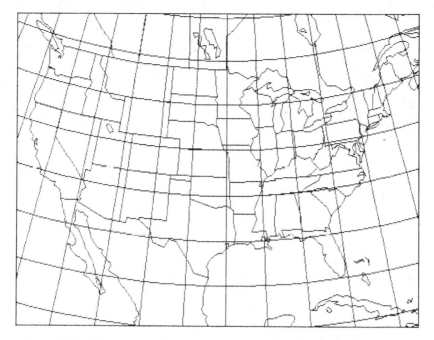

Figure 10-5 Map generated on a dot-matrix printer and reduced photographically from a width of 17.2 cm (6.8 in.). This Albers equal-area conic projection was created on an Atari home computer with an Epson printer. (Courtesy of John P. Snyder.)

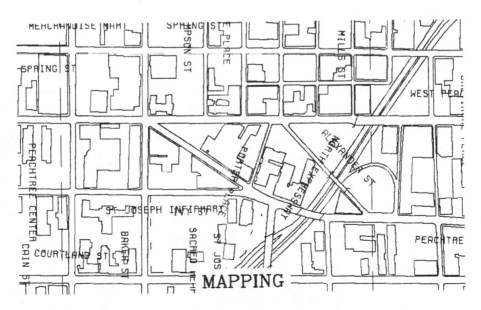

Figure 10-6 Map generated on an electrostatic dot printer. (Courtesy of Versatec, a Xerox company, located in Santa Clara, Calif.)

magenta, cyan, and yellow—and a multipass technique to rapidly generate color images that rival graphics produced with a well-maintained color copier.

Another electronic device for the rapid generation of permanent, or "hard-copy," color graphics is the *ink-jet printer*, which ejects tiny droplets of ink from a nozzle, gives them an electric charge, and directs them by a computer-controlled electromagnetic field to appropriate spots on a sheet of paper.[11] The ink-jet printer generates droplets continuously and, where the image is to be blank or light, deflects them into a gutter (see Figure 10-7). A row of nozzles can direct a stream of densely packed dots along a line, with the image accumulating row by row, as with a typewriter, line printer, or electrostatic dot printer. Plotters with several banks of ink-jet nozzles, one each for black and the three primary ink colors (magenta, cyan, and yellow), can produce high-resolution color graphics.

Images composed row by row are called *raster* graphics, after the term coined to describe the pattern of lines on a television picture regenerated with a cathode ray tube, or CRT. A beam of electrons is directed toward the broad end of a vacuum tube that is coated on the inside with an electroluminescent phosphor (see Figure 10-8, left), which glows in proportion to the strength of the incident electron beam. In a raster CRT display, electromagnets deflect the beam across each row and down the screen, row after row, before repeating the scan (see Figure 10-8, right). The phosphor does not glow indefinitely, and the scan must be repeated 30 or more times per second to avoid a noticeable flicker. Because the image disappears when the CRT display is turned off, the picture is called a "soft copy." Multiple cathode rays, one for each of the three additive primary colors (red, green, and blue), are used to produce a color picture. One electron beam excites a pattern of dots that glow in red, another excites a pattern of intermingled green-glowing dots, and a third addresses a grid of blue dots, interspersed among the red and green dots. The intensities of these tiny, intermingled dots can be varied to produce colors of any hue or brightness. For high-resolution color graphics, however, a specially designed *color monitor* is preferable to the standard television display.[12]

Of all the graphic display devices yet developed, the CRT has had the most significant effect on mapping. Because the CRT has no moving parts, it involves no mechanical inertia and can generate maps so rapidly—in a matter of seconds, in some cases—that users can conveniently interact with the computer by inspecting an image and then selecting a new design, a new geographic distribution, or a new analysis. When the response time is rapid—say, half a minute or less—the wait is not agonizing and the analyst is not distracted by boredom, impatience, or daydreaming.

---

[11] See, for example, Catherine Cramer, "Color Graphics Hard Copy Comes of Age," *Computer Graphics World* 6, no. 1 (January 1983), 29–42.

[12] Philip E. Bonice, "How to Evaluate Raster Scan CRT Monitors," *Computer Graphics World* 6, no. 4 (April 1983), 29–40.

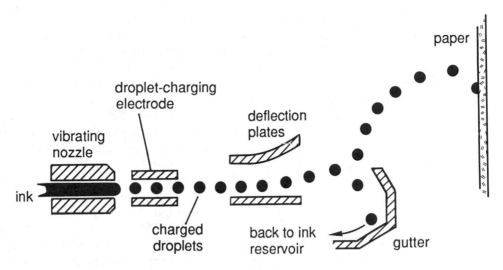

Figure 10-7 Ink-jet plotter forms an image with a stream of tiny droplets of ink that are given an electrostatic charge and then deflected individually to their intended spots on the image by variable-charge, microprocessor-controlled deflection plates. Droplets not needed on the image are deflected into a gutter for return to the ink reservoir.

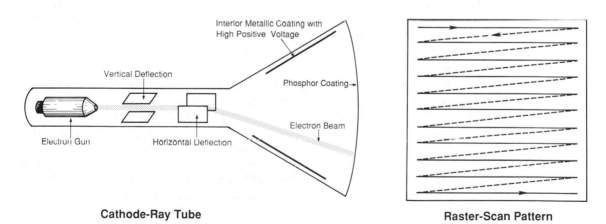

Cathode-Ray Tube   **Raster-Scan Pattern**

Figure 10-8 A raster display is generated by a beam of electrons deflected horizontally and vertically (right) across the screen of a vacuum tube coated on the inside with an electroluminescent phosphor. The raster-scan pattern of the electron beam is controlled by sets of variable-voltage deflection plates and a high-voltage metallic coating inside the tube.

The size of the screen, the fineness of detail (screen resolution), and the complexity of the image all limit response time. Many CRT displays are not larger or more detailed because of the need to continually "refresh" the screen from a digital representation of the image, stored on a solid-state-memory "refresh buffer." The more rudimentary graphics systems represent each independent grid cell—or *pixel*, for picture element—in memory by 8 bits, which may be used to code up to 127 colors or levels of gray. Yet fewer colors and gray levels are generally used. Each color is given a code that is matched with a set of intensities for red, green, and blue in a *color look-up table*. Advanced raster graphics systems with 24 bits per pixel allocate 8 bits each to red, green and blue, to permit a virtually unlimited number of colors (over 16.7 million, or 2^{24}). Because machine memory is expensive and large pictures would retard processing and increase flicker, images larger than 1,280 by 1,024 pixels, which requires a large amount of storage for its 1,310,720 cells, have been uncommon. Similarly, except where a large image is needed to accommodate many viewers at once, screens are seldom larger than 28 by 21 cm (16 in. along the diagnonal).[13]

The raster-mode, refresh CRT is but one of many rapid electronic display devices. A once widespread but now less common variation is the vector-mode, storage CRT, so called because the picture is generated as a series of straight-line segments, or *vectors*, on a screen with a phosphor that retains its glow for several minutes, or longer. The image is composed from a list of x, y-coordinates by moving the cathode ray in two dimensions—as with an "Etch-a-Sketch" toy—instead of in the faster, more easily controlled raster pattern. An advantage here lies in an image that need only be lighted in its linear elements, the line segments of its letters, numbers, and graphic symbols. A disadvantage lies in the need to redraw the entire picture if even a single small feature is to be deleted. Although vector displays are less common now than in the infancy of computer cartography, many data bases are organized as vector data because of the convenience of this format for processing individual features, such as roads and boundaries.

Computer engineers have designed many other display devices, such as the *plasma panel*, which represents an image through a matrix of tiny cells filled with neon gas. These cells can be illuminated or extinguished individually, without need for refresh memory.[14] The plasma panel is one of a variety of possible wall screens and is considered more convenient than the CRT because it need be no thicker than a few centimeters. Because the current ascendance of the CRT in soft-copy graphic display is by no means assured, the general term VDU, for *visual display unit*, is perhaps a more durable, forward-looking term.

[13] For an introduction to color CRT graphics, see James D. Foley and Andries Van Dam, *Fundamentals of Interactive Computer Graphics* (Reading, Mass.: Addison-Wesley, 1983), pp. 93–136.

[14] See, for example, Donald K. Wedding and Roger E. Ernsthausen, "Large-Area Flat Panel Displays," *Computer Graphics World* 6, no. 4 (April 1983), 68–70.

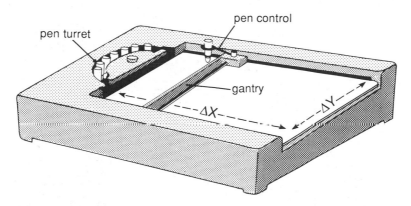

Figure 10-9 Using vector data, a pen plotter draws line maps through coordinated movements of a gantry that moves across the paper in the *x*-direction and a pen control that moves along the gantry in the *y*-direction. Pen can be lowered (to draw) or raised (to slew, or move without drawing). Pen control can return to the pen turret to exchange active pen for one of a different color.

The soft-copy storage CRT is not the most prominent vector-mode display: older and more widespread is the electromechanical hard-copy *pen plotter*, a device that moves a pen in the orthogonal *x*- and *y*-directions on a plane, lowers the pen to draw, and raises it to move to a new image element (see Figure 10-9). Early pen plotters were crude devices that drew diagonal lines with small but noticeable steps, but the contemporary pen plotters can generate unwavering diagonals and position the center of the pen point to within 0.25 mm (0.01 in.). As with the vector CRT, a picture is composed of straight-line segments, which can, if sufficiently short, yield curved lines and almost esthetically pleasing labels, as in Figure 10-10. The computer can instruct some pen plotters to fetch a new pen from a selection of eight or more colors or widths. Still more advanced is the high-resolution film plotter, equipped with a *photohead* to draw with light on photographic film, rather than with ink on paper. High-quality labels and point symbols are possible when the photohead is equipped with a lettering template so that the images of graphic-arts-quality type can be exposed, or "flashed," onto the film, which can then be used to generate press plates for lithographic printing.[15] The two photohead plots in Figure 10-11 are indistinguishable in appearance from artwork prepared by a skilled pen-and-ink draftsperson.

[15] For an example of software strategies for the automatic placing of labels for point, line, and area features, see J. Ahn and H. Freeman, "A Program for Automatic Name Placement," in *Proceedings of Auto-Carto Six: the Sixth International Symposium on Automated Cartography, the National Capital Region of Canada, October 16–21, 1983*, vol. 2 (Ottawa: Steering Committee of Auto-Carto Six, 1983), pp. 444–53.

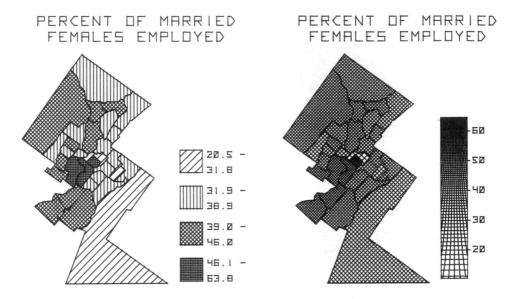

Figure 10-10 Choropleth maps of Scranton, Pennsylvania, census-tract data on female employment plotted by a pen plotter. Map at left is a traditional, classed choropleth map, whereas map at right is a nonclassed, continuous-tone version of the same distribution.

An important part of digital cartography called *data capture* relies on automated hardware that enters positional data for map features into computer memory for storage, further processing, and ready retrieval and display. Some data entry devices are designed principally for interactive graphics, to point to specific features or symbols, to edit data files, and to select specific instructions from a *menu* of commands.[16] Prominent among these "pointing devices," as Figure 10-12 shows, are the *light pencil*, which indicates position on the screen of a CRT display by recording the time the electron beam passes beneath a sensor held against the screen and then using the speed and pattern of the raster scan to convert this elapsed time into *x, y*-screen coordinates; the *mouse*, which rests on a nearby flat surface and can be moved left, right, or in any other direction to specify the movement on the screen of a crossed-line or arrow target; the *joy stick*, a common two-dimensional lever used with video games; and the *digital tablet*, with which the user follows linear features and records *x, y*-coordinates by moving a cursor or stylus along the feature in question. More expensive and precise are the large digitizing tables government agencies and private database

---

[16] For a comparison of various pointing devices used in computer graphics see Vic Kley, "Pointing Device Communication," *Computer Graphics World* 6, no. 11 (November 1983), 69–72.

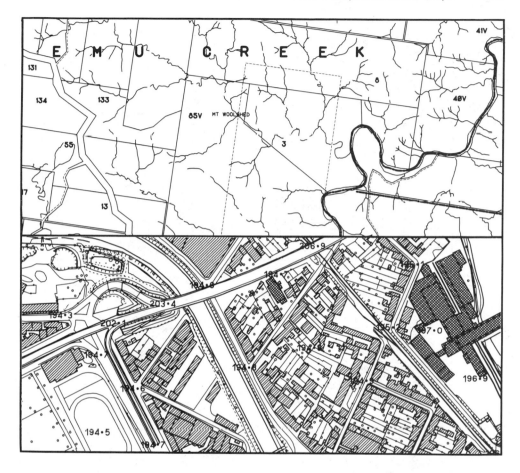

Figure 10-11 Portions of maps drawn with a photoplotter head by a Gerber
model 78 precision drafting system. (Courtesy of Gerber Scientific, Inc.)

firms use to measure coordinates to the nearest 0.025 mm (0.001 in.). Sophisticated production digitizers commonly are part of a graphics work station that
might include two CRTs, one displaying the features already recorded and another for examining, at a larger scale, selected parts of the data base, to correct
errors or assign feature codes (see Figure 10-13).

Cartographic data also can be collected in raster format by an electronic
scanner that senses the amount of light reflected from a map mounted on a
large, rapidly rotating drum. As Figure 10-14 shows schematically, the map is
treated as a grid, with rows wrapped around the drum and columns parallel to
its axis. With every rotation, the scan head advances to a new row, and readings
are taken in steps along each row for the cells in successive columns. On a black-

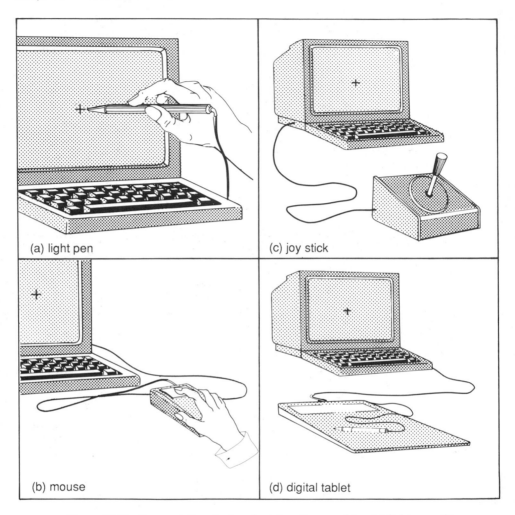

(a) light pen

(c) joy stick

(b) mouse

(d) digital tablet

Figure 10-12   Four pointing devices for interactive graphics: (a) light pen, (b) mouse, (c) joy stick, and (d) digital tablet.

and-white map very little light is reflected from a cell occupied by part of a map symbol printed in black, and a low reflectance would be recorded. Nonimage cells, in contrast, reflect more light, and a higher reflectance would be recorded. A sensing system with color filters and several sensors, one for each subtractive primary hue (yellow, magenta, and cyan) can capture raster data "separated" by color. Scan digitization is more rapid than manual, line-following digitization, but the assignment of digital codes identifying individual features usually requires manual intervention and can be slow and error-prone. Highly advanced systems, with software for automatic feature-extraction and character recogni-

Figure 10-13 Interactive Graphics Design System (IDGS) Workstation. (Courtesy of Intergraph Corporation.)

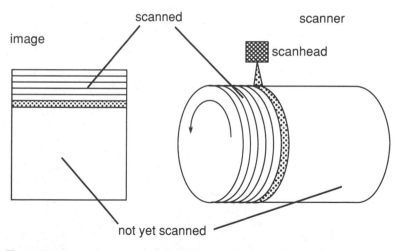

Figure 10-14 Image on drum of raster-mode drum scanner is sensed row by row and pixel by pixel along each row. A row corresponds to one scan track, examined in one rotation of the drum. Scanhead advances along the drum, parallel to the axis, to sense successive rows of the image.

tion, may well render manual digitization obsolete in the development of large cartographic data bases.[17]

Some drum scanners can be operated in reverse, so to speak, to generate film separations used to make press plates for lithographic printing. In this case, the sensing head is replaced by a photohead that can "write" with a "light spot" rather than measure reflectance. Usually several light spots are used to generate multiple, adjacent rows with each rotation of the drum, so that the cells can be sufficiently small to provide high graphic resolution without greatly increasing the time required to plot a map. A laser generator, producing light with a nearly uniform wavelength, is preferable because "coherent light" is less likely to spread and produce slightly fuzzy images than is white light, composed of a variety of wavelengths. Laser plotters able to generate from 150 to more than 400 individual spots for each linear cm (400 to 1,000 spots per in.) can produce type characters indistinguishable from standard typeset text. Moreover, laser plotters can be more precise and consistent than traditional graphic-arts screening processes in generating dot-screened images for graytone area symbols and color lithography.[18]

In computer cartography, the software (a general term for both the computer programs and the data bases) is as important and necessary an element of a successful system as the computing machinery, or hardware. Perhaps the most crucial illustration of the critical role of program software is the conversion of data from vector format to raster mode, or vice versa. Because many data bases, particularly those composed of boundary lines and other linear features, are stored principally in vector form, and because most rapid, high-resolution graphics devices display a raster image, vector-to-raster conversion is especially important. In a sense, the software must draw the map in the computer's memory, before display, and each mark on the map must be rearranged for easy plotting from top to bottom, rather than in sequence along individual features.[19] Equally necessary is raster-to-vector software, which can identify and track linear features in scan-digitized raster data. In this application the computer assumes the role of the cartographic technician and traces the path of a linear feature

[17] For a discussion of the value and principles of scan digitization, see A. R. Boyle, "Developments in Equipment and Techniques," in *The Computer in Contemporary Cartography*, ed. D. R. Fraser Taylor (Chichester, Eng.: John Wiley & Sons, 1980), pp. 39–57. For an example of the post-processing needed to produce a useful cartographic database from raster-scan data, see J. F. Harris et al., "A Modular System for Interpreting Binary Pixel Representations of Line-Structured Data on Maps," *Cartographica* 19, no. 2 (Summer 1982), 145–75.

[18] For an example of the use of a laser scanner and plotter in the production of printed road maps, see Martin Brunner, "The Production and Update of Road Maps by Means of Computer-Assisted Procedures," *International Yearbook of Cartography* 21 (1981), 23–29. Also see Kathleen Edwards and R. M. Batson, "Preparation and Presentation of Digital Maps in Raster Format," *American Cartographer* 7, no. 1 (April 1980), 39–49.

[19] Donna J. Peuguet, "An Examination of Techniques for Reformatting Digital Cartographic Data. Part 2: The Vector-to-Raster Process," *Cartographica* 18, no. 3 (Autumn 1981), 21–33.

through the scanned, gridded image. Format conversion is but one of many possible manipulations of cartographic data, for maps represented electronically can be searched, analyzed, and measured, as well as reordered and displayed.

THE COMPUTER AND TRADITIONAL CARTOGRAPHY

Computer cartography has had a wide usage in the established roles of traditional cartography, where it has been applied for over three decades. One of digital cartography's most obvious assets, of course, is the ease with which a geographic information system can update a data base and produce new, more timely maps. Another obvious and widespread application is the generation of statistical maps, an especially convenient use when areal-unit data are already in digital form for statistical analysis and when a digital outline map is also available for the corresponding set of states, provinces, counties, or census tracts. This section explores a few of the many ways in which computer cartography has improved the map author's ability to make traditional cartographic products and analyze geographic distributions.

Map Projections

An early, and perhaps the most obvious, application of the computer in cartography was in the computationally demanding task of projecting the earth's curved surface onto a plane. As any student who has struggled through a cartography course with a heavy emphasis on map drafting and map projections will attest, laying out some of the more curvilinear grids and then transforming coastlines, boundaries, and other features is not only tedious but also a reason why some geographers have harbored distaste for and resentment of cartography. (More unfortunate, however, is the class time these manual tasks might have taken away from a fuller treatment of how projections distort and how this distortion can be managed to promote analysis or communication.) Moreover, many hand-drawn projections are impotently simplistic, particularly when the projection might more appropriately be centered on a locally significant point— as in the oblique Mercator projection in Figure 10-15, for which a photohead plotter generated in minutes a grid that would have taken days to calculate, lay out, and draft by hand. Although southern Africa and other places on the map's periphery are noticeably distorted, this is a good projection for general reference and meteorological maps of Europe.

Topographic Mapping

Digital computing has many roles to play in the development of the modern topographic map, including the calculation of the precise location of geodetic control points shown on air photos used in compilation and, in some cases, the

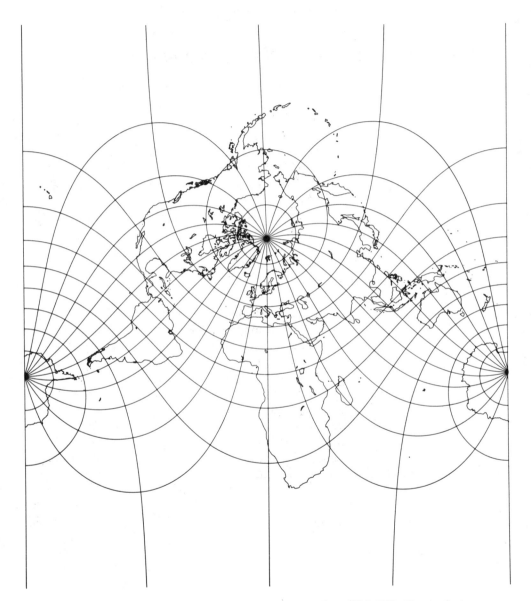

Figure 10-15   Oblique Mercator projection centered on 45°N, 15°E. (Courtesy of the U.S. Geological Survey.)

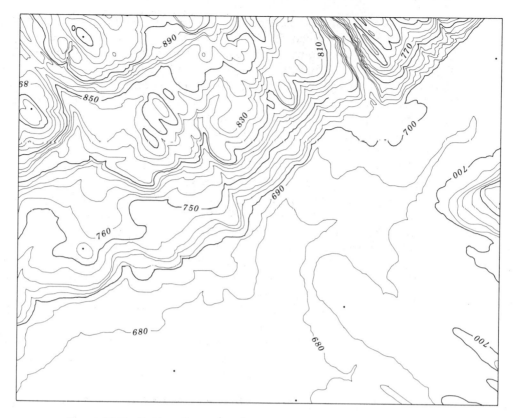

Figure 10-16 Portion of a contour-line "separation" plotted with a high-resolution photohead plotter from digital terrain data. Photohead produces fine lines for regular contours, wider lines for index contours, and graphic-arts-quality type for elevation labels. (Courtesy of the Topographical Survey Division, Surveys and Mapping Branch, Energy, Mines and Resources Canada.)

computer-controlled removal of distortion from aerial photography, the calculation of elevations, and the automatic plotting of contour lines. The contour map in Figure 10-16, for instance, was generated from elevation data collected directly from aerial photography with a digital stereocompilation system and plotted on film by a plotter with a photohead.[20]

In the 1970s government mapping agencies began to consider seriously a much fuller role for computer data systems in the management of basemap data. Stereoplotters such as the Analytical Plotting System shown in Figure 2-7, for

[20] For a discussion of the photogrammetric capture of digital cartographic data, see Lewis J. Harris, "The Application of Computer Technology to Topographical Cartography," in *The Computer in Contemporary Cartography*, ed. D. R. Fraser Taylor (Chichester, Eng.: John Wiley & Sons, 1980), pp. 59–92.

instance, can be used to extract contours and the positions of terrain features and to record the x, y-coordinates and feature codes in data files for editing, conversion to a standard projection system, and plotting. More important, when the map needs to be updated because of changes in terrain or settlement, the database can be made current without the complex and costly operations needed to add or delete features on a base map stored on many sheets of photographic film. The raster-format laser plotter, able to generate "final negatives" for each printing ink, expedites dissemination, and lowers the cost of storage, revision, and reproduction.[21]

The first digitally produced topographic base maps of the 1970s were mere experiments, but by the mid-1980s many government mapping agencies were routinely printing topographic quadrangle maps drafted not by humans, but by computer-controlled plotters. For example, in the 1970s the Surveys and Mapping Branch of Canada's Department of Energy, Mines and Resources used manually digitized data to generate all artwork except typography for an experimental 1:50,000-scale topographic map; now the Surveys and Mapping Branch collects digital data during photogrammetric compilation and generates linework, typography, and area symbols using automatic drafting tables.[22] Experiments with digital cartography at the U.S. Geological Survey have led to a variety of new systems and products, including a program to expedite the completion of the nation's 7.5-minute topographic map series. Data collection, data editing, and the plotting of all artwork are computer assisted. The first experimental sheet, the Birch Tree, Missouri, 7.5-minute Provisional Edition, 1982, is indistinguishable in graphic-arts quality from manually produced maps.[23] Digital cartography is now a vital part of the day-to-day operations and cost-control strategies of government mapping agencies.

Statistical Mapping

Geographers, policy analysts, and other social scientists have been making maps of quantitative areal-unit data since the rise of censuses and scientific societies in the nineteenth century. By reducing substantially the time and effort required,

[21] See, for example, Doyle G. Smith, "Raster Data Development in the National Mapping Division, U.S. Geological Survey," *Technical Papers*, American Congress on Surveying and Mapping, Fall Technical Meeting, San Francisco, September 9–11, 1981, pp. 284–88.

[22] See L. J. Harris, "An Approach to Automatic Cartography for Topographic Mapping in Canada," in *Computer Cartography in Canada*, ed. Aubrey L. leBlanc, published as *Cartographica* monograph no. 9, 1973, pp. 10–15; and J. M. Zarzycki, "A Digital Topographic Data Base System," *Computer Graphics World* 5, no. 10 (October 1982), 49–53.

[23] See L. H. Borgerding, F. E. Lortz, and J. K. Powell, "Computer-Assisted Map Compilation, Editing, and Finishing," in *Proceedings*, Fifth International Symposium on Computer-Assisted Cartography, Crystal City, Va., August 22–28, 1982 (Falls Church, Va.: American Society of Photogrammetry and American Congress on Surveying and Mapping, 1983), pp. 141–46; and *Research, Investigations, and Technical Developments: National Mapping Program, 1982* (Reston, Va.: U.S. Geological Survey, open-file report no. 83–568, 1983), pp. 2–8.

digital computers and graphics-display devices have increased greatly the use in business, government, and academia of statistical maps such as Figure 10-17. Although most of the maps produced are for exploratory data analysis by individuals, numerous others are viewed more widely in oral presentations or published reports.

Perhaps the biggest impetus in the 1980s toward an enhanced use of statistical graphics has been the availability of software systems that include not only the computer programs for generating graphic symbols, but also the geographic databases for defining the geometric extent of these symbols on plot or screen. Particularly influential has been the SAS/GRAPH software, which links a sophisticated library of computer routines for data processing and statistical analysis to a small but generally useful library of mapping functions and a powerful geographic database with which the user can produce, among other graph-

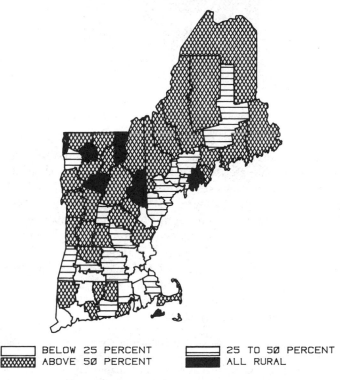

RURAL NEW ENGLAND
**Rural Percentage of the
1980 County Populations**

☐	BELOW 25 PERCENT	☰	25 TO 50 PERCENT
▨	ABOVE 50 PERCENT	■	ALL RURAL

New England average is 25 percent

Figure 10-17   Choropleth map generated with SAS/GRAPH.

RURAL NEW ENGLAND
Rural Percentage of the
1980 County Populations

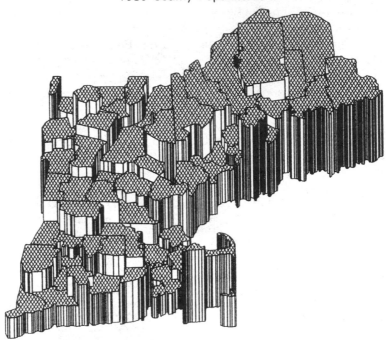

Figure 10-18   Prism map generated with SAS/GRAPH.

ics, choropleth maps of the world or selected continents by country, of Canada by province, and of the United States by state or county (see Figure 10-17). SAS/GRAPH and other statistical mapping systems can display these maps on a pen plotter or VDU, in black-and-white or in color, with or without supporting non-cartographic statistical diagrams.[24] The program can be run on a large, centralized mainframe computer, supporting many users simultaneously in a time-share mode. With an interactive computer, either a time-share system or a "stand alone" microcomputer, the user can quickly preview a display and decide to alter the specifications or to plot the map "as is." Business graphics systems with hard-copy devices that produce 35-mm color slides are particularly advantageous to the analyst who wants to include statistical maps in presentations to clients or corporate managers.[25]

[24] SAS/GRAPH capabilities are outlined in *SAS/GRAPH User's Guide* (Cary, N.C.: SAS Institute, 1981). For a critique of SAS/GRAPH, see James R. Carter, *Computer Mapping: Progress in the '80s* (Washington, D.C.: Association of American Geographers, 1984), pp. 54–62.

[25] See, for example, John Cool, "Presentation Graphics on the IBM PC," *Computer Graphics World* 7, no. 5 (May 1984), 57–60; and Leslie Blumberg, "Communicating with Computer-Generated Slides," *Computer Graphics World* 5, no. 6 (June 1982), 57–58.

Although the choropleth display, which preserves the familiar network of areal-unit boundaries, will probably remain the dominant type of statistical map, many other cartographic displays are possible with the same data. One highly dramatic option is the *prism map*, in which a "stepped statistical surface," with each area elevated above a base plane in proportion to its value for the mapped distribution, is plotted as if viewed from a selected vantage point above the base plane (see Figure 10-18). The diagram is treated as a solid figure, with hidden lines removed to enhance the three-dimensional effect.[26] Interactive graphics systems promote experimentation with viewing azimuth and vertical scaling, the principal design elements of the obliquely viewed statistical surface.

THE COMPUTER AND THE FUTURE OF CARTOGRAPHY

In addition to promoting more pertinent map projections, increased cost-effectiveness in topographic mapping, and wider use of statistical maps, the digital computer is altering how people think about "the map" and expanding the kinds of issues cartographers regard as important. Perhaps most revolutionary is the emerging recognition that the geographic information contained in the map is more basic, and hence more important, than the graphic symbols that present it.[27] Moreover, the digital cartographic database is rapidly replacing the paper map as the principal vehicle for storing and analyzing geographic data. The traditional graphic map, whether displayed on paper or as soft copy on a VDU screen, will depend increasingly on the availability of the data in digital form, and cartographers will design many maps primarily to be searched or "read" by a computer rather than viewed by human eyes. This section examines a few important effects of cartography's electronic transition—namely, how cartographers must develop new concepts to describe the structure of digital maps, how electronic representations of the terrain surface will enhance landscape analysis and earth science, and how telecommunications systems and electronic publishing may routinely deliver timely map information to classrooms, laboratories, offices, and even homes.

Databases and Cartographic Objects

Information stored in computers is organized into lists, in which, for example, the *x, y*-coordinates of points representing a feature are stored in "vector" sequence, starting at one end and continuing through to the other. To expedite

[26] For examples of other computer-produced statistical graphics, see Carter, *Computer Mapping*, pp. 41–62; and Alan M. Baker, Rowan Faludi, and David R. Green, "An Evaluation of SAS/GRAPH Software for Computer Cartography," *Professional Geographer* 37, no. 2 (May 1985), 204–14.

[27] For a discussion of the imminent effects of the "electronic transition" in cartography, see Mark Monmonier, *Technological Transition in Cartography* (Madison: University of Wisconsin Press, 1985).

processing, other lists are often used; for example, tables cross-referencing areal units on opposite sides of a common boundary can specify the geometric framework of the digital map and form what computer scientists call a *data structure*. By linking parts of the database that the computer might want to manipulate in the same step, the data structure in a sense gives the computer the eyes to identify related pieces of information that might be nearby on the ground but widely separated in computer memory.

Because data structures can be quite complex, it is important that persons using or describing them rely on a common set of terms and definitions. Particularly basic to the documentation of a data structure is the identification of a set of fundamental cartographic objects. As outlined in the mid-1980s by the National Digital Cartographic Data Standards Committee, there are ten elementary cartographic objects, shown schematically in Figure 10-19.[28] These definitions are based on the concepts of the *point*, which has a position specified by its x, y-coordinates, and a *node*, at which two or more linear features, such as boundaries, meet. In some data structures, of course, the nodes also are points. The various cartographic objects identified in Figure 10-19 differ in whether they terminate at nodes or at mere points; whether the intermediate part of the feature is represented by a list of points or, in the case of the *arc*, by a mathematical function; and whether features are directed, as for a *link* representing a portion of one-way street. Basic cartographic objects in two dimensions include the *pixel*—essentially a grid cell, but defined concisely by the committee as "an element of an area on the ground in a nondivisible measurement, organized in an array to form a regular tessellation of a plane"—and the *polygon*, which is a closed figure formed by a closed circuit of either line segments or links and nodes. These definitions are part of a larger set of generic and specialized definitions that should promote the exchange of cartographic data and computer programs by eliminating the confusion that can arise in a rapidly developing new technology in which evolving terms often acquire different, conflicting meanings.

Another set of terms and definitions necessitated by cartography's electronic transition addresses the map's permanence and graphic tangibility. A primary distinction is made between a *real map*, defined as "any cartographic

---

[28] For a discussion of elementary cartographic objects, see Harold Moellering, "The Challenge of Establishing a Set of National Digital Cartographic Data Standards for the United States," *Technical Papers*, American Congress on Surveying and Mapping, 42nd Annual Meeting, Denver, March 14–20, 1982, pp. 201–12. The original set of 10 elementary objects was enlarged to 20 cartographic objects and six "special implementation objects" reflecting terms in use or preferred by federal mapping agencies. For definitions and illustrations of this larger group of cartographic objects, see Harold Moellering, "Evaluating and Testing the Interim Proposed Standard for Digital Cartographic Objects," *Issues in Digital Cartographic Data Standards*, Numerical Cartography Laboratory, Ohio State University, for the National Committee for Digital Cartographic Data Standards, report no. 7, April 1986, pp. 9–20.

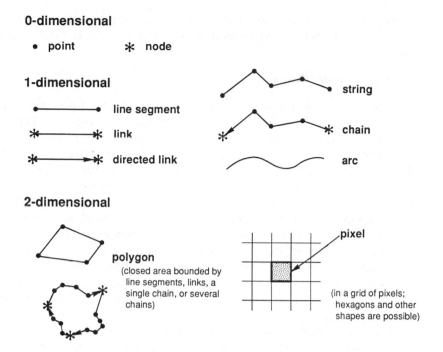

Figure 10-19 Basic cartographic objects.

product with a directly viewable image and a permanent tangible reality," and a *virtual map*, which is either temporary or not directly viewable.[29] Maps printed on paper in books, newspapers, and magazines, or as folding road and street maps are considered real maps, as are hard-copy maps drawn by computer. But three classes of virtual maps are required to address fundamental differences in electronic maps. The *virtual map—type I*, which has a "directly viewable cartographic image but only a transient reality," includes maps displayed on a CRT.[30] Somewhat more abstract is the *virtual map—type II*, which "has a permanent tangible reality," as with laser disk data, "and is not directly viewable."[31] Still more abstract is the *virtual map—type III*, which is neither tangible and permanent nor directly viewable, and which thus includes digital data stored magnetically on disk or tape. This kind of map is intended principally to be examined by a computer and need not even be used to generate a graphic display. Because these databases commonly contain numerous linkages among geographically and topologically related cartographic objects, they are said to

[29] Harold Moellering, "Strategies of Real Time Cartography," *Cartographic Journal* 17, no. 1 (June 1980), 12–15.

[30] Ibid.

[31] Ibid.

represent "cartographic deep structure."[32] In contrast, other forms of the map, with symbols that can be viewed or touched, constitute "cartographic surface structure."

Digital Terrain Data

Computer-readable maps of the land surface will make possible many types of scientific and engineering analysis, including such diverse applications as modeling flood hazards, estimating the costs of cutting and filling for highway construction, and evaluating the visual impact of a proposed electric power line. The military has carried out much of the basic research, given its concern with applying digital terrain data to real-time battlefield applications, Cruise Missile guidance systems, tactical "war games" simulation models, and real-time interpretation of airborne radar imagery, for convoy tracking and camouflage detection. But the civilian effort is progressing as well, albeit in the more placid direction of acquiring digital cartographic data when new or completely revised large-scale topographic maps are prepared.[33] Although progress may seem slow and somewhat uncertain, the digital topographic database is likely to emerge as the core of our national base mapping program, with the traditional, printed topographic map sheet relegated to a secondary position, and possibly even turned over to the private sector for preparation and publication.

Digital terrain data consist of two basic types. The *digital line graph* (DLG) is essentially a file of vector data that can be used to draw contour lines, highways, boundaries, and other linear features common to the conventional topographic map. Many different types of feature are included, each type identified with a unique *feature code* so that it can be suppressed or included in a specific display or analysis.[34] In contrast, the *digital elevation model* (DEM) is a grid of elevation estimates, organized in raster fashion for convenient retrieval and analysis but not readily displayed without invoking either a contouring program to thread contour lines through the grid or an oblique-view program to plot a three-dimensional "block diagram." DEM data the U.S. Geological Survey provides for 7.5-minute quadrangles consist of elevations estimated at the intersections of rows and columns 30 m (100 ft) apart and permit not only intricately detailed oblique views, as in Figure 10-20, but also plan views showing areas with slopes that meet a stated criterion for steepness or direction.[35]

[32] "Deep structure" is a term borrowed from linguistics. See Timothy L. Nyerges, "Representing Spatial Properties in Cartographic Data Bases," *Technical Papers*, American Congress on Surveying and Mapping, 40th Annual Meeting, St. Louis, March 9–14, 1980, pp. 29–41.

[33] For information on the variety of digital cartographic databases compiled by the U.S. Geological Survey, see Robert B. McEwen, Hugh W. Calkins, and Benjamin S. Ramey, *Overview of USGS Activities*, Circular no. 895-A (Reston, Va.: U.S. Geological Survey, 1983).

[34] For a list of feature codes for DLG data, see William R. Allder et al., *Digital Line Graph Attribute Coding Standards*, Circular no. 895-G, (Reston, Va.: U.S. Geological Survey, 1984).

[35] For detailed information on DEM data, see Atef A. Elassal and Vincent M. Caruso, *Digital Elevation Models*, Circular no. 895-B (Reston, Va.: U.S. Geological Survey, 1983).

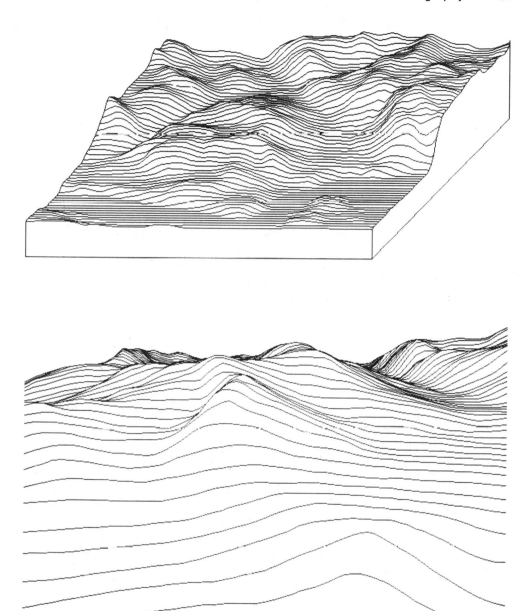

Figure 10-20 Oblique views of the West Point, New York, area from high
(above) and low (below) angles. Ink-jet plots are based on DEM data. Top view,
from the northeast, shows the Hudson River in the foreground, and bottom
view, looking due south, simulates view from elevation of 300 m (1,000 ft).
(Courtesy of Computer Graphics Laboratory, Department of Geography and
Computer Science, U.S. Military Academy.)

When combined with digital cartographic data for population and for land use and land cover, a digital elevation model can be a powerful resource for computerized site analysis by landscape architects, real-estate developers, regional planners, or forest managers.[36] In selecting a route for an electrical transmission line, for example, a planner might begin by preparing a list of constraints: densely settled areas, excessive gradients, marshlands and other sensitive wildlife habitats, and specialty croplands. Each constraint is represented by a digital grid map and assigned a weight reflecting its estimated relative impact (see Figure 10-21). If registered to the same grid system, these maps can then be added together in the computer to yield a composite constraint map, which should be particularly useful in selecting among alternative paths in avoiding sensitive areas. Overlay analysis is also useful in geographic, epidemiological, ecological, geological, and other kinds of research in which an investigator searching for cause-and-effect relationships can benefit by exploring the spatial coincidence of various sets of possibly relevant factors.

Videotex and Digital Atlases

For many applications, particularly in journalism and business, data are of little use if not timely. Although most users of digital elevation models can be content to wait weeks for delivery, persons or corporations interested in the current state of the weather or the commodities market must have their information within hours or minutes. Videotex, a two-way telecommunications system carrying queries and replies by satellite, telephone, TV cable, or broadcast television, is a promising vehicle for meeting demands for timely cartographic data.[37] Although the early one-way "teletext" systems of the 1970s were proficient only in providing access to one of a limited number of screens of alphanumeric text, videotex technology has developed rapidly in the 1980s and promises to offer a variety of services that depend on detailed graphics, including current news, financial data, at-home video-catalog shopping, and "down-loaded" video games that can be played on the user's personal computer. As an electronic clearinghouse for information of many types, the videotex system will make possible tailor-made "newspapers" suited to the subscriber's unique needs and interests and thus alter drastically the roles and operations of the print and broadcast media.[38]

---

[36] Land-use and land-cover data available from the U.S. Geological Survey are described in Robin G. Fegeas et al., *Land Use and Land Cover Digital Data*, Circular no. 895-E, (Reston, Va.: U.S. Geological Survey, 1983). These data are stored in vector format, but can be converted to grid format for overlay analysis. Similar data are provided for census county subdivisions, with which the land-use and land-cover data can be linked to demographic and economic data.

[37] For an introduction to videotex systems, see Jan Gecsei, *The Architecture of Videotex Systems* (Englewood Cliffs, N.J.: Prentice-Hall, 1983).

[38] See Anthony Smith, *Goodbye Guttenberg: The Newspaper Revolution in the 1980's* (New York and Oxford: Oxford University Press, 1980); and Benjamin M. Compaine, *The Newspaper Industry in*

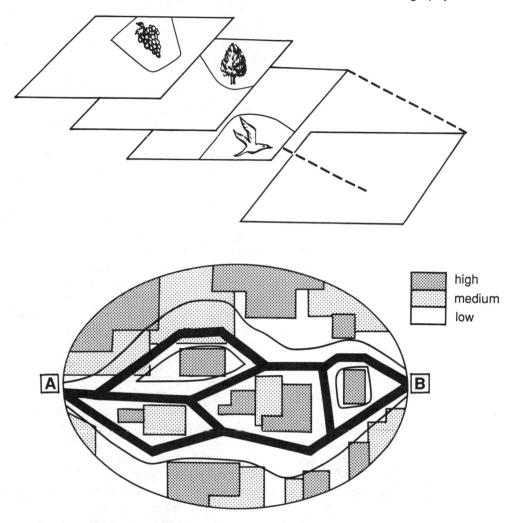

Figure 10-21 Steps in the preparation of a composite constraint map for planning transmission-line corridors. Overlays representing constraints are weighted and summed to yield composite constraint map. (From diagrams in Ontario Hydro, *Right-of-way Planning: Avoiding Sensitive Areas* [Ontario, Can., May 1983].)

Early large-scale commercial videotex systems, such as Ceefax in Britain and Antiope in France, were one-way systems carrying a limited amount of information in the "vertical blanking interval" separating two successive televised pictures. In Europe each individual picture composed of 625 raster-scan

---

the 1980s: An Assessment of Economics and Technology (White Plains, N.Y.: Knowledge Industry Publications, 1980).

lines includes 25 "blank" lines, which can be coded with useful information. (In the United States and Canada televised pictures consist of only 525 scan lines and appear slightly more grainy.) With Ceefax an individual "teletext" screen consisted of up to 24 lines of text, with up to 40 characters per line.[39] On each of the two BBC channels, 100 different screens were broadcast, one after the other, in a series repeated every 25 seconds. The subscriber's television set was equipped with a decoder, connected to a keypad for entering the digits 0 to 9 and a few control symbols. The first screen displayed was a *menu* offering several general categories of information, each identified by number. The user would then select a category, enter its number with the keypad, view a more specific menu, and then enter a code for, say, the latest currency exchange rates or a listing of executive job openings. When each number was entered, the system would wait for the appropriate screen, or "page," and "grab" it to display. Hitting the hashmark on the keypad would display additional information stored for the same topic on the next, "continuation" screen, which could be retrieved without returning to the menu. Because retrieval time would increase significantly if the number of available screens were increased, one-way videotex systems tended to be unattractive to many subscribers, even when an entire TV channel was dedicated to teletext. In the late 1970s, Prestel, a somewhat similar two-way system using telephone lines, replaced Ceefax as the principal British videotex system.

Canadian experiments with two-way videotex in the late 1970s suggested that intricately detailed graphics such as the map outline in Figure 10-22 could be transmitted efficiently, even along low-speed, "voice-grade" telephone lines.[40] The Canadian videotex system, Telidon, is based on *alpha-geometric* coding, in which a picture is decomposed into basic geometric elements such as circles, sectors, rectangles, and triangles. Each element is represented by a *picture description instruction* (PDI) specifying the type of element and its color, size, position, and orientation. A sequence of appropriate PDIs transmitted by airwave or telephone in response to a specific request can be recreated by a decoder attached to the user's television set. By avoiding the "jaggies" (see Figure 10-23, left) common to the *alpha-mosaic* coding used with Prestel, Antiope, and other European videotex systems, Telidon's alpha-geometric coding can take full advantage not only of the graphic-arts resolution inherent in the 525-line raster scan of current North American television sets (see Figure 10-23, right), but also of the even finer resolution of color monitors and high-definition digital television sets, which might eventually replace conventional low-resolution TV.[41]

[39] See A. E. Cawkell, "The Paperless Revolution," *Wireless World* 84, no. 1511 (July 1978), 38–42, and no. 1512 (August 1978), 69–74; and Rex Winbury, ed., *Viewdata in Action* (London: McGraw-Hill, 1981), pp. 3–32.

[40] For further information on Telidon, see Richard H. Veith, *Television's Teletext* (New York: North-Holland, 1983), pp. 25–27, 91–99.

[41] See Gerry Walter, "Raster Image Communication," *Journal of Micrographics* 15, no. 5 (May 1982), 30–35.

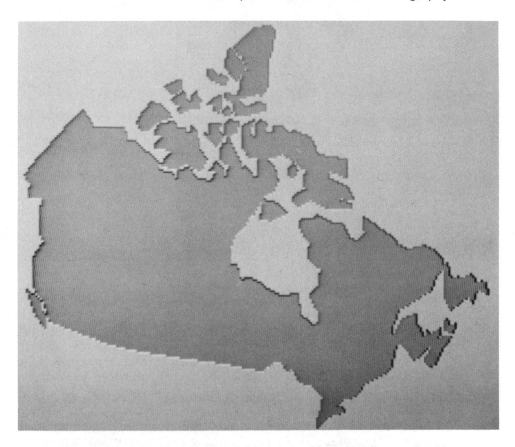

Figure 10-22 Canadian coastline and international boundary illustrate graphic detail possible with Telidon. (Courtesy of Department of Communications, Government of Canada.)

Videotex may well revolutionize map use not only by providing ready access to an electronic atlas of timely virtual maps, but also by giving the map author greater control over the sequence in which the user views individual map elements. Sequencing, after all, is unavoidable when PDIs are transmitted over low-speed channels, but this otherwise frustrating delay can be used to program the viewer's introduction to the map and to call attention to major image elements.[42] With a typical choropleth map, the first element displayed might be the title, to focus attention on the theme or to enable the user to abort early an inappropriate display. Next the system might display the outline of the area, to draw attention to the region and the map's scale. After the legend is

---

[42] D. R. F. Taylor, "The Cartographic Potential of Telidon," *Cartographica* 19, nos. 3 and 4 (Autumn and Winter 1982), 18–30.

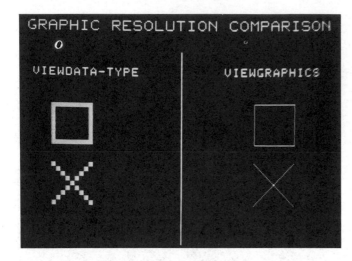

Figure 10-23 Comparison of graphics-art resolution of alpha-mosaic (left) and alpha-geometric (right) coding. (Courtesy of Department of Communications, Government of Canada.)

developed, each category might be displayed individually, starting with the highest and lowest groupings. Additional attention might be drawn to important aspects of a distribution by symbols that blink or flash after the entire map is on the screen.

Symbol sequencing is but one of many graphic enhancements promoted by videotex systems. A third coding standard, called *bit mode* or *photographic coding*, permits transmission and display, pixel by pixel, of high-resolution graphics such as satellite images and detailed geologic maps. Users may store these graphics on floppy disk for later display or for manipulation on a personal computer. Videotex is by no means tied to the conventional television set, after all, and maps received through a videotex network may also be used to generate a hard copy on a home or office printer. The possibility of receiving overnight, when transmission rates are low, large amounts of data may well transform publishing in general, and with it, atlas publishing.[43] Still more radical is the distribution of mapping software through either a videotex system or conventional retail outlets, to assist the user in experimenting with cartographic data, designing his or her own maps, or creating dynamic displays, as in a series of maps to illustrate the historical geography of settlement.[44] In addition to making maps more timely, electronic publishing is banishing the notions that the map is inherently static and that one map is sufficient for most applications.

[43] See, for example, Paul Starr, "The Electronic Reader," *Daedalus* 112, no. 1 (Winter 1983), 143–56.

[44] See Harold Moellering, "The Real-Time Animation of Three-Dimensional Maps," *American Cartographer* 7, no. 1 (October 1980), 67–75; and Carl Rosendahl, "Designing for Computer Animation," *Computer Graphics World* 6, no. 10 (October 1983), 38–40.

CHALLENGES AND CAVEATS

The electronic transition in cartography will not ensure maps that are more meaningful, more economical, and in general better than those produced by conventional, less automated technologies. Recent experience, in fact, suggests that many users of computer-produced maps are overly tolerant of rigid, "lazy" software that yields awkward, unaesthetic maps. During the early 1980s, for instance, the SAS Corporation was enormously successful in marketing SAS/GRAPH, despite the program's inability to plot easily visible legends when users requested a relatively small-scale map. Moreover, the system offered twenty different typefaces, yet failed to provide two innovations accepted almost a decade earlier by cartographic scholars: continuous-tone, no-class choropleth shading (see Figure 5-9) and a classification algorithm to optimize the internal homogeneity of categories on choropleth maps.[45] Although cartographic theorists had long warned against quantitative choropleth maps with symbols varying widely in hue, many naïve users rejoiced in maps adorned with a garish array of unordered, illogically organized hues.[46] If anything, by placing a powerful tool in the eager but clumsy hands of "cartographers" who knew almost nothing about mapping and graphic design, computer-assisted cartography has led to an abundance of shoddy or marginal maps.

Three groups are uniquely suited to fight this abuse. Educators in geographic cartography and other fields concerned with graphics should not only instill in their students an appreciation of graphic logic and aesthetics, they should also carry more widely the argument that every educated adult should be graphically literate. Software authors and publishers, the second group of defenders, should not only provide program documentation that clearly and thoroughly describes their product's limitations as well as its uses, but also incorporate algorithms to warn the user who inadvertently violates graphic principles. The astute "user-cartographer" must maintain high standards for both software products and finished graphics displayed in public. The constructive critic can attempt to warn and inform at a variety of levels by offering polite, private hints to close associates and by engaging in vigorous public challenge

[45] See W. R. Tobler, "Choropleth Maps Without Class Intervals?" *Geographical Analysis* 5, no. 3 (July 1973), 262–65; George F. Jenks and Fred C. Caspall, "Error on Choroplethic Maps: Definition, Measurement, Reduction," *Annals of the Association of American Geographers* 61, no. 2 (June 1971), 217–44; and Mark Monmonier, "Flat Laxity, Optimization, and Rounding in the Selection of Class Intervals," *Cartographica* 19, no. 1 (Spring 1982), 16–27.

[46] See, for examples, Arthur E. Robinson, "Psychological Aspects of Color in Cartography," *International Yearbook of Cartography* 7 (1967), 50–61; and David J. Cuff, "Impending Conflict in Color Guidelines for Maps of Statistical Surfaces," *Cartographic Journal* 11, no. 1 (June 1974), 54–58.

to vendors selling conceptually defective software and analysts touting conceptually defective finished graphics.[47]

Compatibility of software with software and of software with hardware must be an equally important public concern if computer-assisted cartography is to realize its true potential. Digital cartography is expensive, particularly in the development of large geographic databases. Much of the potential benefit of a data set can be lost if it (the data set) cannot be related to other data sets because of an incompatible format or potential users ignorant of its existence. When public money is used to compile digital cartographic data, as is generally the case, millions of tax dollars can be wasted through the duplicative efforts of mutually isolated federal agencies. In the early 1980s the U.S. General Accounting Office identified poor interagency coordination and lack of a uniform federal standard for exchanging cartographic data as severe and ominous problems.[48] But even though compatibility and coordination are being addressed on the federal level, the needs of local government and private-sector users remain.

A final but related concern is cost and pricing, particularly for federally developed databases. Should these data be treated as scientific information, to be developed at the public expense and priced only to recover the marginal cost of duplicating and mailing a tape or diskette—a policy in effect since the U.S. Geological Survey started producing topographic maps in 1882? Or should these data be copyrighted and priced to recover almost all costs, in the traditional policy of Britain's Ordnance Survey? Or might some intermediate strategy be appropriate, such as different prices for private and commercial users? An increased concern in government about cost recovery through user fees, as well as increased expectations among users of federally produced maps, serves only to heighten anxiety about pricing policy for digital cartography. Perhaps the main concern of cartographers and map users must now shift from the graphic design and geometric accuracy of maps that are made to the uninformed decisions and missed opportunities resulting from maps that are not made.

FOR FURTHER READING

BURROUGH, P. A., *Principles of Geographical Information Systems for Land Resources Assessment*. Oxford, Eng.: Clarendon Press, 1986.

CARTER, JAMES R., *Computer Mapping: Progress in the '80s*, Resource Publications in Geography Series. Washington, D.C.: Association of American Geographers, 1984.

[47] An excellent critique in this vein, albeit addressed principally toward graphics of all types, without special reference to computer graphics, is Edward R. Tufte, *The Visual Display of Quantitative Information* (Cheshire, Conn.: Graphics Press, 1983). For a constructive critique of SAS/GRAPH mapping, see D. R. Green et al., "SAS/GRAPH for Cartography: Map Projections and Labelled Choropleth Maps," *Cartographica* 22, no. 2 (Summer 1985), 63–78.

[48] Controller General of the United States, *Duplicative Federal Computer-Mapping Programs: A Growing Problem*, report no. GAO/RCED-83-19 (Washington, D.C.: General Accounting Office, 1982).

FOLEY, JAMES D., and ANDRIES VAN DAM, *Fundamentals of Interactive Computer Graphics.* Reading, Mass.: Addison-Wesley, 1982.

MARBLE, DUANE F., HUGH W. CALKINS, and DONNA J. PEUGUET, eds., *Basic Readings in Geographic Information Systems.* Williamsville, N.Y.: SPAD Systems, 1984.

MONMONIER, MARK, *Computer-assisted Cartography: Principles and Prospects.* Englewood Cliffs, N.J.: Prentice-Hall, 1982.

MONMONIER, MARK, *Technological Transition in Cartography.* Madison: University of Wisconsin Press, 1985.

RHIND, DAVID, and TIM ADAMS, eds., *Computers in Cartography.* London: British Cartographic Society, 1982.

SNYDER, JOHN P., "Map Projection Graphics from a Personal Computer," *American Cartographer* 11, no. 2 (October 1984), 132–38.

SNYDER, JOHN P., *Map Projections Used by the U.S. Geological Survey.* (Geological Survey bulletin no. 1532). Washington, D.C.: U.S. Government Printing Office, 1982.

TAYLOR, D. R. FRASER, ed., *The Computer in Contemporary Cartography,* Progress in Contemporary Cartography Series. Chichester, Eng.: John Wiley & Sons, 1980.

TEICHOLZ, ERIC, and BRIAN J. L. BERRY, eds., *Computer Graphics and Environmental Planning.* Englewood Cliffs, N.J.: Prentice-Hall, 1982.

APPENDIX A

Temperature Conversions

TEMPERATURE CONVERSIONS

The Celsius (C) temperature scale, also called Centigrade,
is used in most countries of the world. A temperature conversion
scale is shown on the left.

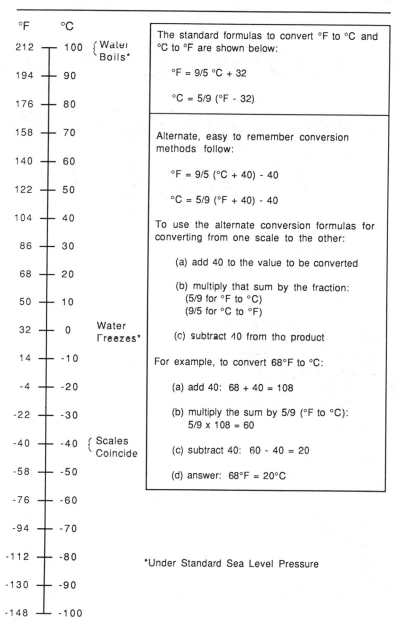

°F	°C	
212	100	Water Boils*
194	90	
176	80	
158	70	
140	60	
122	50	
104	40	
86	30	
68	20	
50	10	
32	0	Water Freezes*
14	-10	
-4	-20	
-22	-30	
-40	-40	Scales Coincide
-58	-50	
-76	-60	
-94	-70	
-112	-80	
-130	-90	
-148	-100	

The standard formulas to convert °F to °C and
°C to °F are shown below:

$$°F = 9/5 \ °C + 32$$

$$°C = 5/9 \ (°F - 32)$$

Alternate, easy to remember conversion
methods follow:

$$°F = 9/5 \ (°C + 40) - 40$$

$$°C = 5/9 \ (°F + 40) - 40$$

To use the alternate conversion formulas for
converting from one scale to the other:

    (a) add 40 to the value to be converted

    (b) multiply that sum by the fraction:
       (5/9 for °F to °C)
       (9/5 for °C to °F)

    (c) subtract 40 from the product

For example, to convert 68°F to °C:

    (a) add 40: 68 + 40 = 108

    (b) multiply the sum by 5/9 (°F to °C):
       5/9 x 108 = 60

    (c) subtract 40: 60 - 40 = 20

    (d) answer: 68°F = 20°C

*Under Standard Sea Level Pressure

APPENDIX B

Sources of Maps and Cartographic Information

Aerial Photography Field Office
Agricultural Stabilization and
   Conservation Service
U.S. Dept. of Agriculture
P.O. Box 30010
Salt Lake City, UT 84125

air photo prints, indexes

American Congress on Surveying
   and Mapping
210 Little Falls Street
Falls Church, VA 22046

professional organization with student members; publishes *The American Cartographer*

American Geographical Society
   Collection
Golda Meir Library
University of Wisconsin–Milwaukee
P.O. Box 399
Milwaukee, WI 53201

extensive collection of North American and foreign maps, current and historical; publishes *Current Geographical Publications* (10 times a year)

American Society of
  Photogrammetry and Remote
  Sensing
210 Little Falls Street
Falls Church, VA 22046

professional organization with student members; publishes *Photogrammetric Engineering and Remote Sensing*

Association of American
  Geographers
1710 Sixteenth Street, N.W.
Washington, DC 20009

professional organization with student members; *Resource Publications* series includes short books on mapping

Canada Map Office
Surveys and Mapping Branch
Dept. of Energy, Mines and
  Resources
Ottawa, Ontario K1A 0E9
Canada

information about a wide variety of Canadian maps; index maps, topographic maps, photomaps, thematic maps, and atlases

Canadian Cartographic Association
c/o Department of Geography
University of Ottawa
Ottawa, Ontario K1N 6N5
Canada

professional organization with student members; publishes *Cartographica* (with the University of Toronto Press) and a newsletter

Chadwyck-Healey Inc.
623 Martense Avenue
Teaneck, NJ 07666

high-quality microfilm copies of Sanborn Fire Insurance Maps (1867–1950) at the Library of Congress

Earth Observation Satellite
  Company (EOSAT)
4300 Forbes Boulevard
Lanham, MD 20706
(toll-free: 1-800-344-9933)

photographic prints and digital tapes of Landsat multispectral scanner and Thematic Mapper imagery; information about EOSAT

EOSAT
EROS Data Center
Sioux Falls, SD 57198
(toll-free: 1-800-367-2801)

Landsat imagery, including pre-EOSAT scenes

Geography and Map Division
Library of Congress
Washington, DC 20540

extensive collection of maps of the United States, including historical maps; cartographic bibliographies

Hermon Dunlap Smith Center for the History of Cartography
Newberry Library
60 West Walton Street
Chicago, IL 60610

publishes quarterly newsletter *Mapline*; map collection and research aids; hosts Nebenzahl Lectures in the History of Cartography

Historic Urban Plans
Box 276
Ithaca, NY 14850

facsimile reproductions of nineteenth-century city maps

Imago Mundi Limited
c/o Dept. of Geography
King's College
Strand
London WC2R 2LS
United Kingdom

publishes *Imago Mundi,* annual international journal on the history of cartography

International Bank for Reconstruction and Development
Information and Public Affairs Dept.
1818 H Street, N.W.
Washington, DC 20433

publishes inexpensive *World Bank Atlas* and photomaps of lesser developed countries

Map Collector Publications, Ltd.
Church Square
48 High Street
Tring, Hertfordshire HP23 5BH
England

publishes the *Map Collector* (quarterly) and books on map collecting and the history of cartography

National Archives and Records Service
Pennsylvania Avenue at 8th Street, N.W.
Washington, DC 20408

special collections of historical maps and early aerial photographs

National Cartographic Information Center
U.S. Geological Survey
507 National Center
Reston, VA 22092
(toll-free: 1-800-USA-MAPS)

information on a wide variety of government maps of the United States; map searches; index maps, topographic maps, thematic maps, photomaps; digital cartographic data

National Climatic Data Center
U.S. Dept. of Commerce
Federal Building
Asheville, NC 28801

climatic maps of the United States

National Geodetic Survey
National Ocean Survey
NOAA
Rockville, MD 20852

information about highly precise (geodetic) surveys

NOAA (National Oceanographic
and Atmospheric Administration)
Central Logistics Supply Center
619 Hardesty Street
Kansas City, MO 64124

leaflet "Explanation of the Daily Weather Map"

Physical Science Services Branch,
C513
National Ocean Survey
NOAA
Rockville, MD 20852

information about hydrographic charts and coastal maps

Shoe String Press
P.O. Box 4327
Hamden, CT 06514

publishes books about map librarianship; accepts orders for *Bibliographica Cartographica*

Soil Conservation Service
Information Division
P.O. Box 2890
Washington, DC 20013

soils maps

SPOT Image Corporation
1897 Preston White Drive
Reston, VA 22091-4326

digital data and photographic products from the SPOT satellite

Glossary

active sensor: a sensing system, such as microwave radar, that generates the energy that is reflected back to the sensor; contrast with *passive sensor*.

aerial photograph: a central perspective photographic image of the terrain; the *ground nadir*, where the optic axis strikes the land surface, appears at the *principal point*, or center, of a truly vertical air photo.

analog map: any directly viewable map on which graphic symbols portray features and values; contrast with *digital map*.

area cartogram: a map on which political divisions' areas are changed to relate to their value or rank for a given characteristic, say, population size.

artifact: an object, such as a map, showing the work or modification of a human being and thereby reflecting culture and technology.

azimuthal projection: transformation of the globe's grid to a plane; all great circles converging to the center are straight lines, and at the center of the projection all angles between great circles are correct.

base map: a map showing roads, streets, railroads, public lands, streams, and other water features on which other types of maps may be drawn.

census geography: the areal units shown on maps that report population and other data; these include the blocks, census tracts, urbanized areas, counties (parishes), and election districts.

census tracts: small geographical areas into which central cities and adjacent areas have been divided for statistical purposes.

central meridian: a line of longitude along which a map is centered from east to west.

choropleth map: a map that depicts quantities for administrative units using area-shading symbols.

climate map: a map that depicts average atmospheric conditions or portrays climatic types; contrast with *weather map*.

color-infrared: film or remotely sensed image sensitive to the green and red parts of the visible spectrum and to *near-infrared* radiation, with wavelengths just beyond those of visible red light; visible images produced for color-infrared film commonly invoke a *spectral shift* to portray greens as blue, reds as green, and reflected infrared areas as red.

conformality: true shape in small areas on a map; preservation of angles.

conic projection: transformation of the globe's grid onto a cone; if the apex of the cone is above one of the poles, the parallels are concentric circles and the meridians are straight lines.

contour: an imaginary line connecting points on the ground with the same elevation above a reference plane, or *datum*.

county: the largest governmental and statistical subdivision of a state; called a *parish* in Louisiana and an *organized borough* in Alaska.

cylindrical projection: transformation of the globe's grid onto a cylinder; when the axis of the cylinder coincides with the axis of the globe, the meridians are parallel straight lines, perpendicular to the parallels.

dasymetric map: a map that uses area-shading symbols to show regions of relatively homogeneous density. Unlike choropleth maps, these are not constrained to political or civil boundaries in defining similar areas.

demographic base map: *area cartogram* based upon population size.

digital elevation model (DEM):   a set of elevation data for points at the intersections of either Universal Transverse Mercator (UTM) grid lines or a set of uniformly spaced meridians and parallels.

digital line graph (DLG):   vector data for the boundaries, roads, drainage lines, contours, and other linear features on a topographic map.

digital map: a machine-readable representation of a geographic phenomenon stored for display or analysis by a digital computer; contrast with *analog map*.

digitizer: a device used to capture data in vector format by measuring and recording the plane coordinates of points on a printed or manuscript map.

district map: a map that defines the geographic areas covered by a given municipal service.

dot-distribution map: a map on which dots representing a given quantity of a phenomenon are placed to portray density variations and distribution.

earth resources satellite: a comparatively low-altitude satellite, such as the Landsats and SPOT, used to collect detailed remotely sensed imagery for comparatively small areas.

eastings: the *x*-coordinates in a plane coordinate system; see *northings*.

electoral map: a map showing election results, either as popular or electoral votes, at national, state, county, or local level.

electrostatic printing: a reproduction method whereby the image is formed by small electrical charges that attract a black or colored powder called a *toner*.

environmental satellite: a comparatively high-altitude satellite, such as the Geostationary Operational Environmental Satellites (GOES) and Synchronous Meteorological Satellites (SMS), designed to monitor large areas on a frequent basis, but with much less detail than for a low-altitude *earth resources satellite.*

equal area: true equivalency of areas, large or small, throughout a map.

false origin: an origin other than the center of the grid, or *true origin*, used to provide *x*- and *y*-coordinates that are always positive.

feature code: a numeric code used to describe a cartographic feature, usually by assigning it to one or more categories or standard attributes.

geopolitical map: a map that represents a global situation in the strategic realm.

gnomonic projection: an azimuthal projection constructed by projecting the grid onto a tangent plane from the globe's center; all great circles are shown as straight lines.

graduated circle: a circular symbol whose area represents a quantity of a given phenomenon.

graphicacy: the communications skill involving visual-spatial relations.

graticule: the grid of parallels and meridians on a map.

great circle route: the path followed (approximately) by airplanes on long-distance trips, based upon the fact that shortest-distance routes follow a great-circle arc between any two places.

ground resolution: degree of detail of a remotely sensed image expressed either as the diameter of the circular *ground spot,* or *instantaneous field of view* (IFOV), of the sensor, or as the dimensions of a rectangular *pixel* for which surface reflectance or attributes are recorded.

hachures: a series of short lines used to show the direction and steepness of slopes.

highway map: a map portraying roads that extend between and through civil divisions; contrast with *street map.*

historical cartography: the use of maps to depict and analyze historical events and phenomena.

history of cartography: the study of the historical development of maps, mapping technology, and map use.

hue: the attribute of color related to wavelength and described, for example, as red, green, purple, or tan; useful on maps to portray differences in kind; contrast with *value.*

index map: a map showing the extent and names of quadrangles or other areas portrayed on the various sheets in a map series.

interrupted projection: a map on which the world is portrayed as a discontinuous surface, often interrupted in the oceans.

isobar: a line on a map connecting points of equal barometric pressure.

isohyet: a line on a map connecting points of equal precipitation.

isotherm: a line on a map connecting points of equal temperature.

land cover: concerns the natural or built phenomena found on the land; contrast with *land use.*

land use: concerns the function of the land, that is, humankind's activities on land; contrast with *land cover.*

letterpress printing: a method of reproduction, now seldom used, whereby the inked image areas on the printing plate are raised above the noninked background areas.

line map: a map composed of line symbols and other abstract cartographic marks, in contrast to the continuous-tone symbols of a *photomap*.

lithographic printing: a method of reproduction, now widely used for printing maps, newspapers, and books, whereby a flat press plate is coated with an ink-accepting surface in the image areas.

mappaemundi: highly schematic medieval world maps.

master plan map: a map of a community's comprehensive development plan that portrays land-use categories.

Mercator projection: a conformal cylindrical projection in the equatorial case on which lines of constant direction (*rhumb lines*) are straight lines.

Metropolitan Statistical Area (MSA): a single county or group of contiguous counties that define a metropolitan region, usually with a central city with at least 50,000 inhabitants; in the past these have been called Standard Metropolitan Statistical Areas (SMSAs) and Standard Metropolitan Areas (SMAs); the precise definitions and changes therein are established by the U.S. Office of Management and Budget (OMB).

minor civil division (MCD): the primary political or administrative subdivisions of a county.

multispectral scanner: a passive scanning system that simultaneously measures and records reflected energy in several *spectral bands*, commonly in the green, red, and near-infrared bands.

natural resource inventory maps: maps showing the topographic, soil, and drainage characteristics of a minor civil division, based primarily upon the soil survey, and used to identify development potential.

northings: the *y*-coordinates in a plane coordinate system; see *eastings*.

official map: a map showing streets, highways, and parks already in existence and proposed; drainage also may be shown; once adopted, the map may be changed only through formal action of elected officials.

optical scanner: a device that captures data in *raster* format by systematically recording the intensity of light reflected from a small spot moving across a printed map or other drawing.

orthophoto: a photographic image of the terrain, produced from aerial photographs but with *radial relief displacement* removed to provide a *planimetric* photomap.

passive scanner: a sensing system, such as the Landsat Thematic Mapper, that does not generate the energy that is reflected back to the sensor; contrast with *active sensor*.

photogrammetry: the technical specialty concerned with making measurements from photographs.

photomap: a map with continuous-tone symbols from a photographed or remotely sensed image of the terrain, in contrast to the high-contrast line symbols of a *line map*.

pixel: a picture element, usually a rectangular element of a uniform grid; *pixel* refers to either the smallest nondivisible cell in a *raster*-format image or the corresponding grid-cell area on the earth's surface.

plane-coordinate system: a system for determining location in which two groups of straight lines intersect at right angles and have as a point of origin a selected perpendicular intersection.

planimetric map: a large-scale map with all features projected perpendicularly onto a horizontal datum plane so that horizontal distances can be measured on the map with accuracy.

polar azimuthal projection: a transformation of the globe's grid onto a plane centered at one of the poles so that all meridians are straight lines.

political map: commonly, a map showing boundaries, in contrast to *physical map*, which shows elevations of the land; broadly, a map whose subject treats governmental events or situations.

polygon: a vector representation of an enclosed region, described by a sequential list of intersection points for the bounding straight-line segments.

portolan chart: a sailing chart showing lines of constant direction between ports or landmarks.

primary colors: a set of basic colors that can be combined in various proportions to yield a full range of hues; the *additive primaries* (blue, green, and red) are combined by mixing light, and the *subtractive primaries* (yellow, magenta, and cyan) by mixing inks or dyes.

prime meridian: a meridian (selected arbitrarily) used as the line from which longitude is measured; the conventional prime meridian passes through Greenwich, England.

prism map: an obliquely viewed three-dimensional statistical map in which values for areal units are portrayed by their heights.

propaganda map: a map used to spread particular beliefs, doctrines, or information.

quadrangle: a four-sided region, usually bounded by a pair of *meridians* and a pair of *parallels*.

radial relief displacement: the distortion of positions of landscape features on an air photo resulting from elevation differences and the central perspective of the photograph; features are displaced toward or away from the center.

raster data: machine-readable data that represent a map or picture as a sequence of intensity attributes stored for grid cells and organized sequentially by rows; contrast with *vector data*.

raster display: a graphic display device, such as a CRT or dot-matrix printer, that produces a map or picture by plotting with light or ink a series of closely spaced parallel variable intensity lines.

real map: any hard-copy map, such as a printed map or aerial photograph, that has a permanent tangible reality and is directly viewable as a cartographic image; contrast with *virtual map*.

relief: elevations, elevation differences, peaks, depressions, and other salient attributes of the land surface or sea floor.

remote sensing: the technical specialty concerned with measuring attributes of or mapping the earth's surface by means of an electronic or optical device carried by an aircraft or satellite.

resolution: see *ground resolution*, *pixel*, and *screen resolution*.

rhumb line: a line on a map showing constant geographic direction; on a *Mercator projection* all straight lines are rhumb lines.

Sanborn map: a large-scale map of a city section portraying commercial, industrial, and residential land use, and showing size, shape, and safety and construction features; once used for setting fire insurance rates.

scene: a remotely sensed image formatted for analysis and display as a grid of picture elements; because of distortion or the rotation of the earth beneath the satellite, resampling is needed to convert the recorded image into a rectangular grid of pixels aligned in mutually perpendicular rows and columns.

screen resolution: the detail and quality of a soft-copy display unit expressed as the numbers of rows and columns of the largest grid of *pixels* that can be presented on the screen.

separation: a photographic or digital image containing all features of a particular type (*feature separation*) or all features to be printed with a particular color or ink (*color separation*).

side-looking airborne radar (SLAR): an active microwave sensing system that scans outward, with scan lines perpendicular to the path of the aircraft.

soil survey: maps and written descriptions of the soil characteristics of an area, often a county.

spectral signature: a land cover's diagnostic reflectance values for a set of narrow spectral bands.

standard parallel: any parallel on which the latitudinal portion of a grid system is based.

statistical surface: a continuous three-dimensional surface that can be estimated from areal or point data and portrayed cartographically.

stereomodel: a three-dimensional model of the landscape viewable with a stereoscope or stereoplotter for the area common to a pair of overlapping *aerial photographs*.

street map: a map showing and naming all roads and avenues (streets) within a municipality; contrast with *highway map*.

subdivision map: a map on which the precise division of land into smaller parcels for purposes of sale or development is shown.

synthetic aperature radar (SAR): an active microwave radar system that improves image resolution by electronically simulating the effects of a much longer antenna.

tax map: a map showing ownership of land in a minor civil division parcel by parcel, along with parcel dimensions, area, and other identifying information.

thematic map: a map that illustrates a subject or topic either quantitatively or qualitatively.

tilt: the deviation of the optic axis of an *aerial photograph* from a direction truly perpendicular to a perfectly horizontal *datum*, or reference plane.

topographic map: a map of land-surface features, including drainage lines, roads, landmarks, and usually relief.

transverse cylindrical projection: a cylindrical projection oriented with the axis of the cylinder through diametrically opposite points on the equator and centered on a meridian.

triangulation: a method for determining location through trigonometry and the measurement of the sides and angles of one or more triangles.

true origin: the two-dimensional center of a plane-coordinate system; see *false origin*.

underground facilities map: a map showing the location of and access to buried electrical, gas, water, and sewer lines.

Universal Transverse Mercator Grid (UTM):   the most widely used plane-coordinate system, extending from 84°N to 80°S latitude and based upon a transverse Mercator projection for each of 60 north-south trending zones.

urbanized area: densely settled parts of the Metropolitan Statistical Area, especially a central city and its closely settled periphery; used to delineate more effectively urban and rural populations within MSAs.

value: the attribute of color related to intensity or graytone; useful on maps to portray rates, densities, and percentages; contrast with *hue*.

vector data: machine-readable data that represent a map or drawing by a sequence of plane coordinates, usually with distinct sublists of points for each feature and attributes describing the feature (and possibly pointing to neighboring features as well); contrast with *raster data*.

vector display: a graphic display device, such as a pen plotter, that draws a map or picture by plotting a series of line segments without a common orientation.

videotex: an interactive television message system, carried by telephone or two-way cable, whereby the user makes selections from a *menu* and receives graphic displays of information.

virtual map: any map that either lacks a permanent tangible reality, as does the soft-copy image on the screen of a cathode ray tube (CRT) display, or is not directly viewable; contrast with *real map*.

weather map: a chart or map illustrating meteorological conditions at a given time for a state or nation; contrast with *climate map*.

zoning map: a map that illustrates the areas of permitted uses of land within a minor civil division.

Index